The Mad, the Bad, and the Different

The Mad, the Bad, and the Different

Essays in Honor of Simon Dinitz

Edited by

Israel L. Barak-Glantz
Wayne State University

C. Ronald Huff
Ohio State University

LexingtonBooks
D.C. Heath and Company
Lexington, Massachusetts
Toronto

To Sy,
our mentor and, above all,
our friend,
who in his own way
has taught us much about life

Library of Congress Cataloging in Publication Data

Main entry under title:

The Mad, the bad, and the different.

  Bibliography: p.
  Includes index.
  1. Crime and criminals—Addresses, essays, lectures. 2. Dinitz, Simon.
I. Dinitz, Simon. II. Barak-Glantz, Israel L. III. Huff, C. Ronald.
HV6028.M29   364   80–8316
ISBN 0–669–03997–7   AACR2

Copyright © 1981 by D.C. Heath and Company

Published simultaneously in Canada

Printed in the United States of America

International Standard Book Number: 0–669–03997–7

Library of Congress Catalog Card Number: 80–8316

Contents

Preface   ix

Acknowledgments   xi

Foreword   *Marshall B. Clinard*   xiii

Biography of a Colleague: Simon Dinitz
Russell R. Dynes and *Alfred C. Clarke*   xix

Part I   *Theoretical Approaches to Crime and Deviance*   1

Chapter 1   The Relevance of Classical Criminology Today
                  Leon Shaskolsky Sheleff   3

Chapter 2   Positivism and Neo-Lombrosianism
                  Gideon Fishman   15

Chapter 3   Ethnomethodology and Criminology: The Social
                  Production of Crime and the Criminal
                  Stephen J. Pfohl   25

Chapter 4   Conflict, Radical, and Critical Approaches to
                  Criminology   *Raymond J. Michalowski*   39

Part II   *Forms of Delinquent and Criminal Behavior*   53

Chapter 5   Delinquency Prevention: The State of the Art
                  Frank R. Scarpitti   57

Chapter 6   Containment Theory: An Attempt to Formulate
                  a Middle-Range Theory of Deviance
                  Walter C. Reckless   67

Chapter 7   Female Criminality: An Assessment
                  Ira J. Silverman   77

Chapter 8   The Puzzle of Dangerousness   *John P. Conrad*   101

Chapter 9   Homicide in America: A Research Review
                  Margaret A. Zahn   111

Chapter 10   Reactions to the Questioning of the Mafia Myth
                 Joseph L. Albini   125

Chapter 11   Recent Developments in White-Collar Crime
                 Theory and Research   *Diane Vaughan*   135

Chapter 12   The Pawnbroker: Banker of the Poor?
                 Catherine M. Hartnett   149

Part III   *Punishment and Correction*   157

Chapter 13   Juvenile Corrections: The State of the Art
                 Clemens Bartollas and *Stuart J. Miller*   159

Chapter 14   The Death Penalty and Deterrence: A Review of
                 Recent Research   *Gordon P. Waldo*   169

Part IV   *Interdisciplinary and Comparative Research in
                 Criminology and Deviance*   179

Chapter 15   Sociopathic and Other Mentally Ill Offenders
                 Revisited   *Nancy J. Beran* and *Harry E. Allen*   181

Chapter 16   Schizophrenic Services: Disjunction and
                 Disservice to Schizophrenics in the Community
                 Ann E. Davis   189

Chapter 17   Psychiatric Aspects of Terrorism in Italy
                 Franco Ferracuti and *Francesco Bruno*   199

Part V   *Special Issues in Criminology*   215

Chapter 18   On the Sociology of Law   *Richard L. Schuster*   217

Chapter 19   The Dismantling of an LEAA Exemplary
                 Project: The Parole Officer Aide Program of
                 Ohio   *Joseph E. Scott*   225

Chapter 20   On Teaching Criminology and Criminal Justice:
                 A Case for Undergraduate Experiential
                 Education   *Thomas W. Foster*   239

                 In Celebration of Sy Dinitz   *Gilbert Geis*   249

Simon Dinitz: Milestones to 1981   255

Index   267

About the Contributors   273

About the Editors   280

Preface

On more than one occasion, Sy Dinitz has described his research and teaching interests as "the mad, the bad, and the different." It is appropriate, therefore, that this characterization of his own work provides both the title and the theme of this book. This is a book about crime and social deviance. It is the product of two years of planning, writing, and editing, involving a total of thirty people who know that the only way to apply the principle of *lex talionis* to Sy Dinitz is to seek our retribution via these essays.

Fall 1981 marks the thirtieth anniversary of Sy Dinitz's arrival on the Ohio State University campus. During the first three decades of his distinguished academic career, Professor Dinitz has achieved both international acclaim as a criminologist and local fame as a preeminent teacher and a dedicated campus and community citizen. In this thirty-year period, he has served as an intellectual catalyst for hundreds of graduate students and thousands of undergraduates, encompassing a wide array of academic disciplines on the Ohio State University campus. This festschrift, written and edited by some of his former students and colleagues, is in honor of his remarkable professional accomplishments and his humanity.

Professor Dinitz has always encouraged his students to attend and participate in professional meetings as a normative aspect of professional socialization. It is fitting, therefore, that the concept of this book grew out of our attendance and discussions at the thirty-first annual meeting of the American Society of Criminology, held in Philadelphia in November 1979. During the past two years, what was initially a vague plan to honor our mentor has been transformed into reality because of the tremendous enthusiasm and eager cooperation of those represented in the pages that follow.

The theme of this book follows what Professor Dinitz taught us about the study of crime and social deviance—that it requires a multidisciplinary approach and the blending of many theories and research methodologies. One colleague recently described Sy Dinitz's approach as "elegant eclecticism," that is, an informed, purposeful eclecticism, rather than theoretical agnosticism. The chapters that follow will surely provide ample evidence that no single label or stigma can be attached to those who have worked most closely with Professor Dinitz. Rather, they and their work are reflective of his emphasis on pursuing truth, no matter where that pursuit leads. In fact, many of us who completed our doctoral studies under his supervision are convinced that he regarded intellectual over-conformity as an indication that one was not yet worthy of the designation Doctor of Philosophy.

The organization of this book reflects the diversity of research interests that has characterized the first thirty years of Sy Dinitz's criminological career. The invited contributions were purposively selected to convey this rich theoretical and methodological heritage. Generally, we asked our contributing authors to address substantive areas through which they were originally linked to Sy, either as students or as colleagues. In some cases, the chapters represent extensions of the authors' original research interests, but Sy's influence on their work will be evident to readers who know both Sy and the authors.

The four chapters in part I highlight central issues in the four major theoretical currents in contemporary criminology: the classical school, positivism, phenomenology and ethnomethodology, and the conflict paradigm. Part II consists of eight chapters that encompass disparate forms of criminal behavior. In part III, we consider some of the important historical and current issues in punishment and correction. Part IV mirrors some of Sy Dinitz's interdisciplinary and comparative research interests in the sociology of deviance. Finally, in part V, we have collected several chapters that deal with special issues in criminology—issues whose scope extends beyond any of the other parts of the book.

In addition to these five major components, the book begins with a foreword and a biographical sketch and ends with an epilogue in celebration of Sy Dinitz. It is our hope that what follows will constitute a fitting tribute to a man who continues to outproduce us. We feared that if we did not seize this opportunity to capitalize on our currently high energy levels, we might burn out before he does. Such incapacitation, although it would unquestionably provide empirical support for one of "Dinitz's laws," would also prevent us from subjecting him to his just deserts.

Acknowledgments

All books require the cooperation and collaboration of many people, some of them "behind the scenes." Special books, as this one is intended to be, often are made possible by special behind-the-scenes people. In our case, we worked with a very special editor, Margaret Zusky of Lexington Books. We appreciate Margaret's active support of this project, her enthusiasm, and her willingness to keep it a secret (including delaying all the usual prepublication publicity) so that we could surprise Sy Dinitz on his thirtieth anniversary at Ohio State.

Festschrift projects involve some very complex and highly personalized judgments. In organizing a book in honor of someone with as many colleagues and friends as Sy Dinitz has, painful decisions must be made concerning contributors, content, style, tone of writing, and many other issues, which become all the more problematic because of the special nature of the book. We accept full responsibility for all these decisions, because we made them all. However, on those occasions when we really needed to test our ideas on someone, or when we were not certain how best to handle one of the countless editorial decisions that arose, we frequently depended on several of Sy's closest colleagues for a sympathetic audience and for sage advice. These special sages are Al Clarke, Russ Dynes, and Gil Geis, and we benefited greatly from their wisdom and their experience.

When we initially conceived of this project, we entitled our proposed book *Criminological Inquiry: Essays in Honor of Simon Dinitz*. John Conrad has our thanks for talking us out of that rather sterile title and for suggesting that we try *The Mad, the Bad, and the Different*. John also provided encouragement and enthusiastic support throughout this effort.

The photograph of Sy Dinitz that adds so much to this book was provided by the Ohio State University Office of Communications Services. We gratefully acknowledge their cooperation in making this photo available for our use.

In the final analysis, though, this book exists because twenty-seven contributors agreed in 1980 that Sy Dinitz's thirtieth anniversary at Ohio State, in 1981, represents an excellent opportunity to honor him and his many distinguished contributions to criminology, to our careers, and to our lives. So, to our twenty-seven collaborators, we express our sincere gratitude and respect for their time and efforts.

Finally, our families—Amiah and Edyah; Pat, Tammy, and Tiffany—have been patient with us most of the time as we attempted to organize, coordinate, and edit a book with twenty-seven contributors from three different continents. Our families understood, because they also love the man whom we would honor.

Foreword

Simon Dinitz is recognized internationally as a leader in the study of a wide variety of areas of deviant behavior, in all of which he has made major contributions. One would therefore expect, as is the case for many European professors, that, on retirement, a volume would be dedicated to him, what is known as a festschrift. In this respect, this volume is unique; rather than waiting to honor him at his retirement, his colleagues, his doctoral students, and others in his broad field have chosen to honor him in commemoration of the thirtieth anniversary of his arrival at The Ohio State University, an association that has been his sole continuous university connection. This commemorative volume gives early recognition to the tremendous scope of his career, as well as to the continuing contributions that are anticipated. His work is now at its peak; no decline is imminent.

The organization of this volume of chapters prepared by numerous contributors clearly recognizes the diverse academic interests of Simon Dinitz: theoretical approaches to crime and deviance; forms of delinquent and criminal behavior, including the violent and dangerous offender and white-collar crime; punishment and corrections; and interdisciplinary and comparative research in criminology and deviance. The latter includes a discussion of the work done by Professor Dinitz in the area of community treatment of schizophrenia. Finally, the volume closes with some special issues in criminology.

When I was asked to write this foreword, I replied: "In view of my long association with Simon Dinitz, how can I turn down such an invitation?" This association began thirty-five years ago at Vanderbilt University, where I was teaching after having left the government immediately after World War II. A young and slender enlisted man arrived to complete the B.A. degree, begun at the College of the City of New York, with the goal of becoming a naval officer. This young student was expected to take a degree in the physical sciences, but after exposure to sociology, and as a result of his own nascent independence, he upset the Navy's plans for him and shifted to a major in sociology, of little use to the Navy at that time. Later he went on to study for the M.A. and Ph.D. with me at the University of Wisconsin, where he received both degrees in a record four years. Throughout his graduate work, he never lacked new ideas. He was buoyantly enthusiastic during his years of graduate work, and he was always impatient to do fieldwork.

During the 1940s, the distinguished sociologist Ernest W. Burgess was asked what advice he would give to a young sociologist. He replied that a young sociologist should select one small area in sociology, on which narrow specialty he should spend his entire life studying. Simon Dinitz did not then nor does he now follow this advice. Few sociologists, in fact, have had his wide scope of interests or have been more successful in pursuing research in a greater variety of areas. It is little known, for example, that his first research was done on alcoholism. The dynamics of Alcoholics Anonymous (AA) was the subject of his M.A. thesis, and in his research he attended weekly AA meetings. He once came to the attention of an older member of the AA group, who one night said to him: "Aren't you rather young to be trying to get on the wagon?" Subsequent to this research, his doctoral studies dealt with the relation of public drinking houses, such as bars, to the drinking phases of alcoholics.

The range of his interests since this early research is indicative of a restless, always inquisitive mind; he would never have been content to follow Burgess's dictum. Had he done so, sociology and criminology would have been the real losers. Scientists of more limited vision can plod along year after year on a narrow project, with much of their research all too often somewhat repetitious. In many cases, those who put all their research "eggs" into one basket end up with their eggs becoming spoiled. Let people with the wide vision shown by Sy Dinitz use their brilliance to work out a variety of new paths in the often dense and uncharted vastness of sociological research possibilities.

The titles of his fourteen books and more than one hundred articles reveal his wide range of research pursuits, a range rarely encountered in a professional bibliography. Of equal importance, they constitute quality as well as quantity; most of them were not written to follow the "publish or perish" drive but rather because of a need to say something about an intellectual problem that had been encountered. Frequently, he asked what Herbert Blumer has termed "the significant question." More specifically, his writings have covered such diverse topics as marriage and the family, schizophrenia, mental hospitals, community psychiatry, juvenile delinquency, the dangerous offender, economic crime, and correctional institutions, both juvenile and adult.

Although he is a competent statistician who leans to quantitative methods, he has never settled for the shallow, largely nontheoretical research of many quantitative sociologists who claim to be scientific sociologists simply because they use sophisticated research methods. To them, the method rather than the theoretical problem becomes the real end rather than a means to an end, as it should be. On the contrary, Dinitz's research is characterized by the application of basic sociological theory and concepts. Depending on the research problem, he has widely employed such concepts as levels of aspiration, self-concept, social interaction and isolation, social integration, status perceptions, decision making, social organizations, social class, social predictors, instrumental roles, societal tolerance, value orientations, community, perceptions of stigma, small-group interactions, organizational change, conflict and cooperation, informal conduct codes, dissensus, and cross-cultural perspectives.

As his original mentor, long-time friend, and constant personal and professional admirer, I believe, however, that I should be allowed the liberty of one critical remark, with full cognizance that many will regard my negative comment as one of his distinct assets. I refer to his occasional tendency to be eclectic in his theoretical model of human behavior. Over the years, he has increasingly tried to combine a sociological approach to deviant and therefore human behavior, with limited biological and psychological explanations. This is reflected in his periodic preoccupation with sociopathy, antisocial personality, and the biological and personality-trait histories of deviant and nondeviant persons, as in his study, *Delinquents and Nondelinquents in the Puerto Rican Slum Culture* (1975). In my judgment, this sometimes eclectic, multiple-factor approach simply does not jibe with his pronounced emphasis on learning and social-role processes in human behavior and the role of culture, subcultures, and social groups.

It should be recognized that his occasional theoretical lapse into a multiple-factor approach is not unique today. Unfortunately, eclecticism is beginning to creep once again into sociology and criminology, even into sociobiology, after having been destroyed many times during the past fifty years by empirical research. It may be the price one must pay for trying to be "scientifically broadminded" rather than adhering to strict sociological principles. This trend may also be the result of increasing collaboration with researchers from other disciplines in which the result is often theoretical cooptation by others in an attempt to achieve consensus. Scientific research on human behavior, deviant and nondeviant alike, is far too young for us now to surrender any of our own distinctive sociological and social-psychological perspectives for consensus with those from other disciplines. As I have pointed out, however, Simon Dinitz has only occasionally veered from a sociological perspective.

Professor Dinitz has been the only recipient of the two highest distinctions in criminology and psychiatry, the Sutherland Award and the Hofheimer Prize. It is highly questionable that anyone else will receive both of these awards. He is unique in that he has been equally at home within the areas of criminology and mental disorder, not necessarily because of a bridge between these two fields, as in the case of the typical forensic psychiatrist. In his writings, criminology and psychiatry have tended to be distinct interests—an interest in mental disorder, particularly schizophrenia, mental hospitals, and community treatment, and also in a variety of criminological topics. These two divergent interests may have resulted from the influences of specific individuals at an early stage of his academic development. His criminological perspective came largely from the University of Wisconsin and, later, from Ohio State, under the influence of Walter Reckless; his interest in various aspects of mental disorder came largely from his research association with Benjamin Pasamanick, the distinguished psychiatrist, when he was on the Ohio State faculty.

It is most amazing that, contrary to the usual practice, Sy Dinitz has rarely closed the book on a research project once he has completed it. Instead, he has often revisited it over many years to see what new perspectives have been wrought by time. Of particular concern to him, and one of his major contributions to research methods, has been a continuing interest in longitudinal or follow-up studies of his original samples. This type of research has provided him with new data with which to view his original findings and predictions. Such a preoccupation is rare in scientific research; even more rare is that he has done not one but several follow-up studies. Far too often, the findings of sociological and psychiatric research leave the reader to speculate if they will hold up in the future for a given sample.

Follow-up studies are methodologically difficult, but Sy Dinitz has never been one to shy away from them for this reason. In the late 1950s, he published a number of articles, with Walter Reckless and others, that dealt with the self-concept of a "good" boy as an insulator against delinquency. This work involved construction of a valuable social instrument with which to measure self-concept. In 1960, he published his follow-up research as "The 'Good' Boy in a High Delinquency Area: Four Years Later." In 1967, a research monograph, published jointly with Ben Pasamanick and Frank Scarpitti, dealt with schizophrenics who had been treated in the community rather than in a hospital. This was succeeded by two follow-up studies of the sample, *Women After Treatment* and *Schizophrenics in the New Custodial Community*. Several subsequent articles also dealt with follow-up studies of this sample. Currently, he is directing research for a ten-volume study of the dangerous and violent offender, to which he himself has already contributed three volumes. One can predict with assurance that these studies will be followed up subsequently to ascertain if the conclusions are still valid later. Simon Dinitz believes, moreover, that the use of control groups, wherever possible, is essential. In his follow-up study of schizophrenic women, for example, he compared treated mental patients with people he presumed to be their "normal" neighbors; and in Puerto Rico, with Franco Ferracuti, he compared delinquents and nondelinquents in slum areas.

Throughout his professional career, Sy Dinitz has recognized that the functions of a university, as the distinguished educator Robert Maynard Hutchins frequently emphasized, are not only to create knowledge through research but also to transmit knowledge. Good textbooks are written primarily by those who also have done independent research. This is true of Sy Dinitz: his two textbooks, one on social problems, the other on deviance, both written collaboratively, create theoretical models supported by empirical data. He has been even more effective in his transmission of knowledge through the classroom.

His teaching, particularly his performance over the years in his large criminology classes, won for him the Ohio State Award for Distinguished Teaching (1970). Ohio State University later gave him two additional awards, one for distinguished research (1979), the other for distinguished service (1980).

Many academicians isolate themselves from professional and community responsibilities. This has never been true of Simon Dinitz. He has been president of the American Society of Criminology and the North Central Sociological Association, vice president of the Ohio Valley Sociological Association, and editor of one professional journal and on the editorial board of others. He has been active on many university committees, in various international professional organizations, and has served on a number of task forces to deal with far-ranging social problems in Ohio. These efforts have made him a more realistic sociologist and researcher. Despite all his research and his other achievements, however, I believe that Simon Dinitz is most proud of his effectiveness as a teacher of undergraduate and graduate students and as the proud mentor of a large number of Ph.D.'s who now carry on the "Dinitzian approaches" to the study of deviant behavior.

Finally, those who know him would find me to be much amiss if I failed to comment on his unusually warm, sympathetic, enthusiastic, and loyal personality. These characteristics have greatly enhanced his ability to extract from his students their maximum performance and to have a marked personal influence on others, all of which has gone beyond his writings. Professional prestige has in no way changed his personal behavior; he remains the same modest person who is as much interested in the work of his friends as in his own, which cannot be said of many academic achievers, whose self-importance increases with recognition. This facet of a deep and understanding personality surrounds and magnifies the marks of the unusual writer, researcher, and teacher that Simon Dinitz is.

Marshall B. Clinard
Emeritus Professor of Sociology
University of Wisconsin, Madison

Biography of a Colleague: Simon Dinitz

Russell R. Dynes and
Alfred C. Clarke

In academic circles, it is usual to present someone in terms of his or her curriculum vitae. This has merit; it notes accomplishments, products, degrees, position, social security number, known children, and current spouse.

But every vitae is the residue of the social construction of reality, to be imposed on those who inquire. Over a long career, it is difficult to untangle the person from the accomplishment, the truth from the myth, the fact from fiction. We don't have that problem. We know Sy Dinitz. We have observed him over a number of years and in countless situations. We have tried to educate him— we felt obliged to do that, since he is younger than we are. Looking back on that task, we are pleased with the results and astonished at how much he learned and how well he turned out. We can only provide glimpses of the magnitude of our task and the immensity of our accomplishment.

We know that Sy was born in 1926. He grew up in that stream of Americana that Norman Rockwell studiously avoided in his *Saturday Evening Post* covers— Brooklyn. His early experiences were conditioned by the depression and by World War II. His parents, Russian-Jewish immigrants, tried to make it easier for the next generation by instilling expectations and by providing experiences. Sy helped and worked summers in the factory in the garment district. He saw the changing ethnic composition of New York reflected over time in the workers. He also came into contact with the ideologies of those who have the solutions to depressions and wars. He followed the fortunes of the Dodgers and the Giants, attended bar mitzvahs, and rode subways. Like everyone else, he went to CCNY. He met Mim, listened to big bands, dreamed of becoming a sports announcer, and worried about life and his future. Freudians might make much of these early experiences, but we do know that he dislikes grass, particularly mowing it, and has some difficulty even now in recognizing farm animals, particularly pigs.

Life often provides its own redemptive experiences. This came for Sy when he joined the U.S. Navy. We were never sure why this occurred, since he is an unlikely sailor; perhaps he wandered by the Brooklyn Navy Yard, or perhaps he admired the workmanship in Navy pants. The Navy, hoping to ensure a victory for democracy, sent him first to Great Lakes and then to Nashville, where his linguistic habits would be most appreciated. He was then sent to Vanderbilt University, the home of southern agrarianism. Vanderbilt was beginning to staff up for the postwar boom and had hired several untested faculty members, such as Robert Winch, Karl Schuessler, and Marshall Clinard. Sy was exposed to good sociology, and the others have managed to have distinguished careers despite their encounter with Sy. Marshall Clinard had the most trouble, however. He left to go to the University of Wisconsin, but Sy Dinitz soon followed, insisting that he needed more knowledge, as well as financial support. Wisconsin was an especially interesting place then, with a diverse faculty and a mature set of graduate students coming back after their World War II experiences. But Sy has always been goal oriented. He got the M.A. in 1949 and then the Ph.D. in 1951. Although he and Mim were married in 1949, their sense of permanence was not enhanced by living in student housing on the Wisconsin campus.

Those familiar with the historical contours of higher education in America know that 1951 was not necessarily a good year. The postwar bulge was over, and the reduced fertility rate of the 1930s was being reflected in the decline of the student population. The fact that Sy was in the job market did not evoke any great celebration in the academic world.

Hiring was much more informal at that time. Ohio State had some faculty changes, and Ray Sletto, then chair, went to the ASA meeting in Chicago to hire someone to teach "family." The meetings were small then and someone (William Sewell is usually assigned blame) remarked that a recent Wisconsin graduate might be able to teach "family." Senior faculty members were consulted on the spot, and Sy Dinitz had a job. Those of us who were not involved in the decision assumed that the senior faculty had, as usual, made a mistake. It was also obvious to us, the most junior faculty, that we would have to absorb the penalty of interacting with him. Clarke was an instructor with an interest in the family and would be most directly involved. Dynes was an assistant instructor (which meant he was paid less) and also was teaching the family course, along with the other introductory courses. When Sy Dinitz showed up, several weeks after the meeting, we told him we were his peers, even if he did come in with the pretension of a Ph.D. He accepted that reluctantly, noting that, although we then lacked the degree, we were, in fact, older than he was. Although he did not seek our mature counsel, we have accepted that responsibility over the years.

We wish we could report his meteoric rise through the academic hierarchy, but we cannot. It took him five years to make assistant professor, a rank now assumed by any new Ph.D. Nor was his considerable written productivity evidenced. We brought him along gradually. His first several articles, which were coauthored, were prompted by discussions concerning sex preferences for our children (each of us had a nonpromised firstborn son). Almost thirty years later, these articles are now cited as pioneering efforts in the sociology of gender. To us, they were empirical resolutions of arguments. We then started a pattern of rotating our names as coauthors on whatever we wrote together. That worked over the years, although each of us takes delight in referring to the other two as "et al." Faced with the shared problem of teaching a common course, we conned another colleague into joining us in writing a social problems text. Although we felt good about the final product, the process was even more enjoyable. We rented houses at a summer resort with our families to work on the book. We spent our advance, increased our skill at shuffleboard and mutual insult, and actually produced a manuscript on time.

Any project involving the three of us has always been preceded by long discussions of reasons we should not do it. Sy is always most pessimistic about everything. This is consistent with his general world view. We only become worried when Sy becomes optimistic and enthused about a project, because then we recognize that he probably will not do it. Sy's best work has always been characterized by self-doubt, self-depreciation, and constant worry. If we tell him that something is good, he will immediately wonder what is wrong with it.

From the firm base provided by our wise counsel and association, Sy began to venture out into an expanded world. He did a project for Nationwide Insurance. He began to work with Walter Reckless, whose interests at that time were especially focused on self-concept and juvenile delinquency. Sy's work with Ben Pasamanick began in 1957 at the Columbus Psychiatric Institute. It was a particularly exciting time there, with the development of a wide range of interdisciplinary projects. Of special importance was the initiation of an experiment relating to the prevention of hospitalization (now called deinstitutionalization). The report of this work in 1967 led to its being given the Hofheimer Prize of the American Psychiatric Association. Sy's other interests, in psychiatric diagnosis, in sociopaths, in staff structure of custodial institutions, and in the outcomes of institutionalization, have provided a continuing focus for later research. His collaboration with Franco Ferracuti and the United Nations Social Defense Research Institute spanned several years and continents. His impact on Israeli criminology, through content, interest, and students, is only partially captured in a 1976 volume of *Israel Studies in Criminology*, dedicated to Sy and edited by Shlomo Shoham. His more recent collaboration with John Conrad at the Academy for Contemporary Problems on the Dangerous Offender Project has led to a number of publications. Sy's major scholarly contributions to the field of criminology have been widely cited and were recognized in 1974 when Sy received the prestigious Sutherland Award, given by the American Society of Criminology.

As we knew from the very beginning, Sy has a capacity to get along with diverse and often difficult colleagues. His numerous officemates and collaborators would fill a large auditorium, and they often *do* fill his house. Each has gained much from that association, because Sy always felt that *he* was the recipient.

Some might infer that Sy developed his impressive research record at the expense of teaching. This is not so. Thousands of undergraduate students at Ohio State have known him as a demanding and provocative lecturer. Years later, they probably would greet him with his standard opening line in class: "Welcome to another hour of truth." Over the years, the Arts College, the University Alumni Association, and graduate students have given him teaching awards. Even the Chicago *Tribune* did a feature story on him as one of the Big Ten's "Ten Most Exciting Teachers." He was pleased by the story, though chagrined by his recollection of the *Tribune*'s usual endorsements. We have been with him all over the country when students have recognized him and recalled to him some favorite remembrance of his classes. They sometimes even remember the point he made with the anecdote.

Those who see him in his performing role miss his directorial skills. Many graduate students know that side of him well. He has always carried more than his share of advising, both in the intellectual sense and in the clinical sense. His role is recorded in acknowledgments and prefaces of scores of theses and dissertations. But recorded nowhere, except in the lives of his students, were those who sought him out for general counsel. People with problems seek him out. He has great empathy with the underdog, and his sensitivity to social inequality and injustice makes him an easy mark. He helps all of them in sophisticated ways. His tremendous empathy allows him to deal with an array of personal and social types that staggers the imagination. His help might range from segmented discussions to continuing "therapy" over years. He always takes the cases, not in the clinical sense but in the concerned sense. This means that he usually carries the woes of others with him. He has never been able to abstract himself from the emotional side of life.

Neither his research productivity nor his effective teaching has been a substitute for other obligations. He has served on the Departmental Council and has chaired the undergraduate, graduate, research, and personnel committees. He has served on the Faculty Council and the Conference Committee of the Teaching Staff and has chaired the University Research Council. He has edited *Criminologica* and has been president of the American Society of Criminology. He has chaired the Subcommittee on Institutional Processes for the Governor's Task Force on Corrections and has headed the Youth Services Advisory Committee. He's been on the board of Alvis House, Buckeye Boys' Ranch, Jewish Family Services, and Hillel. He has not simply collected these affiliations; he has worked with them and has agonized over them.

Occasionally, Sy takes a break to do some work somewhere else. Over the years, he has spent several terms at the Institute of Criminology of the University of Tel Aviv, at the University of Southern California, and at the University of Wisconsin. More recently, we have detected a warming trend in his travels to the University of South Florida. But wherever he is, he's at home: from Tel Aviv to Toledo, from Caracas to Chillicothe, from Walla Walla to Worthington, from Sydney to Sidney, and from Brooklyn to Bexley.

It is obvious that Sy has established an enviable research record, for which he is known nationally and internationally. But despite being a cosmopolitan scholar, he does not shirk his civic duties in the local community, whether it is the department, the college, the university, the Jewish community, the voluntary-agency community, the municipal community, the State of Ohio, or other states. He does not confine his teaching activities to the narrow role of advisor to graduate students. He has challenged thousands of undergraduates to think about a range of problems, not all of them strictly sociological. To these students, he has been provoker, counselor, teacher, advisor, taskmaster, and concerned and continuing friend. To the graduate students, he has been a prodder, an editor, a formulator, a stimulus, sometimes an irritant, and has exhibited all the other traits necessary for obtaining good results.

In effect, he is a scholar who is humane, a cosmopolite and still a localite, a researcher who excels in teaching, an accomplished mass lecturer who can still relate one-to-one. He is a theorist who insists on being practical. He can be a biting critic who worries that he has gone too far. He usually plays the mediating role in conflict situations because of his capacity to see all sides of an issue. His identification with others is internalized, never abstract. If he cannot resolve a problem, he feels that he has failed. Living in a world in which most problems can't be easily resolved, this means that he's seldom happy. He is cheerful always, but happy seldom. He has never compartmentalized problems nor ignored them. This means that he has never experienced the bliss that ignorance brings and has seldom experienced the thrill of victory, but more often the agony of defeat. We recall his self-description during one particularly difficult period: "It only hurts when I move."

With his great interest in his work (and his work family is immense), his personal family has always been critically important to his life. Over the years, Mim has always been both independent and supportive. She probably wishes he'd slow down, but, knowing Sy better than we do, she recognizes that the likelihood that he'll change significantly is slight. Their children, Jeff, Thea, and Risa, are all independent adults now. Sy continues to worry about them, of course. There is no need to worry, but they would not wish to deprive their father of that satisfaction.

One of the few changes we see in Sy is some increased capacity for reflection. This, of course, is one of the few perquisites of age. The AAUP chapter at Ohio State gives an annual award to the faculty member who has contributed most to academic values. So, to his research and teaching awards, Sy recently added this one. In accepting the Nemzer Award, Sy harked back to Durkheim's perennial concerns about social cohesion and cited some of the destructive changes he has observed during his academic career. This was all done with his usual Old Testament gloom, but he ended with a characteristic affirmation:

> I pledge my continued commitment to the academy and promise to remain a
> dedicated campus citizen, to insist on free and unfettered inquiry, to fight for

faculty autonomy, to espouse faculty governance and the return of a sense of community and purpose to the campus. . . . The academy remains the last bastion of free inquiry and rational discourse. I am honored to serve it.

We have been honored to be his colleagues. The academic community and many other communities have been honored by his service. That's something he does not need to worry about.

Part I:
Theoretical Approaches
to Crime and Deviance

Part I begins with a chapter by Leon Shaskolsky Sheleff in which he summarizes the tenets of classical criminology. He reviews the principal works of Beccaria and Bentham and claims that one can observe the revival of classical thought in contemporary criminal-justice practices and policy debates.

In chapter 2, Gideon Fishman points out that the virtue of positivism in criminology has recently been challenged by the revival of humanistic social science; an increased interest in symbolic interactionism, phenomenology, and ethnomethodology; and the rise of neo-Marxist sociology. Fishman argues that the recent reemergence of biological approaches may be attributed to the shortcomings of the sociological perspective in formulating a comprehensive etiological approach and in what he views as its total failure in the field of correction. The emerging "neobiological" approach, he says, actually reflects an interdisciplinary perspective that incorporates sociological, social-psychological, and biological-organic factors in an attempt to explain behavior, some of which may be regarded as criminal or deviant.

The third chapter, by Stephen J. Pfohl, outlines one of the major alternatives to mainstream positivism—ethnomethodology and its contributions to an "interpretive criminology." In elaborating on some of the answers he gave during his Ph.D. oral examination (administered in part by Professor Dinitz), Pfohl traces the theoretical, methodological, and empirical contributions of ethnomethodology to criminology, contrasts it with labeling theory, and suggests its close intellectual relationship with historically grounded critical criminology.

Part I concludes with a contribution by Raymond J. Michalowski, who offers an analysis of other alternatives to mainstream positivism. Michalowski traces the evolution of a more radical criminology in America since the late 1950s, when a fundamental division began to develop between the more traditional positivist focus on individual pathology and an alternative radical criminology incorporating a "critique of domination." He identifies four variants of nonpositivist criminology—the labeling or societal-reaction perspective; conflict theory; radical criminology; and critical criminology—that have emerged or are in the process of developing, and he attempts to assess each of these perspectives and their contributions to the construction of a critical tradition in criminological theory. Michalowski concludes by outlining a scenario for the evolution of radical criminology into critical criminology; he asserts that the integration of radical criminology and critical sociology offers the potential for significant advances in the development of critical criminology.

As these chapters illustrate, theoretical criminology is dynamic, and no single paradigm has yet achieved consensus. This situation may in itself be interpreted as providing some support for a conflict perspective on the field of criminology and deviance.

1 The Relevance of Classical Criminology Today

Leon Shaskolsky Sheleff

It has become a ritual for criminology textbooks to make a cursory reference to the contribution of the classical criminologists before embarking on a far more extensive and detailed expostulation of what is seen as the foundation of the modern criminological enterprise, the positivist school. The writings of the classical school are often looked upon as little more than a prelude to the more substantive scientific work represented by the big three of the positivist school, Lombroso, Ferri, and Garofalo. Each of these, from his own perspective, provided the framework for the behavioral sciences to become actively involved in the study of crime and the criminal. However, developments in criminology in the last decade have served only to emphasize that the concerns of the classical school are still relevant—and perhaps increasingly so.

As disillusionment sets in about the capacity to fully understand the etiology of crime, as reservations are increasingly being expressed about the rehabilitative goals of penal philosophy and correctional practices, so attention is turning more to issues of the sociology of law, including a reassessment of the workings of the criminal-justice system and of penological principles and policies—the very concerns that find expression in the work of the classical criminologists.

A return to the classical writers, however, does not necessarily mean a return to all the ideas espoused by them. On the contrary, debate over these ideas rages today no less than when they were first propounded as innovative ideas almost two centuries ago. But therein lies much of the attraction and the value of a return to the sources—not in order to adopt uncritically what was laid down, but in order to use these ideas to delineate the nature of the present debate.

The two leading figures of the classical school are Cesare Beccaria and Jeremy Bentham; their lives, no less than their works, hold many interesting parallels, as well as idiosyncratic differences.[1] Both had studied law, though neither practiced it. Both published their first critiques of the criminal law anonymously—Beccaria because of his apprehensions as to possible negative reactions from the Austrian rulers of Lombardy and Bentham for reasons that probably relate to his reluctance to mount a direct attack against one of England's greatest legal luminaries of that time, Blackstone. For Beccaria, the divulging of his name led to instant widespread recognition and invitations to travel and consult with distinguished rulers and writers; for Bentham, the curiosity that had been aroused about the identity of the young author of *A Fragment on Government* was completely dispelled when his name was published, and with it the interest in the content of what he had written was abated. In Beccaria's case, his ideas were compressed into a slim one-hundred-page tract, which remained his major, almost his sole, contribution to the study of criminal law.[2] For Bentham, his treatise was merely the opening salvo of an extensive, continuing appraisal of the law in all its complexities, as part of an overall philosophy; some of his works remain unfinished fragments and to this day languish in archival boxes.[3]

Both writers showed a keen interest in economics. Bentham's philosophy was based on the rational calculations of a *homo economicus;* Beccaria subsequently forsook the law entirely for a career in economics, first as a professor, later as a civil servant. Both were influenced by many French philosophers, such as Montesquieu, Voltaire, and Helvetius, with some of whom they maintained direct contacts. Both toyed with the possibility of having their ideas implemented in the Russia of Catherine the Great, who was bent on introducing reform in many areas, including the criminal law. For Beccaria, this involved an invitation to travel to Russia and to assist directly as consultant in the formation of a new penal code, while for Bentham it involved the hope that his work would be recognized and that the reform-minded Catherine would ask him to participate in the formulation of a new code. After lengthy consultations with friends, family, and colleagues, Beccaria turned down the offer; Bentham actually traveled to Russia to visit with his younger brother, who worked there as a naval architect, but when the opportunity to meet personally with Catherine presented itself, he avoided it.

Both men sought and found patrons who were active in intellectual, legal, and political life. For Bentham, among the most prominent were Lord Mansfield, Chief Justice of the King's Bench, in whose court and chambers Bentham spent many long hours watching critically the system of justice in action, and Lord Shelburne, a leading politician who was prime minister for two years. For Beccaria, they included the group of young intellectuals who gathered around Pietro Verri, who was instrumental in encouraging Beccaria to write his analysis of crime and punishment and, later, with his brother, wrote a spirited defense of it when it was attacked,[4] and Count Firmian, the administrator of Lombardy, who also came to the aid of Beccaria and was instrumental in gaining him a position as a university lecturer in economics.

Finally, although they were not part of any school (the term *classical criminology* was obviously supplied only long after both were dead), Bentham, the younger of the two, clearly indicated his indebtedness to Beccaria for some of his ideas. More specifically, the very definition of utility, bandied about by several people before Bentham latched on to it as the key principle in his philosophy, was taken almost verbatim from Beccaria.

Rationality and Utilitarianism

The classical school represents an attempt to ensure the maximum expression of a rational system of justice within the criminal law by applying the basic ideas of utilitarian ethics, with its overriding concept of the greatest happiness for the greatest number of people.

Both Beccaria and Bentham were men of the Age of Reason, products of the Enlightenment, purveyors of ideas whose time had come—reflecting as well as moulding the climate of opinion. They were humanists and liberals. Their recognition of basic rights and equality for all was based on (or, perhaps, led to) a fundamental principle of philosophy that permeates much of their conceptions of the legal system—the doctrine of free will, of the capacity of each person to control his life, and of the corresponding obligation to bear responsibility for the consequences of exercising such control, including full criminal liability for illegal acts, unmitigated by any individual or group factors.

They developed a penal philosophy based on the precise calculations of rational people. The punishments to be imposed were to be of sufficient severity as to deter the offender, and others, from violating the law in the future. However, their severity was not to extend beyond the minimum that would be sufficient to achieve the declared aim of deterrence. Neither the desire for retribution nor the hope of rehabilitating the individual was to be part of the court's considerations.

In their desire for a rational system of human behavior based on equal treatment for all, they ignored or denied individual differences stemming from differential personal experiences or the impact of social factors. Theirs was a humanism that sought to do away with the influences and the inequities of earlier times; it was a humanism that sought to put all people on an equal basis, at least in terms of their intrinsic worth, their basic rights, and, specifically, their treatment in the courts of law. Neither the hoary traditions of the past nor the honorific privileges of the present were to undermine the processes of the criminal law.

Yet, as Sellin, Geis, and other critics have pointed out,[5] there was no room in their broad humanism for the human being; they failed to take account of the person as an individual. In their attempt to ensure standard procedures and undifferentiated treatment, they ignored the simple fact—which was to become a tenet of mainstream academic criminology and practical administration of justice—that people do differ, whether as individuals or as members of different groups, and that a more sophisticated understanding of equality and justice may actually require differentiated responses. They failed to take into account the personal motivations and needs of the criminals in the judicial system.

In their attempt to eradicate the influences of the whims and prejudices of judges, they tried to impose a uniformity that would pervade all facets of the criminal-justice system, including sentencing procedures. They sought not the promise of rehabilitation of the individual criminal but the prospect of general deterrence of the public at large. In trying to free the criminal-law system of its emphasis on retribution and vindictive measures, they introduced a system that, in its search for an abstract justice and a predetermined system of penalties, was often no less arbitrary and unfair to the recipients of that system.

And so, in the past hundred years, as the behavioral sciences have made us increasingly aware of the subtleties and nuances of human behavior and of its variety, both between individuals, and in groups of people or subcultures, so classical criminology has been relegated to the realm of prescientific criminology, of limited, mainly historical interest.

In addition, Bentham's larger philosophy of utilitarianism—the search for the greatest good and happiness for the greatest number—has fallen by the wayside as the political arena has seethed with the struggles of ideologies that came later—communism, socialism, conservatism, fascism, anarchism. Even the liberal others, which, in some respects, Bentham represented, has been related far more to the work of John Stuart Mill, who is also considered a utilitarian but whose philosophy elucidated liberal principles far more clearly than did that of Bentham.[6]

The Revival of Classical Ideas

As positivist criminology—whether Lombrosian biology, Freudian psychology, or Durkheimian sociology—seems to have reached an impasse and as, for all the accumulation of knowledge and for all the practical experimentation, the crime rate continues to rise, so the basic framework (if not the specific proposals) of Beccaria's and Bentham's ideas, is slowly infiltrating back into criminological studies. Practitioners of the sociology of law are urging vigorously that there can be no understanding of crime without a prior investigation of the criminal-law system, with a special emphasis on the manner in which laws are passed and the political interests involved, rather than on the manner in which the courts operate or the need for penal reform. The whole process of social control through the criminal-law system is also being subjected to intense scrutiny, as in the work of the labeling theorists. Yet, whereas Beccaria and Bentham saw mainly specific injustices *within* the judicial system, today's theorists see also the larger societal implications, including the very social control that Beccaria and Bentham desired only to formalize, rationalize, and equalize, as a causative factor in the etiology of crime.[7]

In a parallel development, more and more penologists are arguing for an end to individualized punishment.[8] However, while they seek standardized penalties, they do so not for deterrence but for retribution, the very concept that Bentham and Beccaria were trying to counter.

Going further afield, denouncements of torture, particularly prominent in

Beccaria's work, have been given renewed interest in recent years—not so much in academic criminology but in the polemic work of human-rights organizations.[9] These organizations have provided a mass of clear evidence that torture is not only an unfortunate holdover from earlier dark ages, as so many have tended to see it, but also sometimes very much a part of the stable machinery used by unscrupulous politicians and their henchmen and hatchetmen to maintain tight control over dissident groups and dissenting opinions.

The torture of the ancient regime that Beccaria condemned has recently been presented in a novel manner by a leading historian of law, John Langbein.[10] In a fascinating analysis, he makes two telling points: first, that torture was used not in an arbitrary manner but only under specific, almost rational circumstances, when proof of the commission of the crime already existed but the accused refused to confess; and second, that the system of plea-bargaining today is an irrational counterpoint to this. Langbein argues: "The European jurists devised what Anglo-American lawyers would today call a rule of probable cause, designed to assure that only persons highly likely to be guilty would be examined under torture."[11] Before torture would be employed, there would have to be partial proof, as the torture would be designed not for punishment but to gain detailed factual information about the crime.

Langbein then carries his argument further by arguing that the essential link between torture and plea-bargaining is that both are coercive. "Like the medieval Europeans, the Americans are now operating a procedural system that engages in condemnation without adjudication. The maxim of the medieval glossators, no longer applicable to European law, now aptly describes American law . . . 'confession is the queen of proof'."[12] Langbein notes that, in the European law, the torture victim would be made to repeat his confession voluntarily "but under the threat of being tortured anew if he recanted."[13]

Of course, Langbein's critique does not relate to the cruelty involved in torture; what he is arguing is that both torture and plea-bargaining are coercive and use similar rules regarding when the processes are to be activated. Moreover, he notes that the modern European system of law has developed a more rational system of seeking proof and of determining guilt or innocence and that the Anglo-American system of law seems to be bogged down in an anachronistic system of logic.

Thus, plea-bargaining has now become central to the criminal-justice system today, wherein so much justice is dispensed in an arbitrary and capricious manner. This is indeed a far cry from the impartial justice advocated by the classic writers. Others, too, have written of the widespread ramifications of discretionary justice, particularly in sentencing but also in other areas, such as administrative law.[14] In all these areas, one finds examples of the lack of clear-cut criteria for decision making, the very capriciousness that the classical criminologists had railed against.

Jurists from the school of legal realism have tried to show, just as the classical criminologists did, how arbitrary the law is and how much it has been influenced by situational factors and the personal characteristics of judges. However, the legal realists argue not for a transformation into a rigid, formalistic, and rational system but for a recognition of its haphazardness. Whereas Bentham devoted much effort to trying to eliminate what he called the ''fictions of the law,''[15] such writers as Jerome Frank argue against the ''myths of the law'' as a rational, predictable, consistent system.[16] For them, what is required is not a change in the system but an awareness of the fact that the judge does not automatically and mechanistically apply the law and that he is a human being with a personal philosophy, perhaps even prejudices, which may intrude on his decisions. Since these cannot be eliminated, as was the proposed solution of Beccaria and Bentham, it would be best to recognize human frailties rather than legislate them away by a rigid and formalistic system of law.

The Debate on Capital Punishment

An issue that has evoked increasing concern in recent years has been that of capital punishment, a topic dealt with by both Bentham and Beccaria. Although Bentham originally was intent only on limiting the excesses of capital punishment, he later, in 1830, published a pamphlet, ''On Death Punishment,'' in which he argued for total abolition. However, earlier, Beccaria had become one of the first writers to mount a concerted attack on the death penalty as an illogical and unfair measure. Echoes of Beccaria's ideas, even where there is no direct acknowledgment of his work, have reverberated in recent years in academic and public debate, in legislative and judicial decisions, in polemic books, and in the deliberations of international conferences.

However, not all of those who have participated in this debate have related to the need to suggest equitable and effective alternatives that would satisfy the various aims of penal philosophy. For instance, Beccaria himself advocated penal slavery. Indeed, the opponents of capital punishment may find that the success of their efforts is questioned by those on whose behalf they have struggled. There may even be grave consequences, either in the imposition of other penalties that may be considered more serious by some, or in the denial of freedom of choice to the accused.

These views have been most pertinently expressed by Jacques Barzun, who argues, from a liberal perspective, that the alternatives to capital punishment may turn out to be more vicious and cruel than the death penalty.[17] A sentence of life imprisonment may well be defined and graded as a lesser penalty by legislators, judges, and criminologists, but it is liable to be seen as more onerous by at least some accused. If one of the concerns of abolitionists is to advance the rights of the accused, then they must earnestly and humbly consider how much attention should be paid to their expressed wishes. The Gilmore case provides a poignant reminder of the fact that even the most persuasive arguments against the death penalty may fail to convince the convicted.[18] The question then becomes whether public-spirited people who are opposed to the idea of capital punishment for deep philosophical and practical reasons are entitled to impose their wishes on a convicted criminal who asks that he be judicially executed.

Barzun has his own solution to this dilemma—allowing the accused to choose the penalty. Surely, for those who place the maximum emphasis on the individual's free will, as Beccaria did, this could be a real test of their ideas. Certainly, many of liberal persuasion who are opposed to capital punishment concede the right of an individual to commit suicide. Why should this right be denied a convicted criminal, especially when his own conception of just deserts or expiation demands such a punishment? (Of course, there are clear problems in deciding if an accused person is really exercising free will. Further, it could be that other prisoners, who are sentenced for noncapital offenses, might also request such a right.)

In any event, Beccaria recognized the connection between suicide and capital punishment, but for him the argument went in an opposite direction. According to him, since suicide was a crime, there should also be no death penalty, because the prohibition on the taking of life was absolute and applicable in all cases. As Maestro argues: "It is clear that Beccaria's opposition to the death penalty would be weakened by his recognition that man does have the right to take his own life."[19] However, with suicide no longer a crime in many modern jurisdictions, this part of Beccaria's argument on the death penalty takes on a different dimension. Does the right to take one's life (the decriminalization of suicide) affect the issue of the death penalty?

Beccaria's work on capital punishment, however, becomes even more problematic and disturbing when seen in relation to the alternatives he suggested. As Sellin points out, Beccaria's alternatives sometimes involved a "penalty worse than death."[20] Seeking a rational means of deterring others, he suggested that "the intensity of the punishment of penal slavery, as substitute for the death penalty, possesses that which suffices to deter any determined soul," since "the evildoer begins his sufferings instead of terminating them."[21]

Sellin describes the practices of penal slavery: "The alternatives were forced labor of excruciating kinds or frightful imprisonment, for life or long terms." Many convicts, forced into hard labor, such as barge-towing on the Danube, subjected to the whips of their guards, deprived of adequate nutrition, "actually were subjected to a prolonged death penalty,"[22] many of them dying in an emaciated condition. Other penalties that replaced the death penalty were various corporal punishments, from chaining in a confined space to public whipping. Sellin also notes that, in his zeal for reform of the criminal law, Beccaria "left no room for the reformation of the offender." More sadly, "his advocacy of penal slavery encouraged the invention of horrid forms of imprisonment believed to be more deterrent than death."[23]

Whatever the reservations about Beccaria's work, it is interesting to note that the very criterion that Beccaria attempted to place at the heart of the criminal-justice system has recently been incorporated by the U.S. Supreme Court as the standard by which the constitutionality of the death penalty will be measured. According to recent decisions, there must be clear-cut guidelines as to when the death penalty may be imposed.[24] In particular, the court has tried to eliminate the inconsistencies that criminological research had shown to be characteristic of the utilization of the death penalty. In essence, the court is trying to avoid that very arbitrariness and capriciousness that Beccaria had condemned. In doing so, they may, however inadvertently, have created a legal and logical framework whose ultimate implication seems to be total abolition of capital punishment. The final stage of the death penalty—the pardoning power of the executive—is always capricious and arbitrary, inherently and irrevocably so. By definition, by its very nature, the pardoning power *must* be arbitrary and capricious. It is a personal decision of the highest executive officer. In making this decision, the executive officer is bound by no rules, no precedents, no past practices. It is his personal feelings that are expressed; it is the power of his office that is implemented.

Of course, from a strictly legal point of view, it could be argued that the pardoning power is an executive power, not a judicial one, and thus outside the purview of the court's decision. But this would be more than just sheltering behind a narrow legalism; it would be denying the essence of what the Supreme Court was trying to achieve. At issue were not only the arbitrary decision-making processes of judges and juries but the ultimate consequences for the accused—specifically, that, in fact, this most extreme and final of all penalties was being carried out in a highly discriminatory manner.

Simply, there is no way to avoid this arbitrariness; it is an inherent part of the pardoning process. And, uniquely in the case of capital punishment, the pardoning power is almost always an integral part of the total sentencing process, either because the death warrant requires the signature of the executive officer or because the condemned person, or some public group acting on his behalf, inevitably make appeals for pardon. In a federal state, where different people have the pardoning power, the degree of arbitrariness becomes even more acute.[25]

Thus, I would claim that the arguments advanced by Beccaria against the death penalty may well be on the threshold of official policy in the United

States, not just because his ideas on capital punishment have been accepted, but because of the application of another aspect of his philosophy of criminal justice—the desire to do away with arbitrariness.

One further aspect of Beccaria's strong opposition to the death penalty is of interest, both historical and current. The high regard in which he was held in France led to his ideas being considered when legislation was passed in the heady early days of the French Revolution. In 1791, his works were referred to and his words were quoted by some of the speakers in the debate on capital punishment. One of these was Robespierre, "a deputy from Arras, where he had been appointed criminal judge, but had then resigned as he did not want to pronounce a death sentence. Robespierre spoke for an hour with great eloquence, stressing all of Beccaria's reasons for the abolition of capital punishment."[26]

However, neither the force of Beccaria's logic nor Robespierre's eloquence was sufficient to convince the members of the Constituent Assembly, and they voted to retain the death penalty. Only a few short years later, Robespierre, reneging on his earlier beliefs, instituted the Reign of Terror, in the culmination of which he himself, because of his excesses, was finally put to death.

This, too, has a lesson for modern times. Today, many of Beccaria's ideas on the death penalty are slowly being accepted. Many countries are now in the process of abolishing the death penalty or severely restricting its application. Yet, there is an unresolved issue in regard to the death penalty for political ends, including extralegal capital punishment carried out with the prior sanction or subsequent ratification of government authorities.[27] Minor "reigns of terror" continue to blight the landscape of political reality and the criminal-justice system. In fact, so widespread is the practice of extralegal judicial punishment that advocates of civil liberties and human rights in some countries are engaged in deep debate as to whether it would not be desirable to retain a legal death penalty, which might at least afford accused persons, particularly political prisoners, a greater chance of saving their lives through the due process of law. Beccaria had been greatly distressed by the perversions of the French Revolution. He had "followed with a heavy heart the terrible course of events. He had advocated fairness in the administration of justice, and the courts of justice of the nation he admired so much had now become courts of condemnation without trial. He had advocated the abolition of the death penalty even for the worst crimes as a necessary step toward a more civilized society, and thousands of citizens were being beheaded, often without a conviction, in an immense sacrifice to the bloodthirsty men in power,"[28] including those, such as Robespierre, who had once accepted his ideas.

Herein lies a sober message for criminologists, one that the classical writers understood very well. The work of criminology is not merely an academic discipline. Indeed, neither Beccaria nor Bentham practiced criminology as such.

Their work on the criminal-justice system was part of an extension of their overall philosophy and ideology.

They saw the criminal law and judicial practices as being of pivotal importance in determining the nature of a society, the quality of its life, the essence of its morality. Whatever the present-day relevance of the specifics contained in their theories, whatever reservations or criticisms may be advanced, whatever defects may be divulged, modern criminology should take note of the spirit in which their work was conducted.

This is why classical criminology should be seen not as some quaint and antiquated relic from the past but as possessed of vitality and significance for today.

This is its real legacy, with its evergreen message.

Notes

1. Coleman Phillipson, *Three Criminal Law Reformers: Beccaria, Bentham, Romily* (London: J.M. Dent and Sons, 1923).

2. See Cesare Beccaria, *On Crime and Punishment*, trans. H. Paolucci (Indianapolis: Bobbs-Merrill, 1963).

3. Jeremy Bentham, *The Works of Jeremy Bentham* (1816).

4. This work, by Pietro and Alessandro Verri, is often presented and published as authored by Beccaria.

5. On Beccaria, see, for example, Thorsten Sellin, "Beccaria's Substitute for the Death Penalty," in *Criminology in Pespective: Essays in Honor of Israel Drapkin,* ed. Simha F. Landau and Leslie Sebba (Lexington, Mass.: Lexington Books, D.C. Heath and Company, 1977), pp. 3–11; on Bentham, see Gilbert Geis, "Jeremy Bentham (1748–1832)," in *Pioneers in Criminology,* ed. Hermann Mannheim (Montclair, N.J.: Patterson Smith, 1972).

6. John Stuart Mill, *On Liberty* (Garden City, N.Y.: Doubleday, 1961). See also F.R. Leavis, ed., *Mill on Bentham and Coleridge* (London: Chatto and Windus, 1950). For a good and comprehensive account of Bentham's philosophy, see Mary P. Mack, *Jeremy Bentham: An Odyssey of Ideas* (London: Heinemann, 1962); see also David Lyons, *In the Interest of the Governed: A Study in Bentham's Philosophy of Utility and Law* (Oxford: Clarendon Press, 1973).

7. See, especially, Edwin Lemert, *Human Deviance, Social Problems and Social Control,* 2nd ed. (Englewood Cliffs, N.J.: Prentice-Hall, 1972).

8. See, for example, Andrew von Hirsch, *On Justice* (New York: Hill and Wang, 1976), and Ernest van den Haag, *Punishing Criminals* (New York: Basic Books, 1975).

9. See, for example, Amnesty International "Report on Torture," 1973.

10. John H. Langbein, "Torture and Plea Bargaining," *University of Chi-*

cago Law Review 46(1978):3. See also his larger study, *Torture and the Law of Proof: Europe and England in the Ancient Regime* (Chicago: University of Chicago Press, 1977).

11. Ibid., p. 5

12. Ibid., p. 14

13. Ibid., p. 14

14. See, especially, Kenneth Davis, *Discretionary Justice* (Baton Rouge: Louisiana State University Press, 1969).

15. Jeremy Bentham, *Theory of Fictions* (London: K. Paul, Trench, Trubner, 1932).

16. Jerome Frank, *Courts on Trial: Myth and Reality in American Justice* (Princeton: Princeton University Press, 1950).

17. Jacques Barzun, "In Favor of Capital Punishment," in *The Death Penalty in America,* ed. Hugo Bedau (Garden City, N.Y.: Anchor Books, 1967).

18. See Norman Mailer, *The Executioner's Song* (Boston: Little, Brown, 1979).

19. Marcello Maestro, *Cesare Beccaria and the Origins of Penal Reform* (Philadelphia: Temple University Press, 1973), p. 31.

20. Sellin, "Beccaria's Substitute for the Death Penalty," p. 7.

21. Ibid., p. 4

22. Ibid., p. 6

23. Ibid., p. 8

24. Furman v. Georgia, 408 U.S. 238 (1972); Gregg v. Georgia, 428 U.S. 153 (1976).

25. For an analysis of the arbitrariness of the criminal-justice system in capital cases, see Charles Black, Jr., *Capital Punishment: The Inevitability of Caprice and Mistake* (New York: Norton, 1974). Black discusses all stages of the system. To the best of my knowledge, my legal contention as to the inevitable arbitrariness of the pardoning stage has not been argued specifically before the Supreme Court. For the pardon as a personal act of grace, see G.S. Buchanan, "The Nature of Pardon under the United States Constitution," *Ohio State Law Journal* 39(1978):36.

26. Maestro, *Cesare Beccaria,* p. 153.

27. See Eddy Kaufman, "Murder Committed or Acquiesced in by Government" (Paper presented at the Conference on the Abolition of the Death Penalty, Stockholm, 1977, organized by Amnesty International).

28. Maestro, *Cesare Beccaria,* p. 154. See also Larry C. Berkson, *The Concept of Cruel and Unusual Punishment* (Lexington, Mass.: Lexington Books, D.C. Heath, 1975).

2 Positivism and Neo-Lombrosianism

Gideon Fishman

Not long ago, being considered a nonpositivist was almost an insult to the social scientist. Only in the last decade and a half, with the revival of humanistic social science and the increased interest in symbolic interaction, phenomenology, and ethnomethodology, and the rise of neo-Marxist sociology, has the virtue of positivism been brought into question.

During the last century and a half, criminology largely adhered to the principles of positivism as formulated by August Comte, who stated that the positivist stage is the third stage, in which all phenomena, including the social, are subject to natural laws, to observation, and to experimentation. By crowning sociology as the queen of science, he suggested, in fact, that social phenomena must be perceived as on a continuum with natural phenomena; and, since sociology deals with the most complicated matters, its methodological growth as a discipline reaches its peak following the development of less complicated areas of research, such as biology, chemistry, and physics. (Some would undoubtedly consider this an elegant rationalization for inadequate methodology.) What is evident from Comte's evolutionary view of the development of knowledge is that the positivist stage succeeds a metaphysical level of knowledge.

Temporally, the positivist school of criminology did indeed follow a metaphysical school of thought (the classical school) and to a large extent should be viewed as a reaction to it. Positivist criminology represents, in fact, the antithetical critique of classical attempts to explain crime as the willful, premeditated, and controllable act of a rational human being exercising his free will. Such views as those expressed by Bentham and Beccaria were rooted in an extreme, optimistic belief in the human mind and its potential and reflected the theorists' subscription to a radical, nondeterministic view.[1]

For the positivist, such assumptions are totally inadequate. From a deterministic perspective, the idea of free will becomes irrelevant, since it is not the person who, by his own intent and volition, gets involved in crime. The answer to why one gets involved in crime must be sought elsewhere. Positivism, as a general school of thought, provides few clues as to where to look for etiological

The author wishes to thank Professor C. Ronald Huff for his valuable advice and assistance in the preparation of this chapter.

answers. However, it does tell us a great deal about how to go about our search for answers.

Early positivism represented not only an era in which the words *positivism* and *science* became synonyms and the scientific method was superordinate, but also an era in which there was only one "scientific method." The distinction in methods relevant to the knowledge of man, as opposed to the knowledge of natural phenomena (as suggested, for example, by the German idealist school represented by Dilthey Windelband and others), was pushed aside in favor of the unification of all subjects of inquiry under the same scientific method.

Positivism: Definition and Implications

What is meant by the concept of positivism? It has a variety of connotations. In the domain of research and methodology, it entails adhering to the inductive method, painstakingly collecting measurable and verifiable data, subjecting any assumption to empirical verification, and taking nothing for granted. Positivism also has something to say with regard to man and his behavior. Human action is perceived as determined by external forces beyond one's control; the doctrine of free will is categorically rejected.

From a jurisprudential point of view, positivists were concerned with neither guilt, nor criminal intent, nor the seriousness of the offense. These issues, which were so central to classical jurisprudence, were simply beside the point for the positivists.[2] It seems that the only point positivists had in common with classical criminology was the belief that punishment should be no more nor less than what was necessary to prevent crime. However, unlike the classical school, the early positivists were very pessimistic about our ability to reform criminals. This pessimism seemingly stemmed from the conviction that criminals are born, a position that is incompatible with the reformist mission. Rather than corrections, the main concern of the positivist school became society's well being, and this is where the social-defense ideology gained prominence. Under the social-defense principle, we find Garofalo's proposals of total and partial elimination of born criminals as well as Hooton's views concerning effective ways to reduce criminality by reducing the size of the criminal population. It is such ideology that lies at the core of the U.S. Supreme Court's decision in the famous case of *Buck* v. *Bell* (1972), wherein the Court upheld the right of the State of Virginia to carry out sterilization against a person's will under certain circumstances, such as the existence of feeblemindedness.

For positivists, the rationale for punishment is to protect society. Therefore, the proper punishment has little to do with the offense. Unlike the classical view that punishment should fit the offense, positivists assert that it should fit the offender. Further, punishment must be related not only to the harm inflicted but also to the potential danger. This divergence in views results in the classical school's focus on the offense and the positivists' preoccupation with the offender.

For positivists, the way to study the criminal is through the application of the scientific method, but this is not to suggest that uniformity or consensus exists among criminologists as to the proper explanatory variables that should be examined. The controversies within the positivist school center around proper data collection, sampling, and the validity and reliability of measurements.

Traditionally, the inception of the positivist school of criminology has been attributed to Lombroso and his pioneering work *L'Uomo Delinquente*,[3] wherein the term "born criminal" gained fame. His naive and unprecedented attempt led him to state that "in criminal man, the moral insensibility is as great as the physical insensibility; undoubtedly the one is the effect of the other."[4]

For many, the mere mention of Lombroso's name will be sufficient reason to ridicule him, but the fact is that Lombroso did not represent a passing episode, and his contribution goes far beyond his substantive writings. His most important contribution was in the methodological-epistemological realm. The example set by his work, regardless of how incompetent it may be by present-day scientific-research criteria, paved the way for future generations of criminologists, who, although they undoubtedly improved upon his research methods and explanatory variables, have not really altered Lombroso's essential paradigm for studying crime.

The roles played by physicians such as Gall, Spurzhein, Lombroso, Lange, Kretschmer, and Sheldon in the development of positivism greatly affected the search for possible answers to account for criminal behavior. As physicians, it was natural for them to look for clues in the contribution of the body and its chemistry, which they regarded as the major explanatory variables in all human behavior.

In what is generally known as the biological school, one can identify three major, broad lines of inquiry.[5] The first is morphological or anthropological criminology. It began with Lombroso and his evolutionary concept of atavism (borrowed from Darwin), according to which the criminal is supposed to be a throwback in the evolutionary chain, representing both mental and physical inferiority.

Charles Goring, although disputing Lombroso's findings and casting doubts on the validity of that approach, used similar anthropometric measurements for his study.[6] His findings did not bring this line of research to a halt, and we find others, such as Hooton, Sheldon, and even the Gluecks, pursuing similar ideas.[7]

Once biological determinism and the idea that criminals are inferior individuals began to be established, the logical question to pursue was whether such inferiority was hereditary. This line of research represents the second trend in the biological approach. The research began with Dugdale's study of criminal families,[8] and it continued in a much more careful and improved manner by Goddard.[9] These two early works seem to document the degeneration of subsequent generations. This claim was also evident in the early works of others, such as Tarde, Huxley, and Aschaffenburg.[10] Whereas all those early works implied hereditary causation but actually talked about the transmission of traits, it was Lange who tried to posit the definitive answer to the question of heredity in his famous twin study.[11]

From this point on, although some biologically oriented research continued, the biological approach in general was on the retreat, and it took almost half a century for biologically oriented research in criminology to reappear and become an issue again.[12] Its reemergence was in two major directions. One was the continuation of the genetic trend, but employing a much more sophisticated methodology, such as that manifested by Christiansen in his Danish study or by Dalgard and Kringlen in Norway.[13] Of course, one must not omit the highly celebrated research on the XYY anomaly, which flourished during the 1960s and 1970s.[14] It is interesting how this area of research has been summarized recently, in a most carefully designed study by Witkin and his associates:

> No evidence has been found that men with either of these sex chromosome complements [XYY or XXY] are especially aggressive. Because such men do not appear to contribute particularly to society's problem with aggressive crime, their identification would not serve to ameliorate this problem.[15]

The other vein of research represents the third general trend of the biological orientation and takes a physiological perspective. Here the main focus has been on the individual designated psychopathic or sociopathic or, as it stands today, the individual with an antisocial personality. Quay suggested that this individual's behavior should be perceived as manifesting an extreme stimulation-seeking pattern.[16] According to Quay, the behavior indicates sensory deprivation. Other evidence suggests that the abnormal pattern of response to the environment is a result of defective cortical activity, which is the product of dramatically elevated heart rate and blood pressure. The antisocial individual is perceived as a person with an exaggerated cardiovascular-response pattern (a condition known as cardiac lability), who requires a more intensive range of stimuli. In this area, notable and extensive interdisciplinary research has been conducted by Goldman, Dinitz, Lindner, Foster, and Allen.[17] This research also addresses the issue of treatment of the violent sociopathic offender.

Sociological Positivism

What has been described thus far has been a brief sketch of the biological approach in criminology, but it must be mentioned that the positivist school of criminology also contains a dominant sociological orientation, which has functioned as an antithesis to early positivism, especially in the United States. As Don Gibbons points out, most of the accounts offered by social scientists in the

United States near the turn of the nineteenth century were derived from social Darwinism and biological perspectives on social order that dominated that historical period.[18] However, in examining contemporary criminology, one realizes that biological factors are consistently ignored. This switch in perspective is a result of broad, historical sweeps of events in the United States during the first two decades of the twentieth century, a period that is also known as the progressive era. While Darwinism and biologically based perspectives were regarded as conservative and pessimistic, notions that were related to rehabilitation, assistance to the poor, and the social responsibility of the community to its unfortunate members were considered liberal and progressive ideas. Social science became associated with the social-reform movement and categorically rejected ideas that were associated with conservatism.

What we have been witnessing, in fact, has been a substitution for biological determinism—social determinism. Thus, a vast number of criminological accounts of criminal behavior are actually attempts to attribute causality to one or another set of social variables. Whereas the biological approach perceived human behavior as being determined by genetic defects, constitutional factors, or physiological impediments, sociological determinism attributes criminal behavior to economic-class position;[19] social disorganization;[20] cultures, subcultures, and anomie;[21] or the system itself, as implied by the labeling theorists.[22]

To cite all works relevant to our point is obviously impossible under the circumstances, since, as Rennie points out "there are almost as many American theories of what 'causes' crime as there are American automobiles."[23] One thing common to all, however, is the rejection of the notion that causal factors reside within the individual, as implied by biological positivism. Contemporary criminologists prefer to identify the causes of crime as external to the offender. What emerges is the notion of the dangerous society, rather than the dangerous individual. Gibbons suggests that such a view, if held consistently, must adopt the assumption that, generally, most offenders are mentally and biologically normal individuals and that their motivations toward lawbreaking have been shaped mostly by criminogenic conditions.[24]

Criticisms of the Sociological Approach

Some have questioned the adequacy of explanations that make no room for other than sociological variables.[25] Van den Berghe, in his paper "Bringing Beast Back In," claims that many forms of behavior are the product of necessary interplay between biological predispositions and environment, which points to the artificiality of opposing these two sets of behavioral determinants.[26] His reasoning follows the assumption that human behavior is not radically discontinuous from that of other species; therefore, there is no reason to assume that biological makeup does not affect our behavior when it so clearly affects that of other species. Critics of sociological explanations point out that such explanations will continue to be incomplete and inadequate unless the biological bases of behavior are acknowledged and incorporated. Perhaps that is what the vague term *neo-Lombrosianism* means. If we disregard the discomfort and possible stigma associated with the term, what we see is that the new protagonists of biological research, besides offering highly sophisticated research techniques, are also far from pushing aside the sociological variables.

As I have tried to point out, the sociological school represents a normative-ideological antithesis to early positivism, and the question that should be addressed is why we are witnessing the revival of biological approaches. One explanation is the failure of the sociological perspective to formulate a comprehensive etiological approach and its total failure in the field of correction. It was the pragmatic need to control violent behavior and to maintain the "normal" daily routine at correctional institutions that, at the height of the sociological trend, found us dispensing huge amounts of tranquilizers in our institutions.

The new interest in biological factors can be seen as a synthesis of the extreme biological determinism of the early positivists and the contemporary sociological school. The new synthesis offered by the neobiological school (I hope this term sounds less offensive) may incorporate a behavioral approach; any explanation must be based upon behavioral principles. Accordingly, all behavior is a function of the personal characteristics of the individual concerned and the situation in which he finds himself. Buikhuisen suggests a formula to express criminal behavior: *Cf (PjSj),* where:

C = criminal behavior

Pj = the collective expression of personal characteristics relevant to an explanation of criminal behavior, such as genetic factors, endocrinological variables, biological factors related to the brain, neurophysiological variables, biochemical factors, psychophysiological factors, organic factors, psychiatric factors, psychological factors, sociological variables, attitudes, norms, and values.

Sj = the situation at the microlevel at which criminal behavior took place; the situation at the mesolevel where there has been some element of interaction with a third party, such as parents, school, police, probation; the situation at the macrolevel—the social system and the social, political economic, and educational climate in which one lives.[27]

The opposition manifested by mainstream American criminology to the neobiological approach is to a large degree a response to the traditional biological claims of early constitutionalists, European traditionalists, and endocrine criminologists, which were extraordinarily obstructive and hasty. As Dinitz and his colleagues point out, extrapolations have been based on the most meager evidence.[28] They caution us that their conclusions "should not forever be permitted to stand as impediments to the reconsideration of the role of organicity in the more idiosyncratic, bizzare and non-normative forms of deviance.'' They go on to suggest that the reconsideration of organic factors ''in no way diminishes the importance of the comparative, cultural, and interactional perspectives long dominant in American thought.''[29]

Perhaps, if we can divorce ourselves from the bonds of ideological preferences and be more dedicated to arriving at a comprehensive response to the question at hand, we may witness the flourishing of wide-scale, truly integrative, interdisciplinary research in the future.

Notes

1. Jeremy Bentham, *An Introduction to the Principles of Morals and Legislation.* (New York: Hafner, 1948; reprint of the 1823 edition); Cesare Beccaria, *On Crime and Punishment, 1764,* trans. H. Paolucci (Indianapolis: Bobbs-Merrill, 1963).

2. Ysabel Rennie, *The Search for Criminal Man.* (Lexington, Mass.: Lexington Books, D.C. Heath and Company, 1978).

3. Cesare Lombroso, *L'Uomo Delinquente* (1876). Later translated and edited by his daughter, Gina Ferroro, *The Criminal Man* (Montclair, N.J.: Patterson Smith, 1972).

4. From a speech given by Lombroso on the opening of the Sixth Congress of Criminal Anthropology, Turin, 1906.

5. Harold J. Vetter and Ira J. Silverman, *The Nature of Crime* (Philadelphia: W. B. Saunders Co., 1978).

6. Charles Goring, *The English Convict* (London: Her Majesty's Stationery Office, 1913).

7. Earnest A. Hooton, *Crime and the Man* (Cambridge, Mass.: Harvard University Press, 1935); William H. Sheldon, *Varieties of Delinquent Youth: Introduction to Constitutional Psychiatry.* (New York: Harper, 1949); Sheldon and Eleanor Glueck, *Unraveling Juvenile Delinquency* (Cambridge, Mass.: Harvard University Press, 1950).

8. R.L. Dugdale, *The Jukes: A Study in Crime, Pauperism, Disease and Heredity,* 5th ed (New York: Putnam, 1895).

9. Henry H. Goddard, *The Kallikak Family: A Study in the Heredity of Feeblemindedness* (New York: Macmillan, 1912).

10. Gabriel Tarde, *La Criminaliste Comparee* (Paris: Alcan, 1886); Thomas Henry Huxley, ''Evolution and Ethics'' (1894), in *Selections from the Essays of T.H. Huxley* (New York: Crofts, 1948); Gustav Aschaffenburg, *Crime and Its Repression,* trans. Adalbert Albrecht (Boston: Little, Brown, 1913).

11. Johannes Lange, *Crime as Destiny* (London: Allen and Unwin, 1931).

12. Rennie, *The Search for Criminal Man,* p. 92.

13. Karl O. Christiansen, ''A Preliminary Study of Criminality Among

Twins" in *Biosocial Bases of Criminality,* eds. Sarnoff A. Mednick and Karl
O. Christiansen (New York: Gardner Press, 1977); Odds Steffen Dalgard and
Einer Kringlen, "A Norwegian Twin Study of Criminality," *The British Journal
of Criminology* 16(1976):213–232.

14. W. B. Richards, A. Stewart, E. P. Sylvester, and Victoria Jasiewicz,
"Cytogenic Survey of 225 Patients Diagnosed Clinically as Mongols," *Journal
of Mental Deficiency Research* 1965:245–259; H. Forsman and G. Hambert,
"Chromosomes and Antisocial Behavior," *Excerpta Criminologica* (1967):
113–117; Richard M. Goodman, William S. Smith, and J. C. Migeon, "Sex
Chromosome Abnormalities," *Nature* 216(1967):942–943; Sally Kelly, Rydian
Almy, and Margaret Barnard, "Another XYY Phenomenon," *Nature*
215(1967):405; T. Persson, "An XYY Man and His Relatives," *Journal of
Mental Deficiency Research* 11(1967):239–245; David R. Owen, "The 47 XYY
Male: A Review," *Psychological Bulletin* 78(1972):209–233; Ernest B. Hook,
"Behavioral Implications of the Human XYY Genotype," *Science* 179(1973):
139–150; Lissy F. Jarvik, Victor Klodin, and Steven S. Matsuyama, "Human
Aggression and the Extra Y Chromosome: Facts or Fantasy?" *American Psy-
chologist* 28(1973):674–682; Digamber S. Borgaonkar and Saleem A. Shah,
"The XYY Chromosome Male or Syndrome?" in *Progress in Medical Genetics,*
ed. Arthur G. Steinberg and Alexander G. Bearn (New York: Grune and Stratton, 1974), vol. 10.

15. Herman A. Witkin, Sarnoff A. Mednick, Fini Schulsinger, Eskild
Bakkestrom, Karl O. Christiansen, Donald R. Goodenough, Kurt Hirschorn,
Claes Lundsteen, David R. Owen, John Philip, Donald B. Rubin, and Martha
Stocking, "Criminality, Aggression and Intelligence Among XYY and XXY
Men," in *Biosocial Bases of Criminality,* ed. Sarnoff A. Mednick and Karl O.
Christiansen (New York: Gardner Press, 1977), p. 187.

16. Herbert C. Quay, "Psychopathic Personality as Pathological Stimula-
tion Seeking," *American Journal of Psychiatry* 122(1965):180–183.

17. B. Harold Goldman, Simon Dinitz, Lewis Lindner, Thomas W. Foster,
and Harry E. Allen, *A Designed Treatment Program of Sociopathy by Means
of Drugs: Summary Report* (Columbus, Ohio: Program for the Study of Crime
and Delinquency, 1974).

18. Don C. Gibbons, *The Criminological Enterprise* (Englewood Cliffs,
N.J.: Prentice-Hall, 1979).

19. William Bonger, *Criminality and Economic Conditions* (1905; English
edition, Bloomington, University of Indiana Press, 1969).

20. W.I. Thomas and Florian Znaniecki, *The Polish Peasant in Europe
and America* (Boston: Badger, 1920); Cliford R. Shaw and Henry D. McKay,
Juvenile Delinquency and Urban Areas (Chicago: University of Chicago Press,
1942); Edwin Sutherland, *Principles of Criminology* (Philadelphia: Lippincott,

1947); Donald R. Cressey, "The Differential Association Theory and Compulsive Crimes," *Journal of Criminal Law, Criminology and Police Science* 45 (1954):49–64.

21. Thorsten Sellin, *Culture Conflict and Crime* (New York: Social Science Research Council, 1938); Robert K. Merton, *Social Theory and Social Structure* (Glencoe, Ill.: Free Press, 1949); Albert K. Cohen, *Delinquent Boys: The Culture of the Gang* (Glencoe, Ill.: Free Press, 1955); Richard A. Cloward and Lloyd E. Ohlin, *Delinquency and Opportunity* (London: Routledge and Kegan Paul, 1961); Marvin W. Wolfgang and Franco Ferracuti, *The Subculture of Violence* (New York: Barnes and Noble, 1967).

22. Frank Tannenbaum, *Crime and the Community* (New York: Columbia University Press, 1938); Edwin M. Lemert, *Human Deviance, Social Problems and Social Control* (Englewood Cliffs, N.J.: Prentice-Hall, 1967).

23. Rennie, *The Search for Criminal Man*, p. 131.

24. Gibbons, *The Criminological Enterprise*.

25. Saleem A. Shah and Loren M. Roth, "Biological and Psychophysiological Factors in Criminology," in *Handbook of Criminology*, ed. Daniel Glaser (Chicago: Rand McNally Co., 1974), pp. 101–173.

26. Pierre Van den Berghe, "Bringing Beast Back In: Toward A Biosocial Theory of Aggression," *American Sociological Review* 39(1974):777–788.

27. Wouter Buikhuisen, "An Alternative Approach to Etiology of Crime" in *New Paths in Criminology*. Eds. Sarnoff A. Mednick and S. Giora Shoham. (Mass.: Lexington Books, 1979, 27–43).

28. Simon Dinitz, Harold Goldman, Lewis Lindner, Harry Allen and Thomas Foster, "Drug Treatment of the Sociopathic Offender—The Juice Model Approach" in *Deviance: Studies in Definition, Management and Treatment*. Eds. Simon Dinitz, Russell R. Dynes and Alfred C. Clarke. (New York: Oxford University Press, 1975, 455–458).

29. Ibid.

3

Ethnomethodology and Criminology: The Social Production of Crime and the Criminal

Stephen J. Pfohl

An ethnomethodological perspective . . . directs the researcher's attention to the theories of delinquency employed by laymen and particularly to theories employed by police, probation, and court officials. What is needed are studies showing how folk theories articulate with actual practice. —Aaron V. Cicourel, *The Social Organization of Juvenile Justice*[1]

During the oral portion of my Ph.D. examinations, one of my examiners asked whether the theoretical claims of the societal-reaction perspective on deviance were not a bit exaggerated. The examiner prefaced his inquiry with several comments on the utility of this perspective as a sensitizing device. He then queried me about the existence of certain types of behaviors that would be considered "naturally" deviant in any society or culture—homicide, for example. I responded in the negative.

Homicide is a categorization that removes the act of killing from socially redeemable rationalizations. The behavior is essentially the same: killing the police officer or killing by the police officer; stabbing an old lady in the back or stabbing the unsuspecting war-time enemy; a black slave shooting a white master or a white master lynching a black slave; being run over by the drunken driver or slowly dying of cancer caused by a polluting factory. All are forms of killing. Some are called homicide. Others are excused, justified, or viewed, as in the case of industrial pollution, as environmental health risks. The form and context of what is considered homicide thus appear to vary with social context and circumstance. This is hardly what one would expect from a universally recognized form of crime or deviance.

"Well," continued the examiner, "what about hyperkinesis? Certainly the problems caused by hyperkinetic children cause a universal disturbance in any culture." I disagreed. Consider the interpretation of such behaviors in several South Seas island communities. The behavior we normally associate with hy-

I wish to thank Mary Brady, Susan Guarino, and Ron Huff for thoughtful and constructive comments on an earlier draft of this chapter and Sara White for her assistance in preparing the manuscript. I also wish to thank Simon Dinitz. His support and encouragement in developing a diverse range of critical criminological inquiry has been a great catalyst for all of us who studied with him.

perkinesis is revered there with a categorical halo of religious sanctity. Another examiner, an anthropologist who had studied one such community, agreed. "It's no use arguing with you," the first examiner commented.

So what is universal about deviance? It is not its content but the process that gives deviance its social form—the process by which definitions of acts and persons as deviant are socially generated and applied. This was my answer then. My examiner was Simon Dinitz. In this chapter, written for this volume honoring Simon Dinitz, I will expand this response.

My answer is essentially the same now as then. However, it is an answer that attempts to transcend some of the often-cited limitations of the so-called labeling-theory tradition within the societal-reaction perspective. In doing so, it draws attention to a second major but less commonly articulated strand of theorizing within this perspective—ethnomethodology. Specifically, this chapter outlines the contributions of ethnomethodology to the creation of what might be called an interpretive criminology. It briefly traces the theoretical, methodological, and empirical contributions of ethnomethodology to criminology, contrasts it with the more familiar prescriptions of the labeling-factors approach, and suggests its affinity with the concerns of a historically grounded, critical criminological perspective.

Ethnomethodology: Socially Structured Structures

As a sociological perspective, ethnomethodology is generally concerned with the various methods that people, including sociological researchers, use to accomplish a reasonable account of what is happening in social interaction and to provide a sense of structure for the interaction itself. Ethnomethodology differs from other perspectives, which assume the independent existence of a social structure that provides a fairly standardized set of meanings, roles, and normative rules for the individuals who live within them. From the ethnomethodological perspective, social structure is *never* independent of the consciousness of actors who experience its force. A sense that life is governed by standardized meanings, roles, and rules is just that—a sense, common sense. This makes social structure no less forceful. It simply relocates it within, rather than outside, the world of human thinking and doing, talking and acting, working and playing. Structured society is viewed as an accomplished product of concrete social interaction, rather than its overshadowing predecessor.

This is not to say that, from the ethnomethodological vantage point, life is unstructured. Indeed, most ethnomethodologists follow the phenomenological lead of Alfred Schutz in depicting the experience of everyday life as largely taken for granted, prestructured, and shared with others.[2] However, the structures of everyday life experience are never fully independent of the interpretive work that actors do in making sense of this moment and this place in social life.

It is for this reason that ethnomethodologists turn to the small, detailed, practical features of interpretive social interaction for keys to the larger mysteries of structure and of social life in general.

Ethnomethodological Studies of Crime, Criminal, and Criminal Controls

Given its concern with the processes by which people construct believable, acceptable, or defensible accounts of what social life really is, it is no surprise that ethnomethodology has paid particular attention to problems of deviance and crime. In declaring, discovering, or asserting the category of deviance, social actors dramatize the recognizably real boundaries of social life. The recognition of certain acts or actors as outside the accepted rules of structured society permits us ritualistically to pay homage to the reality of both these rules and the structured society that it is assumed is behind them.

The ethnomethodological view of deviance closely resembles certain aspects of Durkheim's description of the boundary-setting functions of crime control.[3] A structured sense of normal social life is produced by apprehending its opposite. George Herbert Mead suggested a similar phenomenon in his classic essay, "The Psychology of Punitive Justice."[4] For Mead, the "majesty of the law," the "solemnity of the criminal court," and the "severity of the penal sanction" combine symbolically to create a sense of belonging for those who ritualistically unite in opposition to crime and the criminal. Once again, a structured sense of rule-governed society is gained by recognizing that which would threaten the way it is organized.

Although certain aspects of the ethnomethodological approach resembles Durkheim's functional and Mead's symbolic interpretations of deviance, its primary focus is on the practical, interpretive work of actors in making imputations of crime and deviance. The theoretical contribution of ethnomethodology in explicating these matters is perhaps best understood by reference to what are conceived as the three central features of all practical interpretive work: indexicality, reflexivity, and documentary interpretation.

Indexicality

The term *indexicality* is used to indicate that all human interpretive work is in certain ways bound to the context in which it occurs. The reality of the same potentially deviant act will be conceived very differently, depending on whether it is viewed from the patrol car of a police department under pressure to make arrests or from the backseat of a fast-moving vehicle full of partying teenagers.

The importance of indexicality is revealed in Sudnow's analysis of the overcrowded and pressurized court context within which public defenders employ commonsense stereotypes about who is and who isn't the "normal" criminal, and who should be offered or refused a certain line of plea-bargaining or defense.[5] A similar analysis of the indexical constraints inherent in the organization of social-control agencies is found in Cicourel's study of juvenile-justice decision-making,[6] Daniels's consideration of psychiatry within the military,[7] and McCleary's examination of career contingencies affecting parole officers' production of "bad records for good reasons."[8]

Reflexivity

Reflexivity refers to the manner in which actors' interpretive accounts (verbal and nonverbal) come to alter the setting in which they are employed. In other words, interpretive accounts are not only bound by the context in which they occur (indexically), but through their very expression they create new contexts and thereby become (reflexively) a part of the phenomenon on which they report.

The omnipresent importance of reflexivity in human interpretive work is increased by its relative inconspicuousness. Reflexive work, once completed, appears to vanish from self-conscious awareness. This unnoticeable character of reflexivity is particularly evident in the production of deviance. The end product of successful imputational work is paradoxically to forget (or at least be inattentive to) the fact that such work was even involved. This reflexive disguising of the created character of deviance is discussed by Melvin Pollner, who suggests: "While a community creates deviance, it may simultaneously mask its creative work from itself."[9]

Empirically, the dynamics of "unnoticed" reflexive work are clearly evident in Weider's study of the inmate code in halfway houses.[10] This code does not operate as an abstract set of rules governing appropriate behavior. Rather, it is invoked as a solution to particular instances of tension. It allows inmates to call one another into question. The code is invoked to order a disorderly situation. In doing so, however, its users divert attention from the subjective, particularistic, or situational nature of conflict. They reflexively recognize, instead, the objective nature of general rules that allegedly cover all situations. Are the rules really like this? No—they are reflexively invoked only when they are strategically useful. This is rarely noticed. The reflexive use of rules to give a sense of structure to life in the halfway house fades as it is enacted.

The paradoxical characteristic of interpretive work is further illustrated in Garfinkel's analysis of the reflexive rule images produced by jurors in the course of deciding a verdict.[11] These quasi-legal rules were announced after the fact, after jurors had already decided a verdict. They were nonetheless reflexively applied backward in time. As such, they came to be viewed by jurors as the standards that had guided their "fair deliberations" from the beginning. A similar hiding of the reflexive character of social-control judgments is revealed in Sacks's analysis of the reality of suicide threats discovered during hot-line crisis conversation[12] and in Douglas's examination of official descriptions of suicide as the cause of death.[13]

Documentary Interpretation

Harold Garfinkel, the central figure in the development of ethnomethodology, uses the term *documentary interpretation* to refer to the manner in which people infer meaningful action patterns from the appearance of simple behaviorial stimuli. Appearances are treated as documents of something deeper, as expressions of underlying patterns or structures. In the words of Garfinkel, "Not only is the underlying pattern derived from its individual documentary evidences, but the individual documentary evidences, in their turn, are interpreted on the basis of 'what is known' about the underlying pattern. Each is used to elaborate the other."[14]

The study of documentary interpretive practices has proved a valuable resource for studying the ascription of criminal or deviant identities. Such practices are evidenced in Egon Bittner's description of the cognitive methods that police use to jump from surface appearances to the recognition of real troublemakers;[15] in Robert Emerson's analysis of the construction of delinquent biographies in juvenile court;[16] in Jacqueline Wiseman's depiction of the typification of individuals charged with public drunkenness;[17] and in my own study of the prediction of dangerousness by psychiatric specialists.[18] In each case, the interpretive work of social-control agents reduces complex and often contradictory social, political, and economic realities into a neatly packaged depiction of the offender as a fixed type of troublesome individual.

Similar observations are made with regard to norms or social rules. The study of documentary interpretations suggests that ideas about fixed norms or rules are also a product of the judgmental work of those who would control the behaviors of others. This is not to say that rules or norms do not exist, but that they exist only as the end product of the interpretive work by which control agents size up a situation, treat it as a document of a more general pattern, and then use this pattern as a device for ordering experience in the present.

From the ethnomethodological perspective, rules are not viewed as existing independent of the documentary interpretations of actors who see them. When understood in conjunction with the principles of indexicality and reflexivity, this aspect of documentary interpretation underscores the ethnomethodological claim that all norms or roles are essentially open or empty until filled in by the context-bound interpretive work of people in the process of social interaction. Through this work, appearances are transformed into patterns, which are then (reflexively) recognized as having a life of their own. According to ethnomethodologists Mehan and Wood, "Without this work a rule has no meaning, no life at all."[19] With this work, social-control agents produce a sense of the world as normative or rule-governed and thereby justify or legitimize their action as required by norms or rules that are independent of the ways they act to restrain, repress, reform, or rehabilitate those who are discovered to be deviant. But are such norms or rules ever fully independent of the interactional occasions in which they are evoked? The ethnomethodological answer is no. Its detailed observations display the interpretive interaction by which believable and justifiable senses of deviance are produced and legitimized. This is its major contribution to the study of crime, deviance, and social control. With such observations, ethnomethodology constructs interpretive or phenomenologically informed criminology.

Ethnomethodology and the Methods
of Criminological Inquiry

Ethnomethodology has contributed to several advances in the methods of criminological inquiry. First, it has questioned the uncritical use of official statistics on crime and deviance as reflective of crime itself. According to Garfinkel, Kitsuse and Cicourel, and others, the production of official statistics suggests more about the organizational work of control agencies than it does about the activities of deviants.[20] As Edwin Schur points out, this means "that official statistics should be considered an object of investigation to be explained in their own right. Our primary interest should not be in what they might tell us about the causation of deviance, but rather in exploring the causation of the rates themselves."[21]

A second methodological contribution of ethnomethodology to criminology concerns the issue of exactly what is to be considered criminal or deviant. Criminologists have argued since the inception of the discipline about what should or shouldn't be considered a crime. Should one follow legal, normative, or ethical definitions? The ethnomethodological position is clear. Do not start with any preconceived definition. Focus, instead, on definitions that are used concretely in specific historical circumstances. This follows from ethnomethodology's assumption that, for all practical sociological purposes, there is no crime or deviance independent of the judgmental work of the control agents who see such things. If this is the case, then an actor's own definitional practices must become the starting point for the study of crime in history. Criminologists and sociologists of deviance are thus freed from the problem of trying to decide on the most appropriate conceptualizations of rule breaking. According to Kitsuse:

Definitions . . . of members . . . must prevail, however 'misinformed,' 'erroneous,' or 'misguided' they may appear to be from the sociologist's stand-point. The alternative of invoking the sociologist's definitions as the standard of assessing normative behavior, is to face the problem of accounting, on one hand, for the failure of members to negatively sanction behavior that is 'ob-viously deviant,' and on the other for the imposition of such sanctions in the absence of 'norm violating' behavior.[22]

A third contribution of ethnomethodology to the canons of criminological inquiry concerns the reflexive nature of the research process itself. Ethno-methodologists recognize that criminologists, like the people they study, are bound in certain ways to the context in which research is done. Similarly, in interpreting the interpretations of others, researchers are forced to employ similar documentary practices. How, then, can they claim any objectivity about their own observations and analyses? The answer is not to be found in the structured havens of survey analysis or fixed-choice questionnaires. These methods also employ situate inferences and context-bound judgments about what is or isn't a likely, plausible, or meaningful answer or response. To claim otherwise is to lie to oneself, to hide behind a false cloak of constructed objectivity. This is a fundamental theme in ethnomethodology's examination of the practical work entailed in doing social research. How, then, can the researcher make any claims as to the objective nature of his or her inquiry?

Ethnomethodology's response is twofold.[23] It acknowledges that objectivity is partial, at best. The task of the disciplined researcher is to approximate objectivity while providing one's audience with a detailed account of the social context and contextual decisions that are a necessary feature of the research process. Two recommendations are made in approximating objectivity: wherever and whenever possible, (1) attempt at least partial replications of one's work and (2) display as much as possible (for example, through verbatim audio or visual transcripts) the verbal or nonverbal actions of those about whose activities one makes interpretative judgments. In other words, display the phenomenon being analyzed. This allows the audience to join the researcher, at least partially, in interpreting the scene being studied. It furthers the quest for objectivity by providing the audience with data by which to reject or modify as well as to accept the researcher's description and analysis.

The second aspect of ethnomethodology's response calls for the criminol-ogist, or any social researcher, to accompany a study of crime, the criminal, or criminal controls with a study of one's study. This is a difficult, time- and paper-consuming task. Yet, once completed and reported on, this analysis of the research project provides a better vantage point from which to assess the empirical claims of the work.

Ethnomethodology and the "Labeling Factors" Tradition

Ethnomethodology is one of two general traditions within the societal-reaction perspective on crime and deviance. This perspective is rooted in Howard

Becker's proposition that "deviance is not a quality of the act the person commits, but rather a consequence of the application by others of rules and sanctions to an 'offender.' "[24] Since the 1963 publication of this statement, there have been numerous applications and critiques of the societal-reaction perspective. Some have usefully advanced, modified, or pointed out its limitations. Others have generated issues that have sidetracked its central contribution—a concern with the processes through which certain acts and people become defined and dealt with as deviant. The centrality of this theme is emphasized by John Kitsuse, who states:

> The distinctive character of the societal reaction perspective . . . leads . . .
> to a consideration of how deviants come to be differentiated by imputations
> made upon them by others, how these imputations activate systems of social
> control, and how these control activities become legitimated.[25]

The concerns of ethnomethodology coincide directly with this distinctive character of the societal-reaction perspective. The same is not true for what might be called the labeling-factors of tradition. Its arguments as to the primacy of social (as opposed to behavioral) factors in the imputation of criminal or deviant labels and its allowance for the possibility of "secret" and "falsely accused" deviants has generated a series of intellectual debates, sidetracking the essential thrust of the perspective. The primacy of social factors has been contested by researchers who claim, instead, the primacy of individual or behavioral factors.[26] This argument has turned into a sort of quantitative debate about which types of factors account for a high percentage of labeling. This debate takes place as if the documentation of influential social factors would mean that acts that were really not deviant had incorrectly come to be labeled as such. Critics appear to argue the opposite—that deviant acts had really occurred and that they were appropriately labeled. Both sides appear to miss the essential thrust of the societal-reaction perspective—that the recognition of deviance is first and foremost a social judgment and that, like any other judgment, a combination of indexical, reflexive, and interpretive processes are constitutive features of what will be seen, acted upon, and legitimized as really deviant. In other words, the process is essentially social, not incidentally social. It is not incidentally social because, when operationalized, such things as race, class, gender, or presence of a good lawyer account for more labeling than a person does. It is essentially social because knowledge of what a person does is an accomplished product of the interactional processes whereby control agents assess the likelihood that someone is, in facts produced in the assessment itself, really a deviant.

The labeling-factors tradition remains bogged down in assessing the correctness of labels, thus lending credence to the assumption that there are basic social norms that define deviance independent of the interaction process through which control agents do their imputational work. Gibbs is quick to point this out regarding the concepts of secret and falsely accused deviance.[27] On what grounds do labeling-factor theorists make such claims regarding the incorrect-ness of labeling? Obviously, they must assume a certain normative character of deviance that is independent of what control agents see or don't see. From within the labeling-factors tradition, the societal-reaction perspective appears contradictory and weak. How can it be both ways—defining deviance in terms of controlling reactions and yet arguing that some reactions are incorrect, that they miss or mislabel deviance?

The ethnomethodological perspective is more radically interpretive. Its concern is not with the correctness but with the success of labeling. It discards the implicit assumption of normativity found in the labeling-factors tradition. It offers a more consistent conceptual structure for the societal-reaction perspective as a whole. The correctness issue becomes a nonissue. Attention is directed, instead, to the essential interactional processes through which imputations of deviance emerge, are applied, and are rationalized as reflective of a legitimate reality independent of the imputer. As Kitsuse argues, "The contention is not that agents of control act without regard to the behavior of the one labeled, but that in labeling, rule breaking behavior is imputed by others to the deviant."[28]

Power, Identity, History, and Interpretive Criminology

Human reality is a product of concrete social interaction. There is no reality independent of what people do to make interpretive sense of life in the here and now. These are fundamental principles of ethnomethodology. They are also the source of much criticism. According to critics, ethnomethodology's emphasis on interpretive work is too subjective or too relativistic. It ignores the role of power, the impact of self-concept, or the influence of historical circumstance in shaping the form and content of interpreted reality. As Dreitzel points out, much ethnomethodological writing appears relatively inattentive to the ongoing "struggle over the rules of interpretation, a struggle . . . dominated by factors alien to the interpretive creativity of the involved parties."[29]

What is ethnomethodology's response to such criticism? Such matters seem of acute importance with regard to the study of crime, the criminal, and criminal-control work. It is unimaginable that one could articulate a plausible criminology devoid of any reference to power, identity, or history. What, after all, is crime or the criminal but the exercise of the power of the state to control certain behaviors or people believed to have a certain criminal identity within particular historical circumstances?

Ethnomethodology's response is twofold. It is generally true that it has made little explicit or systematic reference to problems of power, self-identity, and history. However, ethnomethodology is not incapable of incorporating these issues into its conceptual framework. Each is implied, if not explicitly developed, within its central theoretical imagery. Moreover, in recent years, such matters have become increasingly recognized in the writings of ethnomethodologists and those who are influenced by this theoretical perspective. Douglas's concern with the impact of differentiated power on the production of social research,[30] Kitsuse and Cicourel's discussion of the organizational constraints guiding the construction of official statistics,[31] Molotch and Lester's analysis of power as producing and being produced by media coverage of the Santa Barbara oil spill,[32] and Daniels's study of the uses of psychiatry in a military setting[33] all point ethnomethodology in this direction. So does my own study of predictions of dangerousness.[34] There I take explicit notice of the ways that self-typified identities and power differentials influence the style and results of diagnostic work. Diagnostic control agents routinely respond or defer to the resistance of powerful others. Power is an ever-present part of the context of indexicality of their interpretive work. The same holds for identity. In their diagnostic work, psychiatric agents produce images or situated identities that they were this or that kind of "professional," "expert," "humanitarian reformer," "good-guy," or whatever. These identities reflexively feed back on the diagnostic work of those who displayed them. Like power, they become intrinsic features of the interpretive imputation of deviance.

Historical circumstance affects interpretive social-control work in a similar fashion. It is never fully outside the documentary interpretations of people who see general patterns or structures behind interactional specifics. Nonetheless, interpretive work is limited by a finite vocabulary of terms to describe a particular event or person at a particular moment in time. It is limited by language that is available in history.

Control agents literally did not see hyperkinesis before the 1960s, because this interpretive control category was not historically available. As suggested by Peter Conrad, seeing hyperkinesis awaited the medicalization of troublesome childhood behaviors.[35] My own analysis of the discovery of child abuse suggests a similar historical grounding of another currently available control category.[36] Today, hyperkinesis and the battered-child syndrome are seen everywhere. This is a matter of historical circumstance. These terms have become part of the interpretive linguistic repertoire of those who would control others. How such terms emerge and become accepted in history has become an increasingly important question for criminologists and students of deviance.

This historical "discovery" of such categorizing devices is often traced, indexically, to powers that reward linguistic or conceptual innovations and to the identities such discoveries produce, reflexively, for those who produce them (for example, the brilliant professional or great reformer). The interpretive use of such concepts, once historically available, further advances or modifies such alignments of power and identity. Historical circumstance passes interpretively into its next moment. Like power and identity, it both shapes and is shaped by the interpretive work of actors in everyday life. Each becomes an additional dimension of the process through which social reality is created, lived within, legitimized, or changed. Regarding crime, the criminal, and criminal controls, each expands ethnomethodology's contributions in creating a criminology that is informed both phenomenologically and by the simultaneous shaping of power, identity, and history.

Concluding Remarks

I began this chapter with a question about what is universal about crime or deviance. Ethnomethodology assists the criminologist in answering this question by drawing attention to interpretive interactional judgments that designate as criminal certain events and people and that activitate and legitimize controlling actions against them. Avoiding certain conceptual pitfalls of the labeling-factors tradition, ethnomethodology has contributed significantly to substantive and methodological aspects of the study of societal reaction to crime. When expanded to include a consideration of power, situated identity, and historical circumstance, ethnomethodology represents a powerful framework for examining what is universal about crime and deviance—the process by which events and people are defined and sanctioned as offenses and offenders.

Notes

1. Aaron V. Cicourel, *The Social Organization of Juvenile Justice* (New York: Wiley, 1969), p. 24.

2. Alfred Schutz, *Collected Papers I: The Problem of Social Reality*, ed. Maurice Natunson (The Hague: Martinus Nijhoff, 1962).

3. Emile Durkheim, *The Rules of the Sociological Method*, trans. Sarah A. Solovay and John W. Mueller, ed. Sir E.G. Catlin (New York: Free Press, 1965), pp. 65–73.

4. George Herbert Mead, "The Psychology of Punitive Justice," *American Journal of Sociology* 23(1918):577–602.

5. David Sudnow, "Normal Crimes: Sociological Features of the Penal Code in a Public Defender Office," *Social Problems* 12(Winter 1965):255–276.

6. Cicourel, *The Social Organization of Juvenile Justice*.

7. Arlene Kaplan Daniels, "The Social Construction of Psychiatric Diagnosis," in *New Sociology No. 2*, ed. Hans Peter Dreitzel (New York: Macmillan, 1970), pp. 182–205.

8. Richard McCleary, "How Parole Officers Use Records," *Social Problems* 24(June 1977):576–589.

9. Melvin Pollner, "Sociological and Commonsense Models of the Labeling Process," in *Ethnomethodology*, ed. Roy Turner (Middlesex, England: Penguin Books, 1974), p. 39.

10. D. Lawrence Weider, "Telling the Code," in *Ethnomethodology,* ed. Roy Turner (Middlesex, England: Penguin Books, 1974), pp. 144–172.

11. Harold Garfinkel, *Studies in Ethnomethodology* (Englewood Cliffs, N.J.: Prentice-Hall, 1967), pp. 104–115.

12. Harvey Sacks, "On Initial Investigation of the Usability of Conversational Data for Doing Sociology," *Studies in Social Interaction,* ed. David Sudnow (New York: Free Press, 1972).

13. Jack D. Douglas, *The Social Meaning of Suicide* (Princeton: Princeton University Press, 1967).

14. Garfinkel, *Studies in Ethnomethodology,* p. 78.

15. Egon Bittner, "The Police on Skid-Row: A Study of Peace Keeping, *American Sociological Review* 32(1969):669–715.

16. Robert M. Emerson, *Judging Delinquents: Context and Process in Juvenile Justice* (Chicago: Aldine, 1969).

17. Jacqueline P. Wiseman, *Stations of the Lost: The Treatment of Skid Row Alcoholics* (Englewood Cliffs, N.J.: Prentice-Hall, 1970).

18. Stephen J. Pfohl, *Predicting Dangerousness: The Social Construction of Psychiatric Reality* (Lexington, Mass: Lexington Books, D.C. Heath and Company, 1978).

19. Hugh Mehan and Houston Wood, *The Reality of Ethnomethodology* (New York: Wiley, 1975).

20. Garfinkel, *Studies in Ethnomethodology,* pp. 186–207; John I. Kitsuse and Aaron V. Cicourel "A Note on the Use of Official Statistics," *Social Problems* 11(Fall 1963):131–139.

21. Edwin M. Schur, *Interpreting Deviance: A Sociological Approach* (New York: Harper and Row, 1979), p. 363.

22. John Kitsuse "The 'New Conception of Deviance' and Its Critics," in *The Labeling of Deviance: Evaluating a Perspective,* ed. Walter Gove (New York: Halstead Press, 1975), p. 278.

23. Stephen J. Pfohl, "Social Role Analysis: The Ethnomethodological Critique," *Sociology and Social Research* 59, 3(April, 1975):243–265.

24. Howard Becker, *Outsiders: Studies in the Sociology of Deviance* (New York: Free Press, 1963), p. 9.

25. Kitsuse, "The 'New Conception of Deviance' and Its Critics," p. 274.

26. Travis Hirschi, "Labelling Theory and Juvenile Delinquency: An Assessment of the Evidence," in *The Labelling of Deviance: Evaluating a Perspective,* ed. Walter R. Gove (New York: Halstead Press, 1975), pp. 181–203; Charles R. Tittle, "Labelling and Crime: An Empirical Evaluation," in *The Labelling of Deviance: Evaluating a Perspective,* ed. Walter R. Gove (New York: Halstead Press, 1975), pp. 157–179; Walter R. Gove "Societal Reaction as an Explanation of Mental Illness: an Evaluation," *American Sociological*

Review 35(October 1970):873–874; A.R. Mahoney, "The Effects of Labeling Upon Youths in the Juvenile Justice System: A Review of the Evidence," *Law and Society Review* 8(1974):583–614.

27. Jack P. Gibbs "Issues in Defining Deviant Behavior," in Robert A. Scott and Jack D. Douglas, eds., *Theoretical Perspectives on Deviance* (New York: Basic Books, 1972), pp. 56–64.

28. Kitsuse, "The 'New Conception of Deviance' and Its Critics." p. 280.

29. Hans Peter Dreitzel, *Recent Sociology No. 2: Patterns of Communicative Behavior* (New York: Macmillan, 1970), p. xviii.

30. Jack Douglas, *Understanding Everyday Life: Toward a Reconstruction of Sociological Knowledge* (Chicago: Aldine Publishing Co., 1920), p. 30.

31. Kitsuse and Cicourel, "A Note on the Use of Official Statistics."

32. Harvey Molotch and Marilyn Lester "Accidental News: The Great Oil Spill as Local Occurrence and National Event," *Americal Journal of Sociology* 81(September 1975):235–260.

33. Daniels, "The Social Construction of Psychiatric Diagnosis."

34. Pfohl, *Predicting Dangerousness.*

35. Peter Conrad, *Identifying Hyperactive Children: the Medicalization of Deviant Behavior* (Lexington, Mass: Lexington Books, D.C. Heath and Company, 1976).

36. Stephen J. Pfohl, "The 'Discovery' of Child Abuse," *Social Problems* 24(February 1977):310–323.

4 Conflict, Radical, and Critical Approaches to Criminology

Raymond J. Michalowski

During its first thirty-five years—from the early 1920s until the late 1950s—criminology was characterized by an almost exclusive concern with the etiology of criminal behavior. As Gibbons observed of this era in criminology:

> Greater attention was given to questions centered on offenders and the genesis of criminal careers than to attempts to identify the social-structural root causes of criminality.[1]

The domain assumptions of this early criminology were (1) that the state and its legal institutions were natural and inevitable responses to the needs for social order, and (2) that deviant and criminal behaviors represented maladaptations at the individual, familial, or cultural level. The role of the state and the socioeconomic arrangements that determine its shape and character received little attention within mainstream criminology.

In the late 1950s, there began to emerge the first signs of what became by the 1970s a fundamental division within criminology. On one side of this division is positivist criminology and the field of criminal justice, with their respective orientations toward understanding the individual deviant and improving the system designed to identify, process, and rehabilitate him or her. On the other side are more distinctly radical versions of criminology, which seek to understand law, crime, and justice through conceptual formations that are both part of, and contribute to, an emerging critique of domination, that is, a "reflective critique of socially unnecessary constraints of human freedom."[2]

The major perspectives that have been part of the process toward a critique of domination within criminology are (1) the labeling or societal-reaction school of thought, (2) conflict theories of law, (3) radical criminology, and (4) critical criminology.

The Labeling Perspective

Although the labeling perspective is not specifically the focus of this analysis, it is difficult to examine conflict and radical approaches to crime in America without some reference to its role in forcing a wedge between criminological theory and uncritical acceptance of state law. The labeling perspective owes its parentage largely to the symbolic-interaction school of social psychology, which held as its fundamental precepts that individuals act toward social objects on the basis of the meaning those objects have for them, and that the meaning of social objects is derived through the process of social interaction.[3] The reformulation of these ideas within criminology led in two directions: one concerned primarily with the effect of a criminal or deviant label on the future behavior of individuals so labeled, and another concerned largely with the process of creating and applying those labels.

The labeling perspective has been criticized by more-radical criminologists for its tendency to "ignore a world of events and structures independent of the social actor's consciousness" and for its failure to break effectively with the reformism, cynicism, and acceptance of a state definition of crime characteristic of liberal criminology.[4] Despite these criticisms, however, the labeling perspective did put into place two important building blocks upon which a more radical version of criminology could be built. First, the labeling perspective introduced into American criminology what Matza calls an awareness of irony (and what more Marxist criminologists might call contradiction), by suggesting that the very attempts we make to control and reduce deviant and criminal behavior can generate additional criminality as a consequence of formal institutionalized application of deviant and criminal labels.[5] Second, the labeling perspective served to demystify the definition of certain behaviors as naturally deviant or criminal by demonstrating that such definitions are created and applied within a process of *real* social interaction, not through the larger, more mysterious workings of social consensus.

Conflict Theories of Law

The conflict theories of law derive from conflict sociology, or what has sometimes been called functional-conflict sociology. The main ideas of this functional-conflict perspective in sociology are (1) that, as a function of both natural human diversity and the group nature of human social existence, society consists at all times of a number of groups with divergent goals and interests,[6] (2) that this diversity of goals and interests places various groups in conflict with one another, (3) that this conflict is characterized by a constant process of moves and countermoves as groups seek to achieve their own goals and thwart the efforts of those who would jeopardize this achievement, and (4) that this process of checks and balances tends toward an equilibrium that is recognized as social order while providing the underlying forces for social change.[7]

This view of human social life was first reformulated into a general theory of law by Vold and later by Turk.[8] Although Sellin's *Culture, Conflict and Crime* is sometimes treated as a similar attempt to develop a conflict theory of law and crime, this work concerned itself mostly with the consequences of contact between extant, culture-based conduct norms.[9] Sellin describes two forms of conflict: a primary form, arising from the contact of ethnic groups, as in the cases of colonization or immigration, and a secondary form, which occurs when a homogeneous culture is transformed into several subcultures.[10] Depending, as it does, on the existence of specific conduct norms as an a priori condition for conflict, Sellin's analysis does not address the role of conflict in shaping the norms of domination and deference within a culture,[11] nor does it provide particular insight into the role of conflict in creating subcultures—for example, class conflicts as a source of subcultural variation. Conflict for Sellin is a consequence of social differences, not a cause of it.

In contrast to Sellin, Vold and Turk accept as a starting point the view that group conflict is endemic to social life. Vold, for example, says that society is "a congerie of groups held together in a shifting but dynamic equilibrium of opposing group interests and efforts."[12] This view is repeated a decade later by Turk, who describes social order as "an always tenuous approximation of an order, more a temporary resolution of conflicting notions about right and wrong and of incompatible desires."[13]

From this starting point, both writers identify legal forms as the expression of the will of those with the power to prevail in any particular conflict. Vold argues:

> The whole political process of law making, law breaking and law enforcement becomes a direct reflection of deep-seated and fundamental conflicts between interest groups and their more general struggles for the control of the police power of the state.[14]

In a similar vein, Turk wrote:

> Legality becomes an attribute of whatever words and deeds are defined as legal by those able to use to their advantage the machinery for making and enforcing rules. Political power determines legality.[15]

Although they espouse essentially similar views of the nature and source of legality, Turk differs from Vold in several areas of emphasis. First, Turk explicitly identifies the possibility that the equilibrium achieved through conflict over law may reflect domination rather than pluralistic accommodation. That is,

> For those groupings who have lost out, *or never really competed,* in the struggle to control legal mechanisms, laws will be edicts. For them to live in a legal order is to be dominated.[16] (emphasis added)

Second, influenced to some extent by the labeling perspective, Turk gives greater attention to the processes of social interaction culminating in the application of deviant labels. In *Criminality and the Legal Order,* he wrote:

> Criminality is not something which anyone *does* but rather something that *happens* in the course of interaction among various parties.[17] (Turk's italics)

The majority of his book is devoted to the dynamics of conflict relations between authorities and subjects.

Whereas Sellin, Vold, and Turk developed theoretical perspectives on the role of conflict in the formation of legality, others have sought to identify empirical indicators that would confirm or disprove the validity of conflict theories of law. Three types of tests of conflict theory emerged in the 1960s and 1970s: studies of sanctioning differentials, analyses of current instances of lawmaking, and attitude surveys.

The general conflict theory of law suggests that, if law does indeed represent the will of the dominant social classes, then enforcement of the law should fall disparately on members of the subordinate classes. This proposition has been tested in a number of studies that sought to determine the extent and nature of differential law enforcement and punishment. These efforts produced a substantial body of contradictory findings in two areas—sentencing disparity and differential arrest rates. One review of the literature on sentencing disparity found that of fifty-three sentencing-disparity studies using data from the years 1951 to 1976, fourteen found support for a conflict hypothesis with respect to race, while thirty-three did not; five had neutral findings. The figures for sentencing disparity by socioeconomic status (SES) were similarly confounded. Of thirty-three studies examined by Williams, eleven found SES to be significant in sentencing, seventeen did not, and five were neutral.[18] Hagan found similar results in an earlier review of sentencing-disparity literature.[19]

Similar controversy surrounds studies of hidden delinquency and crime. Some researchers find evidence of racial and socioeconomic discrimination in police practices, based on the self-reports of juveniles.[20] Others have reported little or no evidence of such selective law enforcement.[21] Thus, clear confirmation or refutation of the discriminatory arrest and sentencing corollary of conflict theory has remained elusive.

Another test of conflict theory has been detailed examinations of contemporary instances of lawmaking. Graham's and Becker's analyses of the origins of drug laws, Roby's study of changes in the New York prostitution law, and Akers's study of professional regulation all fall within this category.[22] Generally, the findings confirm a pluralist-conflict version of conflict theory but contradict the notion that law represents the imposition of a uniform ruling-class will upon the less-advantaged segments of society.

Finally, several studies have sought to use popular opinion as a measure of the existence or lack of conflict surrounding criminal law. Predictably, these studies have found a high degree of uniformity across social classes on the relative seriousness attached to various crime, and this ranking closely parallels the legal definition of seriousness.[23] This has been erroneously interpreted as disproof of the conflict hypothesis. Conflict theory identifies conflict in the creation of law as a historical variable, not a social-psychological one. Measurement of contemporary attitudes toward law ignores the central role of law and law-enforcement practices in defining the social reality through which people come to know the ''truth'' about the crime problem.

Conflict theory, as constructed by Vold and Turk and tested in the various ways mentioned suffers from several shortcomings. First, it is overly abstract. The root cause of conflict is predicated as flowing from a natural tendency for human diversity. The presumed naturalness of this diversity has resulted in little attention by conflict theorists to the concrete ways in which social structures generate more or less diversity of goals and interests at the individual and group level. Second, conflict theories of law tend to be overly microsocial. The tendency has been to focus on specific instances of lawmaking and law enforcement within democratic institutions, with little attention to the larger processes that determined the shape of those institutions. Conflict theories tend to look at conflicts over laws and law enforcement within the state but have little to say about the nature and formation of the state itself. Finally, conflict theory and research have tended to treat such factors as race and socioeconomic status as categorical variables rather than recognizing that they represent socially structured relations. Poverty, for instance, is not a status; it derives from a relationship between haves and have-nots. Similarly, the second-class status of nonwhites derives from their relationship with whites. The tendency to focus on social categories rather than social relations has removed from conflict theories much of their potential for analysis of the dynamic, historical process of legal evolution.

Conflict analysis has tended to be political science (that is, analysis of activities within a given political framework) rather than sociology (that is, examinations of society as a whole). By taking particular state forms as a given, conflict theories of law fall short of their initial promise of a genuine critique of law.

Despite its shortcomings, conflict theory has played a major role in the demystification of what had been the more generally accepted view that law was consensually created and implemented with value-neutrality. At least partly as a result of the conflict position in criminology, a pluralist-conflict view of law—that is, the view that any particular piece of legislation is the outcome of a struggle between countervailing interest groups—has become the more common model of legal formation within mainstream criminology. Although this perspective deemphasizes the fact, as Quinney noted, that certain social groups are almost wholly excluded from direct participation in this conflict,[24] it does challenge the view of law as strictly value-neutral.

Radical Criminology

Partly in reaction to the inadequacies of the functional-conflict and labeling perspectives in criminology, and partly in response to the social turmoil of the 1960s, some criminologists in the United States, England, and Europe began developing approaches to the study of law and crime that drew heavily upon Marxist and neo-Maxist social theory. The various representatives of this generally Marxist approach to the study of law, crime, and justice came to be loosely identified as radical criminologists. This emergent radical criminology in America diverged from its most direct antecedents—labeling and conflict theories—as well as from more traditional criminology in four important ways: (1) its methodology, (2) its transformation of criminology into a unit of analysis, (3) its critique of state law, and (4) its emphasis on radical praxis.

Radical Methodology

At the scholarship level, radical criminologists embraced the methodologies of historical materialism and dialectical thought that are characteristic of Marxist study and expressly rejected the more positivist technical research strategies that are dominant within contemporary criminology. Historical materialism required "doing basic historical research to fill the enormous gaps in our understanding of the 'contours of American history' "[25] This meant that "the crucial phenomenon to be considered is not crime per se, but the historical development and operation of the capitalist economy," particularly as it related to the emergence of state law as the primary mechanism for controlling and ameliorating the contradictions of capital accumulation.[26]

   The centrality of radical criminology's historical analysis of the interaction between the economic substructure and the law represented a significant break with the more conventional ahistorical criminology, which tended either to ignore economic processes within the substructure altogether or to deal with them only in terms of their immediate phenomenal forms, such as the existence of socioeconomic strata, as opposed to examining the dynamics of class relations.

   Radical criminology is also characterized by an emphasis on the methodology of dialectical thought. Specifically, radical criminology accepted the dialectical proposition: "In the investigation of the social world, it is impossible to separate analytically the formation of concept and theory from the field of inquiry."[27] This orientation toward dialectical thought generated within radical criminology strong criticism of the positivist methodology of traditional criminology, and this criticism became a central part of the debate between radical and traditional criminology. The central issues in radical criminology's criticism of positivism (and conversely traditional criminology's defense of it) are (1) the existence of a knowable but not necessarily obvious objective reality, (2) the method whereby this reality can become known, (3) the objectivity that results from the application of positivist methodology, and (4) the relationship of this objectivity to the status quo social order.

Although all the epistemological nuances of this debate cannot be considered here, several points bear mentioning. First, dialectical thought does not deny the existence of objective social conditions, although radical criminologists have sometimes been accused of holding this position. The central issue is not whether objective social conditions exist, but rather the method whereby they can become known. Positivism seeks objectivity through knowledge of phenomenal forms as stable categories of existence. Dialectical thought, by contrast,

> is focused on the generation of new phenomenon, on all that is associated with emergence, creation and novelty. The basic modality of existence for objects of the dialectical case is becoming rather than being.[28]

In order to understand objective conditions, then, dialectical thought requires transcending the phenomenal forms by piercing the very structure of consciousness that gives those phenomenal forms their everyday meaning. From the perspective of dialectical thought, the real task is to transcend the existing consciousness of social forms through a reflective critique of the dynamics that generate that consciousness, which, as Schroyer notes, ultimately requires a "phenomenological reconstruction of the constitutive experiences of the history of mankind."[29]

The question of how social creatures can objectively investigate the social environment from which their consciousness is constructed is a well-recognized problem among European philosophers and social scientists.[30] Given the lack of dialectical tradition within American scholarship, however, radical criminology's critique of positivism is perhaps the least well understood of its elements.

Radical Critique of Criminology

Dialectical methodology, with its emphasis on reflexive critique of the formation of consciousness, requires that radical criminology transform the forms of knowledge characteristic of criminology into objects of study. This led to a critique of traditional criminology that was characterized by frequent criticisms of the "technocratic nature" of positivist criminology and its tendency to promote "gradualist programs of amelioration."[31] Less common have been analyses of the formation of liberal consciousness as it affected the development of positivist criminology. Although analyses of the evolution of liberal consciousness in a somewhat broader context are not uncommon,[32] less effort has been devoted by radical criminologists to expanding the critique of the formation of liberal consciousness in criminology than their orientation toward dialectical thought would seem to suggest. This may in part be because the lack of a tradition of dialectical thought in American scholarship does not enable such analyses to fall easily to hand. Furthermore, reflecting the general pragmatism that is characteristic of American academia, radical criminologists have devoted substantially more energy to analysis of the concrete institutions of repression rather than to the ideological consequences of these and of other legal institutions.

Critique of State Law

Radical criminologists generally accept the neo-Marxian view of the state as having two primary and contradictory functions in relation to capitalism: (1) the facilitation of capital accumulation and (2) legitimation of the world of social relations created by a capitalist mode of production.[33] A third function is that of insuring its own legitimacy in order to achieve the political stability necessary to meet its primary tasks.[34] Actions taken under state law can encompass both direct, instrumental forms of social-class domination and ideologically necessitated concessions to working-class concerns. These concessions are usually aimed either at protecting the legitimacy of the world of social relations appropriate to capitalism (for example, equal employment opportunity legislation) or at maintaining the legitimacy of the state itself (for example, advancing due process rights). Quinney, for example, argues in *Class, State and Crime* that state domination under late monopoly capitalism "is in the first instance ideological, in restricting our conception of life chances and the problems of capitalism," and that the state itself has become a quasi-independent "middle structure."[35] However, radical criminologists have generally given more attention to the instrumental, repressive functions of state law than to its more subtle ideological functions.[36]

Quinney follows his own comment on the ideological functions of state law with the statement that state domination "is exercised in the physical control of our daily lives, in the practice of criminal justice."[37] As a result of this emphasis, the bulk of radical research has focused on the more instrumental elements of class domination, such as police[38] and imprisonment,[39] rather than on

> the extent to which the demands and interests of the dominant class must take into account the limits of direct manipulation imposed by a historical social formation: internal state structure, state-economy relations and economic structure.[40]

These latter functions of state law—social welfare and due process—have received only limited attention from radical criminology. The result is that the pluralist argument, that such reforms demonstrate an absence rather than a tempering of capitalist class will in the law,[41] has been less well answered than it might be by radical criminologists.

Radical Praxis

Another theme central to radical criminology is that criminologists should participate in political struggles against exploitation and domination rather than "in service of the state or liberal reform." Specifically, this means such things as "supporting defendants in political trials, participating in campus protests . . . and helping to develop programs such as community control of the police."[42] In short, radical criminologists should enter into struggles against "exploitation, alienation, racism, sexism and imperialism," in both the large and small ways available to "socialists within the university."[43] The ease with which radical criminologists claim to study objective social conditions while espousing partisanship with human struggles to eliminate dominance and repression is confusing to positivist criminologists.

Such partisanship is, of course, antithetical to positivist notions of objectivity. However, from the radical perspective, participation in partisan struggles is both a cause and an effect of dialectical thought. Dialectical epistemology emphasizes the connectedness between action and thought. Understanding is created not in the abstract but by participating in actions that negate the dominant consciousness. Within this framework, one can only begin to understand domination by opposing domination. Thus, for radical criminologists, praxis is not the application of dialectical methodology to contemporary institutions of domination, it is itself part of the methodology for understanding those institutions.

Critical Criminology: The Future of Radical Thought

It is not my intention to speak here of critical criminology as a theoretical and methodological entity distinct from radical criminology. Critical criminology, as it is used here, refers to a scenario for the evolution of radical criminology, which as yet is only partially unfolded.

The Frankfurt school of critical sociology developed a form of Hegelian-Marxism that placed greater emphasis on dialectical concerns with the formation of consciousness than did most other versions of Marxism.[44] During the late 1960s, particularly through the writings of Habermas and Marcuse, the critical school was rediscovered by the academic left in America.[45] To the extent that criminology is a derivative discipline, this suggests that renewed interest in critical theory within sociology should eventually be reflected in the study of law and justice.

Some movement in this direction can be detected. Three works in particular—Pepinsky's *Crime and Conflict,* Edelman's *Ownership of the Image,* and Hirst's *On Law and Ideology*—in somewhat different ways seek to expand our understanding of the relationship between law and consciousness.[46] Pepinsky's book examines the different legal forms that derive from individualist versus collectivist visions of social order. Hirst and Edleman both develop broad theoretical models for the dialectic between legal forms and consciousness. At a microempirical level, Scimecca has attempted to construct a theory of the self that is amenable to Marxist analysis in criminology through adaptation of Kelly's personal-construct theory.[47]

In addition to the theoretically useful but relatively abstract mentalistic concerns of those under the tutelege of the Frankfurt school, works have appeared in recent years that attempt to place the study of crime and justice within the larger framework of the relationship between legal forms and economic-community forms. Pearce's *Crimes of the Powerful,* Tigar and Levy's *Law and the Rise of Capitalism,* and the Critique of Law Group's *Critique of Law: A Marxist Analysis* each contributes in its own way to broadening the scope of critical criminology beyond examination of the repressive functions of police, courts and corrections.[48]

Finally, as critical criminology moves away from its radical birth, the amount of attention devoted to the critique of traditional criminology appears to be declining. This indicates not so much a rapprochement as an emerging identity for critical criminology. Radical criminology in its early years in America was defined as much by its critique of traditional criminology as by its own substantive analyses. Although the death of radical criminology is periodically announced by its more traditional opponents, many Marxist criminologists have discovered a broad national and international community of scholars wherein dialectical epistemology is both a strong and a legitimate part of intellectual inquiry. This has tended to produce an identity for critical criminology that is less dependent on convincing, converting, or criticizing traditional criminology than was previously the case.

Conclusion

Domination in capitalist and socialist societies occurs both by force and by idea. A critical analysis of law and justice should likewise examine, probably in equal measure, both these sources of domination. Domination by idea is a political state's first choice, for it is less disruptive of social peace and more productive of legitimation than is force. However, it is also best not forgotten that, when hegemony fails and order is threatened, states resort to force, and that at any given time both ideology and force are part of the in-place apparatus for managing the contradiction of class society, be it capitalist or socialist.

A fully mature critical criminology in America has yet to emerge; however, a blending of radical criminology and critical sociology, with their respective focuses on the instrumental and ideological functions of state law, would be a significant advance and would contribute to the modification and eventual elimination of those structures that render human freedom and growth subservient to the vested interests of privileged classes.

To speak of the elimination of economic, political, and social domination is often considered naive, utopian, or unreasonable by those who consider themselves realistic observers of the human condition. However, because the reasonable person is prone to making accommodations to the world as it is, rather than seeking to change it, as George Bernard Shaw rightly observed, "All progress depends upon the unreasonable man" and, I would add, the unreasonable woman as well.

Notes

1. D.C. Gibbons, *The Criminological Enterprise* (Englewood Cliffs, N.J.: Prentice-Hall, 1979), p. 73.

2. T. Schroyer, *The Critique of Domination* (Boston: Beacon Press, 1973), p. 15.

3. H. Blumer, *Symbolic Interactionism* (Chicago: University of Chicago Press, 1969), p. 2.

4. R. Quinney, *Criminology* (Boston: Little, Brown, 1979), p. 15; T. Platt, "Prospects for a Radical Criminology in the United States," *Crime and Social Justice,* No. 1 (Spring-Summer 1974), pp. 2–3.

5. D. Matza, *Becoming Deviant* (Englewood Cliffs, N.J.: Prentice-Hall, 1969).

6. G. Simmel, *The Web of Group Affiliations,* trans. Reinhard Bendix (Glencoe, Ill.: Free Press, 1955).

7. For detailed presentation of the functionalist-conflict perspective in sociology, see L. Coser, *The Functions of Social Conflict* (Glencoe, Ill.: Free Press, 1956); and R. Dahrendorf, "Toward a Theory of Social Conflict," *Journal of Conflict Resolution,* No. 2 (1958), pp. 170–183.

8. G.B. Vold, *Theoretical Criminology* (New York: Oxford University Press, 1958), pp. 203–242; A. Turk, *Criminality and the Legal Order* (New York: Rand McNally, 1968).

9. T. Sellin, *Culture, Conflict and Crime* (New York: Social Science Research Council, 1938).

10. Ibid., pp. 104–105.

11. Turk, *Criminality and the Legal Order,* p. 43.

12. Vold, *Theoretical Criminology,* p. 204.

13. Turk, *Criminality and the Legal Order,* p. xii.

14. Vold, *Theoretical Criminology,* pp. 208–209.

15. Turk, *Criminality and the Legal Order,* pp. 31–32.

16. Ibid., p. 32.

17. Ibid., p. 53.

18. F.P. Williams, "A Review of the Evidence on Class and Racial Differentials in Criminal Justice Processing" (Paper presented at the American Society of Criminology Annual Meeting, Tucson, 1976).

19. J. Hagan, "Extra-Legal Attributes and Criminal Sentencing," *Law and Society Review,* No. 8 (1974).

20. M. Gold, "Undetected Delinquent Behavior," *The Journal of Research in Crime and Delinquency,* No. 3 (January 1966), pp. 27–46; I.F. Nye, J. Short, and V.J. Olson, "Socioeconomic Status and Delinquent Behavior," *The American Journal of Sociology,* No. 63 (January 1958), pp. 381–389; H. Voss, "Socioeconomic Status and Reported Delinquent Behavior," *Social Problems,* No. 13 (Winter 1966), pp. 314–324; J. Williams and M. Gold, "From Delinquent Behavior to Official Delinquency," *Social Problems* 20(Fall 1972): 209–229

21. R.M. Terry, "The Screening of Juvenile Offenders," *Journal of Criminal Law, Criminology and Police Science,* No. 58 (June 1967), pp. 173–181; A.W. McEachern and R. Bauzer, "Factors Related to Disposition in Juvenile Police Contacts," in *Juvenile Gangs in Context,* ed. M.W. Klein (Los Angeles: Youth Studies Center, University of Southern California, 1964), pp. 192–210.

22. J.M. Graham, "Amphetamine Politics on Capitol Hill," *Society* 9 (1972):14–23; H.S. Becker, *Outsiders: Studies in the Sociology of Deviance* (New York: Free Press, 1963); P. Roby, "Politics and Criminal Law: Revision of the New York State Penal Law on Prostitution," *Social Problems,* No. 17 (Summer 1969), pp. 83–109; R. Akers, "The Professional Association and the Legal Regulation of Practice," *Law and Society Review,* No. 2 (May 1968), pp. 463–482.

23. P.H. Rossi, E. Waite, C.E. Bose, and R.E. Berk, "The Seriousness of Crime: Normative Structure and Individual Differences," *American Sociological Review* 39(1974):224–237.

24. R. Quinney, *Criminology* (Boston: Little, Brown, 1979).

25. B. Krisberg, "Teaching Radical Criminology," *Crime and Scoial Justice,* No. 1 (Spring-Summer 1974), p. 64.

26. Quinney, *Criminology,* pp. 31–32.

27. Schroyer, *The Critique of Domination,* p. 104.

28. M. Albrow, "Dialectical and Categorical Paradigms of a Science of Society," *Sociological Review* 22(1976):184.

29. Schroyer, *The Critique of Domination,* pp. 103–168.

30. Ibid., p. 112.

31. See, for example, Platt, "Prospects for a Radical Criminology," p. 3; Mary Marzotto, T. Platt, and A. Snare, "A Reply to Turk," *Crime and Social Justice,* No. 4 (Fall-Winter 1975), pp. 44–45; H. Schwendinger and J. Schwen-

dinger, "Defenders of Order or Guardians of Human Rights?" *Issues in Criminology* 5(Summer 1970).

32. A. Gramsci, *Selections from Prison Notebooks,* trans. Q. Hoare and G. Nowell (New York: International Publishers, 1972); I. Balbus, "Commodity Form and Legal Form: An Essay on the Relative Autonomy of the Law," *Law and Society Review,* No. 11 (1977), pp. 471–481; L. Althusser, "Ideology and Ideological State Apparatuses," in *Lenin and Philosophy and Other Essays* (London: New Left Books, 1970).

33. J. O'Connor, *The Fiscal Crisis of the State* (New York: St. Martin's Press, 1973).

34. A. Syzmanski, *The Capitalist State and the Politics of Class* (Cambridge, Mass.: Winthrop, 1978), pp. 196–197.

35. R. Quinney, *Class, State and Crime* (New York; David McKay, 1977), p. 86.

36. See, for example, R. Quinney, *Criminal Justice in America* (Boston: Little, Brown, 1974), p. 24; J.F. Galliher and J.F. McCartney, *Criminology* (Homewood, Ill.: The Dorsey Press, 1977), p. 1; H. Schwendinger and J. Schwendinger, "Defenders of Order," p. 6.

37. Quinney, *Class, State and Crime,* p. 89.

38. See, for example, P. Takagi, "A Garrison State in a 'Democratic' Society," *Crime and Social Justice,* No. 1 (Spring-Summer 1974), pp. 27–33; S.L. Harring and L. McMullin, "The Buffalo Police 1872–1900: Labor Unrest, Political Power and the Creation of the Police Institution," *Crime and Social Justice,* No. 4 (Fall-Winter 1974), pp. 5–14; *The Iron Fist and the Velvet Glove* (Berkeley: Center for Research on Criminal Justice, 1975); S. Hall, C. Critcher, T. Jefferson, J. Clarke, and B. Roberts, *Policing the Crisis* (London: Macmillan, 1978).

39. See, for example, P. Takagi, "The Walnut Street Jail: A Penal Reform to Centralize the Powers of the State," *Federal Probation* 39(December 1975):18–25; R. Hogg, "Imprisonment Under Early British Capitalism," *Crime and Social Justice,* No. 12 (Winter 1979), pp. 4–18; J.H. Reiman, *The Rich Get Richer and the Poor Get Prison* (New York: Wiley, 1979); I. Jankovic, "Social Class and Criminal Sentencing," *Crime and Social Justice,* No. 10 (Fall-Winter 1978), pp. 9–16.

40. G. Esping-Anderson et al., "Modes of Class Struggle and the Captalist State," *Kapitalistate* 4(1976):189.

41. See G. Kolko, *The Triumph of Conservatism* (Chicago: Quadrangle Books, 1963), for a historical analysis of this tempering function.

42. Platt, "Prospects for a Radical Criminology, p. 6.

43. Marzotto et al., "A Reply to Turk," p. 44.

44. Schroyer, *The Critique of Domination,* p. 134.

45. P. Connorton, *Critical Sociology* (New York, Penguin Books, 1976), p. 12.

46. H. Pepinsky, *Crime and Conflict* (New York, Academic Press, 1976); B. Edelman, *Ownership of the Image*, trans. Elizabeth Kingdom (London: Routledge and Kegan Paul, 1979); P. Hirst, *On Law and Ideology*, (Atlantic Highland, N.J.: Humanities Press, 1979).

47. J.A. Scimecca, "Toward a Theory of Self for Radical Criminology" (Paper presented at the American Society of Criminology annual meeting, November 1980).

48. F. Pearce, *Crimes of the Powerful: Marxism, Crime, and Deviance* (London: Pluto Press, 1976); M.E. Tigar and M.R. Levy, *Law and the Rise of Capitalism* (New York: Monthly Review Press, 1977); Critique of Law Editorial Collective, *Critique of Law: A Marxist Analysis* (University of New South Wales, 1978)

Part II:
Forms of Delinquent
and Criminal Behavior

The theme of diversity is again evident in part II, which encompasses a broad sampling of essays on delinquency and criminality. This section begins with a focus on juvenile delinquency, a field of study with a long and productive history of research at Ohio State University. It is fitting that two of the principals involved in much of the early research, Frank R. Scarpitti (who was then a graduate student) and Professor Emeritus Walter Reckless, are represented in this section.

Scarpitti's chapter provides a concise review of the state of the art in delinquency prevention. The rapidly escalating official rates of juvenile delinquency in the past thirty years have led to a proliferation of delinquency-prevention programs. Scarpitti contends that the principal focus of these programs has been on interpersonal and social-psychological factors, despite some attention to systemic-structural variables and some efforts to reduce the secondary deviance generated by the system's reactions and social-control efforts. Although research in this area has been hampered by both theoretical and methodological problems, adequate evaluation typically suggests that delinquency-prevention programs do not make any significant difference, at least insofar as can be measured by objective indicators. Scarpitti cites the series of studies conducted by Reckless and Dinitz as an illustration of the frequent discrepancy between objective indicators (usually suggesting little or no impact) and subjective measures (usually supporting the experimental intervention). Finally, the chapter concludes with a discussion of some current research and policy issues surrounding this subject.

Professor Emeritus Walter C. Reckless is widely known for his pioneering work in the formulation of containment theory and for his efforts with Professor Dinitz in applying that theory to the prevention of delinquency. Because of the historical importance of containment theory in criminology and its place in the Ohio State criminological heritage, we sought and received permission to reprint the original statement of containment theory as it appeared in 1961. This essay represents Professor Reckless's attempt to develop a middle-range theory of deviant and nondeviant behavior to address such questions as the factors that explain the difference between the criminal and the noncriminal, or the delinquent and the nondelinquent, when both live in a high-crime neighborhood.

A great deal of attention and controversy has recently surrounded the subject of female involvement in crime and delinquency. Ira J. Silverman devotes his chapter to this controversial topic, examining both the magnitude and the etiology of this phenomenon. Silverman contends that data from both official and self-report studies fail to prove the popularly held assumption that female crime and delinquency is escalating rapidly. This perceived increase, he argues, is more apparent than real. In the second part of his chapter, he reviews and critically evaluates four major etiological perspectives that have been used to explain female crime and delinquency: the individualistic, multifactor, social-factors, and female-emancipation perspectives.

Murder and mayhem seem to occupy much of the news we see, hear, and read these days. Although it is not always clear that the media's focus on these events is proportionate to their frequency of occurrence, the perceptions of the public and its elected legislative policymakers suggest that violent crime is out of control in our society and in some others as well. Chapters 8 and 9, by John P. Conrad and Margaret A. Zahn, address violence and dangerousness, though in somewhat different ways.

Conrad, drawing on his research with Dinitz on the Dangerous Offender Project, analyzes "the puzzle of dangerousness" in urban America. He argues that the problem of preventing violent crime is beyond the capabilities of the criminal-justice system acting by itself; rather, prevention is the responsibility of the entire community. The current preoccupation with violent crime, he asserts, distorts the criminal-justice system's operations and similarly affects virtually every aspect of urban life. Conrad sees a new war on crime emerging. However, this new war is a limited war; its target is violent crime. It also is a war that is limited in its tactics, since Conrad sees little likelihood that effective handgun controls will be adopted. The puzzle, then, is what can be done about violent crime if it cannot in fact be controlled by the criminal-justice system. Conrad calls for a major federal effort to attack the problems of the underclass in American society—those economically redundant, unskilled laborers who are disproportionately represented in statistics on violent crime (both as offenders and as victims). He is not optimistic that the recent calls for the private sector to become more involved will result in much assistance to the underclass, since private industry has little use for unskilled labor and is unlikely to assume responsibility for training unskilled workers. Conrad argues that the only feasible approach is a major federal effort to employ underclass youth in conservation programs and other jobs that must be done but are not easily accomplished by a profit-oriented system of labor. In the final analysis, the current level of urban fear and crime may only be lowered when we are able to raise people out of the underclass.

Zahn's essay represents a concise review of the major research findings concerning homicide in America. She notes a number of serious problems that impede our ability to compare the results of different studies: noncomparability of data, inadequate conceptualization, definitional problems in constructing categories of homicide, and other constraints. Nevertheless, she reviews the major findings concerning homicide, focusing on such important variables as the frequency, both temporal and spatial, with which homicide occurs; the characteristics of those who are participants in homicide events (offenders and victims); and the social organization, ideology, technology, and process of homicide events. Finally, Zahn offers a review and assessment of the adequacy of the three major sociological perspectives on homicide—cultural-subcultural, structural, and interactionist—and concludes by raising some stimulating questions to be addressed in future research that is designed to develop a more fully integrated and comparative sociology of homicide.

Shifting our focus a bit from conventional murder and mayhem to organized crime, we next present a chapter by Joseph L. Albini, who shares with us some of his experiences following the publication of his book on the American Mafia. The book questioned some of the popular conceptions about organized crime in America, and its publication resulted in his being challenged, both personally and professionally, by the public and by some scholars. In his discussion, Albini contends that America's belief in a secret criminal society serves several functions, which in turn nourish the faith itself.

A form of criminal behavior that has consistently fascinated Sy Dinitz, ever since his early experiences with it as a participant-observer in a New York sweatshop, is the phenomenon of white-collar crime. Two of Dinitz's former students, Diane Vaughan and Catherine Hartnett, provide analyses of this type of criminal and deviant behavior. Vaughan reviews the major contributions to white-collar-crime research and theory construction. She assesses the two major historical periods of inquiry and concludes by noting that the study of organizational crime and deviance remains in its theoretical and methodological infancy. Hartnett, in her fascinating pioneering study of the deviant occupation of pawnbroking, reviews its history and functions and constructs profiles of the typical pawnbroker and his clients.

The wide range of criminality and delinquency discussed in part II may be viewed as a continuum of dangerousness, which both threatens and solidifies the social order. In part III, we shall turn our attention to some of society's responses to these perceived threats.

5 Delinquency Prevention: The State of the Art

Frank R. Scarpitti

Every American grows up knowing that "an ounce of prevention is worth a pound of cure." There is obvious logic to that belief and, indeed, each of us can cite numerous instances of how implementing that cliché has kept us, individually and collectively, from experiencing unpleasant, tragic, even terrifying consequences. Since juvenile delinquency has been defined as unpleasant, tragic, and even terrifying by many lay and professional persons, it comes as no surprise to learn that programs designed to prevent such behavior have been and continue to be prolific. Although prevention efforts can be identified at least since the 1920s, they have flourished in the last thirty years, even in the face of no demonstrable success.

The recent proliferation of delinquency-prevention programs has received both moral and financial support from the federal government. Although rapidly increasing rates of delinquency in the 1950s encouraged both private and public agencies to intensify their prevention efforts, the 1961 Juvenile Delinquency and Youth Offenses Control Act marked the beginning of a long series of federal efforts in this area.[1] A few years later, the President's Commission on Law Enforcement and Administration of Justice called repeatedly for more crime and delinquency prevention, expressing the view that preventing youthful crime was the only successful way of dealing with it.[2]

On the basis of the commission's report and recommendations, Congress passed the Juvenile Delinquency Prevention and Control Act of 1968 and the Juvenile Delinquency Prevention Act of 1972. The 1974 Juvenile Justice Act created the Office of Juvenile Justice and Delinquency Prevention within the Law Enforcement Assistance Administration (LEAA), with the specific tasks of diverting youths from the juvenile-justice system and developing prevention programs.

As a result, large amounts of money, in a wide variety of programs, are currently being spent on juvenile-delinquency-prevention programs. A recent LEAA report, for example, states that over $42 billion was spent on the problem of juvenile delinquency in fiscal year 1976 and that about 98 percent of the expenditures were for prevention.[3] Further, the majority of delinquency-prevention programs appear to be privately funded, prompting the authors of a recent report to the LEAA to state that not only are delinquency-prevention programs

extensive but their actual magnitude can only be estimated.[4] Using extensive
search procedures, however, Dixon found 6,500 attempts at delinquency prevention between 1965 and 1974.[5] Most prevention programs relate to delinquency in only the most general way. Some 40 percent of the federal money
spent on delinquency in 1976, for example, was for health and health-related
programs, while 78 percent of such funding went to family-related programs as
opposed to youth-centered programs.[6]

Types of Prevention Programs

Prevention refers to providing services to individuals or groups before a delinquent act has occurred in order to reduce the likelihood of such an act. Lejins
has distinguished three types of preventive efforts: punitive, corrective, and
mechanical.[7] Punitive prevention is thought to deter potential lawbreakers by
threatening them with punishment. Corrective prevention rests on the belief that
crime and delinquency are the result of identifiable causes and attempts to
eliminate these factors. Mechanical prevention assumes that the placement of
obstacles (police surveillance, street lighting) in the way of potential offenders
will deter crime.

In addition, prevention services have also been classified as primary, secondary, and tertiary, based on types of target populations.[8] Primary prevention
is directed at all potential delinquents within a specific service area. The objective of this strategy is to insulate the entire population at risk without regard to
individual characteristics. Secondary prevention is aimed at specific groups
because it is believed that they are more vulnerable than the rest of the population. Tertiary prevention focuses on those youngsters who have already had
difficulty with control officials. Status offenders or those manifesting school
behavior problems are often the recipients of tertiary prevention efforts.

A review of delinquency-prevention programs reveals that juveniles involved in these efforts are remarkably similar.[9] In terms of the aforementioned
classifications, most prevention efforts are of the secondary type; the juveniles
involved are male, lower or working class, preadolescent to early adolescent,
and frequently of minority status. The demographic characteristics of known
delinquents are similar, of course, making this group a logical target for preventive efforts.

Other selection criteria are also used, however. Some projects select juveniles whose school behavior is thought to be predictive of future delinquency.
Teacher nominations of youths who are "headed for trouble," are potential
drop-outs or are performing at below average levels are often used to identify
this target group. A number of projects select clients based on gang or pregang
play-group involvement. Youths identified by social agents and agencies as
being delinquency-prone have also become involved in a number of prevention

programs. What is interesting, though, is that, despite the criteria used for selecting program participants, juveniles involved in prevention programs are remarkably similar demographically.

Lejins has maintained that corrective prevention has dominated such efforts. An extensive review of the literature on delinquency prevention by Lundman, McFarlane, and Scarpitti confirms Lejins's observation.[10] In all the programs reviewed, delinquency prevention was attempted by manipulating the variables thought to be responsible for causing delinquent behavior. Neither punitive nor mechanical preventive efforts were used in the programs reported in the professional literature.

The single most frequent type of corrective prevention involves some sort of interaction between an adult worker and a juvenile. Groupwork or casework techniques are very popular, and psychotherapy and counseling are also used, but not as extensively. In all these attempts at delinquency prevention, the basic assumption is that "the causes of delinquency can be corrected by involving juvenile subjects in interaction with adults who seek to alter the behavior or personality of the juvenile subjects."[11]

Alteration of the school environment is the second most frequent type of corrective prevention. This approach is based on the assumption that school often fails to meet the needs of certain children, who then become frustrated and embittered and turn to delinquency as a solution to their unhappy school experiences. Such school-related behaviors as truancy, vandalism, underachievement, classroom disruption, and dropping out are seen as precursors of more serious misconduct. In addition, the school is seen as a convenient location for working with large groups of problem youths.

School-based prevention projects may involve enriched, small classes, with diversified and expanded curricula, as well as remedial work in basic academic subjects. Teachers in such programs act as conforming role models, often as parent surrogates, attempting to make the selected potential delinquents more like youths who are not so labeled.

Other forms of corrective prevention include recreation, based on the belief that athletic activities steer juveniles away from delinquency; providing employment opportunities so that youngsters have access to legitimate means of satisfying desires; parent counseling; and combinations of several of these and other services. Miller's Midcity Project combined detached gang workers, social workers, psychiatrists, family counseling, and group work in an attempt to prevent delinquency.[12]

It should be noted that the history of delinquency-prevention programs has been one of changing emphases along several dimensions. In terms of general theoretical orientation, the progression has been largely one of initial emphasis on personality variables, shifting in the 1960s to a greater concern with providing legitimate educational and employment opportunities for low-income-area youth, followed by programs emphasizing greater concern with the juvenile-justice system itself, particularly the consequences of labeling in the handling of juveniles. Changing emphases of this sort should not be surprising, since there remains a general lack of agreement on what delinquency is and what accounts for it. This is aggravated by the diversity of actual behaviors included in the legal term *delinquency* and the consequent possibility that a single general theory cannot explain all youthful law violation.

Although other theoretical emphases have shown up in recent prevention efforts, it can be said that most current prevention programs retain a primary concern with personality factors and continue their attempts to change individual behavior. This is true because social-work practitioners and their techniques continue to dominate the field and because of the practical problems involved in affecting any larger factors beyond the individual. Even those opportunity programs that remain now define their purpose in terms of assisting individual youths with educational or personality-adjustment deficiencies rather than in terms of the availability of opportunities in the society.[13] Thus, delinquency-prevention efforts remain, by and large, efforts to change individuals rather than social institutions.

The focus on individuals, however, has changed in two major ways from the emphasis that was typical of earlier programs. First, the theoretical under-pinnings of current programs are likelier to be social-psychological rather than purely intrapsychic. Hence, there is more concern, for example, with the impact of family structure, social class, and racial or ethnic identity on adolescent personality formation and less emphasis on the psychodynamics of early child-hood or on delinquency as a variety of psychopathology. The second major change in delinquency programs is that the work of labeling or societal-reaction theorists has had a major impact on policies concerning both prevention and treatment of delinquency. Backed up by self-report studies indicating that probably 95 percent of all adolescents have committed delinquent acts,[14] the emphasis on the role of the juvenile-justice system in determining who is declared delinquent has led to the realization that most delinquents are probably not that different from nondelinquents. Further, self-report studies also indicate that delinquent behavior occurs at all socioeconomic levels and among both boys and girls. The result of these realizations has been a broadening in the definition of what should be considered as delinquency prevention and, again, a shift away from the view of delinquency as a function of abnormal personality development.

As a net result of these changes, the thrust of prevention emphasis has shifted from a negative to a positive focus. That is, rather than aiming at reducing delinquent behavior (especially among high-risk youths), prevention services have increasingly been aimed at promoting positive growth among all adolescents. This change is illustrated in the current federal government philosophy on delinquency prevention, recently stated: *"Until that time when we know how to fine-tune programs to prevent delinquency, let us at least provide the services which are known to be important to the normal, positive development of the child."*[15] Hence, the new orientation has led to greater concern for the processes by which youths acquire acceptable social roles and self-identities.

A number of theoretical arguments and policy recommendations have been made in support of this general prevention orientation, most notably those of Pearl, Empey, and Polk and Kobrin. Pearl's recommendations for preventing delinquency relate to "the cultivation of three human social 'senses': the sense of competence, the sense of belongingness, and the sense of usefulness."[16] If these three senses grow, then the adolescent can develop a healthy self-image, can attain positive goals, and will, ostensibly, be nondelinquent. Empey's recommendations are similar but broader, including four mechanisms for healthy personal growth and delinquency prevention. He advocates the development of (1) legitimate identities, (2) the three senses discussed by Pearl, to enhance the youth's control over his or her own future, (3) "socially acceptable, responsible, and personally gratifying" roles, and (4) changes in social institutions that will result in their assisting with these efforts.[17] Accepting the emphasis on the positive development of the child as the most fruitful delinquency-prevention orientation now available, Polk and Kobrin argue for change in both research and policy. They state that work is needed on how legitimate goals are realized by adolescents rather than the negative emphasis of prior research; and their recommendation is that prevention should be aimed at institutional reform. That is, they believe, that those institutional features that provide positive experiences, rewards, and identities for youth, especially in the schools, should be emphasized for effective prevention.[18]

Actual research on delinquents and nondelinquents, however, has been more limited in scope than that recommended by Polk and Kobrin. The major sets of variables explored in exisiting comparative research generally fall into three categories: self-concept, family dynamics, and peer-group ties. Little of this work is directly connected to prevention tactics, and little of it is even tied to theory; rather, it tends to be strictly empirical in orientation, with theoretical interpretation done on a post hoc basis and with only the most general references to utility for prevention. Further, many studies tend to be rather narrow in focus, especially in the sense that often the major and sometimes only subject breakdown is between delinquents and nondelinquents, with no attention paid to differences in this breakdown by sex, race, age, socioeconomic status, and so forth. Similarly, studies of only one subgroup (for example, only young working-class boys) are only rarely interpreted in terms of the significance of that subgroup's membership. In short, research in this area is both limited in scope and difficult to interpret in a way that would be helpful in a delinquency-prevention effort.

Assessing Prevention Programs

Given the number of prevention programs that have been implemented and the massive amounts of money spent on them, the question of program effectiveness must be addressed. Two recent, independent reviews of such programs reached the same conclusion: this is a very difficult question to answer because of inadequate present technology and general lack of concern with evaluation by program implementers.[19] Technical difficulties include problems of trying to demonstrate that something that didn't occur would have occurred without intervention, of getting adequate measures for delinquent behavior, and of isolating the effects of a program from the many other factors that may influence delinquent or nondelinquent behavior.[20] The failure to use the evaluation technology that does exist has been well documented, in terms of both the adequacy of studies that have been done[21] and the training and attitudes of prevention practitioners.[22]

In an attempt to identify and apply relevant criteria for assessing prevention programs, Lundman, McFarlane, and Scarpitti found that the most prevalent type of program evaluation was the single case study, employing subjective evaluations of goals and intervening variables.[23] Such studies, usually done by program staff members, seem to report positive results but, of course, are extremely unreliable. Such factors as failing to control relevant variables, vested interests of the evaluators, and use of nonsystematically derived definitions of success cause evaluations of this sort to be dismissed. No scientific proof exists that programs evaluated in this way actually prevent delinquent behavior.

Another frequent type of evaluation is similar to the case-study type but employs objective measurements of intervening variables or delinquency. Evaluations of this type typically fail to control variables, however, so it is impossible to distinguish the effects of independent variables, which presumably are manipulated, from the effects of uncontrolled, extraneous variables. It is not surprising that these evaluations generally report positive results, at least on measures of intervening variables thought to be associated with delinquency. Hence, we find reports of improvement, objectively measured, in such things as truancy, school performance, and attitudes, with the assumption that such changes are necessarily linked to changes in delinquent behavior. It must be pointed out that there is no foundation for assuming this relationship. Although it is an improvement over evaluations using solely subjective measurements of impact, the design employed and assumptions made in evaluations of this type do not permit much confidence in the reported results.

Although they are not abundant, some delinquency-prevention-program evaluations do employ experimental designs, usually featuring both subjective and objective indicators of success. In the Lundman, McFarlane, and Scarpitti study, all such projects, with only one exception, report little or no success in preventing delinquency.[24] The lack of positive findings in nearly all reported evaluations using a rigorous experimental design casts even greater doubt on the validity of the many studies that claim program success on the basis of unreliable methods and data.

To illustrate the use of careful design and measurement techniques as well as the frustration of delinquency-prevention efforts, we shall focus briefly on a project by Walter C. Reckless and Simon Dinitz.[25] For nearly fifteen years, Reckless and Dinitz had been working on the hypothesis that a positive self-concept insulates potential delinquents in high-crime areas against actual involvement in law violation. In order to implement their research findings and to subject their hypothesis to a crucial test, they designed a prevention program that attempted to strengthen the self-concepts of selected male juveniles so that they would be better equipped to resist delinquency.

Subjects were nominated by sixth-grade teachers in inner-city schools because, in the teacher's view, they were "headed for trouble." Another group, not headed for trouble, was also nominated. Those boys identified as headed for trouble were randomly assigned to both experimental and control groups, while those selected as not headed for trouble comprised another control group. Experimental-group subjects were placed in self-contained seventh-grade classes with specially trained male teachers, who supposedly served as positive role models. Special lessons were developed, enrichment programs were devised, and discipline was used to reinforce basic program objectives. All experimental- and control-group subjects were followed for four years.

In order to assess the impact of the program, four sets of data were identified in advance: subject and teacher evaluation of the project, school performance, attitudes toward self, and police arrest records. It is not surprising that both the youths and the teachers evaluated the program highly. The juvenile subjects were sure that they had benefited from the project and that other kids headed for trouble could also benefit. Teachers saw significant improvement in school performance as well as overall behavioral change. Based only on these subjective evaluations by program participants, the program was a success.

Objective indicators told a different story, however. Although the experimental subjects did register some positive change on a number of variables, there were no statistically significant differences between them and the control groups of similar youths who were also considered headed for trouble. The special prevention program made no difference in such crucial indicators as arrest, dropping out, attendance, grades, school achievement, and attitudes toward self. The boys in the good-boy control group also showed trends toward greater delinquency involvement and poorer school performance, although they remained superior on these dimensions throughout the study.

Like many experimental studies, this one was operationally successful in that the subjects were provided individual treatment by specially trained teacher-counselors in enriched classrooms. But operational success does not necessarily mean that other intervening variables or delinquency involvement will be altered. Further, this study illustrates the hazard of judging success on the basis of subjective evaluations only. Lundman, McFarlane, and Scarpitti found, without exception, that, when both subjective and objective evaluations were available, the objective data failed to support successful subjective evaluation.[26]

On the basis of this and other reviews of the delinquency-prevention literature,[27] it is apparent that most programs do not permit assessment of results. When design and measurement techniques do permit reliable assessment, the results are most discouraging, since it is clear that no significant differences between experimental and control groups exist. Thus, one may conclude, with some degree of surety, that delinquency-prevention programs have been failures in that no evidence now exists that they successfully prevent delinquent behavior.

Conclusions

Obviously, major problems exist with the implementation and evaluation of delinquency-prevention programs. Fortunately, these problems have been recognized and brought to the attention of the professional community. Relatively little effort has been expended on discussion and analysis of other, perhaps even more important, issues. Chief among these is the problem of protecting individual rights in an effort to identify and treat the potential delinquent.

In our zeal to help, it must not be forgotten that the typical subject in a prevention program has not necessarily violated any laws and is usually guilty only of possessing characteristics upon which selection has been based. Being subjected to a preventive effort, even one of the most benign sort, may pose some danger to the child. Tripodi argues, for example, that any prevention effort can conceivably injure the participant by subjecting him or her to early negative identification and subsequent segregation.[28] Isolating and stigmatizing youths in this way may well create delinquency-fulfilling prophesies, actually increasing the probability of delinquency involvement rather than diminishing it.

Labeling theorists would surely agree. Schur points out how, through the process of retrospective interpretation, the individual identified as delinquent (or potentially so) is seen by others in a new light.[29] He is invested with new personal characteristics and personal identity and finds it difficult to shed such social branding. Rather than imposing potential hardship on a youth through such well-intentioned measures, Schur advocates the consideration of radical nonintervention, that is, in his words, "leave kids alone wherever possible."[30] Rather than attempting to intervene in individual behavior, prevention programs should focus on collective action; such efforts should be voluntary rather than compulsory.

Given the documented failure of prior prevention efforts and the real potential for harm in many programs, the future of delinquency prevention is unclear. Perhaps such efforts should be abandoned in favor of attempts to change the social structure and values that seem to produce delinquency. However, given the monumental nature of that task, it is likely that we shall continue to overlook the failures of past attempts and go on searching for some way to change those who are identified as potential delinquents so that they will conform to the expectations of adult society. For these reasons, the future of delinquency prevention may be similar to its past.

Notes

1. S.L. Wheeler, S. Cottrell, Jr., and A. Romasco, "Juvenile Delinquency: Its Prevention and Control," in *Juvenile Delinquency and Youth Crime,* President's Commission on Law Enforcement and Administration of Justice, (Washington, D.C.: U.S. Government Printing Office, 1967).

2. President's Commission on Law Enforcement and Administration of Justice, *The Challenge of Crime in a Free Society* (Washington, D.C.: U.S. Government Printing Office, 1967).

3. U.S. Department of Justice, Law Enforcement Assistance Administration, *Second Analysis and Evaluation: Federal Juvenile Delinquency Programs* (Washington, D.C.: U.S. Government Printing Office, 1977), pp. 60–65.

4. A.P. Cardarelli, *The Theory and Practice of Delinquency Prevention in the United States: Review, Synthesis and Assessment* (Washington, D.C.: U.S. Government Printing Office, 1976), pp. 125–126.

5. M. Dixon, *Juvenile Delinquency Prevention Programs* (Washington, D.C.: National Science Foundation, 1974).

6. U.S. Department of Justice, *Second Analysis and Evaluation,* pp. 60–63.

7. P. Lejins, "The Field of Prevention," in *Delinquency Prevention,* ed. W. Amos and C. Wellford (Englewood Cliffs, N.J.: Prentice-Hall, 1967).

8. National Advisory Committee on Criminal Justice Standards and Goals, *Juvenile Justice and Delinquency Prevention* (Washington, D.C.: U.S. Government Printing Office, 1976), pp. 25–26.

9. R. Lundman, P. McFarlane, and F. Scarpitti, "Delinquency Prevention: A Description and Assessment of Projects Reported in the Professional Literature," *Crime and Delinquency* 22(July 1976):301.

10. Ibid., pp. 299–300.

11. Ibid., p. 300.

12. W. Miller, "The Impact of a 'Total-Community' Delinquency Control Project," *Social Problems* 10(Fall 1962):168–191.

13. Cardarelli, *Theory and Practice of Delinquency Prevention,* p. 201.

14. U.S. Department of Justice, *Second Analysis and Evaluation,* p. 143.

15. U.S. Department of Justice, Law Enforcement Assistance Administration, "Background Paper: Programs to Prevent Juvenile Delinquency," Apprendix IV in *Programs to Prevent Juvenile Delinquency* (Washington, D.C.: U.S. Government Printing Office, 1976), p. 6.

16. Ibid., p. 7.

17. Ibid., p. 8.

18. K. Polk and S. Kobrin, *Delinquency Prevention Through Youth Development* (Washington, D.C.: U.S. Department of Health, Education and Welfare, 1972).

19. See Dixon, *Juvenile Delinquency Prevention Programs,* and Lundman, McFarlane, and Scarpitti, "Delinquency Prevention."

20. U.S. Department of Justice, "Background Paper," p. 5.

21. C. Logan, "Evaluation Research in Crime and Delinquency: A Reappraisal," *Journal of Criminal Law, Criminology and Police Science* 63(September 1972):378–387; see also Dixon, *Juvenile Delinquency Prevention Programs,* and Lundman, McFarlane, and Scarpitti, "Delinquency Prevention."

22. Cardarelli, *Theory and Practice of Delinquency Prevention,* pp. 145–146, 153–156.

23. Lundman, McFarlane, and Scarpitti, "Delinquency Prevention," p. 304.

24. Ibid., p. 305.

25. W.C. Reckless and S. Dinitz, *The Prevention of Juvenile Delinquency: An Experiment* (Columbus: The Ohio State University Press, 1972).

26. Lundman, McFarlane, and Scarpitti, "Delinquency Prevention," pp. 306–307.

27. See Dixon, *Juvenile Delinquency Prevention Programs,* and U.S. Department of Justice, "Background Paper."

28. T. Tripodi, "Review of Reckless and Dinitz, *The Prevention of Juvenile Delinquency," Social Work* 19(January 1974):119–120.

29. E.M. Schur, *Radical Non-Intervention: Rethinking the Delinquency Problem* (Englewood Cliffs, N.J.: Prentice-Hall, 1973), pp. 117–130.

30. Ibid., p. 155.

6

Containment Theory: An Attempt to Formulate a Middle-Range Theory of Deviance

Walter C. Reckless

Containment theory is an explanation of conforming behavior as well as deviancy.[1] It has two reinforcing aspects: an inner control system and an outer control system. Are there elements within the self and within the person's immediate world that enable him to hold the line against deviancy or to hue to the line of social expectations? The assumption is that strong inner and reinforcing outer containment constitutes an insulation against normative deviancy (not constitutional or psychological deviancy), that is, violation of the sociolegal conduct norms.

A Middle-Range Theory

Containment theory does not explain the entire spectrum of delinquency and crime. It does not explain crime or delinquency which emerges from stronger inner pushes, such as compulsions, anxieties, phobias, hallucinations, personality disorders (including inadequate, unstable, antisocial personalities, etc.), from organic impairments such as brain damage and epilepsy, or from neurotic mechanisms (exhibitionists, peepers, fire setters, compulsive shop lifters). All told these cases are minimal. And containment theory does not explain criminal or delinquent activity which is a part of "normal" and "expected" roles and activities in families and communities, such as the criminal tribes of India, Gypsy vocations and trades (very similar to the former), begging families, and certain phases of delinquency subculture and organized crime. Between these two extremes in the spectrum of crime and delinquency is a very large middle range of norm violation, perhaps as big as two thirds to three quarters of officially reported cases as well as the unreported cases of delinquency and crime. Containment theory seeks to explain this large middle range of offenders. According to its place on the spectrum of delinquency and crime, one might say that it occupies the middle position.

Originally published as "A New Theory of Delinquency and Crime"; reprinted, with the permission of Professor Reckless and the publisher, from *Federal Probation* 25(December 1961):42–46.

A Quick Review of Criminological Theories

Before proceeding further, it might be a good idea to see in what directions theory in criminology is pointing at present. Since the early nineteenth century we have had a long succession of theories, most of which have not stood the test of time. It is possible to assemble these theories into three main camps of schools: (1) biological and constitutional theory—often called the school of criminal biology—in which the mainsprings of deviancy are sought in the inherited physical and mental makeup of man; (2) psychogenic theory, in which the formation of antisocial character is traced to faulty relationships within the family in the first few years of life; and (3) sociological theory, in which the pressures and pulls of the social milieu produce delinquent and criminal behavior.

Mention should be made of some of the specific theories. The dominating theory in Europe today is still the all-inclusive one which falls into the school of criminal biology. It points to the inheritance of weaknesses or pronenesses toward crime and delinquency (plus pressure from a bad environment).[2] Many variants of this theory have shown up in recent years: The attempt to prove inheritance of proneness through the method of studying criminal twins (Lange);[3] the attempt to identify body-mind types (Kretschmer);[4] the general acceptance throughout Europe in the past twenty-five years of several criminally-oriented types of psychopaths, based on inherited proneness (according to Kurt Schneider);[5] the attempt to identify and explain habitual (serious) offenders as contrasted with occasional offenders or offenders of opportunity, according to early onset which in turn points to inheritance of proneness (Irwin Frey);[6] the specification of the mesomorphic somatotype (muscular) as the type of consti-tution which is most usually related to delinquency (first according to William Sheldon[7] and later to the Gluecks).[8]

The psychogenic school probably claims August Aichhorn as its fountain-head. According to Aichhorn,[9] faulty development in the first few years of life makes it impossible for the child to control his impulses. The child lingers on as a sort of aggrandizing infant, living in the pleasure principle and failing to develop the reality principle in life. Friedlander[10] indicates that this faulty development in the first few years of life adds up to an antisocial character structure, incapable of handling reality properly. Redl,[11] who is also a disciple of Aichhorn, calls attention to the failure of the child to develop a management system over his impulsivity; that is, fails to develop a good ego and super ego.

The sociologists, ever since Ferri[12] (Italy, c. 1885), have been calling attention to bad environmental conditions. This was echoed by Bonger,[13] who placed the blame for disproportional crime and delinquency among the prole-tariat on the pressures of the capitalistic system. However, the American soci-ologists in the twenties pointed to conditions of social or community disorganization, rather than factors related to poverty. They became engrossed with identifying the location and characteristics of high delinquency areas of the city, specifying family disruption and conflict instead of broken home, and calling attention to the modal importance of companionship in delinquency.

It was not until around 1940 that a basic American sociological theory of delinquency and criminal behavior was propounded. This was done by Sutherland and it was called differential association.[14] According to this theory, delinquent or criminal behavior is learned as is most other kinds of behavior—learned in association with others, according to the frequency, intensity, priority, and duration of contacts. Sutherland's theory really is not basically different from the one announced by Tarde[15] fifty years earlier, which regarded criminal behavior as a product of imitation of circulating patterns. Glaser[16] fairly recently proposed differential identification as a substitute for differential association. One takes over the models of behavior from those (reference) groups with which one identifies. But this does not have to be a face-to-face or person-to-person identification. (One can identify with the Beatniks without having actual physical contact with them.)

Still more recently Albert Cohen,[17] picking up the lead from Whyte's *Street-Corner Society,* contended that working class boys who turned their backs on middle class virtues and values, found the solution for their status problems in the delinquency subculture of the gang. And most recently of all is the theory propounded by Cloward and Ohlin[18] that urban slum boys gravitate to delinquency subculture when they discover they do not have access to legitimate avenues of success.

Comment on the Theories

Working backward in commenting on these theories, one might say that Cloward's theory only applies to those forms of delinquency which are part and parcel of the role structure of delinquency subculture. Jackson Toby[19] makes the estimate that this might only be 10 percent of the whole spectrum of delinquency. Assuming that Cloward's focus is very restricted, his theory does not account for the boys who do not gravitate toward the fighting gang, the criminal gang, and the retreatist groups (drugs). It does not specify that the ones who do gravitate to the three types of subculture have internalized an awareness of inaccessibility to legitimate success goals. It does not indicate that there are degrees of participation in gangs and that delinquency involvement of some members might be nil.

Cohen's theory has somewhat more merit. Somewhere and somehow in the growing-up process, slum boys turn their backs on middle-class values and look to street-corner groups to come to their aid. But Cohen is not able to specify the boys who do or do not turn their back on middle-class virtues and opportunities and gravitate to the street corner. He does not indicate whether only some of the boys in the street corner get involved in delinquent acts, as Shaw and Thrasher did a generation ago. So we have two interesting sociological formulations here, but not much realistic applicability.

Sutherland's differential association theory was meant to be a general theory, applying to the entire spectrum of delinquency and crime, from low to high in the class structure and across the board in personality. The trouble with Sutherland's theory (as well as Tarde's and Glaser's) is that it does not explain who *does* and who *does not* take up with carriers of delinquent patterns or who internalizes and who does not internalize delinquent models of behavior.

Coming now to the contributors to theory in the psychogenic school (Aichhorn, Redl, et al.), one should observe that at the most they only occupy a small end of the total spectrum of delinquency and crime. It is granted that there are some individuals whose ego and super ego development is too weak or poor to control impulses and to handle ordinary expectancies. But it is not at all clear just which children succumb to or are recipients of faulty socialization in the first few years of life. And it is not clear just which of the children, teenagers, late adolescents, and adults who are supposed to have little control over their impulse system run afoul the laws and regulations of society and those who do not.

One certainly finds it difficult to specify just exactly what the proneness is that is supposed to be the mainspring of serious, habitual, and early-starting offenders (criminal biology). It seems to be a sort of weakness in character. The evidence for the inheritance of proneness is very skimpy and most unimpressive, a sort of unreliable family-tree assessment by clinicians.

William Sheldon was able to specify the different kinds of somatotypes, much more definitely than Kretschmer was able to specify his body-mind types. A group of 200 problem youth in a Boston hostel, according to Sheldon, tended to have mesomorphic (athletic) body types along with several related forms of mental deviancy. The Gluecks discovered that among 500 delinquent and 500 nondeliquent boys the delinquents showed up very much more mesomorphic than the nondelinquents. The mesomorphs were found by the Gluecks to have a higher delinquency potential than other body types. Associated with mesomorphy were strength, social assertiveness, uninhibited motor responses, less submissiveness to authority. While mesomorphy does not explain all of delinquent behavior in the Gluecks' sample, it is certainly associated with a large segment of it and seems to reinforce many of the mental, emotional, and family traits connected with delinquency. Future studies will have to confirm the mesomorphic potential in delinquency.

Gluecks: 4 to 1 Causal Law

Out of their research on 500 delinquent and 500 nondelinquent boys, the Gluecks[20] proposed a five point causal law. According to this formulation, delinquents are distinguishable from nondelinquents (1) physically, in being essentially mesomorphic; (2) temperamentally, in being restless, impulsive, aggressive, destructive; (3) emotionally, in being hostile, defiant, resentful, assertive, nonsubmissive; (4) psychologically, in being direct, concrete learners; (5) socioculturally, in being reared by unfit parents. This might be looked upon as a 4 to 1 law: four parts individual and one part situational. Items 2, 3, and 5 were chosen from among more than 100 overlapping traits, which distinguished delinquents from nondelinquents. The use of more sophisticated statistical methods would have enabled the Gluecks to find the two or three components within this maze of overlapping items which basically differentiate the delinquents from the nondelinquents. Nevertheless, the 4 to 1 causal law still stands as one of the few formulations which is worth attempting to confirm, qualify, or disprove by more rigorous research methods in the future. The law covers most of the spectrum of juvenile delinquency as we know it in the United States, certainly insofar as the full spectrum is represented by 500 boys from Boston who had been committed by juvenile courts to state schools in Massachusetts for delinquency.

Ingredients of Inner and Outer Containment

In contrast to the buck-shot approach of the Gluecks, that is, shooting out in all directions to explore and discover, containment theory seeks to feret out more specifically the inner and outer controls over normative behavior. It is attempting to get closer on the target of delinquency and crime by getting at the components which regulate conduct.

Inner containment consists mainly of self components, such as self-control, good self-concept, ego strength, well-developed superego, high frustration tolerance, high resistance to diversions, high sense of responsibility, goal orientation, ability to find substitute satisfactions, tension-reducing rationalizations, and so on. These are the inner regulators.

Outer containment represents the structural buffer in the person's immediate social world which is able to hold him within bounds. It consists of such items as a presentation of a consistent moral front to the person, institutional reinforcement of his norms, goals, and expectations, the existence of a reasonable set of social expectations, effective supervision and discipline (social controls), provision for reasonable scope of activity (including limits and responsibilities) as well as for alternatives and safety-valves, opportunity for acceptance, identity, and belongingness. Such structural ingredients help the family and other supportive groups contain the individual.

Research will have to feret out the one or two elements in inner and outer containment which are the basic regulators of normative behavior. Undoubtedly in the lists cited above there are items which, if present, determine the existence of other items and cause most of the regulation of conduct. Likewise, research must indicate the way in which the inner and outer regulatory systems operate conjointly. How much self-strength must be present in a fluid world with very little external buffer? How much weakness in self components is an effective external buffer able to manage?

Supporting Research

The research and observations so far which give support to containment theory are the following:

1. According to Albert J. Reiss,[21] as a result of a study of Chicago delinquents who failed and succeeded on probation, the relative weakness of personal and social controls accounts for most cases of delinquency. Reiss found, however, that the personal controls had more predictive efficiency than the social controls as far as recidivism was concerned.

2. Nye[22] presented evidence to the effect that trends toward delinquent behavior are related to four control factors: (a) direct control which comes from discipline, restrictions, punishments; (b) internalized control which is the inner control of conscience; (c) indirect control which is exerted by not wanting to hurt or go against the wishes of parents or other individuals with whom the person identifies, and (d) the availability of alternative means to goals. Nye contends that his social control theory should not be applied to compulsive behavior or the behavior influenced by delinquency subcultures. He feels that the more indirect control is effective, the less need for direct control; the more internalized control is effective, the less need for any other type of control.

3. Reckless and Dinitz[23] found that a favorable concept of self insulated 12-year-old boys in the slum against delinquency, including perceptions about self, companions, home, and school. A poor concept of self, including perceptions that one is likely to get into trouble, his friends are in trouble, his family and home are unsatisfactory, that he will not finish school, and so on, was associated with delinquency vulnerability in 12-year-old slum boys. Four years later, followup contact revealed that the good self concept group had pretty much held the line and the favorable direction, while the poor self concept group had gravitated in unfavorable directions, 35 percent being involved with the law three times on an average. Reckless and Dinitz look upon a good or poor self concept as an internalization of favorable or unfavorable socialization.

4. As a result of his observations on hyperaggressive, hostile children, Redl[24] identifies twenty-two functions of the ego in managing life situations. He conceives of the ego as the manager in the behavior control system, while the super ego is looked upon as the system which gives the signals to the ego. Redl, as is true of Aichhorn disciples, recognize, particularly at the extremes, ego shortage and ego strength as well as a sick conscience and a healthy one.

Containment theory points to the regulation of normative behavior, through resistance to deviancy as well as through direction toward legitimate social expectations. It may very well be that most of the regulation is in terms of a defense or buffer against deflection. At any rate, it appears as if inner and outer containment occupies a central or core position in between the pressures and pulls of the external environment and the inner drives or pushes. Environmental pressures may be looked upon as conditions associated with poverty or deprivation, conflict and discord, external restraint, minority group status, limited access to success in an opportunity structure. The pulls of the environment represent the distractions, attractions, temptations, patterns of deviancy, advertising, propaganda, carriers of delinquent and criminal patterns (including pushers), delinquency subculture, and so forth. The ordinary pushes are the drives, motives, frustrations, restlessness, disappointments, rebellion, hostility, feelings of inferiority, and so forth. One notices at once that Bonger as well as Cloward fall into pressure theory, while Tarde, Sutherland, and Glaser fall into pull theory.

In a vertical order, the pressures and pulls of the environment are at the top or the side of containing structure, while the pushes are below the inner containment. If the individual has a weak outer containment, the pressures and pulls will then have to be handled by the inner control system. If the outer buffer of the individual is relatively strong and effective, the individual's inner defense does not have to play such a critical role. Likewise, if the person's inner controls are not equal to the ordinary pushes, an effective outer defense may help hold him within bounds. If the inner defenses are of good working order, the outer structure does not have to come to the rescue of the person. Mention has already been made of the fact that there are some extraordinary pushes, such as compulsions, which cannot be contained. The inner and outer control system is usually not equal to the task of containing the abnormal pushes. They are uncontainable, by ordinary controls.

Seven Tests of Validity

1. Containment theory is proposed as the theory of best fit for the large middle range of cases of delinquency and crime. It fits the middle range cases better than any other theory.

2. It explains crimes against the person as well as the crimes against property, that is the mine run of murder, assault, and rape, as well as theft, robbery, and burglary.

3. It represents a formulation which psychiatrists, psychologists, and sociologists, as well as practitioners, can use equally well. All of these experts look for dimensions of inner and outer strength and can specify these strengths in their terms. Differential association and/or pressure of the environment leave

most psychiatrists and psychologists cold and an emphasis on push theory leaves the sociologists for the most part cold. But all of the experts can rally around inner and outer weakness and strengths.

4. Inner and outer containment can be discovered in individual case studies. Weaknesses and strengths are observable. Containment theory is one of the few theories in which the microcosm (the individual case history) mirrors the ingredients of the macrocosm (the general formulation).

5. Containment theory is a valid operational theory for treatment of offenders: for restructuring the milieu of a person or beefing up his self. The most knowledgeable probation workers, parole workers, and institutional staff are already focusing to some extent on helping the juvenile or adult offender build up ego strength, develop new goals, internalize new models of behavior. They are also working on social ties, anchors, supportive relationships, limits, and alternative opportunities in helping to refashion a new containing world for the person.

6. Containment theory is also an effective operational theory for prevention. Children with poor containment can be spotted early. Programs to help insulate vulnerable children against delinquency must operate on internalization of stronger self components and the strengthening of containing structure around the child.

7. Internal and external containment can be assessed and approximated. Its strengths and weaknesses can be specified for research. There is good promise that such assessments can be measured in a standard way.

Finally, it is probable that the theory which will best supplement containment theory in the future will be "damage theory," according to which a light to dark spectrum of damage produces maladjustment and deviancy. The problem here is to find measures to isolate the less serious and less obvious damage cases and to estimate how far into the middle range of delinquency and crime the lighter impairments go.

Notes

1. For the complete statement on Containment Theory, see Walter C. Reckless, *The Crime Problem,* 3rd ed. (New York: Appleton-Century-Crofts, 1961), pp. 335–359.

2. Franz Exner, *Kriminologie* (Berlin, 1949), pp. 115–120.

3. Johannes Lange, *Crime and Destiny,* trans. Charlotte Haldane (New York: C. Boni, 1930).

4. E. Kretschmer, *Physique and Character,* trans. W.I.H. Sprott (New York: Harcourt, Brace, 1925).

5. Kurt Schneider, *Psychopathische Persönlichkeiten,* 6th ed. (Berlin, 1943).

6. Irwin Frey, *Die Frühkriminelle Rückfallsverbrecher* (Basel, 1951), pp. 95–98, 103, 253.

7. William H. Sheldon, *Varieties of Delinquent Youth* (New York: Harper and Brothers, 1949), p. 727.

8. Sheldon Glueck and Eleanor Glueck, *Physique and Delinquency* (New York: Harper and Brothers, 1956), p. 219.

9. August Aichhorn, *Wayward Youth* (New York, 1936).

10. Kate Friedlander, *The Psycho-Analytic Approach to Delinquency* (New York: International Universities Press, 1947).

11. Fritz Redl and David Wineman, *Children Who Hate* (Glencoe, Ill.: Free Press, 1951).

12. Enrico Ferri, *Criminal Sociology* (New York: Appleton, 1896).

13. W.G. Bonger, *Criminality and Economic Conditions*, trans. H.P. Horton (Boston: Little, Brown, 1916).

14. Edwin H. Sutherland, *Principles of Criminology,* 4th ed. (Philadelphia: Lippincott, 1947), pp. 6–7.

15. Gabriel Tarde, *Penal Philosophy,* trans. R. Howell (Boston: Little, Brown, 1912).

16. Daniel Glaser, "Criminality Theories and Behavioral Images," *American Journal of Sociology* 61(1956):440.

17. Albert K. Cohen, *Delinquent Boys: The Culture of the Gang* (Glencoe, Ill.: Free Press, 1955), pp. 128–133.

18. R.A. Cloward and Lloyd Ohlin, *Delinquency and Opportunity* (Glencoe, Ill.: Free Press, 1960).

19. Private circulated comment on the Cloward and Ohlin book, 1961.

20. Sheldon Glueck and Eleanor Glueck, *Unraveling Juvenile Delinquency* (New York: The Commonwealth Fund, 1950), pp. 281–282.

21. Albert J. Reiss, Jr., "Delinquency as the Failure of Personal and Social Controls," *American Sociological Review* 16(1951):196–206.

22. F. Ivan Nye, *Family Relationships and Delinquent Behavior* (New York: Wiley and Sons, 1958), pp. 3–4.

23. Walter C. Reckless, Simon Dinitz, and Ellen Murray, "Self Concept as an Insulator against Delinquency," *American Sociological Review* 21(1956):745; "The Self Component in Potential Delinquency and Potential Non-Delinquency," Ibid. 22(1957):569; Simon Dinitz, Barbara Ann Kay, and Walter C. Reckless, "Group Gradients in Delinquency Potential and Achievement Score of Sixth Graders," *American Journal of Orthopsychiatry* 28(1958):598–605; Frank Scarpitti, et al., "The 'Good' Boy in a High Delinquency Area: Four Years Later," *American Sociological Review* 25(1960): 555–558.

24. Redl and Wineman, *Children Who Hate,* pp. 74–140.

7 Female Criminality: An Assessment

Ira J. Silverman

Interest in the female criminal offender is comparatively recent. Until little more than a decade ago, female involvement in crime, in terms of both volume and seriousness, was relatively insignificant as compared with male criminality. However, crime statistics between 1960 and 1970 showed a steep rise in the number of crimes committed by women.[1] During that period, female arrests for index offenses, for example, rose 202 percent, in contrast to an increase of 73 percent for males. Throughout the rest of the 1970s, particularly up to the middle of the decade, arrest rates tended to rise much faster for females than for males.[2]

Part of the burgeoning interest in female criminality can be attributed to scientific curiosity about the reasons for this startling increase in female crime rates. The emergence and subsequent growth of the feminist movement generated interest in whether the gains registered by women in the economic and psychological spheres might have been paralleled by a rise in the incidence of illegitimate activities. As women achieved access to such traditionally male bastions of labor as the construction trades and policing, questions were raised concerning the nature and frequency of their involvement in burglary, auto theft, and robbery—crimes that have long been regarded as an exclusively masculine preserve.

In the past, academic interest in the crime problem was largely confined to a few people in college and university sociology departments. The rapid proliferation of criminal-justice programs and departments during the 1970s produced a marked increase in the number of academicians with interests in crime, criminals, and the functioning of the criminal-justice system. These new programs developed at a time when more and more women were seeking advanced degrees in order to pursue academic careers. The availability of positions in such programs, together with affirmative-action hiring policies, added a substantial female complement to the criminal-justice work force. This provided a constituency with natural interest in and curiosity about female offenders. It had proved difficult in an earlier period to arouse much interest among graduate students in crime as a topic area for theses and dissertations.[3] But growing

I wish to thank Harold Vetter for his comments and editorial assistance on this chapter. Thanks are also dué Gideon Fishman for his advice on the manuscript.

concern on the part of both male and female faculty members for systematic study of the crime problem has been reflected in increased interest by graduate students. This chapter is devoted to an examination of changes in the nature of female crime and a review of the explanations that have been offered to account for the involvement of women in criminal behavior.

The Nature and Frequency of Female Crime

The last few years have witnessed the development of both scientific and popular literature on changing levels of female involvement in crime.[4] Spurred by large percentage increases in major offenses and fueled by headlines describing the participation of women in some rather dramatic crime episodes,[5] there has been a tendency to perceive female crime as rising at a pace so rapid that, if it continued, it would soon result in a major reduction in the disparity between male and female crime rates.

Although accounts in the popular media and examination of the increased female involvement in the major offenses suggest that we are experiencing a female crime wave, the crime wave is more apparent than real. The misleading impression of a female crime wave results from a superficial analysis of statistics on female crime. It is true that there have been large percentage increases in the number of women involved in crime as compared with a decade or more ago. These large percentage increases, however, represent relatively small increases in actual numbers. For example, there was a 288 percent increase in the female burglary rate from 1960 to 1975.[6] This large bulge resulted from the fact that, whereas females committed only 3,600 burglaries in 1960, the number had risen in 1975 to approximately 14,000. During this same period, there was over a 100-percent increase in the male burglary rate. This increase in percentage, however, reflected an increase of 130,000 actual crimes, which tends to reduce to comparative insignificance the increase of slightly more than 10,000 female offenses in the same period.

Although *Uniform Crime Report* (UCR) statistics have been used (or rather misused) to convey a distorted picture of the nature and extent of female criminality, their proper utilization can provide some worthwhile insights into the current status of this offender category. These data will be used in the next section to examine trends in adult female crime; in the section following that, the information will be used, along with self-report data, to scrutinize juvenile female crime patterns.

Adult Crime Data

It is possible to analyze changes in female crime either by using raw UCR arrest figures or by converting these data to arrest rates. The latter method is preferable, since it considers population size and composition and is not affected by differences in the base levels by arrest.[7]

Steffensmeier has taken UCR data for two time periods, 1960–1975[8] and 1965–1977,[9] and converted them to arrest rates. Using the newly computed arrest-rate information, a number of questions concerning female criminality over the past two decades will be examined: (1) how female and male arrest patterns changed for the two data sets 1960–1975 and 1965–1977; (2) whether there were any major changes in the types of offenses committed by women during these periods, particularly in terms of offenses considered violent, male-dominated, masculine, or serious; and (3) whether there are any data to support the hypothesized relationship between expanded occupational opportunities and increased female crime, that is, as reflected in white-collar or economic crimes.

*Male and Female Arrest Patterns for 1960–1975
and 1965–1977*

In the first set of data, there were substantial increases in the rates of female involvement in violent crimes, but these increases were generally matched by those of males. Of greater significance was the fact that the percentage that females contributed to total arrest (%FC) during this period remained approximately the same. In the case of property offenses (burglary, auto theft, fraud, embezzlement, larceny-theft), there was a substantial overall increase as well as a specific percentage increase. However, with the exception of larceny-theft (87 to 380) and, to a lesser extent, fraud/embezzlement (14.7 to 67) these increases were the result of the relatively small size of the initial base. There was also a narrowing of the %FC overall as well as for each specific offense except stolen property.

Data analysis for the second data set, 1965 to 1977, was more extensive; it dealt with twenty-seven offenses.[10] During this period, the %FC for specific offenses changed less than 2 percent for most offenses; the exceptions were larceny (9 percent), embezzlement (5 percent), fraud, forgery (11 percent), and vagrancy (27 percent).

Another important question is whether there has been a shift in types of offenses committed by women. When offenses are rank ordered for both period, it was found (1) that for both sexes, the only major increases in rank position were fraud, stolen property, and narcotics violations; (2) that female arrest patterns, as measured by rank-order correlations, remained fairly stable and did not shift; (3) that the patterns of change were the same for both sexes (that is, male and female rates rose, fell, or remained stable on the same offenses); and (4) that there was no shift toward more similarity between the sexes in the types of crimes committed—the male-female rank-order correlation was .83 for 1965 and .84 for 1977. .

Feminine Participation in Violent Male-Dominated,
Masculine, and Serious Offenses

Steffensmeier noted that increases in arrest rates for males and females in the
violent-offense category were similar from 1965 to 1977 and that the %FC
increased negligibly. In other offenses that traditionally have been considered
masculine because they are viewed as requiring male skills, strength, and techniques, the relative gap between the sexes changed very little (see table 7–1).
Further, for male-dominated offenses, aggregate arrests for males declined—
largely as a result of decreasing arrests for drunkenness—while female rates
remained the same. Nevertheless, the relative gap remained fairly stable. The
inescapable conclusion is that females have not increased their involvement in
violent, masculine, or male-dominated crimes.[11]

Regarding serious offenses, there was a substantial narrowing of the relative
gap, and the percentage these offenses contributed to total female arrests increased to a much larger extent than did the percentage for male arrest. However,
when larceny-theft, which in the case of female criminality is largely shoplifting,

Table 7–1
Aggregate Arrest-Rate Percentage Changes for Adult Males and Females,
1965 and 1977

Type	%FC[a]		Female Total		Male Total	
	1965	1977	1965	1977	1965	1977
Violent	9.9	10.8	7.8	8.2	8.1	10.9
Masculine	8.2	9.5	9.7	11.0	12.4	16.8
Male-Dominated	7.7	8.7	50.6	38.5	69.3	65.0
Serious	14.7	21.1	15.0	25.5	9.9	15.4
Serious without Larceny	7.4	8.5	4.4	5.1	6.3	8.9
Petty Property	23.2	33.8	14.4	29.2	5.4	9.2

Source: Darell Stefensmeier, "Sex Differences in Patterns of Adult Crime, 1965–1977, A review
and Assessment." *Social Forces* 58(June 1980):1092.

Definitions are as follows:
  Violent crimes are murder, aggravated assault, other assaults, weapons, and robbery.
  Masculine crimes are murder, aggravated assault, other assaults, weapons, robbery, burglary,
  auto theft, vandalism, and arson.
  Male-dominated crimes include the masculine crimes, plus stolen property, gambling, driving
  under the influence, liquor-law violations, drunkenness, narcotic drug law, sex offenses (except
  forcible rape and prostitution), and offenses against the family.
  Serious crimes are murder, robbery, aggravated assault, burglary, larceny-theft, and auto theft.
  Petty Property crimes are larceny-theft, fraud, forgery, and embezzlement.

[a]Percentage that female rate contributes to the proportion of total arrests (male rate and female rate).

is excluded from the category of serious crime—a procedure that is more than justified by the fact that shoplifting is primarily petty theft—the picture of comparative criminality is considerably changed.[12] It is clear from the data that claims of increased female involvement in serious offenses are false and result from the inappropriate inclusion of petty theft in this category.

Female Involvement in White-Collar or Economic Crimes as a Function of Expanded Occupational Opportunities

Research on such white-collar or economic crimes as fraud, forgery, and embezzlement has suggested that these offenses are rarely committed by women in the course of their occupations.[13] With regard to embezzlement, female perpetrators tend to be found in comparatively low-level positions (cashiers, bank tellers, sales clerks, and the like).[14] Thus, it is difficult to claim that any increases in this offense are a reflection of increased employment opportunities for women. For these reasons, Steffensmeier has labeled these offenses petty property crimes. It should be noted that the major changes in female offense patterns have actually occurred among these offenses. Table 7–1 shows that the relative gap narrowed and, more importantly, that the total female arrests accounted for by these offenses increased during this period, as compared with the slight male increase in this offense category.

Juvenile Crime and Delinquency

It has also been argued that the movement toward sexual egalitarianism has produced changes in the patterns of female delinquency to the extent that they now more closely approximate those of male juveniles.[15] Although changes in female roles may not be fully reflected in patterns of adult criminality, because of the traditional socialization patterns experienced by many female offenders, the emphasis on role convergence in the socialization experiences of contemporary teenagers should be reflected in patterns of delinquency that parallel those of males in both frequency and offense. It is also important to examine delinquency rates, since they may give us an indication of future patterns of female criminality.

Official Statistics

Steffensmeier and Steffensmeier computed arrest rates for juveniles on twenty-nine offenses for the period 1965 to 1977.[16] They added the categories of drugs and drinking, status, and sex-related offenses to the classification used in the previous analysis. Our examination of female crime will include the first two questions used in the adult analysis[17] plus the following three questions: (1) are there any data to indicate changes in female delinquency rates in the areas of status offenses and sex-related offenses, which are traditional female delinquency patterns? (2) what is the extent of female involvement in drug and alcohol-related offenses as compared with males? and (3) what is the nature of female involvement in petty property offenses?[18]

Juvenile Male and Female Crime Patterns for 1965–1977. During this period, the relative gap between male and female arrest rates narrowed for most offenses. The magnitude of this change, however, was less than 5 percent for all but five offenses: running away (10 percent); larceny-theft (9 percent); liquor-law violations (8.4 percent); other assaults (5 percent); and vagrancy (6 percent). Despite slight percentage variations, the offenses of larceny-theft and running away accounted for the largest number of juvenile females arrested, with each contributing approximately 25 percent of the total arrests for this category.

Female Participation in Masculine, Violent, and Serious Offenses. In regard to masculine crimes and violent offenses,[19] the relative gap narrowed 4 percent, with slight changes being primarily a result of increased female involvement in other assaults (see table 7–2). The fact that these assaults are not particularly serious, often involving females only as companions and observers to boys involved in fights, leads to the conclusion that changes in female involvement in these offenses are minor and insignificant.[20]

Table 7–2 shows that there was a moderate narrowing of the relative gap for serious offenses. The percentage of total arrests accounted for by serious crime dropped slightly for males, while it increased over 6 percent for females. The inclusion of larceny in this category is just as questionable for juveniles as it was for adults and presents the same distorted picture of juvenile female involvement in this category.[21] Thus, it is not surprising that, when larceny is excluded from this category, the relative gap narrowed only slightly between 1965 and 1977 and the percentage of female arrests accounted for by these offenses showed only a slight increase. These modest increases certainly do not indicate any major shift in the nature of juvenile female involvement in serious crime.

Female Involvement in Status and Sex-Related Offenses. Traditionally, juvenile females have been taken into custody for status offenses and sex-related offenses in order to "protect their virtue" and to prevent their involvement in situations that might lead to sexual experimentation and other "unladylike behavior." Therefore, an analysis of changes in female involvement in these offenses is critical in order to determine if there have been changes in female delinquency between 1965 and 1977. Table 7–2 shows that there was a slight

Table 7–2
Aggregate Arrest-Rate Percentage Changes for Male and Female Adolescents, 1965 and 1977

Type	%FC[a]		Female Total		Male Total	
	1965	1977	1965	1977	1965	1977
Violent	10.5	15.0	3.4	5.5	6.3	8.9
Masculine	5.9	9.4	10.1	12.6	33.8	34.5
Serious	12.8	19.1	27.9	32.6	40.2	39.2
Serious without Larceny	4.6	7.8	4.8	6.2	20.9	20.9
Petty Property	20.2	28.7	23.6	28.0	20.0	19.8
Petty Property without Larceny	19.7	23.5	0.5	1.6	0.5	1.5
Status Offenses	30.6	39.6	34.6	32.4	16.8	14.1
Sex-Related Offenses	14.4	19.2	9.3	5.3	11.8	6.4
Drugs and Drinking	12.4	17.9	5.3	12.1	8.0	15.7

Source: Darell Steffensmeier, "Trends in Female Delinquency." *Criminology*, May 1980.
Definitions are as follows:
  Violent crimes are murder, aggravated assault, other assault, weapons, and robbery.
  Masculine crimes include the violent offenses, plus burglary, auto theft, stolen property, vandalism, arson, and gambling.
  Serious crimes are murder, robbery, aggravated assault, burglary, larceny-theft, and auto theft.
  Petty Property crimes are larceny-theft, fraud, forgery, and embezzlement.
  Status offenses are runaways, curfew, and liquor-law violations.
  Sex-related offenses are disorderly conduct, suspicion, and vagrancy.
  Drug and drinking offenses are narcotic drugs, driving under the influence, drunkenness, and liquor-law violations.
[a]Percentage that female rate contributes to the proportion of total arrests (male rate and female rate).

drop in the percentage that each of these categories contributed to total female arrests during this period. These data would appear to indicate that our protective attitudes toward young girls have certainly not changed. However, the slight drop in the percentage of total juvenile female arrests accounted for by these offenses would appear to reflect the slightly increased involvement of female adolescents in other offenses.

Female Involvement in Drug-Related Offenses. Although aggregate arrest rates for drug-related offenses rose considerably for both males (711.6 to 1,-804.7) and females (100.4 to 393.6) from 1965 to 1977, males still dominated arrests for these offenses. However, there was a 5 percent narrowing of the relative gap, and the change in the percentage of total arrests accounted for by this category was greater for females than for males (see table 7–2). Changes in the relative involvement of females in this category is primarily due to increases in liquor-law violations (65.7 to 179.8) and arrests for narcotic drugs (6.8 to 150.7). Data from the self-report studies, to be presented in the next section, and from other sources suggest that this increased juvenile female drug use primarily involved soft drugs, such as marijuana.[22]

Juvenile Female Involvement in Petty Property Crime. The rationale designating the offenses of larceny, forgery, fraud, and embezzlement as petty property offense is as valid for juveniles as it is for adults. Data on this category showed that, between 1965 and 1977, the relative gap narrowed and there was a slight increase in the percentage of total arrests accounted for by this category. However, it is clear that these changes are due primarily to increased involvement in larceny, which accounted for 25 percent of the arrests in this category in 1965 and 38 percent in 1977. More importantly, when it is excluded from this category, the changes in the relative gap and in the percentage that these offenses contribute to total female arrests were considerably less. Despite the fact that, as noted earlier, there was a 5 percent narrowing of the gap in the case of embezzlement and forgery, these increases are insignificant relative to total female arrests and even to petty theft. This is not at all surprising, since one would not expect that juveniles would be involved in embezzlement, fraud, or forgery-related offenses.

Self-Report Studies

Up to this point, our analysis was limited to the use of UCR data and, as a result, it suffers the biases and limitations of official statistics.[23] There have been enough self-report studies in the juvenile area to provide additional data on (1) convergence between male-female involvement increases and (2) changes in patterning of female delinquency.

An analysis of these studies shows that the difference between the delinquency of boys and girls is less than that which is reported in official statistics.[24] The range in these studies is from a high of 3 to 1 to a low of 1.27 to 1, with the later studies typically showing a closer convergence. Part of the disparity between the self-reported rates and official statistics may be because these studies tend to overemphasize relatively minor status offenses. For example, Zimmerman and Broder report an overall ratio of 1.5;[25] however, these ratios increase to 2.4 for criminal offenses and to 4.7 for violent offenses. This is further reflected in studies that exclude status offenses and develop an index of seriousness using the Wolfgang-Sellin index. For example, the Gold study found that boys had a mean seriousness score of 5.81, as compared with 1.87 for girls.[26]

Although these studies can be examined in several ways, it seems logical to analyze them in terms of their data—national sample versus local samples.

The Gold and Reimer study was the only one that used national samples.[27] This study found that boys were involved in more delinquency than girls, although their frequency of involvement dropped from 7.3 to 6.6 incidents from 1967 to 1973, while delinquency among girls rose from 3.7 to 4.5. However, when drinking and drug use are excluded from the analysis, there is no apparent change over the five-year period in per capita number of offenses among girls (3.16 to 3.09). It is noted that the increase in drug use for both sexes is primarily limited to marijuana. Moreover, a seriousness index showed that, although boys were involved in more serious delinquency than girls were, male scores declined between 1967 and 1972 (3.6 to 3.1), but female scores stayed about the same (1.3 to 1.1).

A second source of self-report data is derived from a variety of local studies, which span the period from the mid-1950s to the late 1970s. Thirteen studies were located that provide comparable data on some offenses.[28] These studies show that the types of offenses girls engage in are similar to those of males; they differ in that females are less involved in serious personal and property offenses. It is interesting to note, also, that, when these data were examined by offense categories, there was a clear progressive disparity from minor to serious offenses. An examination of trends over a fifteen-year period, using studies comparable in procedure and samples, reveals some interesting findings:[29] (1) the ratio of males to females involved in status offenses[30] remained essentially the same (1.35 in 1955; 1.31 in 1972–1977);[31] (2) the disparity between males and females involved in property crime dropped progressively from 3.19 in 1955 to 2.35 in 1964–1965 and 2.11 in 1972–1977;[32] (3) the ratio of males to females involved in violent offenses[33] dropped substantially from 5.76 in 1955 to 2.75 in 1972–1977.[34]

Explanations of Female Criminality

The following sections are devoted to an overview of the explanations offered for female criminality. Since it is impossible to cover every contribution, an attempt was made to discuss a representative selection of interpretations.

Individual Factors

Until recently, systematic efforts to explain female criminality, have been based to a large extent on uncritical commonsense interpretations of female involvement in crime or as an afterthought to theories of male criminality. Early prescientific explanations viewed the female offender as having been corrupted or led astray by others (that is, men) and, in a few instances, as "evil."[35] The attempts at more scientific interpretations of female criminality that emerged in the nineteenth century tended to emphasize inherited physiological and psychological characteristics. Thus, in 1875, van de Warker suggested that men committed crimes when they were poor or hungry, while women committed crimes because of mental traits that drove them to crime.[36]

Lombroso failed to discover as many atavistic characteristics among female offenders as among males and was led to account for female criminality on the basis of childlike or masculine properties that had not been neutralized by normal feminine constraints.[37] Other early studies by Matthews, Burt, and Seagrave were directed toward such factors as physical size, sexual development, illness, and disease, but failed to uncover any causal relationships.[38] Despite these negative findings, constitutional—particularly sex-related—explanations continued to be advanced to explain female crime. Female crime has been attributed to physiological overdevelopment, pregnancy, menopause, and menstruation,[39] although, with the exception of menstruation, little research support has been found to sustain the influence of these factors.[40] The research that shows a relationship between menstruation and crime has been questioned on methodological grounds, such as sample size and reliability, as well as for its failure to determine whether periodic mood changes are characteristic of both sexes.[41] This reflects a major problem with research in this area, that is, its tendency to uncritically equate culturally based gender characteristics—beliefs and attributes—with sex-related biological differences. This is also manifest in the work of Cowie, Cowie, and Slater, who assume that aggressiveness, enterprise, and rebelliousness are masculine traits.[42] This leads them to conclude that female delinquents are physiologically different from normal girls. These and similar views suffer from lack of familiarity with both historical and cross-cultural data. Moreover, as Bole and Tatro point out, so long as the four sexual functions are allowed for—impregnation, lactation, menstruation, and gestation—no particular gender stereotype is unalterable.[43]

Defective intelligence is another factor that was causally related to crime among both sexes. Although some of the early research showed that female offenders were below average in IQ when compared to other women and even to male offenders, their scores in later research were more normally distributed and only slightly skewed toward the lower end.[44] Furthermore, it is plausible that these lower scores result because sampling is limited to apprehended offenders, who may be disproportionately less gifted than their unapprehended counterparts.

Psychoanalytic explanations of female crime are, to a large extent, constitutionally based, because many Freudians view female behavior and personality as anatomically centered—that is, they subscribe to the theory of anatomy as destiny or position.[45] Women are seen as anatomically inferior to men, and this inferiority is rooted in their sex organs. These genital deficiencies are the source of such problems as penis envy, masochism-narcissism, and exhibitionism and are the driving force behind a woman's desire to become a man. Psychodynamic explanations generally center on arrested psychosexual development. Delinquency among girls is attributed to fixation at either the oedipal or pre-oedipal states—the oral (asexual) level or the anal (bisexual) level, which is manifested by premarital sexual relations.[46] Today, as a result of changing sexual mores, teenage female sexual activity is only considered pathological when it is associated with other indications, such as depression and a florid infantile fantasy life.[47] Konopka's research on institutionalized girls aged 14 to 19 reflects this approach.[48] She found four factors that contriubte to female delinquency: biological onset of puberty, complex identity problems, changing cultural position of women, which created role ambivalence, and lack of meaningful adult relationships, resulting in isolation and loneliness.

Multifactor Orientation

A second orientation sought to explain female crime through biological and environmental correlates. The Gluecks studied every aspect of the lives of 500 inmates and concluded that their criminality resulted from a complex of biological, psychological, and social factors, including emotional instability, mental abnormality, psychopathic personality, and economic insufficiency.[49] Most dramatic, although not particularly radical in 1934, was their suggestion that these women be subject to either voluntary sterilization or indefinite incarceration because their pathological conditions made them unfit mothers.[50]

Later research focused primarily on identifying social-background variables. Schulman indicated that court-reported data showed delinquent girls to have more pathological family lives than boys, as manifested by greater dependency, inadequate home furnishings, excessive family mobility, greater proportion of working mothers, and proportionately more broken homes and criminal patterns.[51] Gibbons concludes his review of the research and literature on female delinquency by asserting that family tensions are a major factor in female delinquency, which, in conjunction with social class factors and social liabilities, apparently propels a girl toward delinquency involvement.[52] However, a study by Datesman and Scarpitti provides some evidence that a disruptive family environment (a broken home) is not unequally related to female delinquency, except in cases of girls apprehended for ungovernability and running away from home.[53] Since arrests for these offenses are based on a double standard, taking a more egalitarian view of the sexes suggests that there will be a decline in arrests for these offenses, which should result in less-marked differences in this respect between the sexes.

Social Factors in Female Criminality

Thomas's work represents one of the earliest explanations of female crime to be couched in social terms.[54] He argued that human behavior is directed toward the satisfaction of four fundamental wishes: the desire for new experience, security, response, and recognition.[55] The choice of conventional versus amoral or hedonistic means of satisfying these desires (that is, definition of the situation) was dependent on a girl's ties to the family and community.[56] Those with weak ties became involved in delinquency, sexual or otherwise, in order to satisfy their desire for excitement, pretty clothes, or other amusements.[57]

For over half a century, the research of Shaw and McKay and their colleagues provided a picture of male and female delinquency and associated social conditions in Chicago and other cities.[58] They found that girls were brought to court primarily for sex offenses and boys for larceny. High rates of female delinquency were found to occur in some socioculturally lower-class, depressed areas, as were high male rates.[59]

One of the major works to date on female crime, Otto Pollak's *The Criminality of Women,* concludes that the disparity in official male-female crime rates is misleading because it fails to reflect much female crime that is concealed or masked as a result of its incidental nature to female roles.[60] Female crime is further concealed by a chivalrous attitude, which make male police and victims reluctant to take action against female offenders, and by the propensity of women to select victims unlikely to take action against them.

Since the 1950s, theory and research on crime has focused primarily on male delinquents, with some criminologists also giving attention to females. In this regard, Cohen and Short explained the sexual delinquency of teenage girls as an attempt by girls with limited assets and abilities to hold the attention of males.[61] Like males, they reject conventional yet unreachable status goals in favor of satisfactions that are immediately attainable with present resources. In addition to their participation in sexually oriented subcultures, girls were also found to be involved in violent and aggressive gangs and drug-oriented subcultures, which involve a vicious cycle of prostitution and addiction.

Short and Strodtbeck describe lower-class female delinquents in Chicago and state that, like their male counterparts, these girls are inarticulate and unattractive in both appearance and behavior.[62] They contend that delinquency among these youths results from their entrapment "in a cycle of limited social abilities and other skills, and experiences which further limits opportunities to acquire these skills or to exercise them if acquired."[63] These social disabilities tend to contribute to the status dilemmas of these youths and thus contribute to their delinquency.

Research has also been directed toward ascertaining the applicability of implicit or explicit theories of male crime and delinquencies to females. Datesman, Scarpitti, and Stephenson examined the applicability of self and opportunity theories to delinquent females.[64] They found a relationship between delinquency and self-concept for black females that was not sustained for whites. Delinquency was also found to be more related to limited opportunity for females than for males. Both black and white delinquent females saw their opportunities less positively than did their nondelinquent female counterparts. Public-policy offenders, which, for girls, usually involves sexual behavior, showed the lowest perceptions of opportunity. These researchers argue that the sexual behavior of these girls may represent a pursuit, through less-than-conventional means, of the marriage goal or a rejection of it. A follow-up study by Cernkovich and Giordano found that, although gender-based opportunity—perceptional restrictions to opportunity based on being female—were unrelated to female or male delinquency involvement, blocked general opportunity affected delinquency involvement for both sexes, having more of an impact on whites than on blacks, regardless of sex.[65]

Another study, by Simons, Miller, and Aigner, attempted to determine the applicability of the key variables associated with anomie, labeling, control, and differential-association theories for female delinquency.[66] They found that, with the exception of anomie-opportunity theory, approximately as strong a relationship existed between these theories and self-reported delinquency for girls as for boys. Although neither educational nor occupational opportunity was a strong predictor of delinquency for either sex, it was less so for females. This may occur because these factors are less important for teenage girls than for boys, or because females who are frustrated by blocked legitimate opportunities may also not have access to illegitimate opportunities. They also found that sex-related differences in delinquency rates appear to result from a reduced exposure to deviancy-related factors. In fact, when they controlled for these dissimilarities, the relationship between sex and delinquency was largely eliminated. This provides support for the convergence hypothesis, which argues that crime-rate differences between the sexes will drop as gender roles become more equal. These authors conclude that conventional theories of delinquency are adequate for explaining female criminality; however, they fail to deal adequately with the differential exposure of males and females to criminogenic factors, which is anticipated by their middle-range scope. They assert that this requires explanation on a macro or sociological level, which would specify how sex roles in contemporary society determine the manner in which the sexes are distributed in relation to the independent variables associated with each theory.

Anthony Harris has examined existing theories to determine the extent to which they can incorporate the sex variable.[67] It is his contention that a theory cannot be considered a theory until it starts with the sex variable. He analyzed Merton's strain theory, Cloward and Ohlin's opportunity theory, Sutherland's differential-association theory, subcultural theory, control theory, self-attribution theory, and labeling theory. using four conceptual elements: goal utility, behavior utility, probability, and self-attribution. He concluded that these theories cannot adequately handle the sex variable, and he offered a functional theory of type-scripts, which centers its attention on a stratification of behavior. Type-scripts specify not only the types of actors who commit certain types of crimes but also the types of deviance that are impossible and unlikely for certain types of actors to commit. The value of this position is that it starts with the sex variable, accounts for the empirical variance in both official and hidden criminality, and can account for male-female crime patterns both historically and cross-culturally.

Female Emancipation

Changes in the volume and nature of female crime have also been tied to female emancipation. This raises several questions regarding changes in female involvement in the labor market. First, have there been substantial changes in the rate and pattern of female crime? The data presented earlier in this chapter show clearly that much of the apparent change in female crime and delinquency results from a look at gross percentage changes, without reference to their numerical significance. These data also show that patterns of female crime and delinquency have not changed dramatically over the past two decades. Adult females continue to be primarily property offenders, involved largely in the offenses of larceny, embezzlement, fraud, and forgery. Official juvenile involvement has also remained constant, with the offenses of larceny and running away from home accounting for the vast majority of these offenders taken into custody. Although the juvenile self-reporting data does show a greater trend toward convergence than is evident in official statistics, this must be interpreted in light of other data that show that more serious and persistent delinquents are more likely to be arrested.[68]

A second issue is whether there have been sufficient changes in the female role—that is, expanded employment opportunities, more liberated or feminist attitudes toward self, and masculinization of female behavior—to affect female crime patterns. The attribution of crime to the masculinization of female behavior can be traced back to Lombroso;[69] more recently, it has been linked to role convergence between the sexes.[70] Current research, however, fails to show that female roles have become more egalitarian,[71] and also indicates that traditional female role patterns emphasizing the wife and mother role are still dominant among both American males and females.[72] Further, despite the fact that more women are entering male-dominated fields, attitudes still persist that make their active pursuit and acceptance in these areas a long way off. With respect to crime, although more women not only have become involved in but also have become active participants rather than accessories in male-dominated offenses,[73] their numerical involvement is still relatively minor.

Another indication of the influence of female emancipation on crime is the extent to which female offenders subscribe to more liberal as opposed to traditional role definitions. Existing research on delinquency largely fails to find any positive relationship between these attitudes and crime, and some research actually shows a negative relationship.[74] A study by James and Thornton examined the relationship of attitudes toward feminism and delinquency and controlled for the influence of the women's movement on other delinquency-related variables.[75] They concluded that, while increasing delinquency opportunity and reduced social controls "might contribute to the growth in the rate of delinquency and crime among females, our evidence suggests that the extent of crime among feminist women is similar to, or even less frequent than, that among their more traditional counterparts."[76] Studies of adult females provide remarkably similar results. Leventhal found that female inmates, as compared with college students, were more likely to hold traditional attitudes toward women and their role expectations.[77] However, their scores on the Maculinity-Feminity (MF) scale of the Minnesota Multiphasic Personality Inventory (MMPI) suggested that these inmates perceive themselves as being more masculine than the college sample. The Glick and Neto study also found that the majority of incarcerated women still maintain traditional views regarding the role of women in society.[78]

An assessment of the role-convergence argument also requires an examination of the extent to which the expanded participation of females in the labor market, and particularly in male-dominant offenses, can be related to changes in female crime. First, the evidence shows that expanded female employment is in traditional female rather than male-dominated occupations.[79] Second, a study by Bartol, using an economic model, failed to find any significant relationship between increased female employment and crime.[80] Her data showed that, although increased employment among single women did positively affect property crime, this relationship did not hold for married women, who represented the major portion of this group entering the labor force. Moreover, she found that married women were more likely to commit larceny, which she relates to their diminished legitimate opportunities and to the complementary nature of these crimes to certain household activities. Most important, she attributes the recent rise in female crime to a sharp reduction in "women's value of time at home," which in this case is measured by the number of preschool children in the home. In fact, her data show that the 58 percent increase in the female crime rate between 1960 and 1970 can be accounted for by a drop in the average number of preschool children per husband-wife family during this period.

A final related issue is whether expanded employment opportunities for women have put them in a position to be able to commit white-collar offenses. One cannot commit computer fraud unless one has a job that makes this possible. The data show, however, that women have made only slight gains in the managerial and professional categories.[81] Even these slight gains are overshadowed by the fact that, when women move into these higher-status categories, they typically are employed in less-prestigious and lower-status positions. Therefore, it would appear that women are in little better position now than in the past to perpetrate crimes requiring them to be in relatively high-trust positions. Thus, while female involvement in embezzlement has increased, it is likely, as we noted, that these offenses are committed by women in relatively low-status clerical or sales positions.

Summary and Conclusions

The first part of this chapter was directed toward assessing the changing nature of adult and juvenile female crime. With respect to adult female crime, the inescapable conclusion is that the increase has been more apparent than real. In fact, the large percentage gains in the index and in other offenses have largely resulted from the relatively small size of the initial female base. Female adolescent involvement in crime has also not shown any truly remarkable changes. The self-reporting data show a closer convergence between male-female participation in delinquency than UCR data show. However, these two data sets are not entirely isomorphic, which makes comparisons open to question.

Several predictions can be made with respect to the future of adult and juvenile female crime. Juvenile females will continue to become increasingly involved in violent and property offenses, although there will still be major gaps between their participation and that of adolescent boys. This excludes larceny, which will continue to be the predominant offense for this group, with female arrests probably accounting for between 35 percent and 40 percent of total arrests by the year 2000.[82] Arrests for sex-related offenses will drop as society develops more liberal attitudes toward premarital sexual involvement and as status offenses become removed from the jurisdiction of the juvenile court.

The juvenile data also fail to provide any convincing evidence that, when the current cohort of juveniles reaches adulthood, there will be a change in the nature of female crime. This, along with the adult data set, leads to the conclusion that there will not be a convergence in male-female arrest rates in the near future. Projections show that the relative gap for offenses making the most substantial gains—fraud, forgery, embezzlement, and larceny—will not converge by the year 2000.[83] Female arrests for larceny are projected to account for only 39.1 percent by that point. Although there is little doubt that the numbers of women who are active participants in serious crime will continue to increase, there is no indication that these increases will be of numerical significance in the near future.

The second part of this chapter was devoted to an analysis of explanations regarding female criminality. Until recently, the relatively insignificant involvement of females in crime has resulted in few systematic explanations. Early individualistic explanations of female crime tended be based on stereotypical assumptions, which confused sex-related biological differences with gender-based cultural differences. These views all suffered from an ignorance of historical and cross-cultural data. It is hoped that this type of mythologizing has finally been put to rest. This being the case, we can then expect to see research and theory on the biological and psychological correlates of female crime that will help in understanding and treating this offender category. Initially, multi-factor explanations were imbued with gender misconceptions; however, more recent efforts that have focused on social-background variables appear to recognize the role played by culturally based values in influencing the factors viewed as relevant for explaining female crime.[84] The early sociological explanations of crime (such as Thomas and Pollak) have been criticized for the assumptions made regarding women and their involvement in crime.[85] However, recent research and theory offer very promising avenues for exploration. Several studies found that existing theories can be successfully applied to females. Others have formulated new theories that encompass the sex variable from inception. Both of these pursuits will ultimately assist us in developing a better perspective on the causes of female crime.

Finally, attention has focused on female emancipation as a causative factor in female crime. Following an analysis of the major factors associated with the emancipation or women's liberation position and their influences on female crime patterns, the inescapable conclusion is that these have had little or no influence. Indeed, in some instances, they appear to have had negative consequences. There is also no indication that they will have any influence in the near future. Further concern with this issue is as fruitless as Don Quixote's attack on the windmills. More important, it takes our attention away from the pursuit of avenues of explanations that might better enable us to understand this phenomenon.

Notes

1. U.S. Department of Justice, Federal Bureau of Investigation, *Crime in the United States, Uniform Crime Reports, 1970* (Washington, D.C.: U.S. Government Printing Office, 1971), 120, table 24.

2. U.S. Department of Justice, Federal Bureau of Investigation, *Crime in the United States, Uniform Crime Reports, 1971–1979* (Washington, D.C.: U.S. Government Printing Office, 1972–1980).

3. Christine E. Rasche, "The Female Offender as an Object of Criminological Research," *Criminal Justice and Behavior* 1(December 1974): 301–320.

4. See, for example, Freda Adler, *"Sisters in Crime: The Rise of the New Female Offender"* (New York: McGraw-Hill, 1975); and Rita James Simon, *The Contemporary Woman and Crime* (Washington, D.C.: U.S. Government Printing Office, 1975).

5. This includes the addition of Ruth Eiseman-Schier's name to the FBI's ten-most-wanted list, the involvement of Patty Hearst in the Symbionese Lib-

eration Army, and the attempted assassination of President Ford by Sarah Jane Moore and Annette Fromme.

6. U.S. Department of Justice, Federal Bureau of Investigation, *Crime in the United States, Uniform Crime Reports, 1975* (Washington, D.C.: U.S. Government Printing Office), p. 183, table 31.

7. For a discussion of this method and its justifications, see Darrell J. Steffensmeir, "Crime and the Contemporary Woman: An Analysis of Changing Levels of Female Property Crime, 1960–75;" *Social Forces* 5(December 1978): 566–583.

8. Ibid.

9. Darrell J. Steffensmeir, "Sex Differences in Patterns of Adult Crime, 1965–1977: A Review and Assessment" *Social Forces* 58(June 1980): 1080–1108.

10. The offenses examined were drunkenness, disorderly conduct, larceny-theft, all other offenses, prostitution, other assaults, driving under the influence, liquor-law violations, aggravated assault, vagrancy, fraud, gambling, narcotic-drug offenses, suspicion, sex offenses, offenses against family, forgery, burglary, weapons violations, vandalism, robbery, auto theft, embezzlement, murder, stolen property, arson, and negligent manslaughter.

11. Definitions for these categories can be found in table 7–1.

12. Data to support this view can be found, for example, in Ira J. Silverman and Manuel Vega "Female Criminality in a Southern City," *LAE Journal of the American Criminal Justice Association*, 41(Summer 1978):5160; and John Kramer and Darrell Steffensmeir, "Preliminary Analyses of Pennsylvania Arrest and Court Statistics, 1970–1976" (Unpublished manuscript).

13. See, for example, Dale Hoffman-Bustamante, "The Nature of Female Criminality," *Issues in Criminology* 8(1973):117–136; Dorie Klein and June Kress, "Any Woman Blues: A Critical Overview of Women, Crime, and the Criminal Justice System," *Crime and Social Justice* 1(Spring-Summer 1976):34–49; Rosemary Stanford, Manuel Vega, and Ira Silverman, "The Female Forger," submitted to *The Journal of Criminal Justice;* J.F. Klein and A. Montague *Check Forgers*, (Lexington, Mass.: Lexington Books, D.C. Heath, 1979); and R.G. Denys, "Lady Paperhangers," *Canadian Journal of Corrections* 52(1969):169–192.

14. Alice Franklin, "Criminality in the Work Place: A Comparison of Male and Female Offenders," in Freda Adler and Rita James Simon (eds.) *The Criminology of Women*, ed. Freda Adler and Rita James Simon (Boston: Houghton Mifflin, 1979), pp. 167–176; and Hoffman-Bustamante, "The Nature of Female Criminality."

15. See, for example, Adler, *Sisters in Crime*, and Joseph G. Weis, "Liberation and Crime: The Invention of the New Female Criminal," *Crime and Social Justice* 6(Fall-Winter 1976):17–27.

16. Darrell Steffensmeir and Renee Hoffman Steffensmeir, "Trends in

Female Delinquency: An Examination of Arrest, Juvenile Court, Self Report and Field Data,'' *Criminology* 18(May 1980):62–85.

17. The category of male-dominated offenses is excluded from the analysis of juvenile crime patterns.

18. This last question replaces the white-collar or economic-crime question examined for adults. For obvious reasons, this is more relevant to the juvenile experience.

19. See table 7–2 for the offenses included in each category.

20. Malcolm W. Klein, *Street Gangs and Street Workers* (Englewood Cliffs, N.J.: Prentice-Hall, 1971), pp. 77–78.

21. Larceny in the case of juveniles is even more likely to involve petty shoplifting than it is for adults.

22. Steffensmeir and Steffensmeir in "Trends in Female Delinquency," cite a personal communication from the Drug Enforcement Administration that indicates that, from 1970 to 1975, a constant 15 percent of heroin users were female.

23. Harold J. Vetter and Ira J. Silverman, *Criminology* (Glenview, Ill.: Scott, Foresman, forthcoming).

24. Ronald Akers, "Socioeconomic Status and Delinquent Behavior: A Retest," *Journal of Research in Crime and Delinquency* 1(January 1964): 38–46; Steven A. Cernkovich and Peggy Giordano, "A Comparative Analysis of Male and Female Delinquency," in *Criminal Behavior: Readings in Criminology,* ed. Delos H. Kelly (New York: St. Martins Press, 1980), pp. 112–129; Bill Haney and Martin Gold, "The Juvenile Delinquent Nobody Knows," *Psychology Today,* September 1973, pp. 49, 53; Michael J. Hindelang, "Age, Sex, and Versatility of Delinquent Involvement," *Social Problems* 18(Spring 1981):527–535; Gary Jensen and Raymond Eve, "Sex Differences in Delinquency," *Criminology* 13:427–448; Peter C. Kratcoski and John Kratcoski, "Changing Patterns in the Delinquent Activities of Boys and Girls: A Self-Reported Analysis," *Adolescence* 10(Spring 1975):83–91; Patricia Y. Miller, "Delinquency and Gender" (Unpublished paper, Institute for Juvenile Research, Chicago Department of Mental Health); James Short, Jr. and F. Ivan Nye, "Extent of Unrecorded Delinquency, Tentative Conclusion," *Journal of Criminal Law, Criminology, and Police Science* 49(November-December 1958):290–302; Cyrus S. Stewart, Mary Margaret Zaenglein-Senger, Arthur M. Vener, and L.R. Krupka, "Patterns of Delinquency among Adolescent Girls," *LAE Journal of the American Criminal Justice Association* 41:61–70; Joseph G. Weis, "Liberation and Crime," *Crime and Social Justice* 6(Fall-Winter 1976):17–27; Nancy Wise "Juvenile Delinquency among Middle Class Girls," in *Middle Class Juvenile Delinquency,* ed. Edmund W. Vaz (New York: Harper and Row, 1967), pp. 179–188; Joel Zimmerman and Paul Broder, "A Comparison of Different Delinquency Measures Derived from Self Report Data," *Journal of Criminal Justice* 8(1980):147–162.

25. Zimmerman and Broder, "A Comparison of Different Delinquency Measures."

26. Martin Gold, *Delinquent Behavior in an American City* (Belmont, Calif.: Brooks/Cole, 1970).

27. Martin Gold and David J. Reimer, "Changing Patterns of Delinquent Behavior among Americans 13 through 16 Years Old: 1967–72," *Crime and Delinquency Literature* 7(December 1975):483–517.

28. Akers, "Socioeconomic Status and Delinquent Behavior"; Cernkovich and Giordano, "A Comparative Analysis"; Gold, *Delinquent Behavior in an American City;* Hindelang, "Age, Sex, and Versatility"; Jensen and Eve, "Sex Differences in Delinquency"; Kratcoski and Kratcoski, "Changing Patterns"; Miller, "Delinquency and Gender"; Short and Nye, "Extent of Unrecorded Delinquency" (this study reported data from two samples); Stewart, Zaenglein-Senger, Vener, and Krupka, "Patterns of Delinquency"; Weis, "The Invention of the New Female Criminal"; Wise, "Juvenile Delinquency among Middle Class Girls"; and S. Norland, "Self-Reported Study of Male/Female Delinquency in Nashville" (Unpublished study, cited in Steffensmeir and Steffensmeir, "Trends in Female Delinquency").

29. This comparison involved three time periods and used the following studies: (1) Short and Nye, "Extent of Unrecorded Delinquency" (1955 Western and Midwestern samples); (2) Jensen and Eve, "Sex Differences in Delinquency" (1964–1965 data); and (3) Miller, "Delinquency and Gender" (1972 data), Norland, "Self-Reported Study" (1976 data), and Cernkovich and Giordano, "A Comparative Analysis" (1976 data).

30. Status offenses included runaway, truancy, and driving without a license.

31. No data were provided for status offenses in the Jensen and Eve study.

32. Property offenses included theft—small, medium, and large—and joyriding.

33. Violent offenses included damage to property, fist fight, gang fight, strong-arm theft, and carrying a weapon.

34. The Jensen and Eve study data were excluded because information was only provided on two of the five offenses in this category.

35. Rasche, "The Female Offender as an Object of Criminological Research."

36. Ely van de Warker, "The Relations of Women to Crime," *Popular Science Monthly* 8(1875–1876):246, as cited in Joy Pollock, "Early Theories of Female Criminality," in *Women, Crime, and the Criminal Justice System,* ed. Lee H. Bowker (Lexington, Mass., Lexington Books, D.C. Heath, 1978).

37. Caesare Lombroso and William Ferrero, *The Female Offender* (New York: Appleton, 1897).

38. A.D. Smith, *Women in Prison* (London: Stevens, 1962), as cited in Rasche, "The Female Offender as an Object of Criminological Research."

39. Otto Pollak, *The Criminality of Women* (Philadelphia: University of Pennsylvania Press, 1950), pp. 121–135.

40. Ibid.

41. Lee H. Bowker, "Menstruation and Female Criminality: A New Look at the Data" (Paper presented at the annual meeting of the American Society of Criminology, Dallas, November 1978).

42. John Cowie, Valerie Cowie, and Eliot Slater, *Delinquency in Girls* (London: Heineman, 1968).

43. Jacqueline Bole and Charlotte Tatro, "The Female Offender: The 1980's and Beyond," in *Crime and Justice in America: Critical Issues for the Future,* ed. John T. O'Brien and Marvin Marcus (New York: Pergamon 1979), pp. 255–282.

44. Pollock, "Early Theories of Female Criminality," pp. 113–115; Hermann Mannheim, *Comparative Criminology* (Boston: Houghton Mifflin, 1965), pp. 273–279; Manuel Vega, Ira J. Silverman, and John Accardi, "The Female Felon," in *Reform in Corrections: Problems and Issues,* ed. Harry Allen and Nancy J. Beran (New York: Praeger, 1977), pp. 53–75.

45. Dorie Klein, "The Etiology of Female Crime: A Review of the Literature," in *The Female Offender,* ed. Laura Crites (Lexington, Mass.: Lexington Books, D.C. Heath, 1976), pp. 16–19.

46. Peter Blos, *The Adolescent Passage: Developmental Issues* (New York: International Universities Press, 1979), pp. 217, 245.

47. Ibid., pp. 246–253.

48. Gisela Konopka, *The Adolescent Girl in Conflict* (Englewood Cliffs, N.J.: Prentice-Hall, 1966).

49. Sheldon Glueck and Eleanor T. Glueck, *Five Hundred Delinquent Women* (New York: Knopf, 1934), pp. 299–310.

50. Ibid., p. 310.

51. Harry Manuel Schulman, *Juvenile Delinquency in American Society* (New York: Harper and Row, 1961), p. 475.

52. Don C. Gibbons, *Delinquent Behavior* (Englewood Cliffs, N.J.: Prentice-Hall, 1976), p. 189.

53. Susan K. Datesman and Frank Scarpitti, "Female Delinquency and Broken Homes: A Re-Assessment," *Criminology* 13(May 1975):33–55.

54. William I. Thomas, *The Unadjusted Girl* (Boston: Little, Brown, 1923).

55. Ibid., p. 4.

56. Ibid., pp. 41–44.

57. Ibid., p. 109.

58. Clifford R. Shaw and Henry D. McKay, *Juvenile Delinquency and Urban Areas* (Chicago: University of Chicago Press, 1974).

59. Ibid., pp. 356–358.

60. Pollak, *The Criminality of Women,* pp. 149–161.

61. Albert K. Cohen and James F. Short, Jr., "Research in Delinquent Subcultures," *Journal of Social Issues* 14(1958):20–37.

62. James F. Short, Jr., and Fred L. Strodtbeck, *Group Process and Gang Delinquency* (Chicago: University of Chicago Press, 1965), pp. 242–243. They claim that the females they studied manifested similar characteristics to those

observed by Robert Rice in a New York City girl's gang; see Robert Rice, "The Persian Queens," *The New Yorker,* 19 October 1963, p. 153.

63. Short and Strodtbeck, *Group Process,* p. 243.

64. Susan K. Datesman, Frank R. Scarpitti, Richard M. Stephenson. "Female Delinquency: An Application of Self and Opportunity Theories," *Journal of Research in Crime and Delinquency* 12(July 1975):107–123.

65. Steven A. Cernkovich and Peggy Giordano, "Delinquency Opportunity and Gender," *Journal of Criminal Law and Criminology* 70(1979):143–151.

66. Ronald L. Simons, Martin G. Miller, and Stephen M. Aigner, "Contemporary Theories of Deviance and Female Delinquency: An Empirical Test," *Journal of Research in Crime and Delinquency* 17(January 1980):42–53.

67. Anthony R. Harris, "Sex and Theories of Deviance: Toward a Functional Theory of Deviant Type-Scripts," *American Sociological Review* 42(February 1979):3–16.

68. Jay R. Williams and Martin Gold, "From Delinquent Behavior to Official Delinquency," *Social Problems* 20(Fall 1972):209–229.

69. Lombroso and Ferrero, *The Female Offender.*

70. For example, Adler, *Sisters in Crime.*

71. See, for example, Ann Parelius, "Emerging Sex-Role Attitudes, Expectations, and Strains among College Women," *Journal of Marriage and the Family* 37:146–153; Karen Oppenheim Mason, John L. Czaika, and Sara Arber, "Changes in U.S. Women's Sex-Role Attitudes, 1964–1974," *American Sociological Review* 41(August 1976):573–596, as cited in *Women, Crime, and Justice,* ed. Susan K. Datesman and Frank R. Scarpitti (New York: Oxford University Press, 1980), p. 374.

72. See Frank N. Magid and Associates, "Americans Cling to Traditional Sex-Role Ideas," *Tampa Tribune,* 22 June 1980, p. 21A.

73. Silverman and Vega, "Female Criminality in a Southern City."

74. Miller, "Delinquency and Gender," p. 47; Raymond Eve and Kreelene R. Edmonds, "Women's Liberation and Female Criminality: or Sister, Will You Give Me Back My Dime?" (Paper presented at the Society for the Study of Social Problems meeting, San Francisco (September 1978), as cited in Datesman and Scarpitti, *Women, Crime, and Justice,* p. 361.

75. Jennifer James and William Thornton, "Women's Liberation and the Female Delinquent," *Journal of Research in Crime and Delinquency* 17(July 1980):230–244.

76. Ibid., p. 243.

77. Gloria Leventhal, "Female Criminality: Is 'Women's Lib' to Blame?" *Psychological Reports* 41(1977):1179–1182.

78. Ruth Glick and Virginia V. Neto, *National Study of Women's Correctional Programs,* U.S. Department of Justice (Washington, D.C.: U.S. Government Printing Office).

79. Datesman and Scarpitti, *Women, Crime, and Justice,* p. 362.

80. Ann Bartol, "Women and Crime," *Economic Inquiry* 17(January 1979):29–51.

81. Datesman and Scarpitti, *Women, Crime, and Justice,* p. 362–363.

82. This is based on the assumption that it will continue to rise to the same extent as adults. See Steffensmeir, "Sex Differences in Patterns of Adult Crime."

83. Ibid.

84. Datesman and Scarpitti, "Female Delinquency and Broken Homes."

85. Pollack, "Early Theories of Female Criminality," pp. 44–50.

8 The Puzzle of Dangerousness

John P. Conrad

If he is asked, Sy Dinitz will tell an enquirer that he chooses topics for research because they interest him. That is scarcely a responsive answer; *everything* interests him. A conversation with him can begin on any subject and command his informed attention. Still, he is a criminologist, a student of social deviance, and that commitment narrows his range of choice. He begins a study hoping to contribute to the increase of knowledge and the solution of sociological puzzles. He relishes the intellectual exercise these puzzles impose, and he assumes the classic value-free posture of every scientist, whatever the discipline. To him, the successful solution of a scientific problem is reward enough for all the effort spent. He does not expect that the conclusion of a project will necessarily lead to a beneficial modification of policy, but he will grant that, when such a result ensues, he is not displeased.

Fortunately for criminology, Sy has a predilection for topics that happen to bear on issues that must be resolved if we are ever to make headway in the prevention of crime and the control of the criminal. Fortunately for me, his most recent interests have been fixed on the problems presented by dangerous offenders. For the past six years, we have been jointly engaged in the study of the violence that urban Americans inflict on one another. It is a topic with many repellent and sometimes horrifying aspects, but it has been the foundation of a congenial partnership. I am pleased that the end is not yet in sight.

Our association began in 1972, when a streak of good luck moved me from a bureaucratic career in Washington to academia in Columbus. Sy was one of the first to welcome me; soon after my arrival, we were collaborating in seminars and teaching criminology courses together. What a pleasure it is to work with so irrepressible an enthusiast! Years of teaching and research have not dimmed his eye for a criminological problem nor slackened his eagerness to start solving it. Criminology has become a muddle in which ideologies compete to the great disadvantage of objectivity, but nothing will shake Sy's conviction that rigorous discipline can establish the social facts about crime.

It was no wonder to me that his classes were always full. His office, strategically situated off the lobby of Hagerty Hall, then housing the Sociology Department at Ohio State, was a magnet for students hoping for a word or two with him. As soon as it became known that he was at his desk, trying to perform his academic duties, a line would form, whether or not it was his official office hour. It usually ended at the last possible moment before he would be due in a classroom. The love of learning, displayed so exuberantly, is contagious. Once infected, his students are not likely to recover from the itch of intellectual curiosity.

Of all the foundations for friendship, a scholarly collaboration must be the strongest. The years spent on the Dangerous Offender Project have not been easy. Disappointments, frustrations, and some modest successes led to trust in each other. Both of us had been long inured to habits of liberal thought; that assured a similar outlook on the society in which our phenomena were to be found. When our opinions differed, we found ourselves in a profitable discourse to trace the reasons for our disagreement and to discover how it could be reconciled.

Both of us decry speculation about the facts as a foundation for policy if the facts themselves can be empirically established. Neither of us has much patience with the oversimplified solutions to the crime problem that are advanced by New Criminologists on the left of New Rigorists on the right. We are gradualists, sure that the criminal-justice system must be modified, but also sure that its basic structure will endure for many years to come in spite of obvious shortcomings. Effort will be better spent on its piecemeal improvement than in a vain struggle to replace it.

We share the view, generally held by informed academics and practitioners, that the causes of crime are beyond the reach of the criminal-justice system, which is not to say that improvements in that system are futile. The functionaries of criminal justice must undertake many kinds of tasks, but their principal mission is to respond to the criminal with the imposition of appropriate consequences for his crime. The prevention of crime is a responsibility in which the whole community must share. Unless the social conditions that generate crime are ameliorated, the nation will never be relieved from the fears that obsess so many Americans. It is a platitude that the connections between social injustice and crime are close; the documentation of these connections is one of the major accomplishments of contemporary criminology. It is for the makers of social policy to keep the nation moving in the direction of social and economic justice, even if these goals can never be fully achieved. The difficulty of the task does not diminish its urgency.

Criminologists must attend to their specialties. Simple justice requires that the inefficiency, the confusions, and the outright brutalities inflicted by the system must be put to rights, even though such improvements do little to reduce the prevalence of crime. Most of these deficiencies arise from misconceptions about crime, about the people who commit it, and about the capabilities of the police and the courts to prevent it. To replace these misconceptions with ideas that are grounded in social reality constitutes the main agenda for the criminologist.

Simon Dinitz and I became preoccupied with the dangerous offender because of our shared perception that criminal violence distorts not only the administration of justice but nearly every aspect of urban life. Disputes persist as to whether the rates of violent crime are really increasing, whether criminal violence is as serious a feature of city life as most people believe, but there can be no doubt that fear of violence is general. That fear and the anger it generates create a social morbidity that erodes confidence in our civic institutions. As criminologists, Sy and I saw the strains that unrealistic expectations imposed on criminal justice. Most of these expectations are instigated by the conviction that something must be done to reduce the burden of street crime and that it is the duty of the system of police, courts, and prisons to bring this reduction about. But if this system cannot accomplish this end, how can it be done? Here was our puzzle. Surely social science could shed some light on ways to reduce the dangers of crime in urban life. It was an interesting topic to study. Coincidentally, perhaps, it was a timely choice.

The New War on Crime

It appears that a new war on crime has been declared. During the last two or three years, many states have increased criminal penalties and have mandated prison sentences for the more serious crimes of violence. In many states, the age of juvenile-court jurisdiction over youthful violent offenders has been reduced, and the waiver of its jurisdiction for violent offenders has become common. The number of men and women on the nation's condemned rows has steadily risen and, after a long moratorium, their execution has begun. The Attorney General of the United States has appointed a commission of notables and scholars to advise him as to the proper federal role in response to the persisting crime problem. A survey by a leading newsmagazine in March 1981 found that 58 percent of its respondents thought that crime had increased in their neighborhoods during the past year, and that a large number had consciously changed their daily habits to provide themselves with protection that they could not expect from the police.[1] The chief justice has urged in a major address that the national effort against crime is comparable as a national priority to the defense of the country against a foreign enemy.

If it is a war, it is a limited war. The aim is the reduction of violent crime. Although some attention will be given to the major crimes against property— burglary, larceny, and auto theft—it is clear that the victory so ardently sought would be the reduction, if not the elimination, of the muggings, rapes, assaults, and murders that seem so prevalent to readers of the daily press.

There is a sense of menace in the streets that does not lend itself to easy quantification but to which legislators and judges are attuned as laws are made more strict and sentences more severe. All this anxiety about crime has boiled up nearly a decade and a half after Congress enacted the Omnibus Safe Streets and Crime Control Act of 1967, providing for an unprecedented federal role in street-crime prevention. The streets are believed to be more unsafe than ever.

Not only is the war limited in its aims, it must also be limited in its tactics. More violence is committed by firearms than by all other weapons combined,[2] but it is unlikely that control over the distribution and possession of handguns will be legislated. Probably there will be mandatory prison sentences for those who possess firearms while committing felonies. As with most criminal law based on legislators' judgments of what reasonable and prudent men would do, it has yet to be shown how many robbers and rapists are reasonable and prudent. There can be no compelling moral objection to the imposition of severe sanctions on criminals who threaten the lives of their victims—even if only symboli-cally–but the efficacy of increased sanctions in preventing crime has yet to be shown convincingly.

The war will not be fought on the battlefield of the national economy. The connection between the unemployment of minority youth and the incidence of violence has been obvious for many years, but we do not hear of plans to remedy this destructive injustice. The only hope in sight is that the young men and women who are now redundant to the economy will be drawn into employment as a by-product of the revitalization of industry.

The nation will continue to rely on the criminal-justice system as its bulwark against crime, even though the limits of its capabilities for the conduct of this war are widely recognized. What hope is there for victories in such a limited war? Looking at the conditions that prevail in our cities and the meager prospects for their improvement, most criminologists will deliver a pessimistic opinion. It is impossible to escape the conclusion that a proportionately small social class produces and will continue to produce enough street crime to keep the nation in fear for years to come.

This is the underclass. It is composed of men and women and children who have been excluded at birth from the security system that supports and protects most Americans. They have been born into and have lived all their lives in neighborhoods in which unemployment is the rule. Those who find their ways into occupational careers escape as soon as they can. Their plight has been described, documented, quantified, portrayed in novels and memoirs, and de-plored for many years. It is correctly pointed out that members of the underclass do not starve and that few of them are homeless. Compared to the poor of a century ago in this country or now in the Third World, our underclass is very comfortable.

Nevertheless, this is a class of people who seldom have attractive choices. They are redundant so far as the economy is concerned, and they are a burden to the taxpayers. Engagement in criminal activity is an acceptable gamble; it affords a chance of relief from the monotony of empty days and short rations while allowing the individual a moment of power over others. The streets are the school of crime where young men learn the elements of the simple trades of mugging and theft. The most adroit will find their ways into the more advanced criminal occupations—the hustling of dope, whores, and numbers.

Nothing good is in sight for the underclass in any future that anyone can predict. Their schools are the worst in town. Jobs with a future are a long way from home. A break in the vicious circle in which they are caught is not to be foreseen. They are society's losers; in any competition for the good things in life, they are sure to lose.

Karl Marx called them the *lumpen-proletariat,* the class from which vagrants, criminals, and prostitutes are drawn. He could account for them in his unsparing analysis of the capitalist class structure:

> We have the demoralized, the degenerate and the unemployable. These are persons who succumb owing to their incapacity, an incapacity induced by the division of labor. . . . Pauperism constitutes the infirmary of the active labor army . . . the dead weight which has to be carried by the industrial reserve army. The production of paupers is an inevitable outcome of the production of relative surplus population; the inevitability of the existence of paupers depends upon the inevitability of the existence of relative surplus population; and the two together form indispensable conditions of the existence of capitalist production and of the development of wealth. Pauperism constitutes one of the indispensable expenses of capitalist production.[3]

For Marx the *lumpen-proletariat* was a pathetic class of social casualties created by the injustices of the capitalist industrial system. Other analysts find other ways to account for the underclass but describe it in ways similar to Marx's account and agree that the most troublesome feature of this class is its inclination to criminal behavior. Edward Banfield, a conservative political scientist, devotes several pages to what he calls the lower class, as distinguished from the working class. His cultural anthropology is summarily ethnocentric. The existence of the American underclass is attributed to the immigration of large numbers of present-oriented people from the Catholic countries of southern Europe and Ireland, contrasting with the future-oriented Protestants from Puritan American stock and northern Europe and equally future-oriented Jews from Eastern Europe. Whatever one may think of this analysis, his description of the present-oriented underclass is certainly consistent with Marx's brief account of the *lumpen-proletariat:*

> The lower-class individual lives from moment to moment. If he has any awareness of a future, it is of something fixed, fated, beyond his control; things happen to him, he does not make them happen. . . . His bodily needs (especially for sex) and his taste for "action" take precedence over everything else—and especially over work routine. He works only as he must to stay alive, and drifts from one unskilled job to another, taking no interest in the work. . . . The stress on "action," risk-taking, conquest, fighting, and "smartness" makes lower-class life extraordinarily violent . . . the nature of

lower-class culture is such that much behavior that in another class would be considered bizarre seems routine.[4]

By Banfield's account, efforts to change all this are in vain:

The lower-class forms of all problems are at bottom a single problem: the existence of an outlook and style of life which is radically present-oriented and which therefore attaches no value to work, sacrifice, self-improvement, or service to family, friends or community. Social workers, teachers, and law-enforcement officials . . . cannot achieve their goals because they can neither change nor circumvent this cultural obstacle.[5]

After noting that the lower class of the nineteenth century probably did not reproduce itself because of high death rates at all ages, Banfield considers the anti-Malthusian effects of modern medicine that have made it possible to increase the numbers of the lower class. He hopes that the lower class can be induced to use birth-control procedures to limit their numbers and argues that perhaps the best way to deal with this prodigal growth in its numbers is to take steps to separate children from their parents in early childhood and bring them up in "normal" family environments. He concedes that there is no politically acceptable way of accomplishing this end nor of carrying out any of the other expedients that might eliminate this lower class and thereby eliminate its costs in crime, mental illness, welfare payments, and general disorder. He professes that he is "frightened" by the impulse of upper-class and upper-middle-class persons to "do good" for the lower-class, and he ruefully concludes that not much good can be done.

Probably Karl Marx would have agreed with Banfield's gloomy estimate. Within the structure of the capitalist system, the *lumpen-proletariat* could not be eliminated. No doubt he would have also argued that, if medicine could improve their life exepctancy, then the revolutionary pressures on the capitalist system would increase accordingly. If Marx and Banfield are in accord on the menace of the underclass—as I shall persist in referring to this element of our society—then what hope is there for urban peace?

In the next section, I will consider the implications of the Dangerous Offender Project findings on the resolution of this apparently hopeless dilemma. Complete domestic tranquility is not to be had in the pluralism of America, but I believe our studies suggest ways in which more of it can be found than Banfield expects.

The Dangerous Offender Project

This is not the place to summarize the findings of the Dangerous Offender Project. They are numerous, complex, and fully set forth elsewhere.[6] The project confirms or establishes eight propositions:

1. Over 85 percent of the violent-offender population studied are of the lowest socioeconomic class.
2. In the violent-offender population studied, blacks are overrepresented by four times their percentage in the general population.
3. Chronic offenders begin delinquent careers in early adolescence.
4. Chronic offenders commit a disproportionate number of violent offenses.
5. If incarcerated, chronic offenders resume their delinquencies after periods of "street time" that are briefer after each successive release from custody.
6. There is no class of offenders that can be statistically identified for legislation to reduce violent crime that will not result in a vast expansion of the penal system.
7. Any effort to build a sentencing policy based on the prediction of dangerousness will result in the incarceration of more people who would not commit new violent offenses than of people who would.
8. The extinction of careers of violent crime begins at about age 30. After age 35, there are markedly fewer violent offenders. After age 40, violence is limited to crimes of passion and other interpersonal offenses.

These conclusions are based on research performed in Columbus, Ohio, but we doubt that similar studies in other cities would arrive at significantly different answers. Violent street crime is a phenomenon of the urban and youthful underclass, a class in which blacks are heavily overrepresented in the middle and late twentieth century. Had we undertaken these studies in England when Karl Marx was writing *Capital,* the population studied would have been white and predominantly Protestant. A century ago in any American city, the social composition of the underclass would have been found to be predominantly white and Catholic immigrant, as Banfield argues. Blacks are the latest immigrants, and it cannot be doubted that modern medicine has facilitated the creation of a large black youth population in the underclass. The problems thus created range far beyond the prevalence of crime. Various kinds of welfare programs for the support of chronically unemployed persons, a high incidence of mental illness, and a disproportionate demand for publicly supported medical services are only some of the most prominent burdens imposed by this large and growing underclass. The need for purposeful action to draw families out of the underclass and into productive society is pressing, and its fulfillment becomes ever more difficult as the years go by without remedial measures being designed and put into action.

Perhaps the clues for a solution can be found in history. Banfield speculates that high mortality rates resulting from medical inefficiency probably created a situation in the nineteenth century underclass that canceled it out; this class did not reproduce itself until the medical breakthroughs of the mid-twentieth century. That, Banfield admits, is a speculation; nineteenth-century statistics do not make a confirmation of this hypothesis possible.

Without any better means of reaching the realities of a century ago, I will interpret the draining of white members from the underclass by a different hypothesis. Nineteenth-century America was advertised as a land of opportunity, and it was exactly that. Work was not hard to find, and a white member of the underclass could emerge from his unfavorable condition without struggling with the handicap of race.

Further, Banfield surely underestimates the organizing power of the Catholic church. Ethnic communities in our metropolises were tied closely to the Church, which had a powerful influence in their socialization. There was an alternative to life in the underclass, and the power of the Church was such that the route into productive society was apparent and not hard to choose. In spite of the mortality rates that Banfield nostalgically cites, the underclass probably lost members to opportunities of a flourishing economy in great need of unskilled labor and to the socialization impact of the Church, to which he attributes a present-orientation.

To me, living in an America in which opportunity has lost its universality and the Church its formidable influence, some hard but hopeful lessons are to be drawn from this hypothesis. If this is primarily a problem of bringing large populations of unskilled blacks and Hispanics into the economy, we can be sure that this solution cannot depend on the private sector of the economy alone. Private employers cannot use unskilled labor in the numbers required, nor can they take the responsibility for training them. The last time the nation had to face an unemployment rate as high as it is now in the large minority populations was in the depression of 1930–1939. Then it was a large and overwhelmingly white population that had to be provided for. An innovative administration created the Works Progress Administration, the Public Works Administration, the National Youth Administration, and the Civilian Conservation Corps to assure that a chronically unemployed sector of the American people would not develop. American political leadership during the past twenty years has not been so provident, even though some botched efforts at community organization and some halfhearted efforts to train youths for employment have been mounted. As the years go on, the problem will not disappear, nor will its solution become easier to stage.

What is clearly needed now is a major federal effort to employ underclass youth. It must be federal; no state has the tax base or the organizational resources to create its own program. There is much work to be done that no one is doing. The dilapidation of nearly every major American city is frequently described and universally deplored, especially by those who have traveled in or visited comparable European cities. Who would be more suited to the rehabilitation of our inner cities than the young people who have to live in them?

Not all the work has to be urban. There is much to be done in the country-side. Reforestation is urgently needed in many parts of the country. Fire fighters and fire preventers are seldom in sufficient supply. Land-reclamation projects, rehabilitation of the national parks, and rural road maintenance have fallen far behind in an economy that cannot manage such activities within the profit system. A great deal of unskilled labor needs to be done. Most of it cannot be handled by private employers. Conservation of human and natural resources is an economic requirement that does not lend itself to the free-enterprise system, but unless it is undertaken, and soon, the free-enterprise system is bound to face new and even more intractable problems than it now faces. We cannot brush aside as inconsequential the administrative, organizational, economic, and social difficulties of a new program of national conservation. Those difficulties are great, but they are within the capability of American talents for innovative design. It is not to be believed that a nation that was capable of the organizational feats of the New Deal years cannot manage the lesser requirements of vitalizing the underclass.

Who will take on the role of the Catholic Church, which socialized the immigrant population of a century ago? Again, we may rely on the same church for some of the needed organization and normative influences. There are many black churches already actively carrying out these tasks. Obviously, not enough is being done. But most of these churches are poor and in need of support they cannot get from their parishioners. Private philanthropy has not been as generous to them as their need requires. There can be no question that the black and Hispanic minorities can produce the leadership needed to influence their communities. Hardly any cause is as good.

The problem belongs first to the minorities, and it is the solutions that are generated within these minorities that will be the most hopeful. The nation as a whole must find ways to make these solutions as rapidly and as fully effective as possible.

This obvious program will not transform the country into a new Utopia. There will continue to be racial conflict, crime, horrifying violence, and all the other unwelcome phenomena that the underclass inflicts on comfortable Americans. There are serious problems for criminal justice to dispose of far beyond the foreseeable future. But the only way to lower the level of urban fear is to raise as many people as we can out of the underclass. Rummaging through the statistics of crime in search of a magic and cheaper alternative will keep criminologists out of mischief, but it will not keep the underclass out of crime.

Notes

1. *Newsweek,* 23 March 1981, pp. 46–54.
2. According to the Uniform Crime Statistics, 1977, murder by firearms constitutes over 60 percent of all murders committed. This figure has been constant for many years.

3. Karl Marx, *Capital* (London and Toronto: J.M. Dent and Sons, 1930), pp. 711–712.

4. Edward C. Banfield, *The Unheavenly City* (Boston and Toronto: Little, Brown, 1968), p. 53.

5. Ibid., p. 211.

6. The propositions in this section are drawn from two of our publications: Donna Martin Hamparian, Richard Schuster, Simon Dinitz, and John P. Conrad, *The Violent Few* (Lexington, Mass.: Lexington Books, D.C. Heath and Company, 1978); and Stephan Van Dine, John P. Conrad, and Simon Dinitz, *Restraining the Wicked* (Lexington, Mass.: Lexington Books, D.C. Heath and Company, 1979).

9

Homicide in America: A Research Review

Margaret A. Zahn

This state-of-the-art presentation summarizes basic knowledge of criminal homicide in America and reviews some characteristics of homicide, including its frequency in time and space; characteristics of participants; and the social organization, ideology, technology, and process of homicide. Sociological theories used to explain the findings are also briefly reviewed, along with some suggestions for resolving problems in the area. The brevity of the chapter necessitates a distillation rather than a full description of available studies. A more complete review of the studies themselves may be found in a companion piece.[1]

The first problem in completing a summary of homicide studies is conceptualizing criminal homicide and rendering available materials comparable. What is considered a homicide, as opposed to accidental death or death by natural causes, varies by historical period, jurisdiction, and agency dealing with or reporting the death. For example, when cars were first introduced, the deaths that resulted from them were classified by some coroners as homicides, although they would now likely be called accidental deaths. Jurisdictional differences, too, affect the definitions of homicide and thus affect resulting information. Some states (Texas, for example) consider killing in defense of property justifiable homicide, while others do not.[2] Further, the agency dealing with and reporting the death may include different categories as homicides. Medical-examiner sources, for example, include justifiable homicide in the total of homicides, while many police departments do not, especially if the homicide involved an officer killing someone in the line of duty. These many differences in definitions of homicide make comparisons across studies and across time periods extremely problematic. Further, since there has been no systematic framework for analyzing homicide, studies do not contain the same variables. Some studies, for example, analyze alcohol use of victims and offenders, while others do not. Even when variables presumed to be the same are included (such as victim-offender relationships), the categories contained and the definition of the categories may vary markedly. For example, Wolfgang classified victim-offender relationships into eleven categories, while Boudouris classified them into nine, and Lane into three.[3] How each set of categories relates to the others is difficult to determine. These problems of comparability partially explain why the sum of the homicide literature seems repetitive but is not cumulative. It also indicates the cautions that must be kept in mind when summarizing available materials.

The Frequency of American Homicide in Time and Physical Space

There were no fully national homicide statistics prior to the early 1930s; therefore, it is difficult to establish the rate of American homicide prior to that time. Local studies of the late 1800s show that the rate was high in the mid-nineteenth century but decreased in the last part of the century.[4] Ferdinand, in a study of Boston from 1849 to 1951, found that the highest murder rate for Boston was in 1855–1859, at 7.3 murders per 100,000 population. Lane, studying Philadelphia from 1839 to 1901, also found the years 1853–1859 to be the most violent for the period covered, with a long-term decline after that. Both authors independently attribute the downward rate of homicide to a growing middle class and structural changes accompanying urbanization. Lane, specifically, explains the decrease by the march of industrialization and the progressive attachment of working-class male populations to the machines and their routine, plus the growth of a middle class and of unified police departments.

The homicide rate in the South, based on a study of Atlanta from 1865 to 1890, was much higher than in the Northeast, although it, too, showed a downward trend during the later part of the nineteenth century. According to Russell, in the years 1865–1870, the homicide rate in Atlanta was 62.6 per 100,000, which decreased to a steady 16.5 for the twenty years following that period. In general, based on these local studies, the rate seemed then to be declining in the last part of the nineteenth century. It began to increase again, however, in the early part of the twentieth century, reaching one peak in the late 1920s (about 1928) or early 1930s and another peak in the late 1970s. Nationally based studies for the 1920s and 1930s, as well as those focused on local sites, support the peak of the late 1920s and early 1930s.[5] Homicide data, both in Vital Statistics and in the Uniform Crime Reports, became fully national in the early 1930s. These two sources show the homicide rate declining in the early 1930s and remaining low and stable during the 1940s, 1950s, and early 1960s. Both national data sources and local studies show a pronounced rise beginning again around 1965, with the homicide rate continuing to remain high: 9.0 in 1978 and 9.7 in 1979 (Uniform Crime Reports, 1978 and 1979).

The homicide trend, then, has varied through time. It varies in space as well. The spatial dimensions of American homicide have been examined in many ways, including its variation by geographic region and by city versus rural area or small town.[6] Regarding regional variations, studies uniformly show higher rates of homicide in the South, although, over time, there has been some small decrease in the degree of difference.[7] There is a wealth of literature on cities and homicide. A recent study that reviews those studies and analyzes longitudinal data relating cities to homicide suggests that the United States is characterized by a J-shaped homicide curve, with large cities having the highest rates but rural areas having higher rates than small towns.[8]

Participants in the Homicide Event

Studies of participants in the homicide event have usually been restricted to studies of the victim and the offender. Although many homicides may be witnessed events, the witnesses and their characteristics, the role they play, and the consequences to them of witnessing the event are seldom examined. Further, although the principal participants have many characteristics by which they can be described, generally only their age, race, and sex have been studied. Other characteristics—such as occupational history, welfare status, and marital history—may be equally important but are relatively unexplored.

In terms of race and sex, findings consistently show that homicide victims and offenders are disproportionately black as opposed to white and male as opposed to female. All studies find homicide to be primarily an intramale event. Although cases of infanticide complicate the homicide picture regarding female homicide offenders (especially in the early twentieth century), females are generally less likely to kill and to be killed. Furthermore, females almost never kill other adult females. In a 1967 study of seventeen American cities, Curtis found that only 4 percent of homicides involved a female killing a female.[9] The racial composition of homicide is also somewhat complicated, especially for earlier data; for example, some Ku Klux Klan killings of blacks may not have been recorded as homicides. In general, however, available studies show black males disproportionately involved as victims and as offenders.

The Social Organization and Ideology of Homicide

The literature on homicide, especially since Wolfgang's classic study, has attempted to describe both the social organization and the ideology of homicide events. Social organization refers to the structured role relations within which homicide most frequently occurs. It is important to note that, although there are many repetitive role relationships (for example, employer-employee; merchant-customer; husband-wife), only some relationships seem to be persistently associated with homicide. Seldom in the literature, for example, is an employer-employee relationship associated with homicide, while frequently a husband-wife relationship is. Further, it is less frequent for a patron to kill a bartender than to kill another patron, even though they are all in the same situation and may all have the same demographic characteristics.

In addition to social organization, each homicide event is usually characterized by an ideology, that is, an attempt to interpret the experience.[10] Although most homicide researchers discuss this as *motive*, the broader term, *ideology*, may more accurately reflect the complexities of the interpretation. An ideology of the event is recorded by the police, the courts, and subsequently by researchers. What is officially transcribed as the motive by official sources may not be the motive according to the actual participants. Further, the evaluation of the motive by researchers may bear a different relationship to the event than that recorded either by official sources or by those directly involved. Although this discussion cannot encompass the relationship between the ideology and the social organization of the event, I would suggest that it is not accidental that the structural form of lower-class male killing lower-class male in nonwork, barroom argument is usually described as the result of "trivial" arguments, while husband-wife conflicts over the same issue are infrequently described that way.

With these caveats, the findings regarding the social organization (social relationships) and imputed motives (ideology) of homicide can be described. Findings are arranged according to each historical period for which studies are available.

Two studies of America in the late nineteenth century, Lane's and Russell's, show that, for both Philadelphia and Atlanta, the modal type of homicide relationship was a male killing another male as a result of an argument, usually—in Lane's and Russell's terms—a trivial argument.[11] Specifically, Lane found that the modal homicide incident in nineteenth-century Philadelphia began as a brawl or quarrel, typically originating in a saloon and reaching a climax in the street. Murder was most likely to involve an acquaintance (48 percent), followed by a stranger (30 percent), then by a family member (22 percent). During the period in question, infanticide occurred with some frequency (55 per year), and women were indicted more frequently than men for this type of murder. Most homicide indictments, however, were of males, and murder in early Philadelphia usually involved an argument between two men who were either acquaintances or strangers who encountered each other in the bars or streets of the city.[12]

In Atlanta during that period, the major type of homicide was also a quarrel between males, associated with avenging insults and settling personal disputes. According to Russell, homicide was a publicly sanctioned system of individual combat to settle "remarkably petty quarrels." According to him, only 9.5 percent were family disputes and another 9.5 percent were felony-related.[13]

Only two studies classify victim-offender relationships in the early twentieth century. They suggest that, in Detroit and Chicago, the criminal-transaction homicide and those considered justifiable became prominent forms. Both these types were apparently related to bootlegging and the enforcement of prohibition laws. In Detroit, when the large category of justifiables was removed, there remained almost equal proportions of homicides involving domestic relations

(18.2 percent); friends and acquaintances (18.2 percent); and criminal transactions (16.6 percent). Chicago showed a similar pattern, with justifiable homicide, gang and criminally related homicide, and altercations and brawls being most prominent. Domestic homicides comprised only 8.3 percent of the total for Chicago in 1926–1927. Neither study from this period describes arguments between males as trivial, even those occurring in recreational settings, such as barrooms.[14]

The 1940s, 1950s, and early 1960s consistently showed domestic and love-related homicides as an important category, more important than in any earlier time.[15] Although males killing males in trivial arguments also continued as important homicide types during this period, those related to criminal transactions became few in number. Using Wolfgang's classic study as representative of the period, motives are classified as trivial altercations (35.0 percent), domestic quarrels (14.1 percent), jealousy (11.6 percent), altercations over money (10.5 percent), robbery (6.8 percent), revenge (5.3 percent), accidents (3.9 percent), self-defense (1.4 percent), halting a felon (1.2 percent), escaping arrest (1 percent), concealing birth (1 percent), other (3.4 percent), and unknown (4.8 percent).[16]

The social organization and ideology of homicide changed again in the late 1960s, especially in northeastern and midwestern cities, and continues in the same vein today.[17] The most comprehensive study of the period, the Violence Commission's report, with subsequent analyses by Curtis, shows that husband-wife killings accounted for 15.8 percent of criminal homicides.[18] Approximately 9 percent involved other family members. Lovers, close friends, and other primary relations also totaled 9 percent, while slightly less than 30 percent, although known to each other, were nonprimary. In the remainder of the cases, they either were strangers (15.6 percent) or the offender was unknown (20.9 percent). Minor altercations were the most frequent motives (35.7 percent), followed by unknown (21 percent), other reasons (10.6 percent), and robbery (8.8 percent).

The pattern demonstrated by Curtis and confirmed by many other studies of the Northeast and Midwest shows that, while a dominant form is an argument between two male acquaintances, a close second is a stranger killing someone under unknown circumstances. This period, with its increase in robbery-related and stranger homicides in the Northeast and Midwest, exhibits fewer references to the homicide context as trivial.[19]

In sum, the social organization of homicide varies over time, although, in all periods, males arguing in a nonwork setting over presumably trivial matters is a major type. Domestic feuds, in most periods, represent a small but persistent percentage of cases, and the ideology linked to this organizational form is often said to involve sexual matters (infidelity) or money. Criminal and victim-stranger relations have claimed large percentages of lives at some times (the late 1920s and the 1970s) and in some places; the ideology of the victim-stranger event is not particularly well-defined, but is most frequently thought to involve robbery or other criminal behavior.

The Technology of Homicide

Apart from the social organization and ideology of homicide, the event is also characterized by technology and a process. Technology includes those implements directly used to kill—guns, knives, clubs—and those substances, such as drugs and alcohol, which directly cause or indirectly contribute to the event. Most sociological studies, with the exception of Wolfgang's, attribute some importance to gun use.[20] Most also agree, however, that availability of guns has not been adequately studied, so we do not know if availability alone is the primary issue. Researchers indicate that factors associated with the willingness to use guns are also important.[21] Block illustrates this viewpoint well when he states that "support for gun control legislation (i.e., controls on availability) will come only when the circular escalation of crime, fear and self-protection is broken."[22]

The association between alcohol and homicide has also been explored in the literature. The manner of exploration most commonly used involves reporting the percentage of offenders or victims who had been drinking at the time of the fatal attack. Wolfgang's study, for example, found that in 64 percent of the homicide cases in Philadelphia in 1948–1952, alcohol was used by either the offender or the victim immediately prior to the final assault. However, a review of these kinds of studies finds that the percentage of victims who had been drinking varies widely.[23] Further, although much of the literature finds some association between alcohol and homicide, the manner of the association remains unclear. Wolfgang's report and the Violence Commission's report, for example, caution that there is no direct causal connection between alcohol and homicide.[24] The nature of the linkage, then, needs to be examined to determine whether the association is the result of weakened behavioral controls, for example, or, as Gelles contends, of the learning of drunken behavior as a "time out" from norms and demands of civility.[25] If the latter proves to be the case, then research needs to focus on the expectations and learning attached to drinking and drunkenness among black males and other subgroups of society.

The relationship of drugs, other than alcohol, and homicide poses some of the same problems, although there is even less known association between drug use and homicide.[26] If drugs are related to homicide, it appears to be via one of two connections: either by combining some drugs with alcohol, aggressiveness is increased,[27] or, by being involved in the illegal-drug-using life-style, the user has greater risks of being killed by an unhappy customer, an ambitious dealer wishing to increase his turf, or a citizen or law officer attempting to control robbery associated with some drug-use life-styles. A study conducted in Philadelphia by Zahn and Bencivengo establishes this latter possibility.[28]

The Process of Homicide

Until recently, homicide has not been analyzed in terms of process. In the 1970s, however, some researchers attempted to describe the interaction sequence.[29] Based on a study of seventy cases, Luckenbill, for example, concluded that the criminal homicide process begins with a victim engaging in some behavior or event that the offender defines as an offense to "face." (This often takes the form of an insult.) The offender, often with the aid of bystanders, interprets this as personally offensive and decides to restore face through a retaliatory move. In retaliating, the offender expresses contempt for the opinion of the victim and judges him or her an unworthy person. The most common retaliatory move is the ultimatum. The victim escalates the transaction by accepting the ultimatum and establishes a working agreement that violence is appropriate to the situation. Commitment to battle is enhanced by the availability of weapons, and death is the result.[30]

Other studies focus on the process of robbery-related injuries, especially as affected by victim resistance and by weapon choice.[31] Block describes the robbery-related injury as one in which a victim attempts to resist a robber's threat, with the robber's reaction to resistance being use of force with resulting injury (sometimes death) to the victim.[32]

The interactional or process accounts of homicide, though relatively new, are extremely provocative and very useful, especially for policy purposes. Existing sociological theories have incorporated some of the facts reported here but not others.

Sociological Explanations of Homicide

Three major sociological theories of homicide are the cultural-subcultural, the structural, and the interactional. Cultural theorists see homicide as resulting from learned, shared patterns of behavior that are specific to a given group. The basic causes are in the norms and values, transmitted across generations, that are learned by members of this group. Certain subgroups exhibit higher rates of homicide because they are participants in a subculture that has violence as a norm. Wolfgang and Ferracuti, the famous founders of this approach, have used the explanation to account for high homicide rates among young black males.[33] A variant of the explanation has also been used to explain the high homicide rates in the southern region of the country.[34]

There are a number of theoretical as well as evidential problems with the subculture-of-violence approach. First, it often fails to explain how or why the subculture emerged in the first place. It fails, also, to explain why some who are exposed to the subculture become violent and others, similarly exposed, do not. Additionally, it is tautological. The proponents of the theory first observe that homicide is differentially distributed in the social structure and then say that this is so because these components of the social structure are violent.

These theories have often used inappropriate data to test the theoretical position. For example, although learned normative-value systems are said to account for the different rates of violence among black males, the data used are demographic, with few or no individual-level values or group-level normative data. When individual-level data have been used, they have failed to confirm a subculture of violence among black males.[35] Such findings have led some researchers to conclude that the subculture-of-violence explanation may be in-adequate to explain interpersonal violence among these groups.[36]

The structuralist position is more amorphous, with no clear intellectual spearhead. This disparate set of explanations asserts that broad-scale social forces, such as lack of opportunity, institutional racism, demographic transi-tions, and population density, are the structures that shape homicide rates. These forces operate independently of human cognition and do not require the inter-vention of individual learning to explain their impact. One illustration of a structuralist approach is that of Van den Berghe, who argues that resource competition is at the heart of aggression. When populations or their needs increase, resource competition also increases, and aggression (including homi-cide) results. This aggression is, at times, regulated by territoriality, which establishes monopoly over resources within space, and hierarchy, which creates an order of precedence in access to and distribtuion of resources. In Van den Berghe's terms, keen resource competition leads to territoriality and hierarchy, but territoriality and hierarchy also occasion many instances of aggression.[37]

In general, the myriad of structural explanations suggest parameters affect-ing homicide rates. They do not specify, however, the conditions under which these variables lead to violence rather than alternative outcomes (for example, when population density leads to violence and when it leads to passivity). They do not explain the occurrence of differing types—for example, family versus robbery-related murder—in differing periods of time or the structural reasons for them. Further, they often have not constructed adequate tests or evidence for proving their assertions. Evidence using comparative, historical materials seems most appropriate for evaluating notions regarding changing resources, demographic transitions, and the like. Securing good cross-cultural and historical data on homicide, however, remains extremely problematic and thus hampers attempts to test some structural explanations of homicide.

Whereas structuralists concentrate on macrostructure, interaction theorists focus on microstructure or the nature of the interaction that escalates into a homicide.[38] They do not try to explain differential rates of homicide but rather describe the process through which a given homicide occurs. Interaction theorists link theory and data much more closely than do the other two types, and their descriptive accounts provide information of interventional and preventive value. They do not explain, however, why certain escalating conflicts result in murder while others may result in divorce. Further, why do certain groups have a higher incidence of repetitive conflict, with violence as the favored solution? More descriptive accounts, using comparison groups in conflict situations that do not result in homicide, would further their attempts.

Although each of these approaches has offered some aid to understanding, each also leaves much to be desired. Attempts at integrating these disparate viewpoints have recently been made and are suggestive for future research. Gelles and Straus have attempted to accomplish this in the area of family violence, while Curtis has attempted such a synthesis for violence committed by blacks in the contemporary United States.[39] According to Curtis, culture is the intervening interpretive variable between structural determinants and violent outcomes. The structural determinants of the behaviors of poor blacks are economic marginality and institutional racism. These structural conditions are filtered through a series of contracultural values and behaviors (for example, physical prowess and thrill-seeking) and, when coupled with weapons possession, alcohol, and drug consumption, lead to conflict generation.[40] It is not yet known just how fruitfully integrated approaches can be researched. Their inclusiveness, however, is both suggestive and appealing.

In sum, homicide research and theorizing have established both some persistent findings—for example, that males generally kill males more than females kill females—and some interesting etiological leads. However, the field often seems redundant and stagnant. To increase the productivity, I suggest three major activities. First, certain persistent findings need to be more closely examined, utilizing appropriate data. For example, we do know that males are dominant in homicide and that they commit homicide because of arguments. Do males argue more than females, and, if so, why? If not, why do men's arguments become lethal, while those of women do not? Obviously, to answer these kinds of questions criminologists will have to use data sources other than those traditionally associated with the criminal-justice system. In my opinion, some official data sources, such as police records, though valuable for many components of homicide research, have been used too exclusively. Often data have been collected that are clearly inappropriate to the theoretic suggestions (sometimes simply because they are in the police record). The link between data and theory in homicide research has been tenuous, and myopia about data sources may be one of the reasons.

Second, the literature often fails to clarify the genre of human activity that homicide represents. Those studying homicide often do not compare it to any other related forms of behavior. When comparisons have been made, criminologists have generally linked homicide to other forms of interpersonal physical violence, such as assault and rape.[41] Such comparisons have been illuminating and require extension. Further, comparisons to collective forms of interpersonal violence may also be instructive.[42]

I also suggest that other previously unexplored comparisons be attempted. For example, homicide is one form of terminal relationship and one way of reducing conflict. There are other ways of terminating relationships (for example, divorce, graduation, geographic mobility) and other methods of resolving conflict (such as withdrawal and compromise). Research and conceptualization using these comparative comments might lead to new understandings and to a genuine sociology of homicide.

Finally, empirical and theoretical efforts regarding American homicide need to be extended to establish the extent to which these patterns obtain in different historical periods and in different countries. In sum, until we resolve some of the conceptual problems involving the genre of homicide and until we have a more historically informed and fully comparative account of its character, the understanding of American homicide will remain illusive, as will the principles governing this genre of human activity. These seem to be our next steps for developing a sociology of homicide.

Notes

1. See Margaret A. Zahn, "Homicide in the Twentieth Century United States," in *History and Crime: Implications for Criminal Justice Policy,* ed. James A. Inciardi and Charles E. Faupel (Beverly Hills, Calif.: Sage, 1980), pp. 111–131.

2. See Henry P. Lundsgaarde, *Murder in Space City* (Oxford University Press, 1977).

3. Marvin Wolfgang, *Patterns in Criminal Homicide* (Philadelphia: University of Pennsylvania, 1958); James Boudouris, "Trends in Homicide, Detroit 1926–1968" (Ph.D. dissertation, Wayne State University, 1970); and Roger Lane, *Violent Death in the City: Suicide, Accident and Murder in Nineteenth Century Philadelphia* (Cambridge, Mass.: Harvard University Press, 1979).

4. Theodore N. Ferdinand, "The Criminal Patterns of Boston Since 1840," *American Journal of Sociology* 73 (July 1967):84–99; Roger Lane, *Violent Death in the City;* and James M. Russell, "Homicide and the Violent Ideal in Atlanta, 1865 to 1890" (Unpublished paper, University of Tennessee at Chattanooga, 1978).

5. Nationally based studies of this period were conducted by H.C. Brearly, *Homicide in the United States* (Chapel Hill: University of North Carolina Press, 1932), and by Frederick Hoffman, *The Homicide Problem* (San

Francisco: Prudential Press, 1925). Examples of locally based studies of this time period include Edwin H. Sutherland and C.E. Gehlke, "Crime and Punishment," in *Recent Social Trends in the United States* (New York: McGraw-Hill, 1933), pp. 1114–1167; and James Boudouris, "Trends in Homicide."

6. Regional studies of homicide include Raymond D. Gastil, "Homicide and a Regional Culture of Violence," *American Sociological Review* 36(1971):412–427; Collin Loftin and Robert H. Hill, "Regional Subculture and Homicide: An Examination of the Gastil-Hackney Thesis," *American Sociological Review* 39(1974):714–724; Sheldon Hackney, "Southern Violence," in *Violence in America: Historical and Comparative Perspectives,* ed. Hugh D. Graham and Ted R. Gurr (Beverly Hills, Calif.: Sage, 1969). A review article on homicide and cities is in Dane Archer, Rosemary Gartner, Robin Akert, and Tim Lockwood, "Cities and Homicide: A New Look At An Old Paradox," *Comparative Studies in Sociology* 1(1978):73–95. Intracity area variation of homicide has also been studied—see, for example, Richard Block, *Violent Crime* (lexington, Mass.: Lexington Books, D.C. Heath, 1977)—but will not be reviewed here.

7. Alvin L. Jacobson, "Crime Trends in Southern and Nonsouthern Cities: A Twenty Year Perspective," *Social Forces* 54 (1976):226–241.

8. Archer et al., "Cities and Homicide."

9. Lynn A. Curtis, *Criminal Violence* (Lexington, Mass.: Lexington Books, D.C. Heath, 1974), p. 32.

10. The definition of ideology has been drawn from Gerhard Lenski and Jean Lenski, *Human Societies: An Introduction to Macrosociology* (New York: McGraw-Hill, 1978), p. 48. The idea of using social organization, ideology, and technology as descriptive elements also derives partly from their work.

11. See Lane, *Violent Death in the City,* and Russell, "Homicide in Atlanta."

12. Lane, *Violent Death in the City.*

13. Russell, "Homicide in Atlanta," pp. 13, 16.

14. Boudouris, "Trends in Homicide," and Arthur V. Lashly, "Homicide in Cook County," chapter 13 in *The Illinois Crime Survey* (Chicago: Illinois Association for Criminal Justice, 1929).

15. Examples of studies of the 1940s and 1950s are Wolfgang, *Patterns in Criminal Homicide;* Howard Harlan, "Five Hundred Homicides," *Journal of Criminal Law and Criminology* 6(1950):736–752; and Robert C. Bensing and Oliver Schroeder, Jr., *Homicide in an Urban Community* (Springfield, Ill.: Charles C Thomas, 1970).

16. Wolfgang, *Patterns in Criminal Homicide.*

17. Numerous studies from this period include Block, *Violent Crime;* Margaret A. Zahn and Glenn Snodgrass, "Drug Use and the Structure of Homicide

in Two U.S. Cities," in *The New and the Old Criminology,* ed. Edith Flynn and John Conrad (New York: Praeger, 1978), pp. 134–150.

18. Donald J. Mulvihill and Melvin H. Tumin, *Crimes of Violence,* vols. 1, 11, 12, 13 (Washington, D.C.: U.S. Government Printing Office, 1969); and Curtis, *Criminal Violence.*

19. Studies of southwestern cities for the same period show a different pattern, with family-related homicides more dominant. See Lundsgaarde, *Murder in Space City,* and Zahn and Snodgrass, "Drug Use and the Structure of Homicide."

20. Block, *Violent Crime;* Franklin E. Zimring, "Determinants of the Death Rate from Robbery: A Detroit Time Study," in *Lethal Aspects of Urban Violence,* ed. Harold M. Rose (Lexington, Mass.: Lexington Books, D.C. Heath and Company, 1979), pp.31–50; Zahn, "Homicide in the Twentieth Century United States."

21. For example, Block, *Violent Crime,* pp. 103–105; Zahn, "Homicide in the Twentieth Century United States," p. 126–129.

22. Block, *Violent Crime,* p. 103.

23. Wolfgang, *Patterns in Criminal Homicide,* pp. 136–138; Stephanie W. Greenberg, "Alcohol and Crime: A Methodological Critique of the Literature," In *Research on the Relationship Between Alcohol and Crime,* ed. J. Collins (Draft overview and state-of-the-art papers for LEAA project) (Research Triangle Park, N.C.: Research Triangle Institute, 1979).

24. Mulvihill and Tumin, with Curtis, *Crimes of Violence,* vol. 12, p. 648.

25. Richard J. Gelles, *The Violent Home: A Study of Physical Aggression Between Husbands and Wives* (Beverly Hills, Calif.: Sage, 1972).

26. Mulvihill and Tumin, with Curtis, *Crimes of Violence,* vol. 12, pp. 667–683.

27. Jared R. Tinkelberg, "Alcohol and Violence," in *Alcoholism: Progress in Research and Treatment,* ed. Peter G. Brown and Ruth Fox (New York: Academic, 1973), pp. 195–210.

28. Margaret A. Zahn and Mark Bencivengo, "Violent Death: A Comparison Between Drug Users and Non-Drug Users," *Addictive Diseases: An International Journal* 1(1973):283–296.

29. David F. Luckenbill, "Criminal Homicide as a Situated Transaction," *Social Problems* 25(December 1977):176–186; Lonnie H. Athens, "A Symbolic Interactionist's Approach to Violent Criminal Acts" (Ph.D. dissertation, University of California at Berkeley, 1975); Lonnie H. Athens, "Violent Crime: A Symbolic Interactionist Study," *Symbolic Interaction* 1(1977):56–70.

30. Luckenbill, "Criminal Homicide," pp. 185–186.

31. Block, *Violent Crime,* pp. 29–60; and Zimring, "Determinants of the Death Rate from Robbery," pp. 31–50.

32. Block, *Violent Crime*.

33. Marvin E. Wolfgang and Franco Ferracuti, *The Subculture of Violence: Towards an Integrated Theory in Criminology* (London: Tavistock, 1967).

34. Gastil, "Homicide and a Regional Culture," pp. 412–427.

35. Sandra J. Ball-Rokeach, "Values and Violence: A Test of the Subculture of Violence Thesis." *American Sociological Review* 38(1973):736–749; Howard Erlanger, "The Empirical Status of the Subculture of Violence Thesis." *Social Problems* 22(1974):280–292; Howard Erlanger, "Is There a 'Subculture of Violence' in the South?" *Journal of Criminal Law and Criminology* 66(1976):483–490.

36. Ball-Rokeach, "Values and Violence"; Erlanger, "Empirical Status"; Erlanger, "Is There a 'Subculture of Violence' in the South?"

37. Pierre L. Van den Berghe, "Bringing Beasts Back In: Toward a Biosocial Theory of Aggression." *American Sociological Review* 39(December 1974):777–787.

38. Luckenbill, "Criminal Homicide"; Athens, "A Symbolic Interactionist's Approach."

39. Richard J. Gelles and Murray A. Straus, "Toward an Integration Theory of Intrafamily Violence. Unpublished paper, University of New Hampshire; Lynn A. Curtis, *Violence, Race, and Culture* (Lexington, Mass.: Lexington Books, D.C. Heath and Company, 1975).

40. Curtis, *Violence, Race, and Culture*, p. 56.

41. Block, *Violent Crime;* Curtis, *Violence, Race, and Culture*.

42. Dane Archer and Rosemary Gartner, "Violent Acts and Violent Times: A Comparative Approach to Postwar Homicide Rates," *American Sociological Reveiw* 41(December 1976):937–963; this is a very informative attempt of this type.

10 Reactions to the Questioning of the Mafia Myth

Joseph L. Albini

It has often been said that one can never fully understand the reality of situations such as prejudice, intimidation, and other negative aspects of life until they are experienced on a personal level. Of those negative aspects, suspicion and false accusation have come to be realities for me as a result of having written a book that argues against the existence of a secret criminal society known as Mafia or Cosa Nostra.

When I undertook research into the phenomenon of organized crime, I did so with a great deal of apprehension. This apprehension came because I believed in the existence of a Mafia. Why not? After all, the few books I had read on the subject argued definitively that such an organization (called by different names) did exist. A probably even more important factor that stimulated this belief was my Italian background. Mafia was for me, as I am certain it has been for other Italian-Americans, a household term. Yet I never realized until I delved fully into the research that both my usage of the word and my conception of what it consisted of was nebulous. As many people still do, I had a vague idea of a secret criminal society consisting of Sicilians who were bound together by secret ceremonies and codes—a society whose most powerful weapon was intimidating and ruthlessly killing anyone who did not do what it demanded.

It became obvious by the end my field-data collecting, as well as from reading the literature in both Italian and English, that I was dealing with a subject in which the data were grossly contradictory and that governmental sources, despite these contradictions, seemed to have taken a rather unified public position concerning its structure—a secret criminal society called, synonymously, Mafia and Cosa Nostra.

This chapter is a discussion of my experiences following the publication of my book, *The American Mafia: Genesis of a Legend*.[1] By examining these experiences, I hope to address personally certain issues regarding the role and conflicts confronting social scientists whose findings contradict a conditioned construction of social reality.

From the moment my book appeared, I began to realize that I had called into question or attacked a popular belief in American society—the existence of a secret criminal society called Mafia or Cosa Nostra. I never had realized, however, how powerfully grounded this belief was in the average American's mind. Also, I had never realized how little factual knowledge the average American had about the subject. I learned not only that most people believed in a Mafia but, more interesting, that they did not fear whatever it was that they defined as Mafia and were actually excited by it. While I was writing my book I believed, as did most criminologists, that syndicated crime, regardless of the name given to it, was a menace and that both the government and the general public viewed it as such and hence desired to have it destroyed. I have since become more realistic in my understanding of this phenomenon, not only as a result of my personal experiences after the publication of my book but also from what I learned from my later study of organized crime in Great Britain. This study, which involved interviews with underworld informants in Glasgow and London, gave me further interesting insights into myths that criminals believe about themselves and the socially accepted beliefs regarding criminals that are generally accepted by the Scottish and British publics.

The first reality was revealed in one of the questions that was asked of me after my book appeared, in my first television interview on a news broadcast in Detroit: "Is it true that the Mafia paid you to write this book?" My immediate reaction was laughter, as I thought the question was being asked in jest. It soon became apparent, however, that many people believed this because they believed in a secret criminal society.

Yet this belief in a secret criminal society, I have come to realize, serves an end in itself—the need to believe that such a society does exist. This illusion fulfills functions that, in turn, serve to keep it alive.

First, a belief in a secret society allows Americans to draw attention away from certain realities that otherwise would make it necessary to place blame upon the American public itself—that is, that syndicated crime exists because large segments of the American public desire and have continuously desired illicit goods and services.

Two major sources of information that I believe are responsible for this continued form of social projection are the journalists and certain governmental bodies. Not only have these two sources been instrumental in exciting the public with so-called proofs regarding the existence of Mafia and Cosa Nostra but, as Galliher and Cain note in a recent article,[2] most textbooks in criminology have drawn their data from these references.

Probably two of the most influential governmental and journalistic sources have been the report of the President's Task Force Commission on Organized Crime and Mario Puzo's novel, *The Godfather*. Although the commission was presented with all manner of convincing evidence, according to one of its consultant-spokesmen, Donald Cressey,[3] the commission report produced no more evidence in terms of new information than that revealed in the government report of 1965, following the famous Valachi testimony. Hawkins and I have presented arguments demonstrating that Valachi's testimony is in direct contra-diction to his own and the government's conclusions.[4]

What I marvel at is the task force's complete lack of reanalysis of the McClelland hearings data. During their testimony in the McClelland hearings, representatives of various police departments differed in their description of how organized crime was structured in their cities. The Chicago structure included an Italian and a non-Italian organization. Yet these different conceptions were simply put aside in the final conclusions of the McClelland committee report and the task force report. Instead, we saw the structure of syndicates in various cities described only in Valachi's conception of twenty-four families, each having a boss, underboss, lieutenant, consigliere, and soldiers.

My major criticism of the task force report is that not only did it give no attention to existing contradictions in the literature and previous governmental reports but it had no historical basis. Rather than noting that, throughout American history, organized crime has undergone various changes in its structure and function (ethnic and otherwise) and that today, as in the past, variations in this structure and function exist in different parts of the country, it focused on a unified conception of syndicate structure throughout the country. Surely the Task Force must have been aware that there were syndicates operating throughout the country that did not fit the conception of Cosa Nostra in terms of either origin or the ethnicity of its participants. Yet these were not given attention. It is interesting to note, also, that one of the task force consultants, John A. Gardiner, was evidently aware of the existence of one such syndicate, as he had written about it.[5] According to Gardiner, this was a powerful syndicate operating in a city to which he gave the fictional name Wincanton, although another source has defined it as Reading, Pennsylvania.[6] According to Gardiner, this syndicate was under the leadership of a Russian immigrant named Irving Stern. In his description of this syndicate, Gardiner makes it clear that this is not a Cosa Nostra outfit. Yet it is interesting to note that one of his interests seems to be "why the East Coast families of the Cosa Nostra did not attempt to take over Irv Stern's organization?"[7] Equally interesting is Gardiner's noting that one of the reasons may have been that "the East Coast syndicates lacked the muscle or resources to destroy Stern even if they wanted to."[8] I am not concerned here with Gardiner's reasoning as to why these families did not take over Stern's enterprises; rather, I am interested in noting what seems to be a constant bias of the task force report—a belief in the unquestionable power of Cosa Nostra families, as though they were the only powerful syndicates operating syndicated crime. There are hundreds of syndicates operating in the United States, with a variety of ethnic mixtures among their participants. Not only has this been true historically, but any examination of syndicate involvement in illicit drugs, gambling, and other illegal enterprises today reveals involvement of Americans from various ethnic backgrounds, including blacks, Puerto Ricans, Mexicans, Cubans, Chinese, and mixtures of other groups, depending on the part of the country in which the activity is being carried out.[9] Redlinger and Michel note, for example, that the distribution of heroin in San Antonio is in the hands of one minority group—the Mexican-Americans.[10] Yet the task force report focuses attention on a centralized national secret society consisting only of Italians, especially Sicilians. By giving attention to a nationally organized Cosa Nostra, it has drawn attention away from the fact that syndicates in the United States are primarily located in specific geographical areas and thus that their growth and continued existence, changes, and other aspects are best understood in terms of differences in avenues of corruption, variations in the desire for illicit goods in different areas of the country, and other factors of a localized nature, rather than as an overall national blueprint of evil originating with and executed by so-called Mafia chieftains.

Evidence that I have obtained from informants and the police during my research for the book has since convinced me that syndicates are historical and social entities. As such, they can be understood only when they are studied as entities that have a local significance and whose structures vary in terms of the nature of the patron-client relationships that exist, have existed, and are continuously changing, rather than as part of a static structure, such as that described in the task force report. Certainly, the works of Ianni and Chambliss have demonstrated this point further.[11]

This brings us to a second point concerning the function of a belief in Mafia or Cosa Nostra—the simplicity with which the structure of syndicated crime is explained. By giving simple, all-encompassing positions, such as boss, underboss, and the like, the structure is described in such broad terms that it can explain virtually anything. Yet what does this structure (so secret that we had to wait for Valachi to reveal it) show? One gets the impression that without this structure, oaths, rituals, and so forth, criminal syndicates just could not function. We note that Gardiner was able to describe the Stern syndicate without using the common positions of Cosa Nostra familes, but was the Stern syndicate any less effective in its activities and power? I am certain that if we wanted to, or if we were told that it was a Cosa Nostra syndicate, we could easily fit members of the Stern syndicate into such positions as boss, underboss, and so on. The point is that it is not how one describes a position or what one entitles it but rather the essence of the different types of power relationships that exist between the individual participants that realistically portrays the real nature of syndicate functioning in the United States. Syndicate activity involves so many types of relationships (kinship, business-type contracts, friendships, antagonisms, and so forth), which interweave both legitimate and illegitimate areas of society, that they cannot be described in the simple structure presented by the task force. However, the task force's conception has the advantage of simplicity, which allows writers to explain the structure very easily. Also, because it is a secret phenomenon, writers can virtually say anything about it and still retain credibility.

Cressey, for example, notes that Cosa Nostra families have a "corruptor."[12] This is another attempt at simplicity, but it brings us to another function served by a belief in Mafia and Cosa Nostra—the separation of society into "good guys" and "bad guys."

In the position of corruptor, as well as in the entire conception of Cosa Nostra, we receive the impression that it is the syndicate criminal who goes out and corrupts and thus forces his goods and services upon the American public. Corruption can and does take on many forms. Evidence given by my informants shows that corruption of witnesses, public officials, and others cannot be accomplished by one corruptor in a given area. Corruption of this kind necessitates use of all types of relationships that interweave legitimate and illegitimate members of society. The major objection I have toward the conception of corruptor is that it assumes that it is always the syndicate criminal who approaches the public official. The DeCavalcante tapes have been cited by many believers in the Cosa Nostra as proof of its existence, because these tapes revealed conversations in which its members corrupted police. I do not understand what was so exciting about this information, considering that syndicate criminals in America were paying off police as early as 1865.[13] Corruption is part of the very structure of syndicated crime in America. However, it is not always the syndicate criminal who corrupts the police official. Just as often, corruption originates with the public official or the candidate aspiring to become one. The entire history of machine politics consists of deals between political candidates and syndicate criminals, the latter giving the former financial and other forms of campaign support in return for protection of criminal enterprises upon election to office. To speak of a corruptor reduces the process of corruption to its simplest terms. It makes for a simple definition of the corruptor as the bad guy who forces corruption on the good guys.

The attention given to the Mafia and Cosa Nostra also serves the further function of permitting the American public to cast attention away from itself. It is indeed a gross form of hypocrisy when, as I have heard hundreds of times, a person who gambles in illegal enterprises or a drug user asks, "Why doesn't the government do something to get rid of the Mafia?" These people do not realize that they are part of the system of syndicated crime. Without them, syndicated crime could not exist. Attention on the Mafia as original corruptor has blurred for the American public the fact that that public, along with the government that has made certain goods and services illegal, is the basis on which syndicated crime thrives in America. I have become further convinced of this from my study of organized crime in Great Britain. There I found no evidence of syndicated crime that could match, in any way, the American structure or degree of magnitude. I can only believe that, along with other factors, legalization of addictive narcotics and gambling have largely been responsible for the lack of growth of criminal syndicates in Great Britain.

Basically, then, a belief in Mafia or Cosa Nostra has helped the American public, the government, and other segments of American society to fool themselves in a process of circular reasoning, which allows each to believe that they are innocent bystanders or victims of the corrupting influence of syndicate criminals rather than participants in the very system they profess to fear. As I claimed earlier, I do not believe that the American public really fears syndicated crime. It seems that the American public has become excited by the portrayal of the Mafia by journalists and free-lance writers who, under the guise of informing the public, have helped create an image of the Mafioso as not a feared enemy but rather an admired hero. They have created a stereotype, which, along with the belief in Mafia as a secret society, has become the basis for the average American's conception of syndicated crime. Why has this stereotype so impressed the American public? I think the answer lies in the fact that the stereotype includes entities that Americans admire and seek, that is, money, sex, and violence.

In the boredom of the average American's life, it must serve as some consolation to be able to believe and vicariously live the so-called good life of the Mafioso, who is constantly visualized as being chauffered in the biggest cars and always surrounded by beautiful women. In addition, he does not fear anyone, because all he has to do is pick up the telephone and the person he fears will be dead within a few hours. As ridiculous as this may sound, we must remember that the American public loves mythology, and it has learned to believe in stereotypes.

Here we can enlarge on a statement I made earlier in this chapter—that, along with the task force report, Puzo's novel, *The Godfather,* strongly influenced public belief in the Mafia. I am in no manner imputing any motives to Puzo, nor am I blaming him for how his novel was interpreted. I am certain that he meant it to be the novel that it was. He never implied that it was based on a personal knowledge of syndicate-criminal behavior or syndicate structure. He made it clear that he had never talked with a gangster in his life.[14] The influence of Puzo's book, in my opinion, lies in the interpretation the public gave it—that it was a factual book based on his personal experience with the topic. Puzo, like myself, has been accused both of being paid off by the Mafia and of being a member.[15]

In my opinion, in terms of the popularity it achieved, Puzo's book came at an appropriate time—the period both following the McClelland hearings, where masses of television viewers watched Joseph Valachi, who thrilled them with so-called revelations of the secret society to which he belonged, and following the publication of the task force report on organized crime. There is a definite similarity between Puzo's fictional portrayal of the organization of the Mafia and that noted by the findings of both governmental bodies, despite the fact that the latter referred to the organization as Cosa Nostra.

Puzo, however, brought the characters to life so well that people came to view his book as fact. When the movie was released, it carried the stereotyping process one step further. People could now see how members of the Mafia acted, dressed, ate, joked around, killed, and even made love. The secret society was now exposed, and people lined up for hours at theater box offices to get a glimpse of what life is like in the Mafia. Indeed, from what people have told me, they were thrilled. However, what soon became apparent to me was that, in discussing both the movie and the book, people were not viewing them as fictional but as an actual description of syndicated crime in the United States. Indeed, a very respectable public official from New York told me that a mayor of a major U.S. city refused to believe in the Mafia until he read *The Godfather*.

At this point, it is appropriate to mention the personal experiences I have encountered as a result of having written my book. My most bizarre experiences occurred during a three-day period I spent autographing my book, which was being sold by an ethnic civic organization during the Italian ethnic festival in Detroit in 1972. This allowed me to talk with hundreds of people, who took this opportunity to ask me questions about the book. The questions, attitudes, insults, and other reactions of these people gave me added insight into the American public's conception and level of knowledge concerning syndicated crime.

Many people asked me if I was a member of the Mafia. When I answered no, many of them questioned how I could consider myself qualified to write a book on the topic. These people almost inevitably cited *The Godfather* as their source of information. I pointed out in several of these discussions that *The Godfather* was a novel, to which the reply was that Puzo "had to write it that way," otherwise they (the Mafia) would have killed him. One person said that he knew that both Puzo and I had been paid off by the Mafia. I remarked that his observation was interesting, considering that Puzo's book portrayed the existence of a Mafia, whereas I was arguing the exact opposite. This contradiction at first appeared to bother him, but soon he resolved the issue with the following observation: "Oh, I've got it now. Of course, that is really smart on the part of the Mafia. They pay Puzo to say that there is one and then turn around and pay you to say that there isn't one. That way they keep everyone confused." He walked away happy with his new discovery. Some people were less indirect and polite in their approach. One person called me "an idiot," saying that all I was trying to do was vindicate the Italians. I pointed out to him that several non-Italian writers had also questioned the existence of the Mafia. He replied, "What the hell would they know about it if they aren't Italian?" I soon learned that it didn't make any difference what argument I presented, there was always a counter argument, despite the fact that the logic at times was low-keyed. It seemed that people resented my questioning not only something they believed in but a phenomenon they seemed to like. This included individuals in the Italian community. One Italian-American expressed his belief in the following interesting statement: "Why do you want to say that there isn't a Mafia? Look, it's the only thing we've got. If these cake-eaters respect us at all, it's because they know that we can dump them in the river. Take away that and the Italians will really be dirt."

The height of paranoia was evidenced in the reaction of one man who bought a copy of the book. Caught in the crowd, he stopped momentarily in front of the booth, where he was asked by one of the salespersons if he wished to buy a copy. It was obvious that he interpreted this question as a threat, as if he were really being told, "Buy it or else." The man's hands were trembling as he gave the book salesperson the money. This fear was further evidenced when it came time for me to autograph the book. Feeling sorry for him and feeling that I was correctly apraising his reaction, I asked him if he really wanted to buy the book. He immediately replied, "Yes, it's O.K. Yes." I then asked him his name, as I did everyone whose copy I autographed. At this point he appeared utterly traumatized. He then asked me if it was necessary for me to know his name. I said no but explained that the autograph would be more personal if it included his name. He then said "Frank," only to change it to "Charlie" and again to "Tony" in a matter of seconds. I don't remember which name I finally used, as I realized that I was only torturing the poor fellow by keeping him there. He took the book and disappeared into the crowd as though he had been involved in some criminal conspiracy.

The major lesson I learned from talking to these people was that their factual knowledge of syndicated crime was limited to what they read in the newspapers and primarily to their having read *The Godfather* or seen the movie. Most of them did not seem to be as interested in arguments that contradicted their belief as in repeating their own beliefs. When faced with the contradictions in their thinking, rather than examining these contradictions, they simply turned to insult, walked away, or repeated their original belief. Indeed, I saw the same characteristics in the format of these discussions as in those between individuals arguing over religion.

A belief in a secret society allows people to think virtually whatever they please. It allows them to settle any contradiction by simply arguing, "We do not know everything about how the society works." Yet, without knowing everything, it is surprising how much they profess to know about it. What amazes me is that the very newspaper and magazine stories that tell us that the Mafia is "a secret society" are the ones that then go on to give us the names of the bosses, a full description of the rules and ceremonies, and photographs of the major leaders. The Mafia has served to provide entertainment and excitement for a public that, from what I have observed, is not fearful of its existence, as many writers have argued, but rather wants to believe in it. As one person puts it, "Seriously now, it would be a great feeling to have a Godfather. You can turn over all your troubles to him knowing that you will always be protected. Seriously, it's cool. I just wish I had one."

This illusion is maintained because the public's conception of the Mafia is based on that of the journalist, who in many cases gives the public what it wants. The DeCavalcante tapes, which have been offered as proof of the existence of Cosa Nostra reveal, as Kempton has shown, a mass of evidence that directly contradicts the journalist's and public's glorified conception of the status and power of its members.[16]

I hope this chapter has allowed others to share in the experiences I have had in writing a book on a topic that I thought was scientific in nature, only to find that it was somewhat akin to attacking religious dogma. As a social scientist, I have come to appreciate that, when faced with criticism, one can and must rely on the validity of his or her data. I have presented findings in terms of my interpretation of the data. I do not profess to have the truth, as, in scientific inquiry, one can never speak of absolute truth. All I can say is that I have reported in my book a conception of syndicated crime based on my analysis of this phenomenon. Since then, other works have been published that demonstrate that syndicated crime is a phenomenon that can be empirically studied. My work, along with these, served to take away the mysticism and fear that have kept researchers away from this area of study for so long. If my book made this contribution, along with giving some insight into the essence of the basic structure of syndicated crime in America, then I feel that it has contributed to the literature. Personally, writing the book has served another function—it has helped me learn a great deal about the real needs of American society.

Notes

1. Joseph L. Albini, *The American Mafia: Genesis of a Legend* (New York: Appleton-Century-Crofts, 1971; New York: Naiburg Publishing Corporation, distributor).

2. John F. Galliher and James A. Cain, "Citation Support for the Mafia Myth in Criminology Textbooks," *The American Sociologist* (May 1974).

3. Donald R. Cressey, *Theft of the Nation* (New York: Harper and Row, 1969), p. x.

4. Gordon Hawkins, "God and the Mafia," *The Public Interest,* No. 14 (Winter 1969); Albini, *The American Mafia,* chapter 6.

5. John A. Gardiner, "The Stern Syndicate," in *The Crime Establishment,* ed. John E. Conklin (Englewood Cliffs, N.J.: Prentice-Hall, 1973), pp. 159–175.

6. Gene Friedman, "Crime Fighters Zero in on Us," *Reading Times,* 15 May 1967, p. 1.

7. Gardiner, "The Stern Syndicate," p. 164, footnote 6.

8. Ibid.

9. John Finlator, *The Drugged Nation* (New York: Simon and Schuster, 1973), chapter 10; *The Heroin Trail* (New York: Signet, 1974); "Clamp Down on Hashish Racket," *The Overseas Hindustan Times* (New Delhi), February 28, 1970, p. 2; "16 Detroit Police Accused as FBI Raids Betting Ring," *The Detroit News,* 16 May 1971, p. 6–A.

10. Lawrence John Redlinger and Jerry B. Michel, "Ecological Variations in Heroin Abuse," *The Sociological Quarterly* 11(Spring 1970):219–229.

11. Francis A.J. Ianni, *A Family Business: Kinship and Social Control in Organized Crime* (New York: Russell Sage, 1972); W.J. Chambliss, "Vice, Corruption, Bureaucracy, and Power," *Wisconsin Law Review* 1971: 1050–1173.

12. Cressey, *Theft of a Nation,* pp. 250–251.

13. Albini, *The American Mafia,* p. 178.

14. Mario Puzo, *The Godfather Papers and Other Confessions* (New York: G.P. Putnam's Sons, 1973), p. 35.

15. Ibid., p. 36.

16. Murray Kempton, "Crime Does Not Pay," *The New York Review of Books,* 11 September 1969, pp. 6–8.

11 Recent Developments in White-Collar-Crime Theory and Research

Diane Vaughan

Sociological interest in white-collar crime can be bracketed into two distinct periods. These periods are distinguished from each other not only by time but also by focus. The initial period, from 1940 to the early 1960s, has been called the classic core of white-collar crime investigation.[1]

This classic period of inquiry was intitated by Sutherland's introduction of the concept of white-collar crime in his 1939 presidential address to the American Sociological Society.[2] Despite early criticisms of the expansion of the concept of crime beyond the criminal law,[3] Sutherland's statements had considerable appeal and stimulated attempts at conceptual refinements. There was general agreement that Sutherland's contribution was remarkable. However, his definition was inherently ambiguous and it inhibited, rather than facilitated, research. In addition, by emphasizing the characteristics of the individual offender, Sutherland's definition turned attention away from the organization as violator. Although attempts to refine his concept of white-collar crime were many and varied, no single solution to the problem brought consensus within the discipline.

The dominant theoretical perspective of the classical period was Sutherland's differential association, which was tested by Sutherland himself as well as by Clinard, Cressey, Lane, and Quinney.[4] By the end of the classical period, relatively little empirical support existed for the differential-association perspective, although it did draw attention to the importance of learning certain values and norms, as well as techniques and motives. However, another aspect of Sutherland's theoretical perspective frequently has been overlooked. Sutherland proposed the concept of differential social organization as a complementary concept to differential association.[5] Cressey pointed out that Sutherland was concerned not only with the processes by which one becomes criminal but also with organizing and integrating the factual information about crime rates.[6] Behind differential social organization lay the notion of inconsistent standards of conduct, creating strains for crime. Both differential association and differential social organization, then, could be used to account for variations in rates of crimes between or within social organizations.[7]

Portions of this chapter appeared in Diane Vaughan, "Crime between Organizations: A Case Study of Medicaid Provider Fraud" (Ph.D. dissertation, The Ohio State University, 1979).

Although Sutherland's emphasis on the importance of social organization was obscured by his emphasis on differential association, the issue of social structure gradually began appearing in the theoretical efforts of others. The influence of social structure was acknowledged by recognition of norm and value conflict within and between groups. Aubert, for example, demonstrated that businessmen face contradictory values and norms: a universalistic obligation as a citizen to obey the law and a particularistic obligation as a businessman to avoid only the most blatant offenses and to resist the law whenever possible. They condemn violation of the law in general, but they also justify violations in certain situations.[8] Quinney found that the structure of the occupation produced differential orientations to law violation. Although business values, in general, conflict with universalistic social obligations, occupational role organization can restrain or encourage violation of the law by businessmen.[9]

Although the work of Aubert, Quinney, and others began to point to the relation between structure and illegal behavior, the importance of the organization itself had not yet been explored. The classic period of inquiry offered nothing further in elaborated theory, other than indications by many that the problem extended beyond the social class of the offender. No definitive theory emerged.

The research of the period reflected the amorphous nature of knowledge at the time. Empirical studies groped for some kind of theoretical integration and cumulative insight. Researchers were preoccupied with determining the extent of violations and possible explanations. They examined particular industries or violations of particular laws, resulting in interesting findings in discrete areas but little integration. If any consistency could be found in the research that emerged, it lay in several attempts to test Sutherland's theoretical perspectives. Another common factor was found in several studies examining violations of regulations related to World War II.

Limited access to data was a serious handicap. A high degree of ingenuity was required to secure any information on the topic. Researchers relied heavily on public documents on corporate crime. Important sources of data were the administrative agencies responsible for the enforcement of wartime programs, such as rationing and rent controls. These agencies collected data on violations, which in many instances became public information and therefore were accessible to sociologists. Because of the sensitivity of the subject matter, interview data were seldom available for studies of corporate violations. Given the limited extent of conceptual and theoretical development, and inherent difficulties in empirical work on white-collar crime, the amount of research carried out during the classical period is significant in its own right.

At the close of this period, conceptual development was still in its rudimentary stages, theoretical integration had not been achieved, and research efforts were directed toward the specific rather than the general. However, these are the admitted marks of an emergent interest area. The beginning boundaries were just being established, the dilemmas just being defined. Despite the existence of controversy, or perhaps because of it, the ultimate ramification of Sutherland's presidential address of 1939 was the establishment of white-collar crime as a field of study. Twenty years of scholarly inquiry had followed.

New Trends: From White-Collar Crime to Organizational Crime

Despite promising beginnings, the momentum of these first two decades did not carry into the 1960s. The classical period was followed by a nearly ten-year hiatus, during which inquiry was practically abandoned. In the 1970s, however, interest revived. Not only did scholars reassess the classical work, but contributions were made through research advances and the development of a macroanalytic framework, which emphasized the relation between this form of crime and the social structure.

Although the linkage between social structure and deviance is a persistent theme in the literature, the traditional explanations have been directed at individual crime and deviance.[10] Recent work, however, indicates a shift to the structural level of analysis in studying the crime and deviance of organizations as well. The early focus on the social status of the offender[11] has given way to an emergent paradigm based on macrolevel concepts. This is not new, however. The roots lie in Sutherland's earlier emphasis on differential social organization,[12] Quinney's and Lane's on occupational structure,[13] Aubert's on social structure and values,[14] and Reiss's on the relation between individual and organizational deviance.[15] What *is* new is that a consensus seems to be growing for the structural approach. Although individual researchers are investigating divergent topics, the structural orientation provides a common thread.

It is this structural orientation that distinguishes this new period from the classical period of inquiry. However, as work continues, issues related to definition and theory remain controversial. In fact, the characteristics of the classical period are still applicable: conceptual development is in its rudimentary stages, theoretical integration has not been achieved, and research efforts are directed toward the specific rather than the general. Nevertheless, one fact is clear. Sociologists are developing a framework for the study of the crime and deviance of organizations. Appropriately, we are witnessing the creation of the macrolevel tools necessary for the understanding of a macrolevel phenomenon. This trend is observable in the conceptualization, theoretical perspectives, and research that have appeared since the beginning of the 1970s.

Conceptual Definitions

The first attempt at conceptual definition in the 1970s was by Edelhertz, who renamed white-collar crime "economic crime," in an effort to move from

Sutherland's emphasis on the actor to an emphasis on the act itself.[16] The Edelhertz definition, the first attempt at conceptualization in nearly a decade, had great impact in stimulating thought. Although it offered no basis for conjecture as to the structural influences on the behavior in question, it reemphasized the conceptual problems in Sutherland's work. Other attempts at reconceptualization followed. However, rather than focusing on the nature of the act, as Edelhertz did, subsequent efforts began to note the importance of structure.

Pepinsky first pointed to the importance of structural influences when he redefined white-collar crime as exploitation.[17] With this conceptual definition, he noted that research could investigate structural conditions that result in exploitation or its elimination. Soon after, Meier, objecting to Sutherland's atomism, addressed the conceptual distinctions between white-collar crime, occupational crime, and corporate crime.[18] Since occupational crime, as defined by Quinney, can be an act of individuals of either high or low socioeconomic status, white-collar crime is but one form of occupational crime.[19] Whereas occupational crime is committed by individuals in the course of their occupation, Meier noted that corporate crime is the behavior of groups of persons, organized in common purpose. These groups of persons can be termed *organizations*.[20]

Shover further developed the concept of organizational crime as

> criminal acts committed by individuals or groups of individuals, thus including conspiracies, during the normal course of their work as employees of organizations, which they intend to contribute to the achievement of goals or other objectives thought to be important for the organization as a whole, or some subunit within the organization, or their own particular job duties.[21]

Shover also addressed Quinney's concept of occupational crime. Shover believed that organizational crime and occupational crime exist as two very distinct types of phenomena; he suggested that "occupational crime" should be used to denote violations by the self-employed that occur in the course of occupational activity and that those committed by employees of formal organizations should be considered "organizational crime."[22]

Shrager and Short developed the concept of organizational crime in ways that both paralleled and diverged from Shover. Organizational crime was defined as

> the illegal acts of omission or commission of an individual or a group of individuals in a legitimate formal organization in accordance with the operative goals of the organization, which have a serious physical or economic impact on employees, consumers, or the general public.[23]

This definition is consistent with Shover's in its emphasis on individuals or groups within organizations and the linkage with organizational objectives. The definitions differ in that Shover gives wider variability to types of organizational goals that may be relevant, while Shrager and Short include illegal acts of omission and emphasize harm.

Still another definition aims at distinguishing deviance committed *by* organizations from deviance committed *in* organizations. Sherman suggests that the former is a "collective rule-breaking" action that helps achieve organizational goals, while deviance committed *in* an organization is "individual or collective rule-breaking action that does not help to achieve organizational goals, or that is harmful to those goals."[24] However, as Sherman himself notes, the difficulty lies in determining what the operative goals of the dominant coalition are at a given point in time.[25]

The most recent effort at conceptual definition that facilitates macrolevel analysis of the phenomenon is that of Biderman and Reiss.[26] Although they reject the term *organizational crime* in favor of "white-collar violations," the influence of structural factors is nevertheless made explicit. White-collar violations are

> those violations of law to which penalties are attached that involve the use of a violator's position of significant power, influence, or trust in the legitimate economic or political institutional order for the purpose of illegal gain, or to commit an illegal act for personal or organizational gain.[27]

According to this definition, the violator may be an individual, a group of individuals, or an organization. By emphasizing the violator's "position of significant power, influence, or trust in the legitimate economic or political institutional order," Reiss and Biderman have eliminated the former distinction between organizational and occupational crime, while designating organized crime as falling outside this area of inquiry. Although agreement has not been reached on the definitional problem, structural elements consistently have been included in the work of these sociologists who have grappled with defining the concept over the last decade.

Theoretical Perspectives

Although no formal theory has achieved consensus, three efforts of the present period move toward the development of theoretical frameworks that emphasize the structural elements of the phenomenon. Ermann and Lundman have developed an "organizational deviance" framework.[28] They begin with the assumption that "the recurrent patterns of behavior we call organizations somehow contribute to the occurrence of actions publicly and consensually considered as deviant." Thus, for sociologists, a major task should be to "focus on those acts that have come to be publicly recognized as deviant, and on the processes by which they become labeled and controlled."[29] To facilitate this, Ermann and

Lundman have devised a framework by which an act can be considered organizational deviance. The criteria are as follows:

1. The act must be contrary to norms maintained by others outside the organization.
2. The act must be supported by the internal operating norms of the organization that conflict with the organization's formal goals.
3. New members of an organization must be socialized to accept rationalizations and justifications that support action contrary to external norms.
4. To be organizational deviance, as opposed to individual deviance, the action of an individual must have peer support from fellow workers. This support may be passive or active.
5. Organizationally deviant acts must have support from the dominant administrative coalition of the organization. This support, too, may be passive or active.[30]

Ermann and Lundman's framework offers two advantages: (1) study of the crime of organizations is promoted, also allowing investigation of corporate acts that are defined as deviant but not yet sanctioned by law; and (2) the role of organizational processes, as well as their structure, is emphasized and legitimated as a subject for research.

Clark and Hollinger's theoretical approach emphasizes the importance of normative systems.[31] Clark and Hollinger agree with Ermann and Lundmann that the concept of deviance has more merit than the exclusive focus on criminal behavior. However, their theoretical framework is based on occupational deviance, building on the earlier work by Quinney. In their research on employee theft, Clark and Hollinger note the existence of a relationship between normative systems and occupational deviance. They recognize four normative systems operating in the work setting as sources of occupational rules: (1) society, (2) the formal work organization, (3) the occupational association, and (4) the work-group subculture. Often, these normative systems are in conflict, producing differing interpretations of whether a given act is an example of deviance or conformity. Occupational crime occurs when a normative incongruity exists between society's criminal law and one or more of the other three normative systems.

Sherman supports the construction of integrated sets of propositions as the necessary next step in building a theory of organizational deviance.[32] He suggests we begin by addressing particular problems, thus generating middle-range theories, and sets forth the following propositions to explain why some organizations adopt deviant goals:

1. Organizations that depend on other organizations for survival are vulnerable to the preferences those other organizations have for the organization's operative goals.

2. Internal or organizational coalitions derive power from supporting the preferences of outside organizations on which the organization depends for survival.
3. The more powerful the internal coalition, the more likely it is to prevail in the setting of operative goals.
4. Therefore, when outside organizations on which an organization depends prefer that the organization not adopt deviant goals, the less likely it is that the dominant coalition will adopt such goals.[33]

Research

Research interests since the 1970s in many ways duplicate the characteristics of the classic period. Although an overall examination clearly reveals the development of an organizational paradigm through increased interest in selected structural explanatory variables, an enormous amount of work also has been done that either builds on research of the classic period or explores heretofore unresearched topics. For example, research on attitudes toward white-collar crime (following the work of Newman) has been conducted by Reed and Reed, Vaughan and Carlo, Scott and Al-Thakeb, and Shrager and Short.[34] Similarly, Cressey's embezzlement study has been succeeded by research on internal theft. For example, Clark and Hollinger's research generated data on the broader topic of employee deviance against the formal work organization.[35] In one innovative expansion of Cressey's early work, Edelhertz and Walsh have undertaken research on the theft of nuclear secrets.[36]

A new research interest, without foundation in the classical period, concerns victims of white-collar crime.[37] Other recent work has examined particular types of violations,[38] the relation of law to specific behavior,[39] and white-collar crime as it occurs in other countries.[40] In addition, researchers are continuing to investigate individuals as offenders—their prosecution, defense, and sentencing.[41]

However, the shift to a macroanalytic framework is apparent in the increasing focus on the organization as the unit of analysis. The body of work that is emerging follows the holistic model suggested by organizational theorists, who note the importance of studying not only the organization but also the environment in which organizations exist.[42] The beginnings of this orientation in criminology can be noted in the work of Conklin and Gross.[43] The relevance of the variables suggested by these two authors has been confirmed in recent case studies by Carson, Kramer, Vaughan, and Stone.[44] In addition, many efforts have been directed toward model building by testing selected factors, in both the organization and the environment, that may predict illegal organizational behavior.

In examining the relationships between organizational characteristics and illegal behavior, researchers have frequently focused on the financial performance of the firm. In a sample of firms involved in trade litigation, Staw and Szwajkowski examined the relationship between a firm's economic well-being and its trade violations, such as price discrimination, monopoly, and price fixing.[45] The results indicated an inverse relationship between financial performance and illegal behavior. This finding was confirmed by Asch and Seneca, who found that poor profit performance by firms increased the probability of illegal collusive behavior.[46] Perez, however, in his study of 1,000 industrial corporations, found that profitability was not significantly related to antitrust and other trade-practice violations.[47] Clinard and his associates, investigating enforcement actions initiated by the federal government against the 582 largest publicly owned corporations, found that performance was only slightly associated with violations of the law; the effects were small, but in the hypothesized direction.[48]

Another organizational characteristic that has been frequently tested for its hypothesized relationship to illegal behavior is firm size. In the work of Asch and Seneca, a positive relationship was found between firm size and the commission of antitrust violations.[49] Perez and Salancik found a similar relationship between size and illegal behavior.[50] In the research conducted by Clinard and his colleagues, however, the findings appear to vary with the way in which the data were grouped. Individual firm size did not have the hypothesized relationship with violations.[51] However, when measured in terms of violations per unit size of the firm, larger firms tended to commit more total violations of all types.[52] Moreover, the researchers state:

> When violations are considered in terms of number per unit size, firm size is found to have no additional effects for all but one type of violation, and for manufacturing violations is relatively strongly related in the direction opposite that predicted. That is, the results indicate that, generally, large firms do not have more violations per unit size than do small firms. For manufacturing violations, the results show that while larger firms have more total violations, they have fewer infractions per unit size than do smaller firms.[53]

Although financial performance and firm size have been the organizational characteristics most frequently tested in the research conducted since the beginning of the 1970s, other organizational factors have been examined as well: market power, growth rate, capital invested abroad, relative firm dominance,[54] firm longevity,[55] and firm diversification.[56] In addition, researchers have attempted to sort out the influence of the environment on illegal organizational behavior. The variable most frequently tested is industry concentration. In every case, research has confirmed a positive relationship between industry concentration and illegal behavior.[57] However, Asch and Seneca found that the relationship varied with the type of industry: a positive relationship between industry concentration and collusive behavior in the consumer-goods industry; a negative relationship between industry concentration and collusive behavior in the producer-goods industry.[58]

While other research has investigated the influence of individual environmental factors, such as inelasticity of demand,[59] industry financial performance, and industry growth rate,[60] some studies have focused on the relationship between the organization and the environment. Perez, for example, examined joint ventures and interlocking corporate affiliations as relational characteristics that influence illegal organizational behavior.[61] In addition, Salancik, studying affirmative-action compliance among defense contracting firms, tested the interdependence of the firms and the government as the independent variable.[62]

An overall evaluation of these empirical attempts to verify factors in organizations and their environments that contribute to illegal behavior would clearly be premature. However, a summary description is not out of order. Many variables suggested in the literature have not yet been tested. For those that have, the research exhibits wide variability in industry, violations, enforcing agency, and organizational and environmental variables examined. In addition, there are methodological limitations: sampling is limited to enforcement actions, and operational definitions do not have proven construct validity. Because of these complicating factors, findings are noncomparable.

Clinard and his associates, at the beginning of their report, suggest that, if all or the same set of predicting variables apply to all types of violators, a single causal framework may be indicated. However, if different predictors are relevant for different violations, the concept of illegal organizational behavior may be multidimensional and may require the elaboration of a broad theoretical structure or differentiated structures.[63] Their investigation of firm and industry structure yielded mixed results. In general, except for manufacturing violations, measures of firm and industry characteristics were not strong predictors of corporate violations.[64]

Considering the conceptual and theoretical support for the influence or organizational and environmental factors on the behavior of organizations, these scattered and sometimes contradictory empirical findings may not yet warrant any conclusions about possible theoretical formulations. The findings may simply indicate that the study of organizational crime and deviance is still in its theoretical and methodological infancy.

Notes

1. Gilbert Geis and Robert F. Meier, eds., *White-Collar Crime: Offenses in Business, Politics, and the Professions* (New York: Free Press, 1977).

2. Edwin H. Sutherland, "White-Collar Criminality," *American Sociological Review* 5 (1940).

3. See, for example, Paul W. Tappan, "Crime and the Criminal," *Federal Probation* 11(1947):41–44; Paul W. Tappan, "Who is the Criminal?" *American Sociological Review* 12(1947):96–102; Robert G. Caldwell, "A Re-examination

of the Concept of White-Collar Crime," *Federal Probation* 22(1958):30–36; E.W. Burgess, "Comment," *American Sociological Review* 56(1950):32–34.

    4. Edwin H. Sutherland, *White-Collar Crime* (New York: Dryden Press, 1949); Marshall B. Clinard, *The Black Market* (New York: Rinehart, 1952); Donald R. Cressey, "Application and Verification of the Differential Association Theory," *Journal of Criminal Law, Criminology, and Police Science* 43 (1952):43–52; Robert A. Lane, "Why Businessmen Violate the Law," *Journal of Criminal Law and Criminology* 44(1953):151–165; Earl R. Quinney, "Occupational Structure and Criminal Behavior: Prescription Violation by Retail Pharmacists," *Social Problems* 11(1963):179–185.

    5. Sutherland, "White-Collar Criminality," p. 12.

    6. Edwin H. Sutherland, "Development of the Theory," in *The Sutherland Papers*, ed. Albert Cohen et al. (Bloomington: Indiana University Press, 1956), pp. 13–29.

    7. Richard Quinney, "The Study of White-Collar Crime: Toward a Reorientation in Theory and Research," in Geis and Meier, *White-Collar Crime*, p. 291.

    8. Vilhelm Aubert, "White-Collar Crime and Social Structure," *American Journal of Sociology* 58(1952):263–271.

    9. Quinney, "Occupational Structure and Criminal Behavior," pp. 179–185.

    10. See, for example, Robert K. Merton, "Social Structure and Anomie" and "Continuities in the Theory of Social Structure and Anomie," in *Social Theory and Social Structure* (Glencoe: The Free Press, 1957); and Emile Durkheim, *Suicide* (Glencoe: The Free Press, 1951).

    11. Sutherland, "Development of the Theory."

    12. Ibid., p. 9.

    13. Quinney, "Occupational Structure and Criminal Behavior"; Lane, "Why Businessmen Violate the Law."

    14. Aubert, "White-Collar Crime and Social Structure."

    15. Albert J. Reiss, Jr., "The Study of Deviant Behavior: Where the Action Is," *Ohio Valley Sociologist* 32(1966):60–66.

    16. Herbert Edelhertz, "The Nature, Impact, and Prosecution of White-Collar Crime" (Washington, D.C.: National Institute of Law Enforcement and Criminal Justice, U.S. Department of Justice, Law Enforcement Assistance Administration, 1970), p. 3.

    17. Harold E. Pepinsky, "From White-Collar Crime to Exploitation: Redefinition of a Field," *Journal of Criminal Law and Criminology* 65(1974): 225–233.

    18. Robert F. Meier, "Corporate Crime as Organizational Behavior" (Paper presented at American Society of Criminology Annual Meeting, Toronto, 30 October–2 November 1975).

    19. Quinney, "Occupational Structure and Criminal Behavior."

    20. Meier, "Corporate Crime as Organizational Behavior," p. 4.

    21. Neal Shover, "Defining Organizational Crime," in *Corporate and*

Governmental Deviance: Problems of Organizational Behavior in Contemporary Society, ed. M. David Ermann and Richard J. Lundman (New York: Oxford University Press, 1978), p. 39.

22. Ibid., p. 40.

23. Laura Shill Shrager and James F. Short, Jr., "Toward a Sociology of Organizational Crime," *Social Problems* 25(1978):407–419.

24. Lawrence W. Sherman, *Scandal and Reform: Controlling Police Corruption* (Berkeley: University of California Press, 1978), pp. 4–5.

25. Lawrence W. Sherman, "A Theoretical Strategy for Organizational Deviance" (Paper presented at Conference on White-Collar and Economic Crime, International Scoiological Association, Potsdam, New York, February 1980), p. 9.

26. Albert Biderman and Albert J. Reiss, Jr., "Definitions and Criteria for Selection of Prospective Federal Sources on White-Collar Crime Data," Report No. 1. Grant No. 78-NI-AX-0132 (Washington, D.C.: National Institute of Law Enforcement and Criminal Justice, U.S. Department of Justice, Law Enforcement Assistance Administration, 1979).

27. Ibid.

28. M. David Ermann and Richard J. Lundman, eds., *Corporate and Governmental Deviance: Problems of Organizational Behavior in Contemporary Society* (New York: Oxford University Press, 1978), p. 18.

29. Ibid., p. 17.

30. Ibid., pp. 7–9.

31. John P. Clark and Richard Hollinger, "On the Feasibility of Empirical Studies of 'White-Collar Crime' " (Paper presented at American Society of Criminology Annual Meeting, Tucson, 4–7 November 1976), p. 9.

32. Sherman, "A Theoretical Strategy for Organizational Deviance."

33. Ibid., pp. 23–24.

34. John P. Reed and Robin S. Reed, " 'Doctor, Lawyer, Indian Chief': Old Rhymes and New on White-Collar Crime," *International Journal of Criminology and Penology* 3(1975):279–293; Diane Vaughan and Giovanna Carlo, "Victims of Fraud: Victim-Responsiveness, Incidence, and Reporting," in *Victims and Society*, ed. Emilio Viano (Washington, D.C.: Visage Press, 1976), pp. 403–412; Joseph E. Scott and Fahad Al-Thakeb, "The Public's Perceptions of Crime: Scandinavia, Western Europe, the Middle East and the United States," in *Contemporary Corrections: Social Control and Conflict*, ed. C. Ronald Huff (Beverly Hills: Sage, 1977), pp. 78–88; Laura Shill Schrager and James F. Short, Jr., "How Serious a Crime? Perceptions of Organizational and Common Crimes," in *White-Collar Crime: Theory and Research*, ed. Gilbert Geis and Ezra Stotland (Beverly Hills: Sage, 1980), pp. 14–31.

35. Clark and Hollinger, "On the Feasibility of Empirical Studies of 'White-Collar Crime.' "

36. Herbert Edelhertz and Marilyn Walsh, *The White-Collar Challenge to Nuclear Safeguards* (Lexington, Mass.: Lexington Books, D.C. Heath and Company, 1978).

37. Gilbert Geis, "Victimization Patterns in White Collar Crime," in *Victimology: A New Focus. Volume V, Violence and Its Victims,* ed. Israel Drapkin and Emilio Viano (Lexington, Mass.: Lexington Books, D.C. Heath and Company, 1974), pp. 89–105; Diane Vaughan and Giovanna Carlo, "The Appliance Repairman: A Study of Victim-Responsiveness and Fraud," *Journal of Research in Crime and Delinquency* 12(1975):153–161.

38. Donn B. Parker, "Computer-Related White-Collar Crime," in *White-Collar Crime: Theory and Research,* ed. Gilbert Geis and Ezra Stotland (Beverly Hills: Sage, 1980), pp. 199–221; Michael Maltz and Stephen M. Pollock, "Analyzing Suspected Collusion Among Bidders," Ibid., pp. 174–198; Michael W. Reisman, *Folded Lies: Bribery and Corruption in Multinational Corporations* (New York: Free Press, 1980).

39. W.G. Carson, "The Institutionalization of Ambiguity: Early British Factory Acts," in *White-Collar Crime: Theory and Research,* ed. Gilbert Geis and Ezra Stotland (Beverly Hills: Sage, 1980), pp. 142–173; Neal Shover, "The Criminalization of Corporate Behavior: Federal Surface Coal Mining," Ibid., pp. 98–125.

40. Charles E. Reasons and Colin H. Goff, "Corporate Crime: A Cross National Analysis," Ibid., pp. 126–141.

41. John Hagan, Ilene H. Nagel (Bernstein), and Celesta Albonetti, "The Differential Sentencing of White-Collar Offenders in Ten Federal District Courts," *American Sociological Review* 45(October 1980):802–820. In addition, several projects on white-collar offenders are nearing completion at Yale Law School, under the direction of Professor Stanton Wheeler.

42. William Evan, "The Organization-Set: Toward a Theory of Interorganizational Relations," in *Approaches to Organizational Design,* ed. James D. Thompson (Pittsburgh: University of Pittsburgh Press, 1966), pp. 173–191; F.E. Emery and E.L. Trist, "The Causal Texture of Organizational Environments," *Human Relations* 18(1965):24–36.

43. John E. Conklin, *Illegal but Not Criminal: Business Crime in America* (Englewood Cliffs, N.J.: Prentice-Hall, 1977); Edward Gross, "Organizational Structure and Organizational Crime," in *White-Collar Crime: Theory and Research,* ed. Gilbert Geis and Ezra Stotland (Beverly Hills: Sage, 1980), pp. 52–76.

44. Carson, "The Institutionalization of Ambiguity"; Diane Vaughan, "Crime Between Organizations: Implications for Victimology," in *White-Collar Crime: Theory and Research,* ed. Gilbert Geis and Ezra Stotland (Beverly Hills: Sage, 1980), pp. 77–97; Ronald C. Kramer, "Corporate Crime: An Organizational Perspective" (Paper presented at Conference on White-Collar and Economic Crime, Potsdam, New York, 7 February 1980); Christopher Stone, *Where the Law Ends: The Social Control of Corporate Behavior* (New York: Harper and Row, 1975).

45. Barry M. Staw and Eugene Szwajkowski, "The Scarcity Munificence

Component of Organizational Environments and the Commission of Illegal Acts," *Administrative Science Quarterly* 20(1975):345–354.

46. Peter Asch and J.J. Seneca, "Is Collusion Profitable?" *The Review of Economics and Statistics* 58(February 1976):1–12.

47. Jacob Perez, "Corporate Criminality: A Study of the One-Thousand Largest Industrial Corporations in the U.S.A." (Ph.D. dissertation, University of Pennsylvania, 1978).

48. Marshall B. Clinard, Peter C. Yeager, Jeanne Brissette, David Petroshek, and Elizabeth Harris, *Illegal Corporate Behavior* (Washington, D.C.: U.S. Department of Justice, 1979).

49. Asch and Seneca, "Is Collusion Profitable?"

50. Perez, "Corporate Ciminality"; Gerald Salancik, "The Role of Interdependence in Organizational Responsiveness to Demands from the Environment" (Unpublished manuscript, University of Illinois), cited in Jeffrey Pfeffer and Gerald Salancik, *The External Control of Organizations* (New York: Harper and Row, 1978).

51. Clinard et al., *Illegal Corporate Behavior,* p. 171.

52. Ibid., p. 168.

53. Ibid.

54. Ibid.

55. Perez, "Corporate Criminality."

56. Clinard et al., *Illegal Corporate Behavior;* Perez, "Corporate Criminality."

57. Clinard et al., *Illegal Corporate Behavior;* Asch and Seneca, "Is Collusion Profitable?"; George Hay and Daniel Kelly, "An Empirical Survey of Price-Fixing Conspiracies," *Journal of Law and Economics* 17(1974):13–39; William N. Leonard and Marvin G. Weber, "Automakers and Dealers: A Study of Criminogenic Market Forces," *Law and Society Review* 4(1970):407–424.

58. Asch and Seneca, "Is Collusion Profitable?"

59. Leonard and Weber, "Automakers and Dealers."

60. Clinard et al., *Illegal Corporate Behavior.*

61. Perez, "Corporate Criminality."

62. Salancik, "The Role of Interdependence."

63. Clinard et al., *Illegal Corporate Behavior,* p. 150.

64. Ibid.

12 The Pawnbroker: Banker of the Poor?

Catherine M. Hartnett

In the United States, pawnbroking was a major form of credit for people living in urban centers at the turn of the twentieth century and well into the 1930s. Since that time, the number of pawnshops in American cities has declined steadily. The future of pawnbroking is questionable. For example, there were 300 licensed pawnshops in Ohio in the early 1940s; in January 1978, there were only 74. Will the disappearance of the pawnbroker materially affect the economic scene?

Operating within the legitimate world of finance and in the peripheral world of deviance, the pawnbroker is in a marginal social position. As a financier, he lends money to people who pledge some personal possession as security. As a "poor man's banker," he associates with marginal people who are experiencing money problems. A consequence of this marginality is that the pawnshop and the pawnbroker are usually defined in terms of meanings and values derived from novels, films, and songs that tend to reinforce a stereotype of the pawnbroker as greedy, heartless, and dishonest and of the profession itself as dishonorable. To what extent does this stereotype conform to the real nature and true character of the pawnbroker?

The pawnbroker has a reputation for trafficking in and being a receiver of stolen goods. If the alleged relationship between fencing and pawnbroking is accurate, it would seem reasonable that the incredible increase in burglary, robbery, and larceny in recent years would be reflected in a corresponding increase in the number of pawnshops or at least in the volume of pawning activity. The fact that there is an increase in crimes against property and a decrease in the number of pawnshops challenges the assumption that the pawnshop is mostly a cover for fencing operations involving stolen goods.

Since the pawnbroker has never been a subject of sociological analysis, an empirical investigation of this occupation seemed warranted to answer the foregoing questions and to distinguish fact from fiction regarding individuals engaged in this occupation.

In order to answer the questions, multiple methods were employed in a three-year study of pawnbroking. The historical method was utilized to trace the origin of pawnbroking and the restraints that society has imposed on this practice. Next, a qualitative investigation of all the pawnshops in a large midwestern city was conducted to observe the interaction of pawnbrokers with others: customers, pawnshop detectives, police officers, crime victims, state licensing officials, and journalists. Finally, a systematic documentation of pawn-shop cards at the central police station was employed to determine the patterns of all pawning activities of a large midwestern city for a two-month period. The conclusions in this chapter represent only part of a complete analysis of data gathered.

Development of Pawnbroking

There is no record of the first pawnbroker or the original pawnshop. It is known that the system of pledging personal effects as security for loans has existed since ancient days. Patterson maintains that the pawnshop was the progenitor of the present banking system.[1] He argues that the constant taking of articles in pledge required their safekeeping to secure the repayment of a loan and no doubt led to the deposit of money and valuables in the safe places provided by pawnbrokers.

The Code of Hammurabi is the oldest extant record of man's attempt to maintain order through law.[2] Several sections of the code provide insight into the pawning activities in ancient Babylonia. The laws reveal an acceptance of interest on loans, the protection of creditors under the law, an unfavorable attitude toward debtors, and harsh punishment imposed on the receiver of stolen property. Roman codes also contain references to pledging as a recognized business practice. According to Thomas, the Roman contract of *pignus* referred to the pledging of an object as security for a debt.[3] From early times, it was customary to agree that, if a debt was not paid by an agreed date, the creditor would be entitled to sell the pledge. In later classical law, revisions were made to the effect that a creditor's selling privilege was limited. When an item was sold, any excess over the creditor's due had to be transferred to the debtor. There is no doubt that when the German tribes invaded the Roman Empire, they assimilated the principles and practices of Roman law along with other aspects of culture. The original Goths were tribesmen with little experience in com-mercial matters. Nevertheless, the Visigothic Code, compiled in the seventh century, exemplifies the extent to which the German tribes were influenced by Roman law. Sections of this code relating to articles pledged as security for debts and association with thieves are similar to those in Roman law. Thus, the foundation for the norms associated with pledging personal property were firmly set in ancient days. The need for a written document, specifying the time and manner of repayment of a loan, and the need to control against the acceptance of stolen articles as pledges were as necessary in the days of antiquity as they are in contemporary times.

Although pledging was a universal practice in ancient days, it was condemned by some religious leaders on moral principles. In both the Old and New Testaments one finds negative attitudes expressed toward the practice of charging interest on loans. The turning point in the history of pawnbroking came during the medieval period of Western European civilization. Pawnbroking was opposed by theologians and scholars on the grounds that it was contrary to the ideal of justice. Various restrictions were imposed to limit the extension of this practice. Harsh as the penalties were for those who participated in this activity, it would appear that ecclesiastical injunctions could not regulate morality in commercial matters. Pawnbroking continued because there was a demand for the services rendered by the pawnbroker to the inhabitants of the urban areas. If the work of scholars is to be taken at face value, it would appear that medieval communities were unconcerned with the financially distressed and those who assisted them. For the most part, historical accounts reflect the scholastic interpretation, which was consistently opposed to pawnbroking. Christian merchants either would not or could not satisfy the demands of the urban citizens for credit; therefore, Lombards and Jews were licensed by various communities to service the needy, since these men were not encumbered by Christian scruples. The pawnbrokers were perceived as "public sinners" and became convenient scapegoats for the many problems of society. Toward the end of the medieval period, the Franciscans in Italy established the *Montes Pietatis,* which were charitable pawnshops with low interest charges for loans. Eventually, the *Montes Pietatis* became public pawnshops, operated by the local municipality, and these institutions spread to other European cities, where they may still be found servicing the urban residents.

Though remaining ideologically opposed to the idea of interest, the public pawnshop represented an easing of the ecclesiastical position regarding interest. The extent to which the legacy of religious bigotry generated by ecclesiastical authorities toward the pawnbroker is still a part of the American biblical heritage is not known; however, it may be assumed that part of the failure of pawnbrokers to achieve more than a marginal social status in this secular age is somehow associated with the idea of "public sinner" from medieval times.

In the modern age, pawnbroking has been differentiated along class lines. Certain pawnshops cater to the working class and are known as the industrial trade, while others cater to the middle and upper classes and are referred to as the city trade. The bulk of the pawnbroking trade is with the working class, who live in the central city. The extension of easy credit terms to working-class individuals through credit cards, charge accounts, and other forms has impinged on the pawning business. However, there continues to be a need for pawnshops in large cities to provide loans to individuals who have no established credit but do have some personal item that may be used as a pledge when there is an immediate need for money.

Functions of the Pawnbroker

While observing transactions in the pawnshop, I was impressed by the number of individuals who redeemed their possessions. Gradually, a favorable image of the pawnbroker evolved from the data as an awareness of the various functions he performed for the community became known. A discussion of these functions follows.

First, the pawnbroker functions as a special type of financier in a community. Through his services, an individual may borrow money quickly, with no invasion of his privacy. No investigation is made of the pawner's occupation, credit rating, or purpose for borrowing money. No waiting period is necessary. The pawner receives an amount of money for which he must forfeit, for a time, a personal possession. The borrower has six months to repay the loan. If, after this time period, the pawner does not repay the loan plus interest, he loses the ownership of his possession. However, as long as the pawner pays the monthly interest, for example, $1.75 on a $25 loan, the pawnbroker will keep his possession. Some objects have been in pawn for as long as seven years. Contrasted with other alternatives, such as borrowing from a bank or finance company or selling some personal possession, pawning has certain advantages. When a loan is contracted at a bank or finance company, the amount of debt increases steadily until the loan is repaid. Often, hidden costs and escalating interest rates are included in the amount the borrower must eventually repay. Embarrassment and harassment are often the end result of a friendly loan service from a local finance company. When a personal possession is sold, there is a finality about the transaction. In contrast to borrowing from other financial institutions or outright selling of a possession, pawning has no hidden costs associated with it. Further, the loss of the item is temporary rather than permanent.

Second, the pawnbroker functions as an auxiliary to the police in a community. When the pawnbroker suspects a pawner of possessing stolen merchandise, he employs certain strategies to assist the police in making an arrest. For example, he notes license numbers and immediately calls the pawnshop squad. Police bring mug shots of known or suspected criminals to the pawnshop and request the pawnbroker to be attentive should the suspected individual visit the scene. By means of this type of cooperation, many crimes have been solved.

Closely related to the preceding function is the capacity of the pawnbroker to be a deterrent to crime. Professional thieves do not patronize a pawnshop; novice thieves do. When the daily police report is examined, the novice thief is usually discovered. In those cases in which the novice thief is not detected, the low valuation he receives for his stolen merchandise should discourage him from taking risks for such minimal profit.

Professional thieves know that pawnbrokers will not fence for them. In 1977, undercover fencing operations, known as "stings," were operated by federal government agents in an effort to buy stolen property from thieves, who were later arrested. In July 1977, undercover police in the city where this study was conducted announced that they, too, had operated a fake secondhand store and had recovered $200,000 worth of stolen goods. The brokers expressed the view that these types of operations were successful because word was out among thieves that the places were accepting stolen goods. There is no connection between a sting-type operation and an honest pawnshop, because, in the former, the word is out that one can sell stolen goods, whereas, in the latter, the word is out that stolen goods are reported. A pawnshop detective explained the situation well: "If a person stole something and a broker accepted it as a pawn, he would most likely lose his license if discovered. And sooner or later, he would be discovered. There is no honor among thieves. Thieves in prison have no loyalty to any broker or fence. A thief will squeal on his mother if he thought it would get him out. Here's how the stolen goods get to the shop most of the time. Usually a thief will sell the item to a person in a bar, who then takes it to a shop, unaware, supposedly, that it has been stolen. He gives his correct address; we check his identity and through him the police are led to the regular thieves and their bar connections."

Many other functions are provided by the pawnbroker. He assists in the recovery of stolen goods and thus helps keep theft-insurance rates low. The pawnbroker buys merchandise people no longer want. He sells used goods at a bargain to those who cannot afford new items. He stores valuables for individuals for specific periods of time. And, finally, the pawnbroker enables journalists to write human-interest stories.

Profile of a Typical Pawner

The state law requires that, for every article bought or pawned, a pawnbroker must complete a card that identifies the item and the person who pawns or sells a personal possession. The cards are mailed daily to the intelligence unit of the police department. I examined 3,516 pawnshop cards received by a police department for a two-month period. In addition, I had the opportunity to examine pawnshop books and merchandise while accompanying a pawnshop detective in his routine inspection of pawnshops. When the data from these cards representing the universe of cards for the period were processed and analyzed, the following results were obtained. First, males pawn more than females. It was found that 80 percent of the pawners were male and 20 percent were female.

Second, whites pawn more than blacks; 62 percent of the pawners were white and 38 percent were black. Third, persons under age 30 pawn more than those over 30; the mean age of a pawner was 31, the youngest pawner was 18, and the oldest pawner was 79. Fourth, pawners are distributed over a wide geographic area. Individuals from 103 zip-code areas used the services of the city pawnshops. The majority of pawners live in the "inner belt," an area located in the same or the adjacent zip-code area as the one in which a pawnshop is located. Fifth, it is customary for a pawner to depend on a single personal possession for pawning purposes; less than 5 percent of the customers pawned three or more items at a time. Sixth, the most frequently pawned items are jewelry, guns, and stereos. Seventh, pawnshops depend on regular customers for the operation of their business. Approximately 75 percent of pawn transactions are with regular customers, for whom pawning is a normal, habitual way of borrowing for short periods of time. Finally, the regular customer borrows $25 and is likely to redeem his possession before the loan period has expired.

Although many questions concerning pawners remain unanswered, this study identified the type of person serviced by a community pawnshop. The findings confirm the statements of pawnbrokers that pawnshops service patrons from a wide geographic area, of all ages, all races and both sexes. However, the degree to which pawnshops serve each of these categories is not the same. The young, white male from the central city appears to use the shop most frequently. He is the individual, lacking a credit rating, who finds pawning a convenient means of getting cash. So long as poor, frustrated workers exist in urban centers, there is a need for an available, simple means of obtaining funds in an emergency situation.

Conclusion

Designed to meet the needs of the individual when confronted with a personal financial problem, pawnbroking has faced constraining forces throughout history. In the ancient period, legal and political restraints were imposed on the occupation; in the medieval period, moral and philosophical restraints were attempted; in the modern period, social, psychological, and economic restraints are evident. The consistency of data acquired through the triangulation of data-gathering techniques provided us with the reassurance necessary to confirm the hypothesis that pawnshops are indeed the poor man's banker and are a benefit to a community. It is hoped that this study has succeeded in demythologizing a little-known and long-misunderstood occupation.

Notes

1. W.R. Patterson, "Pawnbroking in Europe and the United States," *Bulletin of the Department of Labor* 21:173–310.

2. C.H.W. Jones, (trans.), *Code of Hammurabi* (Edinburgh: T. and T. Clark, 1903).

3. J.A.C. Thomas, *Textbook of Roman Law* (New York: Oxford University Press, 1976).

Part III:
Punishment and
Correction

Part III offers a blend of sociohistorical-qualitative and empirical-quantitative analyses of punishment and correction. In chapter 13, two of Simon Dinitz's former students, Clemens Bartollas and Stuart J. Miller, who have published extensively in the field of juvenile corrections, provide a historical overview of the rehabilitation and punishment of juvenile offenders. In the American Puritan period (1646–1824), the family was the dominant social-control system. Then came the houses of refuge (1824–1899), succeeded by the juvenile court (1899–1960), and then a period of expanding juvenile rights (1960–1975). Finally, Bartollas and Miller argue that, in 1975–1980, there emerged a collage of reforms and philosophies leading to a state of anomie in juvenile corrections. They view as problematic efforts to restore the American family to its previously preeminent status, because of the disintegration of the American nuclear family.

Some of the most intense public-policy debates in recent years are those that have surrounded the death penalty as a possible deterrent to homicide. Gordon P. Waldo provides an excellent, yet concise overview and assessment of research on this subject. From 1919 to 1975, the hypothesis that the death penalty deters homicide was categorically rejected. Then, with Isaac Ehrlich's highly publicized study, concluding that an additional execution each year might have resulted in seven or eight fewer murders, research on this subject proliferated. Waldo carefully considers this issue by analyzing the Ehrlich study, six other studies that support the deterrence position, and ten studies that are critical of Ehrlich's quantitative methodology, modeling, and conclusions. Waldo concludes that neither the evidence for a deterrent effect nor the claims of a brutalizing effect are persuasive, and he raises the fascinating possibility that these effects may in fact operate simultaneously.

The recent return to the use of capital punishment in Utah, Florida, and Indiana and the widespread public support for such executions underscores the importance of developing and implementing rational penal policy, beginning with the juvenile-justice system. The public's fear of crime and its frustration with the juvenile- and criminal-justice systems have fueled the current preoccupation with the death penalty and other harsh punishments as a means of retribution.

13 Juvenile Corrections: The State of the Art

Clemens Bartollas and
Stuart J. Miller

Juvenile corrections, the stepchild of adult corrections, does not have an easy task today. Public opinion demands that juvenile crime, expecially violent juvenile crime, be reduced. However, governmental concern and funding are meager. The juvenile-justice system has neither unifying philosophy nor simple lines of responsibility. Prevention strategies have proved ineffective. Status offenders and other noncriminal young people are often confined with and treated like hardened criminals. Juvenile institutions have failed, yet communities resist neighborhood corrections programs.

The past is prologue. As in every area of human endeavor, the present and future of juvenile corrections can neither be understood nor prepared for without comparison with what has happened in the past. The philosophy of colonial days still affects public attitudes about the relationship between families and misbehaving juveniles, and philosophies of confinement that emerged with the industrial revolution still structure our response to convicted offenders. Reforms have neither succeeded nor failed. The suggestions about what to do with wayward juveniles have been so numerous, so full of hope, and so ambiguous in outcome that David Rothman's phrase, "reform is the designation that each generation gives to its favorite programs,"[1] could be the slogan for juvenile corrections today.

The Past

American Puritan Period: 1646–1824

The history of juvenile corrections begins in the Puritan period.[2] In those small communities, justice was simple, the law was uncomplicated, and the family was the cornerstone of the community. The only official law-enforcement officials were town fathers, magistrates, sheriffs, or watchmen. The only institutions of corrections were almshouses for the poor, prisons for debtors and political and religious offenders, and jails for prisoners awaiting trial or punishment.[3]

Juvenile offenders in those days did not face a battery of police, probation,

159

or parole officers, nor did they need to concern themselves with teachers, counselors, or social workers trying to remake them. They had only to worry about being sent back to their families for punishment, for the family was considered the first line of defense against deviancy. If they were still recalcitrant after harsh whippings and other deprivations, young delinquents could be returned to community officials for further punishment, which included public whippings, dunkings or placement in stocks, or, in more serious cases, expulsion from the community or capital punishment.

The Refuge Period: 1824–1899

By the early nineteenth century, reformers looked for a substitute for the family, because they believed it failed in its mission of effectively rearing children. They wanted a substitute that would provide an ordered, disciplined environment similar to the ideal Puritan family.[4] Houses of refuge, expected to be homes away from home, were proposed as a solution. There, discipline was to be administered firmly and harshly, for wayward children were to be protected from the corrupting urban environments emerging throughout the nation. These facilities reflected a new direction in juvenile correction. No longer were parents and family the first lines of control for children. The family was to be supplemented, its authority superseded by the state, and its progeny placed in facilities that were better equipped to reform offenders of the public order.

The houses of refuge flourished throughout the nineteenth century. Certainly, they had their detractors. Some had grown unwieldy in size, and discipline, care, and order had disappeared from most. Reformers also began to suspect that their houses of refuge were not as effective as had been hoped. Citizens throughout the nation were well aware that many youths were also confined in jails and prisons—institutions that were filthy, dangerous, degrading, and ill-equipped to manage. A change was in order, and reformers developed a new institution that they believed would help keep undesirables off the street, while assuring humane placement of young delinquents.

The Juvenile Court Period: 1899–1960

The juvenile court, born in Cook County, Illinois, was intended to represent the interests of the state. The *parens patriae* philosophy, upon which the juvenile court was based, is best explained in the words of the Committee of the Chicago Bar Association that created the new court:

> The fundamental idea of the juvenile court law is that the state must step in and exercise guardianship over a child found under such adverse social or

individual conditions as to encourage the development of crime. . . . The
juvenile court law proposes a plan whereby he may be treated, not as a criminal,
or legally charged with crime, but as a ward of the state, to receive practically
the care, custody, and discipline that are accorded the neglected and dependent
child, and which, as the act states, "shall approximate as nearly as may be
that which should be given by its parents."[5]

Proponents promised that the juvenile court would be flexible enough to
give individual attention to the specific problems of wayward children. No
longer were children to be handled en masse. Reflecting the philosophy of
positivism, this generation of reformers believed that, once the causes of deviancy were identified accurately, specific problems could be treated and cured.
Juveniles would be kept out of jails and prisons so that they would not be
corrupted by adult offenders. In short, according to its supporters, the juvenile
court brought protection rather than punishment.

However, the juvenile court period was not accompanied by radical changes
in philosophy. The family continued to be subservient to the state, and youths
could still be institutionalized. The creation of another official agency to aid the
family in controlling children was the only new factor in the juvenile court.
Delinquent youths were to continue under the control of the state until they
either were cured or were too old to remain under the jurisdiction of juvenile
authorities.

The development of the juvenile court was not the only way that modern
society extended its control over the young. Police departments established
juvenile bureaus. The notion of treating juveniles for their specific problems
was extended into both probation and parole agencies, which had become
institutionalized in the correctional process. The industrial school, a carry-over
from the nineteenth century, was reserved for those who could not be treated
in their communities. These industrial or reform schools attempted to establish
discipline in the lives of wayward youth. The family became even more remote
from the correctional system as the state grew stronger and more assertive of its
responsibility for youth.

The Juvenile Rights Period: 1960–1975

In recent years, practices of the past were continued, but with some new twists.
Reformers believed that juveniles too frequently were subjected to curbstone
justice by the police, to capricious and arbitrary justice by the courts, and to
punitive and repressive justice in the training schools. The pressure that these
reformers placed on the federal courts led, in the 1960s and early 1970s, to a
series of decisions by the U.S. Supreme Court that changed the legal norms of
the juvenile court (*Kent* v. *United States,* 1966; *In re Gault,* 1967; *In the Matter
of Samuel Winship,* 1970; and *McKeiver* v. *Pennsylvania,* 1971).[6] The *In re*

Gault decision, the most far-reaching of these cases, stated that a juvenile has the right to due-process safeguards in proceedings where a finding of delinquency could lead to confinement and that juveniles have rights to notice of charges, to counsel, to confrontation and cross-examination, and to privilege against self-incrimination. The intent of these Supreme Court decisions was to protect the fundamental constitutional rights of young people.

The dissatisfaction with the now-traditional methods of juvenile justice was a second development of recent years. Reformers believed that inconsiderate treatment by the police, five-minute hearings in the juvenile court, and degrading and often brutal treatment in training schools fostered rather than reduced juvenile lawlessness. Community diversionary programs were established as alternatives to the juvenile-justice system. Youth Service Bureaus, the most widely used of these diversionary programs, promised to keep youthful offenders out of the formal justice system. Guided by Jerome Miller, who had closed Massachusetts's training schools in the early 1970s, other states began a process of deinstitutionalization in which only deep-end delinquents would be sent to long-term training schools. Enthusiasm for community-based corrections was so widespread in the early 1970s that many observers believed that training schools were about to be retired.

Sociological theory was dusted off, and reformers rediscovered the community and family. Communities were charged to take greater responsibility for their social problems, including youth crime, and to refrain from so quickly referring these problems to the control agencies of society. The family was recognized once again, as in the Puritan and refuge eras, as a contributing factor in delinquency. Programs were developed to help families solve their problems and to regain their stabilizing force in the lives of their children.

Thus, the juvenile-rights era witnessed a deepening involvement of the state in the lives of juveniles while renewing efforts to keep juveniles out of the system.

The Present: 1975–1980

Contemporary juvenile corrections is a collage of older reforms and philosophies. The most prevalent theme is dissatisfaction with the state's role in preventing, treating, and controlling the problem of juvenile crime. Reformers and hard-liners alike lament unfairness in the administration of juvenile justice, the failure of the rehabilitation model, and the ineffectiveness of juvenile institutions.

Unfairness in the Administration of Juvenile Justice

Inconsistency is one aspect of the unfairness with which the juvenile-justice system is charged. The National Juvenile Justice Assessment Center recently found few uniform guidelines for labeling juveniles who enter the system. Informal agency norms and practices are followed, rather than formal rules and procedures. Probation, court, and protective-services intake officers have great discretion in dealing with juveniles under their jurisdiction. Consequently, the way juveniles are classified varies arbitrarily from jurisdiction to jurisdiction.

The classification of juvenile offenders is also branded unfair. Throughout the Puritan and refuge eras, it was commonly assumed that all children got into trouble for similar reasons. Awareness of differences was translated into admissions policies in a few orphanages and training and reform schools, but in most cases juveniles were mixed in either with adults or with other juveniles who might be sane, insane, dependent, neglected, hardened offenders, minor offenders, or simply incorrigible. Not until the 1960s did reformers begin to argue that the abused, the dependent and neglected, the status offender, and the chronic offender were all different and should receive the benefits of different kinds of treatment.

In such policies as the Juvenile Justice and Delinquency Prevention Act of 1974, the federal government expressed its strong stand that status offenders and other noncriminal young people do not belong in institutions. Although this soft-line policy of keeping status offenders out of the system is gaining public acceptance, many jurisdictions are still trying to implement the federal guidelines. The result is that many youths who should never see the inside of a juvenile institution are still confined. The runaway is still housed with the rapist. Juvenile-court judges, who are protective of their responsibilities, have led the movement to keep status offenders under the jurisdiction of the juvenile court. They claim that status offenders, probably as much as any type of youthful offender, need the protection and guidance of the juvenile court. In effect, they say: "If we don't watch over status offenders, who will?"

The variability in juvenile-justice dispositions also troubles many students of the field. About one-third of all juvenile cases are dealt with informally. This means that nonlegal factors influence the ways juvenile offenders are processed through the juvenile-justice system.[7] If a youth is abusive or uncooperative toward law-enforcement officers, the youth will likely be referred to the juvenile court and perhaps be kept in detention regardless of the cause for the referral. Many jurisdictions have given prosecutors ultimate responsibility for deciding if and when a juvenile will be processed through the juvenile court. Written policy is virtually nonexistent.[8] A juvenile-court judge may send a middle-class offender to a local diversion program for the same crime for which a youth from a poor family goes to training school.

Reformers are troubled by social injustice within the juvenile-justice system. It is claimed that white and middle-class children are "saved," while poor and minority children are discarded to training school. The long-term institutions, as one author put it, too frequently become society's garbage dumps for minority children and the children of the have-nots.[9] Another said that the defenseless and beaten children of the poor succumb to "the oppressive ideology of the privileged."[10]

The Failure of the Rehabilitation Model

Under the protection and fatherly guidance of a juvenile judge, the *parens patriae* philosophy promised, youthful delinquents would be cured of their crimes. Psychiatrists and psychologists would help root out the causes of criminal behavior. However, there is little evidence that the rehabilitation model has worked; indeed, this model is ridiculed in most correctional settings today. Empiricists testify that the rehabilitation model has not reduced recidivism. Youthful offenders might well concur with the youth who said, "I don't need therapy; I just want to get out of here."[11]

Those who have studied the problem of reforming juvenile offenders often agree that the noble efforts of the system only made a youth worse and that little can be done until a youth is ready either to walk away from or to mature out of criminal behavior. A young man told one of the authors, "They have messed over me long enough. I'm going home and get my shit together. You won't see any more of me in places like this." In fact this eighteen-year-old went home and turned his life around. He stayed "clean" (out of crime), found and kept a good job, and appeared to be happily married.[12]

Hard-liners have been particularly upset by the failure of the system to rehabilitate violent young people. Practitioners in the juvenile-justice system have long been baffled by the deep-end delinquent who has committed violent acts in the community. Institutional staff members have too frequently resorted to drug therapy to control these offenders. Within community- and institution-based settings, these youth usually intimidate staff and inmates alike, resort to exploitation to attain what they desire, and help create a criminogenic, rather than therapeutic, environment.

The failure of the rehabilitation model has made reformers rethink the role of the family. The original intent of reformers was to supplement the family, but the actual result of their efforts was to preempt the family's authority. Thus, rather than providing the family with a supporting cast to which it could turn in times of need, reforms further undermined the rights of the family. Although the juvenile court was intended to protect and help children, it actually prolonged the dependence of children on the state and, in the process, supplanted the family. Today we are again debating the role of the family in rearing children. It is discouraging that families apparently suffer from such signs of the times as high divorce rates, more working mothers, and the increased involvement of family members outside their homes.

The Failure of Juvenile Institutions

Training schools have fewer friends than they have ever had, for there is more and more agreement that they are violent, dehumanizing, criminogenic, and do far more damage than good.[13] The maximum-security institution in Ohio studied by Bartollas, Miller, and Dinitz was well equipped with programs, staff, and facilities, but one inmate summarized the quality of institutional life when he said, "Only the strong survive in this place." Ninety percent of the young people in this institution were involved in a victimization matrix; 10 percent were chronic sexual victims. Staff members were also caught in the vicious circle of victimization; they used inmate leaders to make their jobs easier and often exploited inmates in more serious ways. Residents, meanwhile, constantly tried to intimidate and manipulate the staff in every conceivable way.[14]

Studies of training schools for girls are no more encouraging, for they generally find that the majority of girls are involved in ongoing lesbian alliances.[15] There is little evidence from these studies that many girls derive positive attitudes or benefits from institutionalization. In a study of coeducational training schools in North Carolina, Sieverdes and Bartollas found little to recommend training schools to this nation's policymakers.[16]

The Future

Juvenile corrections in the 1980s and 1990s will combine softness and hardness. We should go soft on noncriminal and minor offenders and be hard on chronic and violent juvenile criminals. The decline in birthrate of the late 1960s and 1970s should lead both to a drop in juvenile crime in the 1980s and to a softening attitude toward juvenile crime. In the coming decade, the exorbitant cost of juvenile institutionalization should also contribute to this softening attitude. Thus, noncriminal youths may have a better chance to stay out of the juvenile-justice system and youthful offenders who have committed property offenses should find themselves on probation or in residential facilites.

Training schools will be reserved for hard-core and violent offenders. Since inner cities will probably experience less population decline than other areas and the poor will get no richer, violent youth crime will continue to be centered among minority youth. Mandatory sentencing will become more common for violent offenders; an increasing number of hard-core juvenile offenders will also be transferred to the adult criminal courts.

Community-based corrections will probably be more concerned with security than it is at present. Residential facilities, for example, will be used for more youthful offenders, especially those who have committed serious property crimes. Restitution and community-service conditions of probation will probably be required of most probationers.

The quality of training-school life will be no better than it is today. Training schools will be smaller and more security-oriented and will confine deep-end delinquents for longer periods of time. They will also continue to be jungles in which the strong survive. The social hierarchy, with the leaders at the top and the scapegoats at the bottom, will thrive.

Juvenile corrections itself will continue to be a marginal governmental concern, with meager funding and ineffective lobbying. No unifying philosophy will emerge in juvenile corrections, nor will any new method of treatment be recognized as more effective than those presently in use. The fragmentation of the juvenile-justice system will continue to be extensive.

Summary

The history of juvenile corrections in the United States begins with the family. In the colonial period, the family was looked to as the first line of defense against crime. In the refuge period, reformers substituted institutions for the family; their houses of refuge were intended to be homes away from home and to provide the order and discipline that so many families lacked. At the turn of the twentieth century, the juvenile court was created to aid families in controlling children. But instead of aiding the family, the juvenile court came more and more to replace the family. In other words, the state was taking over the process of correcting juvenile lawbreakers. The juvenile-rights era witnessed a continuing and deepening involvement of the state in the lives of juveniles, but there was also a growing awareness of the shortcomings of bringing youths into the net of the system. The present is a time of reevaluating the effectiveness of the system in correcting youthful delinquent behavior. Reformers would like to turn again to the family, but the decline of the nuclear family and the increase in working mothers dampen hopes for the reemergence of the family as a corrective model in juvenile corrections.

Notes

1. David J. Rothman, *Conscience and Convenience: The Asylum and Its Alternatives in Progressive America* (Boston: Little, Brown, 1980), p. 4.

2. The format used in this section is partially adapted from Charles P. Smith, David J. Berkman, Warren M. Fraser, and John Sutton, *A Preliminary National Assessment of the Status Offender and the Juvenile Justice System: Role Conflicts, Constraints, and Information Gaps,* Reports of the National Juvenile Justice Assessment Centers (Washington, D.C.: U.S. Department of

Justice, LEAA, National Institute for Juvenile Justice and Delinquency Prevention, 1980), pp. 6–19. See also the history of juvenile corrections that introduces the second edition of Clemens Bartollas and Stuart J. Miller, *The Juvenile Offender: Control, Correction and Treatment* (Boston: Holbrook Press, Allyn and Bacon, forthcoming).

3. Harry Elmer Barnes, *The Evolution of Penology in Pennsylvania: A Study in American Social History* (Montclair, N.J.: Patterson Smith, 1968), p. 27.

4. For an in-depth look at the refuge of postcolonial days, see David J. Rothman, *The Discovery of the Asylum* (Boston: Little, Brown, 1971).

5. Roscoe Pound, "The Juvenile Court and the Law," *National Probation and Parole Association Yearbook* 1(1944):4.

6. Kent v. United States, 383 U.S. 541 (1966); In re Gault, 387 U.S. 1 (1967); In re Winship, 397 U.S. 358 (1970); McKeiver v. Pennsylvania, 403 U.S. 528 (1971).

7. See Charles P. Smith, T. Edwin Black, and Fred R. Campbell, *A National Assessment of Case Disposition and Classification in the Juvenile Justice System,* Reports of the National Juvenile Justice Assessment Centers (Washington, D.C.: U.S. Department of Justice, LEAA, National Institute for Juvenile Justice and Delinquency Prevention, 1980), p. xv.

8. Ibid., p. xiii.

9. Lois G. Fores, *No One Will Listen: How Our Legal System Brutalizes the Youthful Poor* (New York: John Day, 1970).

10. Barry Krisberg, *Crime and Privilege* (Englewood Cliffs: N.J.: Prentice-Hall, 1975).

11. Interview, February 1979, with an institutionalized Ohio youth.

12. Interview, May 1972, with an institutionalized Ohio youth.

13. Clemens Bartollas, Stuart J. Miller, and Simon Dinitz, *Juvenile Victimization: The Institutional Paradox* (New York: Halsted Press, Sage, 1976); Sethard Fisher, "Social Organization in a Correctional Residence," *Pacific Sociological Review,* 4(Fall 1961):87–93; Howard Polsky, *Cottage Six: The Social System of Delinquent Boys in Residential Treatment* (New York: Russell Sage Foundation, 1970); Barry Feld, *Neutralizing Inmate Violence: Juvenile Offenders in Institutions* (Cambridge, Mass.: Ballinger, 1977).

14. Bartollas, Miller, and Dinitz, *Juvenile Victimization.*

15. Rose Giallombardo, *The Social World of Imprisoned Girls* (New York: Wiley, 1974).

16. Christopher M. Sieverdes and Clemens Bartollas, "Modes of Adaptation and Game Behavior at Two Juvenile Institutions," in *Youth Crime and Juvenile Justice: International Perspectives* ed. Paul C. Friday and V. Lorne Stewart (New York: Praeger, 1977), pp. 22–38.

14 The Death Penalty and Deterrence: A Review of Recent Research

Gordon P. Waldo

The first empirical study on the deterrent effect of the death penalty using U.S. data was published in 1919 by Raymond Bye.[1] In 1925, studies were published by both Sutherland and Kirkpatrick followed by the classic studies of Vold, Sellin, and Schuessler.[2] Over a period of fifty years, a variety of studies were conducted, some comparing states before and after abolition, others comparing states with and without the death penalty, and still others looking at murder rates following well-publicized executions. One thing all of these studies had in common was a rejection of the deterrence hypothesis—that the use or existence of the death penalty reduced the rate of murder.

This situation changed abruptly in 1975 with the publication of an article by Isaac Ehrlich, who used sophisticated statistical techniques and concluded that there appeared to be a deterrent effect.[3] Because his research provided the first empirical support, proponents of the death penalty were quick to seize on his findings. The difficulty in comprehending the statistical techniques, however, led most of the proponents merely to cite his statement that an additional execution per year might have resulted in seven or eight fewer murders per year.

Ehrlich's study set off a virtual avalanche of research aimed at critiquing, refuting, or supporting his findings. This chapter is a very brief, nontechnical review of the large body of research that has developed on this topic in the past six years.

Ehrlich's Research

Ehrlich's approach involved the use of two-stage least-squares regression analysis with time-series aggregate data on executions and homicide rates in the United States. He used the years 1933–1969, with the entire nation as the unit of analysis. In addition to executions and homicides, he also included other variables in his equations—the arrest rate in murder cases, the conditional probability of conviction for arrested murder suspects, the unemployment rate, the rate of labor-force participation, the proportion of the population aged 14 to 24, per capita income, and time (T). It should be noted that he converted his variables into logarithms and did not use the linear form. (The sole exception to this was T, which was not transformed.) Ehrlich constructed a "supply function'' of murders and hypothesized that, as executions increase, murder will decrease.

In the regression model Ehrlich used, the estimated coefficients of the explanatory variables are interpreted as elasticities. This means that the coefficients obtained indicate the percentage of change in murder rates that can be expected from a 1 percent change in the risk of executions. He examined several different models for varying time periods and for variations of the execution variable. He reported elasticity coefficients that ranged from $-.039$ to $-.068$, with several of the larger ones being statistically significant. If an elasticity of $-.068$ is used, this could be interpreted as implying that, for every 1 percent increase in executions, there should be a decrease of .068% in the murder rate. When average figures for murder and executions are used across the time period encompassed, this yields the estimates that are frequently reported—that is, seven or eight fewer murders per year for each additional execution.

In a second study, Ehrlich used a cross-sectional approach, by which he examined the murder rate and executions across states for 1940 and 1950.[4] He used several economic variables and several deterrence variables as they related to the murder rates for these two time periods. He used the ordinary-least-squares estimation procedure and once again made a logarithmic transformation of the data. Ehrlich concludes that his findings are not inconsistent with the deterrence hypothesis, and he estimates a reduction of twenty to twenty-four murders for each execution, based on the cross-sectional data.

In fairness to Ehrlich, it should be noted that he recognizes some of the limitations of his analysis, and in none of his research does he conclude that he has offered convincing evidence for the deterrent effect of the death penalty, nor has he advocated the use of capital punishment as a rational policy. To the contrary, he consistently argues that other factors, such as increased employment and income, should have a much greater preventive effect than would executions.

Ehrlich's Supporters

Although Ehrlich's research examining the deterrent effect of the death penalty was the first to offer support for the hypothesis, it is no longer the only supportive research. A search of the literature located six published articles, in addition to Ehrlich's work, that provide findings supportive of this position. The first three will be mentioned only briefly, since they use different approaches or had different research purposes.

Lester claims to have found a deterrent effect by computing the probabilities for murder in years in which there were no executions.[5] Since his article is only one page long, it is difficult to determine exactly what he did or how to assess his conclusions. Phillips did a study using data from England for twenty-two highly publicized executions from 1858 to 1921 and claims that there is a short-run deterrent effect during the week in which the execution occurs but no long-run deterrent effect.[6] This study is similar in design to those of Savitz and King, using U.S. data, both of whom failed to find a deterrent effect.[7] Because of space limitations, none of these studies will be reviewed further here.

An excellent article by Cantor and Cohen compares the Vital Statistics and Uniform Crime Report data in terms of methodological issues and substantive conclusions that would differ using the various data sets.[8] They found substantial variation in the magnitudes of the coefficients obtained, but most were negative, indicating some degree of support for the deterrence hypothesis. They do not discuss their findings in any depth, since their focus is on the problems inherent in using different data sets. They conclude with a caution to researchers to be wary of the fact that the magnitude of the coefficients differs greatly, depending on which measure is used.

Wolpin did a time-series study of data for England and Wales from 1929 to 1968 that was a direct response to Ehrlich's research.[9] He basically accepted Ehrlich's model and assumptions, although he included some different economic variables in his equations. All the variables are reported in natural logarithms; however, he states that he examined the linear form and that the results were the same. He argues that, if everything else remained constant, an additional execution per year should save four potential victims per year. Wolpin notes that, in his longer, unpublished paper, he explores some of the problems in the analysis and provides alternative explanations for changes in the murder rate. However, he contends that the deterrence hypothesis is consistent with the English data.

In another study that follows Ehrlich, Yunker conducted a time-series analysis using 1933–1972 data for the United States.[10] He used a simultaneous-equation model that postulates that current executions are related to current murder rates and that the current murder rate is inversely related to the past level of executions.

Yunker suggests that Ehrlich misidentified his model. Therefore, Yunker attempts to identify the model in a different manner. He says that data from 1933 to 1959 are appropriate for the estimation of the execution function during that period and that the data from 1960 to 1972 are appropriate for the estimation of the murder function. He obtains a coefficient for the execution variable, which he then translates into a prediction that 156 murders would be deterred for every additional execution per year. He notes that the main factor contributing to the large difference in predictions of murders deterred between Ehrlich's research (7 or 8 murders) and his own (156 murders) is the time period used in the estimation. Since Yunker believes he has correctly identified the model and Ehrlich has not, he apparently believes that the use of the death penalty could have an effect twenty times as great as that proposed by Ehrlich.

Cloninger conducted a cross-sectional analysis of the forty-eight contiguous states in the United States.[11] His research was prompted by that of Ehrlich and Yunker, and he attempted to eliminate some of the criticisms of research by using cross-sectional rather than time-series data and by using ordinary-least-squares regression techniques rather than a simultaneous-equation model. He included many of the same variables that Ehrlich had used but Yunker had excluded. The murder rate was based on data for 1960 by states, but the execution variable was the average of 1955–1959 executions by states. He found a negative coefficient for the execution variable, which, if the necessary computations are made, converts to an estimate that approximately 560 murders would be deterred for each additional execution.

Cloninger does some additional analysis in which he dichotomizes the states into southern and nonsouthern. The deterrence hypothesis is supported for the nonsouthern states, but the relationship disappears in the southern states. Cloninger does not elaborate on this finding, nor does he comment on the fact that the deterrence relationship does not exist in the southern region, which is known for a high murder rate and a large number of executions.

Ehrlich's Critics

Many attempted replications of Ehrlich's research, as well as studies using similar approaches but slightly different data, have appeared in recent years but have not reached the same conclusions as the aforementioned studies. Space will not permit examination of all these studies; however, ten are selected for brief discussion.[12]

One of the early reexaminations of Ehrlich's work was by Passell and Taylor.[13] They found that the deterrent relationship did not exist when linear data were used, but it emerged when the data were converted into logarithms. They note that logarithmic transformations are normally justified on the basis of economic theory or on the basis of statistical tests that indicate that the logarithmic form is more consistent with the data than other forms would be. They conclude that Ehrlich's choice of the log-linear form is not justified on either grounds. Passell and Taylor note that, if the normal linear form is used, the estimated coefficients are positive rather than negative. This runs counter to the deterrence hypothesis and lends itself instead to an interpretation consistent with the brutalization hypothesis—that executions increase murder rates.

Passell and Taylor also found that the logarithmic relationship was greatly affected by the inclusion of the period 1962–1969, during which executions came to a halt. When these years are excluded, the relationship disappears. This is of considerable importance because, as is frequently noted, the use of time-series data assumes that the structure of the model and the coefficients to be estimated remain stable over the time periods selected for analysis. Passell and

Taylor suggest that Ehrlich's equations include time periods in which the causes of murder varied, thus raising strong doubts about the validity of his estimates.

Passell and Taylor proceed to note that, if everything else Ehrlich did in his research were correct, his conclusions would rest on a very dubious assumption—that a change in the rate of executions would have no effect on the behavior of judges and juries in convicting defendants who faced a death penalty. It can logically be argued that, as the risk of execution increases, the probability of conviction decreases. Passell and Taylor suggest that, if a 100 percent increase in execution rates were to reduce conviction rates by more than 17 percent, then any additional executions would lead to an increase, rather than a decrease, in the number of murders.

Bowers and Pierce also attempted to replicate Ehrlich's work.[14] Their findings were consistent with those of Passell and Taylor in that they found that the deterrence relationship held only for the log-linear-transformed data. They also found that the relationship was maintained only when the specific time periods used by Ehrlich were included. If the time period is changed, the relationship disappears or becomes positive. Bowers and Pierce also question Ehrlich's use of FBI data for homicide, citing many of the problems with these data that have been well known to criminologists for years. They conclude that Ehrlich's findings are a result of inadequate data and a misapplication of his statistical techniques.

Klein, Forst, and Filatov were commissioned by the National Academy of Sciences to analyze the Ehrlich study for a national panel that had been established to evaluate the literature on deterrence and incapacitation.[15] They were able to gain access to Ehrlich's original data, which earlier critics had been unable to do. They criticize Ehrlich on theoretical as well as methodological grounds. They state that his theory is strongly contrived, and they have doubts about the insights provided by his approach for the understanding of criminal behavior.

More specifically, they suggest that Ehrlich misspecified his model and omitted from consideration relevant factors that contributed to an increase in murder during this period. They note that, while there was a large increase in murder during the 1960s, there were even greater increases in the rates of other crimes that were unaffected by the death penalty. This suggests to them that Ehrlich's statistical results are produced by other variables, which might explain the general increase in crime and which were excluded from his analysis. This would leave the false impression that the declining use of the death penalty resulted in an increase in murder, when in fact the true cause was still undetermined.

They also note, as did Bowers and Pierce, that, because of the manner in which Ehrlich computed the execution-rate variable, which involves a common term in the execution and murder rates, he could have biased his results so that a deterrent effect appeared to exist when in fact it did not. They note that, because of this bias, the true elasticity may be positive, which would indicate a counterdeterrent effect of the death penalty.

Klein, Forst, and Filatov agree with the earlier researchers that the effect of the death penalty on the murder rate was not significant in a linear-form equation. They also concur that there is nothing in the theory or in Ehrlich's data that would lead one to select a logarithmic transformation rather than a straight linear-regression model.

Forst conducted a study using data from the 1960s.[16] All the studies cited here had concluded that this was the time period that yields the appearance of a deterrent effect in Ehrlich's data. Forst looked at changes over time as well as across jurisdictions. He suggests, in a follow-up to Klein, Forst, and Filatov's study, that the appearance of deterrence in Ehrlich's time-series analysis is the product of several variables that were omitted by Ehrlich. Forst measures the execution variable six different ways and concludes that his finding of no relationship between the execution rate and the murder rate is very robust and is not seriously affected by using the six different operational definitions of the execution variable. He concludes that his findings do not support the deterrence hypothesis.

Passell conducted a cross-sectional study using the years 1950 and 1960.[17] This study was very similar in design to Ehrlich's second study. Passell, however, used three different models in addressing the issue. In addition to examining the deterrence relationship using the frequency of executions, as Ehrlich had done, Passell also looked at the relationship between abolition and retentionist states and the relationship between de facto abolition and the use of executions. He was unable to find a deterrent effect using any of these approaches, and, in fact, many of his coefficients were positive rather than negative. Passell concludes that there is no reasonable way of interpreting the cross-sectional data in his study as supportive of the deterrence hypothesis.

Several of Ehrlich's critics suggest that gun ownership may explain the deterrent effect of the death penalty, but Kleck is the first to examine the question empirically.[18] He conducted a time-series analysis using the period 1947 to 1973. He concludes that his findings do not support a deterrence hypothesis and that Ehrlich's misspecification of his model by the omission of the important variable of gun ownership probably led Ehrlich to the wrong conclusion. The rapid increase in the supply of privately owned guns is probably a better explanation of the increasing murder rate than is the decline in the execution rate.

Knorr used ordinary least squares in an approach called "pooled cross-sectional time-series analysis" for 1950–1960 data.[19] This approach combines some of the features of the time-series, cross-sectional, and paired-comparison approaches in trying to answer the question of the deterrent effect of the death penalty. He used both regional and state data in his analysis and tried to test the deterrence hypothesis in several different models. He argues that his methodology and the models he used were favorably disposed to a confirmation of Ehrlich's conclusions if they could be supported by any set of data. He intentionally designed the study and used the data that he believed would be most supportive of the hypothesis that the decline in executions increases the murder rate. He found no support for the deterrence hypothesis in any of his models and concluded that the hypothesis may have no real basis in fact.

Brier and Fienberg concur with many of the criticisms heretofore noted and also raise three other important questions that are relevant to this issue.[20] First, they question Ehrlich's logic in using a simultaneous-equation model that assumes that the murder rate and the execution rate affect each other in a simultaneous, interactive manner. They argue that it makes more sense to assume that a criminal's subjective perception of punishment affects his current behavior, but that there is a time delay in terms of the effect of the murder rate on the execution rate. They suggest that a recursive model is more appropriate than a simultaneous model. When the recursive model is applied, the coefficients, while still negative, are not significant.

Second, while several other writers point to problems in using the early years in Ehrlich's time-series crime data, Brier and Fienberg suggest that the data for 1934 are particularly troublesome. The residuals for 1934 are extremely large, and they argue that this point should be treated as an outlier and should be eliminated. When this one data point is eliminated, the coefficient of the log-transformed equation goes from negative and significant to positive and approaching significance. Ehrlich's entire relationship is reversed when the data for 1934 are removed from the analysis.

Third, Brier and Fienberg note that Ehrlich had made logarithmic transformations of all his variables except time (T), and they question why. The decision appears to have been an arbitrary one, but one that greatly affects the outcome. When they reproduce Ehrlich's model using T not logged, and compare it to results when T is logged, the coefficients change from negative to positive— once again, a complete reversal in the results as a function of an arbitrary decision in the modeling process.

Black and Orsagh criticize Ehrlich's research because the execution variable is tied to the probability of arrest and the conditional probability of conviction following arrest, so that it is difficult to determine the separate effects of the different sanctions.[21] In their study, they measure the sanction variables separately and use the 1950 and 1960 data for a cross-sectional analysis. They use a log-linear functional form similar to Ehrlich's. They note that two different models are called for, depending on the assumption one makes about whether or not the sanctions are influenced by the murder rate. They use separate models to test for each assumption: ordinary-least-squares regression, assuming that the sanctions are not affected by the murder rate; and two-stage least squares to test the second assumption, that there is a simultaneous or feedback process. Testing either of these models, they obtain positive coefficients in every equation, which runs counter to a deterrence interpretation. They conclude that the death penalty does not have a deterrent effect for the time periods they examined, and they emphatically reject the empirical evidence that has been offered thus far in favor of the death penalty.

One final study is included, which is not a critique of Ehrlich but a critique of Yunker's research. Fox starts by noting that, whereas Yunker's estimate of 156 lives saved makes Ehrlich's estimate of 7 or 8 appear trivial, the errors in Yunker's analysis are so great that they make Ehrlich's research appear flawless by comparison.[22] Fox argues that Yunker's approach to the identification problem is fallacious. He says that, rather than locating a model to fit an existing set of data, as is normally done in the identification process, Yunker perverted the logic of identification and found a set of data to fit his model. Fox is also very critical of Yunker's failure to include other variables in his model. Yunker excluded other variables, arguing that these variables did not vary over the period of the 1960s but were, in fact, constant. Fox says this assumption is simply incorrect, and he provides several illustrations of this. He introduces an age variable into the equation, and the execution coefficient changes from significantly negative to slightly positive. Fox rejects Yunker's claim of having found any support for the deterrence hypothesis.

Conclusion

It is clear that the vast amount of research generated in the last few years has not settled to everyone's satisfaction the controversy over the death penalty as a deterrent to homicide. The evidence of a deterrent effect is very suspect, and the same should be said about the evidence of a brutalization effect. It may be, as suggested by Zeisel, that the reason proponents have not been able to offer a convincing case is that, if there is an effect, it is so minute as to defy measurement using the tools available to the social scientist.[23] At this point, it might well be argued that, if we had better measurement tools, the results might just as likely prove the brutalization hypothesis as the deterrence hypothesis. A point that most writers on this topic ignore is that it can be argued logically that deterrence and brutalization can occur simultaneously, so that some people are deterred and some are brutalized by the same event. The possibility of this outcome greatly complicates the issue and reinforces Zeisel's conclusion that we may never know the true relationship. It would seem, however, that, for those who advocate the use of the death penalty as a deterrent, the responsibility is once again upon them to provide empirical support for their position.

Notes

1. Raymond T. Bye, *Capital Punishment in the United States* (Philadelphia: The Committee on Philanthropic Labor of Philadelphia Yearly Meeting of Friends, 1919).

2. Edwin H. Sutherland, "Murder and the Death Penalty," *Journal of Criminal Law and Criminology* 15(1925):522–529; Clifford Kirkpatrick, *Capital Punishment* (Philadelphia: The Committee on Philanthropic Labor of Philadelphia Yearly Meeting of Friends, 1925); George Vold, "Can the Death Penalty Prevent Crime?" *The Prison Journal* 12(1932):3–8; Thorsten Sellin, *The Death Penalty* (Philadelphia: American Law Institute, 1959); Karl Schuessler, "The Deterrent Influence of the Death Penalty," *The Annals of the American Academy of Political and Social Science* 284(1952):54–62.

3. Isaac Ehrlich, "The Deterrent Effect of Capital Punishment: A Question of Life or Death," *American Economic Review* 65(1975):397–417.

4. Isaac Ehrlich, "Capital Punishment and Deterrence: Some Further Thoughts and Additional Evidence," *Journal of Political Economy* 85(1977): 741–788.

5. David Lester, "Executions as a Deterrent to Homicides," *Psychological Reports* 44(1979):562.

6. David P. Phillips, "The Deterrent Effect of Capital Punishment: New Evidence on an Old Controversy," *American Journal of Sociology* 86(1980): 139–148.

7. Leonard Savitz, "A Study in Capital Punishment," *Journal of Criminal Law, Criminology and Police Science* 49(1958):338–341; David R. King, "The Brutalizing Effect: Execution Publicity and the Incidence of Homicide in South Carolina," *Social Forces* 57(1978):683–687.

8. David Cantor and Lawrence Cohen, "Comparing Measures of Homicide Trends: Methodological and Substantive Differences in the Vital Statistics and Uniform Crime Report Time Series (1933–1975)," *Social Science Research* 9(1980):121–145.

9. Kenneth I. Wolpin, "Capital Punishment and Homicide in England: A Summary of Results," *American Economic Review* 68(1978):422–427.

10. James A. Yunker, "Is the Death Penalty a Deterrent to Homicide? Some Time Series Evidence," *Journal of Behavioral Economics* 5(1976): 45–81.

11. Dale O. Cloninger, "Deterrence and the Death Penalty: A Cross-sectional Analysis," *Journal of Behavioral Economics* 6(1977):87–105.

12. Some of the other recent studies using econometric techniques that have failed to find a deterrent effect of the death penalty are Burley V. Bechdolt, "Capital Punishment and Homicide and Rape Rates in the United States: Time Series and Cross Sectional Regression Analyses," *Journal of Behavioral Economics* 6(1977):33–66; William J. Boyes and Lee R. McPheters, "Capital Punishment as a Deterrent to Violent Crime: Cross Sectional Evidence," *Journal of Behavioral Economics* 6(1977):67–86; David McKee and Michael Sesnowitz, "Capital Punishment: The Canadian Experience," *Journal of Behavioral Economics* 6(1977):145–152.

13. Peter Passell and John B. Taylor, "The Deterrent Effect of Capital Punishment: Another View," *American Economic Review* 67(1977):445–451.

14. William J. Bowers and Glenn L. Pierce, "The Illusion of Deterrence

in Isaac Ehrlich's Research on Capital Punishment," *Yale Law Journal* 85(1975):187–208.

15. Lawrence R. Klein, Brian Forst, and Victor Filatov, "The Deterrent Effect of Capital Punishment: An Assessment of the Estimates," in *Deterrence and Incapacitation: Estimating the Effects of Criminal Sanctions on Crime Rates,* ed. Alfred Blumstein, Jacqueline Cohen, and Daniel Nagin (Washington, D.C.: The National Academy of Sciences, 1978).

16. Brian E. Forst, "The Deterrent Effect of Capital Punishment: A Cross-State Analysis of the 1960's," *Minnesota Law Review* 61(1977):743–767.

17. Peter Passell, "The Deterrent Effect of the Death Penalty: A Statistical Test," *Stanford Law Review* 28(1975):61–80.

18. Gary Kleck, "Capital Punishment, Gun Ownership, and Homicide," *American Journal of Sociology* 84(1979):882–910.

19. Stephen J. Knorr, "Deterrence and the Death Penalty: A Temporal Cross-Sectional Approach," *Journal of Criminal Law and Criminology* 70(1979):235–254.

20. Stephen S. Brier and Stephen E. Fienberg, "Recent Econometric Modeling of Crime and Punishment: Support for the Deterrence Hypothesis?" *Evaluation Review* 4(1980):147–191.

21. Theodore Black and Thomas Orsagh, "New Evidence on the Efficacy of Sanctions as a Deterrent to Homicide," *Social Science Quarterly* 58(1978): 616–631.

22. James A. Fox, "The Identification and Estimation of Deterrence: An Evaluation of Yunker's Model," *Journal of Behavioral Economics* 6(1977): 225–242.

23. Hans Zeisel, "The Deterrent Effect of the Death Penalty: Facts vs. Faith," in *The Supreme Court Review, 1976,* ed. Philip Kurland (Chicago: University of Chicago Press, 1977), pp. 317–343.

Part IV: Interdisciplinary and Comparative Research in Criminology and Deviance

Throughout the first three decades of Sy Dinitz's academic career, he has been extensively involved in and committed to interdisciplinary and comparative research. The "elegant eclecticism" to which we referred earlier is by definition not attainable within the parochial constraints of one theoretical perspective, one method of analysis, or one cultural arena. Dinitz has transcended such constraints, and in so doing has managed to transmit these values to his students, who tend to display similar respect for the research contributions of other disciplines, other perspectives within their own field, and work of foreign scholars.

The chapters that follow have been written by Sy Dinitz's former students (Beran, Allen, and Davis) and a close research collaborator and colleague (Ferracuti, joined by his research colleague in Rome, Francesco Bruno). These contributions reflect research topics that the former students pursued with Dinitz at Ohio State (mentally disordered offenders and the deinstitutionalization of schizophrenics) or that have recently occupied much of his attention (violence and terrorism).

In chapter 15, Beran and Allen review the history of the insanity defense and devote special attention to some of the problems that have troubled this interdisciplinary field of inquiry, where sociology and criminology meet psychiatry and law. In the second part of their chapter, Beran and Allen discuss some of the research conducted by Dinitz, with various collaborators, on the sociopathic offender. An important component of that research was its incorporation of bioneuroendocrinological factors. The implications of this line of study are identified and discussed by the authors.

Ann E. Davis, who has collaborated with Dinitz on his research concerning schizophrenics in the community, asks, in chapter 16, whether the community-mental-health movement has really led to a system that is more humane and less costly, as was intended, or whether the noble intentions of this reform movement have been perverted by fiscal materialism and the bureaucratization that pervades the social-welfare system more generally. In essence, she asks if it is possible that our actions in the area of mental health are paralleling a national-welfare mentality geared to the survival of the least fit at a minimally humane subsistence level. She argues that, as we have shifted our approach from custodialism and overprotection to neglect and abandonment, we may have made many things worse, not better. She suggests that we confront the unintended consequences of our reform efforts, and she offers a discussion of the main problems to be addressed if the community-mental-health concept is to work as it was intended.

Finally, Franco Ferracuti and Francesco Bruno discuss a phenomenon that is variously regarded around the world as crime, deviance, madness, or badness—terrorism. Certainly, terrorist events in recent years have occupied an increasingly important place in the news and in world politics. Italy, the home of the authors, has been extensively victimized by terrorism, as exemplified in recent years by the kidnapping and murder of Aldo Moro and the bombing of the Bologna railroad station. And, although stepped-up efforts by the Italian police to arrest terrorists in 1980 and 1981 have met with much success, and the total number of terrorist events has declined, terrorism still poses a serious threat to the stability of Italian society, as well as to the domestic tranquility of other nations. This is exemplified by the recent arrest (after the Ferracuti-Bruno chapter was written) of Mario Moretti, the alleged mastermind of the Moro kidnapping and murder and the leader of the Red Brigades. Moretti was wanted by the Italian police on at least fifty-one criminal charges. However, this major triumph by the Italian police was tempered somewhat by the murder, three days later, of an Italian prison guard as he left his home. This murder was said to be part of the Red Brigades' campaign against the Italian prison system. And so the war goes on—in Italy and elsewhere.

Ferracuti and Bruno provide a thorough, rich discussion of the history and current status of terrorism in Italy, incorporating psychiatric, sociological, and political aspects of Italian terrorism. They discuss "red" (left-wing) and "black" (right-wing) terrorism, compare political ideologies and characteristics of each type of terrorist group, and discuss the attraction of each group for certain segments of Italian society. The threat of terrorism is real, and Ferracuti and Bruno propose that Italy and other nations must implement, in a democratic manner, the necessary changes to incorporate marginal groups; otherwise, nations such as Italy may be faced with increasingly unstable conditions and uncontrolled violence.

Ferracuti and Bruno's call for the incorporation of marginal groups into the mainstream of Italian society is reminiscent of Conrad's argument for an expanded federal commitment to allow the American underclass to escape into the expanded opportunity system available to most Americans. It is interesting that both essays focus on violent crime; the major distinction between them is the motivation of the offender.

15 Sociopathic and Other Mentally Ill Offenders Revisited

Nancy J. Beran and
Harry E. Allen

People caught up in the criminal-justice system who subsequently evidence mental disturbances have long been accorded a special status. Designated most often as the "criminally insane," this category of deviants has generated a unique set of policies, procedures, and institutions within the larger criminal-justice and mental-health systems. With one foot in each of the two parent systems, mentally ill criminal offenders have been conceptualized as doubly stigmatized by some and doubly afflicted by others. The fact that still others debate the respective merits of doubly manipulative and doubly manipulated highlights the unique problems involved in the definition and management of this unique category of persons.

Competence to Stand Trial

Although many types of mentally ill offenders can arguably be identified, much attention has been directed toward those who are incompetent to stand trial, those who are not guilty by reason of insanity, and the sexual psychopaths, or sociopaths. The discussion that follows will focus on the current state of the art regarding each of these types, with special emphasis on the sociopath. Other current issues that concern all types of mentally ill offenders will also be briefly considered, including the right to treatment and the right to refuse treatment.

The question of a defendant's competence to stand trial is traceable to the common law and reflects the common sense of justice that would be violated by subjecting a disoriented person to criminal proceedings. If a defendant does not understand the nature or object of these proceedings, or the nature of the criminal charges being made, or is unable or unwilling to assist counsel in a defense, then the typical test of competency to stand trial would have been met.

Although the specific criteria for incompetency have rarely been challenged, the motives of those invoking the procedure and the procedure itself are currently under fire. Critics are contending that a latent goal of the incompetency procedure is to serve as an "easy way in" to institutionalization, especially for indefinite and often interminable periods of time. This goal is described as an odious denial of the constitutional right to trial and as tantamount to preventive detention. Under assault is the widespread practice of automatically institution-alizing people who are found to be incapable of standing trial and the equally widespread failure to provide treatment directed toward resumption of compe-tency and to provide periodic review.

In response to these criticisms, adjustments to procedural abuses are in-creasingly evident. Courts and legislatures are beginning to mandate that those to whom incompetent defendants are committed must provide treatment pro-grams designed to restore competency. Correlatively, while defendants are under treatment for restoration, their cases are to be periodically reviewed, and those defendants who are judged not likely to regain comptency within a reasonable period of time are to be either released or committed under civil procedures to civil institutions. The mental illnesses of incompetent defendants are being conceptualized as not unlike the mental illnesses of anyone else.

The Insanity Plea

Less frequently raised but more widely discussed than the incompetency issues is the insanity plea. Although its historical roots in English law go back at least as far as the thirteenth century, the test for sanity most widely employed in the United States derived from the 1843 M'Naghten case. Under the M'Naghten test, a defendant is not guilty by reason of insanity if he does not have the capacity to know right from wrong with respect to the particular act charged. The most common criticism of the M'Naghten rule is that its focus on purely cognitive variables excludes many mentally ill defendants whose disorder is more emotive. This criticism has led some jurisdictions to adopt the ''irresistible impulse'' test, especially in conjunction with the M'Naghten test.

The criticism was also instrumental in the 1954 emergence of the Durham rule. Under the Durham test, a defendant is not criminally responsible if his or her unlawful act was the product of mental disease or mental defect. In estab-lishing this standard, the court was attempting to reflect more modern clinical approaches and to expand the role of clinical input into the final decision. However, the inability of clinicians to agree on definitions of such key concepts as mental disease was one of the major problems that led to the rejection of the standard in 1972 by the very court that earlier had established it. In place of the Durham rule, the court adopted a rule that is steadily growing in popularity and use in the United States—the American Law Institute Model Penal Code test, first introduced in 1966. This test holds that a person is not guilty by reason of insanity if, at the time of the commission of the crime, the accused lacked substantial capacity to appreciate the wrongfulness of his conduct or to conform his behavior to the requirements of the law.

What constitutes the best test for insanity continues to be a hotly debated issue, as does the question of whether or not all versions would best be abolished. It is often suggested that there is a close relationship between the insanity plea and capital punishment. The insanity defense is merely a ploy, some say, for avoiding infliction of the death penalty. To the extent that this statement is true, the use of the insanity defense is currently in a state of disarray.

In large measure because of its juxtaposition of free will and determinism, the insanity plea highlights a strain between the mental-health and criminal-justice systems, between the clinician and the jurist. Correlatively, the appropriate role of the clinical perspective is a topic of debate with regard to both the insanity plea and the question of incompetency to stand trial. Clinicians are often not well versed on either issue (including their distinguishing characteristics) and are inclined to define capabilities and incapabilities in mental-health and mental-illness terms. As a result, requests for evaluation on these legal questions often solicit reports containing only psychiatric diagnoses or other clinical assessments of the defendant's affliction with psychiatric disorders.

A current issue that concerns all types of mentally disordered offenders is the right to treatment. Traditionally, one of the justifications for creating separate categories of offenders as criminally insane and for consigning them to special institutions for the criminally insane has been to provide them with treatment for this condition. The treatment has not been provided, and the courts are beginning to mandate that it must be if these special categories and institutions are to remain.

A court order on right to treatment is a two-edged sword. The courts have clearly stated that concepts of adequate care can be defined, operationalized, and implemented within the current state of the psychiatric arts. In short, the courts are telling institutions that they can and will move from nineteenth-century to twentieth-century standards of care. However, for some institutions, the roots of substandard care are a century deep, and the necessary alterations in physical structure, staffing, and orientation are therefore enormous. In these circumstances, right-to-treatment orders are actually functioning to close some institutions.

In contrast to all this, the right to refuse treatment is gaining in relevancy as therapies that are tantamount to behavioral engineering become ever more finely tuned. And, as the risks and ramifications of new treatment procedures increase, informed consent becomes an issue. Some argue that the way to deal with the sticky ethical questions of behavioral engineering is to leave the entire matter up to the individual offender's choice. Others argue that being incarcerated and giving informed consent may be contradictions in terms.

In the criminal-justice system at large, there has been a recent trend toward the resurrection of punishment as an acceptable and even desirable goal of the system. It is now becoming fashionable to be categorically cynical about treatment in corrections. The utilitarian principles of the classical school are being reiterated in calls for calculated rationality in the assignment of punishments. In short, the trend is toward blaming criminals and punishing them.

These developments could have serious implications for the management of mentally disordered offenders. The emphasis on blame might consider mental aberrations loopholes for avoiding punishment. Thus, greater interest might be directed toward tightening up tests for assessing criminal responsibility and even for determining competency to stand trial. However, less interest might be directed toward the identification and treatment of special categories of offenders, such as sociopaths, whose mental status has been defined as questionable yet who nonetheless have been held criminally responsible. Perhaps courts will decide that justice is best served by assuming that *all* people should be punished for their criminal deeds, regardless of their mental status. Such an extreme outcome appears unlikely, since it would require legal philosophy to relinquish its long-standing commitment to the concept of *mens rea* as a component of crime. But we are clearly witnessing nothing less than a reassertion of the notions of free will, choice, responsibility, and accountability in the administration of criminal justice.

Incarcerated Sociopathic Offenders

Nowhere in the study of mentally disordered offenders is the issue of free will versus reduced responsibility more obvious than with the antisocial personality or sociopath. Clinicians cannot agree even on the definitions of the clinical entity, whose etiology is variously attributed to heredity, defective role-taking ability, insufficient anxiety and fear arousal, delayed maturation (on several levels), and autonomic dysfunctions, among others.[1]

Part of the disagreement and dissensus on what to do with and for such offenders lies in the fact that the clinical entity commonly called the sociopathic personality may not, in fact, be unitary but may actually include offenders whose behavioral manifestations are the result of at least two etiologic or causal processes. Sociopathic offenders are frequently defined as chronically antisocial people who are frequently in legal trouble, who do not learn from punishment or experience, and who do not seem to have loyalties to common normative expectations, people, groups, or codes. They are described as hedonistic, self-centered, callous, and emotionally immature, with a low sense of responsibility evincing both a lack of judgment and an uncanny ability to rationalize their behavior so that it appears not only reasonable but also justified and warranted.

In the late 1960s, Simon Dinitz and his collaborators attempted to replicate an earlier study, which showed that incarcerated sociopaths had a hyperreactivity to epinephrine and, paradoxically, learned faster while under the influence of the drug.

Those who are interested in the details of the several experiments on the drug regimen should refer to the previously published literature, which describes in great detail the procedures used in the Ohio Penitentiary and Chillicothe Correctional Institution projects.[2] We are concerned here with the basic findings and implications of the results for the treatment and handling of sociopaths.

The Ohio Penitentiary project data (1967–1969) did not initially support the fairly consistent findings of the relationships of epinephrine to heightened arousal and learning. What quickly emerged was the conclusion that the experimental group of sociopaths—carefully selected using rigorous criteria—was in fact composed of not one but at least two distinct groups, only one of which showed hyperreactivity to the injected drug.

Comparisons of the two groups on approximately twenty parameters revealed significant and consistent empirical and theoretical differences and suggested that it was possible for an incarcerated sociopathic offender to become sociopathic through a medical (autonomic defect) as well as a social (learning) process.

Much of the confusion about causation and considerable discussion about handling sociopathic offenders may previously have been predicated on erroneous assumptions about the nature of the disorder or disorders. The legal issues of diminished responsibility, free will, and punishment versus treatment were refocused, partly as a result of the work of Dinitz and his collaborators.

The ensuing research at the Chillicothe Correctional Institute employed more refined and sensitive techniques to investigate the underlying autonomic defect, which reflects a diminished function of catecholamine-secreting neurons, particularly those involving sensory input. The second experiment utilized imipramine pamoate, a "psychic arouser" whose functions and effects are specific and medically well known.

By way of analogy, most readers will recall that hyperkinetic children are frequently administered amphetamines as part of the medical treatment for their disorder. The paradoxical result is that many such children become more normal and are treatable and educable. The same paradoxical results were found in the second experiment.

Incarcerated sociopathic offenders in the second experiment quickly showed remarkable improvement, as indicated by weight gain, increased learning abilities, reduced custody levels, improved behavior as rated by correctional officers, and subjective states as reported to the experimenters. Unfortunately, a lawsuit initiated by a person excluded from the experiment (for medical reasons), coupled with legal issues dealing with abuses in behavior-modification programs, led to a premature termination of the experiment.

In sum, what Professor Dinitz and his collaborators have demonstrated in a convincing way is

1. That sociopathic personality is not a unitary disorder;
2. That one type of sociopathic personality results from a medical dysfunction (an autonomic defect);
3. That social forces can also create an antisocial sociopathic personality; and
4. That medical intervention—to cure a medical illness—is one response to the treatment needs of some incarcerated sociopathic offenders.

These findings have ramifications for the emerging issues of determinate sentencing; presumptive sentencing; rehabilitation; right to treatment and right to refuse treatment; *mens rea* and reduced criminal responsibility; coercive versus voluntary treatment; and certain ethical, moral, and legal issues that would gravitate around balancing the right to be left alone with the need for social-control agencies to require medical treatment after incarceration.

The issues have not been settled. Indeed, it will require decades for legal scholars to identify adequately the issues and the related legal problems. The U.S. Supreme Court will utimately be called upon to resolve these burning questions on a case-by-case basis. Nevertheless, we are indebted to Professor Dinitz and his collaborators for research that has contributed markedly to our understanding of the etiology of sociopathic behaviors, as well as to a sharpening of both the definition of the issues and the treatment of such disorders.

Notes

1. Harold Goldman, Lewis A. Lindner, Simon Dinitz, and Harry E. Allen, "The Simple Sociopath: Physiologic and Sociologic Characteristics," *Biological Psychiatry* 3(1971):77–83; Lewis A. Lindner, Harold Goldman, Simon Dinitz, and Harry E. Allen, "Antisocial Personality Type with Cardiac Lability," *Archives of General Psychiatry* 23(September 1970):260–267.

2. Harry E. Allen, "Bio-Social Correlates of Two Types of Anti-Social Sociopaths" (Ph.D. dissertation, Ohio State University, 1969); Harry E. Allen, Eric W. Carlson, and Patrick S. Dynes, "Career Life Patterns: A Cohort Analysis of 274 Criminal Careers" (Paper presented at the Twenty-Third Annual Southern Conference on Corrections, Tallahassee, Florida, 6 March 1978); Harry E. Allen, Lewis A. Lindner, Harold Goldman, and Simon Dinitz, "The Social and Bio-Medical Correlates of Sociopathy," *Criminologica* 6(February

1969):68–75; Harry E. Allen, "Hostile and Simple Sociopaths: An Empirical Typology," *Criminology* 9(May 1971):27–47; Simon Dinitz, "Chronically Antisocial Offenders," in *In Fear of Each Other,* ed. John P. Conrad and Simon Dinitz (Lexington, Mass.: Lexington Books, D.C. Heath and Company, 1977), pp. 21–42; Simon Dinitz and John P. Conrad, "Thinking About Dangerous Offenders" (Columbus, Ohio: Academy for Contemporary Problems, 1978); Simon Dinitz, Harold Goldman, Harry E. Allen, and Lewis A. Lindner, "Psychopathy and Autonomic Responsivity: A Note on the Importance of Diagnosis," *Journal of Abnormal Psychology* 82(1973):533–534; Simon Dinitz, Harry E. Allen, Harold Goldman, and Lewis A. Lindner, "The Juice Model: A New Look at Sociopathy," *et al.* 3(1972):20–28; Patrick Dynes, Eric Carlson, and Harry E. Allen, "Aggressive and Simple Sociopaths: Ten Years Later," in *Biology and Crime,* ed. C. Ray Jeffery (Beverly Hills, Calif.: Sage, 1979), pp. 65–76; K. Gatten, Simon Dinitz, Harold Goldman, Lewis Lindner, and Harry E. Allen, *Pre-Institutional, Intramural and Parole Careers of Sociopaths: An Outcome Study* (Columbus, Ohio: Program for the Study of Crime and Delinquency, 1973); Harold Goldman, "Sociopathy and Diseases of Arousal," *Quaderni di Criminologia Clinica* 2(1973):113–125.

16 Schizophrenic Services: Disjunction and Disservice to Schizophrenics in the Community

Ann E. Davis

In 1967, the landmark Hofheimer Prize winning study *Schizophrenics in the Community: An Experimental Study in the Prevention of Hospitalization* was published.[1] That experiment in the home care of schizophrenic patients clearly demonstrated that a chronic patient population could be kept successfully at home if they were given medications and supportive home-care services and that hospitalizations, costly both in terms of dollars and in terms of the patient's psychic anguish, could substantially be reduced if not avoided completely. Now, in 1981, the community-mental-health program has been in progress for at least half a decade. Schizophrenics have been moved (some say dumped) into the community. But serious questions remain. What are the benefits to the community and what are the benefits to the patients? In what aspects is community care really better than custodialism? Is it more humane? Is it less costly? Or is it possible that we, as a nation, have taken good theory and ideology and allowed it to achieve a metamorphosis that blends with fiscal materialism and with the compartmentalization and technological scatter of our welfare programs? Is it possible that our actions in the area of mental health are paralleling a national-welfare mentality that is geared to the survival of the least fit at a minimally humane subsistence level? In brief, are we kidding ourselves about the new millennium in mental-health care?

It is my position that no sane person could be an advocate for the resumption of custodialism, but neither can anyone find great merit in the present disarray of care being given to schizophrenics in the community. In true accord with past historical shifts, mental-health programming appears to have moved from the total overprotection of schizophrenics (custodialism) to neglect in the current community program. It is ironic that such a pendulum swing approximates that of the schizophrenogenic mother, who at first smothers and then abandons. Neither action, of course, is advantageous to the patient.

Schizophrenia remains a high-priority health problem in the United States. There are roughly three million diagnosed schizophrenics in the United States, and the direct and indirect cost to the community is more than \$14 billion.[2] Because schizophrenia is often described as a lifetime disorder, the prevalence rate is high (2 to 10 per 1,000 population). Also, each year, 100,000 to 200,000 additional persons become affected by this condition.[3] Schizophrenics account for 50 percent of our institutionalized population, and the disorder remains among the main reasons for psychiatric hospitalization.[4] There is controversy over the extent to which such patients absorb our outpatient mental-health services, with estimates ranging from 15 percent of services to its being the second most frequent diagnostic category seen in these facilities. The clinical experience is probably closely related to the practices of the state mental hospitals in a given region.

There is little doubt that the shift from the hospital custodial era to community care has indeed taken place. Over the last 15 years, it is estimated that there has been more than a 30 percent decrease in the number of beds occupied by hospitalized schizophrenic patients. However, although the number of beds has decreased, the total number of patients involved in hospital readmissions has risen. One author addressses the problem in this manner: "Schizophrenia is not a benign condition. With the best aftercare in the world more than 40% of the sufferers fail to achieve even a social remission five years after its onset."[5] Another states that readmission in the two- to four-year period after discharge is a 40 percent to 60 percent probability for each patient.[6] It is also estimated that only 15 percent to 40 percent of the schizophrenics in the community achieve an average level of adjustment.[7] Yet, despite continued high incidence and prevalence rates and despite the high hospital-readmission rates, as well as the poor prognosis for social adjustment, we maintain a staunch, positive philosophy supportive of community care. What is it, in fact, that we are supporting?

Community Mental Health: Ideology and Reality

The goal of community-mental-health care is to prevent or curtail hospitalization, theoretically limiting inpatient care to thirty days, or less when possible, and in turn offering treatment to patients in their communities through a network of extensive and coordinated community-based services. The ultimate goal is the prevention of chronicity and the restoration of the patient as a functioning member of society. The shift from the hospital to the community, as previously mentioned, has indeed taken place. The number of patients in hospitals has decreased dramatically, but the readmissions have created what is commonly termed the "revolving-door syndrome." One study states: "It has been shown with existing aftercare facilites, 33% of patients discharged return to the hospital within six weeks."[8] Bleuler reports the following results based on forty years of study of a population of some 950 schizophrenics. At least 25 percent recovered entirely, 10 percent remained permanently hospitalized, and 50 percent to 75 percent alternated between acuteness and recovery. He also notes that the 25 percent who recovered were neither those under drug treatment nor those cared for by welfare agencies. Bleuler concludes that it is somewhat discouraging that the number of long-standing recoveries has not increased in this century, and also that the prognosis for severe deterioration has hardly diminished.[9] If he is correct, and if we have not actually altered the course of the illness but have merely shifted to the community mode of care, the question still remains—who has benefited?

With large numbers of schizophrenics in the community and with nominal development of aftercare and community-based treatment facilities, where, in fact, are the schizophrenics and how are they surviving? Answers to these questions are both sketchy and disheartening. In our follow-up study on schizophrenics, we found that patients were most likely to use the community-mental-health centers in last-ditch efforts to prevent rehospitalization, and that those with the greatest need seemed least likely to use the clinics consistently for aftercare support.[10] The most frequent difficulty was a breakdown in the referral network between hospital and clinic, plus a lack of aggressive follow-through on the part of clinic staff members to find clients who failed to keep their appointments or who were noncooperative.

The community-mental-health centers have been regarded as more effective in dealing with the neurotic and less-disturbed patient population (and recently with the paying population), and, in rural areas, as too sophisticated in purpose and ideology for the rural populations.[11] The centers are deficient in the number of psychiatrists on their staffs; they are staffed primarily by social workers and psychologists, whose skills are better suited to the less-disturbed, ambulatory-care clientele.

There are some extensive studies on the level of adjustment of schizophrenics in the community, which do not provide much encouragement. The most optimistic reports show that 69 percent have a good or fair social outcome; the most pessimistic see an 8 percent recovery or consider no patient symptom-free.[12] Given our follow-up findings and the general consensus of others, it appears that most patients make marginal community adjustments, remain financially dependent on welfare or other family members' monies, and remain socially dependent in their homes, boarding homes, nursing homes, or run-down, hotel-type facilities. A speaker in Louisville, Kentucky, summed up the current critique of community care as follows: "All over the land we in the mental health field are being criticized because we get patients out of state hospitals, and we get them out of the mental health centers, and then they go into filthy nursing homes, broken-down hotels, and just lie about in the streets. It is a valid criticism."[13]

If we conclude that community care has done little to alter the prognosis or the marginal functioning of patients, we may legitimately ask what impact it has had on the community and specifically on the families of the patients, who bear the major burden of patient care. Our original study as well as our follow-up indicated that families experience a great deal of stress in coping with the patients.[14] Clair Creer cites more recent work with families, which shows problems with patients include bizarre eating habits, bizarre interactions, sleeplessness, embarrassments in front of neighbors, perplexing delusions, threats of violence, threats of suicide, unpredictability, and excessive dependency.[15] We would be blind to expect that these disturbed hospital patients would become well adjusted in their homes. In reality, patients impose problems on their families, on the neighbors, and on the community. It is inappropriate that little or none of our community care is focused on the family or is given in the home. We continue to fail to develop aggressive outreach efforts for patients whose reality-testing skills are so poor that they are limited in their ability to cooperate and to keep clinic appointments.

Further, even though we in mental health choose to ignore it, schizophrenics in the community add to our rising rates of deviance. The annual incidence of suicide for expatients is 5.3 times the expected figure, or higher.[16] Increased alcoholism rates have also been seen, as well as increases in drug abuse and in sexual deviance.[17] At worst, it is suggested that we have increased the possibility of mating and thus have increased the incidence of schizophrenic offspring. Obviously, too, we are subjecting more children to care by schizophrenic parents. It is a commonly accepted fact that genetics and child-rearing in disordered homes form the basic etiology of schizophrenia. We currently seem to be in the business of promoting an increase in schizophrenia by failing to contend with these issues. One possible conclusion is that, although custodialism was disadvantageous to the patient, community care, as practiced, is disadvantageous to the families, the communities, and perhaps to the patients as well.

Speculations on the Dialectics of Care of the Mentally Ill

Consonant with dialectical shifts in many other areas of the social world, there have been historical shifts to diametrically opposing styles of care in the treatment of the mentally ill. Custodialism and punitive care have previously alternated with ideologies of humane care, such as the challenge to the early state-hospital system during the moral-treatment era of the Quakers. Also, history gives evidence of good philosophies that have produced treatment practices that were destructive and antithetical to the ideologies on which they were based. State hospitals originally were established for the purpose of removing the mentally ill from poorhouses and from their status as beggars, with the intent of placing them in an environment of good, clean living in the country, where the asylum would provide the peaceful, tranquil environment necessary for recovery. Instead, what happened was the growing horror of the overcrowded "snake pits" of custodialism in the 1940s and 1950s.

A similar ideological miscue is occurring today. Patients moved from the large state hospitals now live in mini-institutions, such as nursing homes, boarding homes, and halfway houses, or apartments for the mentally ill. In these facilities, they often lack grounds where they can venture out in safety. They lack recreational resources, such as those provided in the mental hospital. The same is true for deficiencies in the availability of vocational and occupational therapies. In many cases, patients do not receive adequate physical and psychiatric medical attention. In decentralizing, then, we should ask if the current facilites, often small and isolated, can offer such dependent populations the resources that the infamous custodial facility, despite its flaws, did provide. Also, does smallness alone mean anything, given a population that is socially and physically dependent for their life needs on these very facilities? It ought to be added that we must frequently accept the fact that we have neither built nor coordinated the needed resources in the community.

Another curious aspect is that the financial burden for care, once handled exclusively by the states in the form of subsidies to the hospitals, has now been shifted to the federal and local governments and can no longer be clearly or directly ascertained. The costs, now more effectively hidden, are carried by social security payments to the disabled, by medical care provided to the medically indigent, and by the departments of vocational rehabilitation, visiting nurses' associations, halfway houses, and other agencies that provide services to discharged patients.

A final irony may be found in the rebuilding of new institutions. Some community-mental-health centers with inpatient beds have become minicomplexes of care and are gowing; old state hospitals have converted to mental-health centers; and tuberculosis sanatoriums have become nursing homes primarily intended for the care of the chronic mentally ill. Try as we may, we appear unable to ignore the problem of dependent populations in need of subsidized housing and support. Nor have we been able to shake our edifice complexes. Thus, the question still remains—what has actually changed, if not the condition and future prospects of the patient with schizophrenia? We are still geared to provide care that is custodial in nature, though perhaps in smaller institutions.

Realistic Confrontation of the Illness

Requisites for Care as Dictated by the Nature of the Illness

It is commonly accepted that schizophrenia has a genetic component (that there is, at least, a predisposition) and that the social environment, from birth on, plays a critical role. Concerning the genetic factor, as a nation we have done very little in the area of primary prevention (that is, genetic counseling or advice about childbearing), and we have judiciously avoided the issue of sterilization.

At worst, children of schizophrenic parents have at times been adopted without full knowledge of the risk assumed by the adoptive parents.

The social realm is easier to contend with, but we again fail to confront the enormity of the task. We are beginning to address the question of identifying at-risk populations. But, given that we have yet to accomplish prevention or such identification, let us address how the current treatment plans relate to the nature of this illness. The schizophrenic patient exhibits: (1) impaired social relationships, (2) impaired affective expression, (3) impaired communicative skills, (4) an impaired sense of self, and (5) uneven development and disjunctive behavior.[18] In more common phraseology, few areas of life and function are untouched by the disorder. In even greater simplicity, Pao says that schizophrenics cannot allow themselves to love. They feel acutely that their love for others can only bring rejection and pain to themselves, and they are therefore withdrawn and have a sense of futility about existence.[19] The world is unable to comprehend their plight; the patients, in turn, are unable to assess the world realistically, and the frustrations of patients are thus exacerbated.[20] These patients, who have poor boundaries between their inner and outer worlds, are a highly sensitive and vulnerable population. Chronicity is often seen as a progressive deadening of the human senses in response to an uncomprehending and incomprehensible world; it is a mode of avoiding further pain. It is interesting that some of the most creative people in history have been psychotic. Buck and Kramer state: "While the difficulties in living demonstrated by schizophrenics cannot be denied, their capacity for creative expression should neither be ignored."[21] From a purely humanistic point of view, then, and given our awareness that this is a population with creative potential, we ought to be obliged to improve our service.

From a sociological perspective, it is interesting to note that the high-risk populations are those in which powerlessness and detachment from society are at their zenith; among the divorced, the rate is 1.9 per 1,000 in contrast to the rate among the married of 0.5 per 1,000. Among black males, it is 1.44 per 1,000, and among black females it is 1.37 per 1,000, which contrasts markedly to the white male rate of 0.74 and the white female rate of 0.53 per 1,000.[22] Other high-risk groups include migrants, immigrants, and the lower socioeconomic classes. Again, these are the powerless and the alienated in our society. Those in the low-socioeconomic-status groupings are often said to be there because of their downward drift in economic status, but this explanation does not easily apply to the black, the immigrant, or the migrant; thus, the answer may more properly lie in the etiology of disorders in low-status positions that promote alienation and powerlessness.

These genetically and environmentally handicapped persons show their combined inabilities to cope with life by being timid or shy, by being without friends, by having poor school and work records, and by making inadequate sexual and marital adjustments. They also migrate to areas that tolerate and enfold them—the disorganized inner-city areas.[23] What do the nature of the illness and the problems of those patients tell us about more appropriate modes of care?

Toward the Improvement of Services to Schizophrenics

In general, the needs of the schizophrenic include a need to establish relatedness, to conquer withdrawal, and to establish interpersonal relationships. Therapists working with such patients should present the posture that they are there— tangible, reasonable, benevolent, and strong. This involves active intervention and reassurance; it is necessary to offer the patient what he or she previously lacked interpersonally in sufficient quantity or degree.[24] This is obviously the ideal and is the mandate assumed by therapists who undertake analytic psychotherapeutic approaches with patients. However, it is impossible to handle large numbers of chronic schizophrenics in this manner because of cost, time limitations, and the lack of sufficient therapists. We can better address the needs of these patients in other ways.

The family, though often the culprit in the exacerbation of the illness, is nonetheless the environment of primary community care for the patients. We have persisted in ignoring this fact, and services to the family are insufficient. A highly excitable and critical home environment is related to patient relapse. It is further postulated that relapses can be avoided by "cooling off" the home environments through counseling, thus lowering patients' arousal levels.[25] The assessment of home environments should be completed more systematically before hospital discharges, and counseling contact should take place periodically and consistently throughout the course of the patient's lifetime of follow-up care. Studies indicate that relatives of schizophrenics often receive virtually no sensible advice about the patient's condition, about medication, about outcomes, or about the best ways of responding to disturbing behavior.[26] This oversight is obviously a treatment error.

It has been suggested that patients do better if there is a limit on the number of treatment people they must trust. If at all possible, it would be advantageous to attempt to retain the same doctor for both hospital and posthospital care. If this is not possible, then a nurse or social worker should be assigned to help maintain the primary treatment contact with the patient between hospitalizations and among aftercare agencies—again, over a long period of outpatient contact. In our follow-up study it became obvious that additional strains are placed on patients who must relate to numerous treatment and rehabilitative persons who are unfamiliar with the patient and his or her social environment and who may exacerbate problems by making conflicting or inappropriate recommendations. Studies have also suggested that making a definite appointment with a specific therapist can noticeably increase the rate of compliance.

Hospitalization and other interim-care facilites, such as day care, foster care, night care, and halfway houses, are poorly coordinated—or even non-existent in some communities. Referrals should be tailored specifically to the needs of each patient. Obviously, meeting the patient's total needs is impossible, and fine-tuning is impossible when interagency cooperation is lacking and the facilities themselves are lacking. Perhaps hospital discharges should be evaluated more stringently in terms of the availability of resources for the patient in each specific community.

One other controversy has become obvious in the course of extensive research over the last decade: the issue of the maintenance of patients on medications. It bears repeating and underscoring: "In general it is an accepted therapeutic technique to keep schizophrenic patients for the rest of their lives on the drug that has helped rescue them from crises and that has maintained them over long-term supportive care."[27] Although some advocate an occasional drug vacation of one month per year if it doesn't disorganize the patient, it is generally believed that patients do best if they take adequate amounts of phenothiazines over long periods.[28] Due to the lack of follow-through on aftercare referrals and due to the misconceptions of some treatment persons, we continue to fail in providing adequate supervision of medications for community-care patients.

Finally, though most difficult of all, it is necessary that we continue the effort to employ patients actively either in sheltered-workshop settings or in the marketplace. We also need to be certain that social activities are available to them. Often, our system of welfare benefits mitigates against employment, and legal requisites adversely affect our ability to employ patients in other than full-time work. A review and revision of disability-benefit laws and regulations would be advantageous.

Thus, the positive interractive effect between the continued and carefully supervised prescription of medications, a supportive home environment, the use of limited and appropriate hospitalizations, and the availabilty and use of networks of rehabilitative and supportive services are proper foci for the community care of patients. Given an illness that results from disordered and inconsistent environments, surely treatment personnel will defeat their purposes by allowing the current disjunctive, discordant, and often nonexistent community-care efforts to feed into the problem of the illness. Although little is coordinated or centrally organized in the realm of health care in the United States, our systemic deficiency becomes a real culprit in the care of schizophrenics. It is time for us to address this issue directly and to attempt to rectify these problems. Otherwise, we are merely contributing to inhumane care and to the perpetuation of the schizophrenic disorder.

Notes

1. B. Pasamanick, F. Scarpitti, and S. Dinitz, *Schizophrenics in the Community: An Experimental Study in the Prevention of Hospitalization* (New York: Appleton-Century-Crofts, 1967).

2. Leopold Bellak, "Nature and Interaction of Community Psychiatric Treatment and the Schizophrenic Syndrome," in *Treatment of Schizophrenia: Progress and Prospects,* ed. Louis Jolyon West and Don E. Flinn (New York: Grune and Stratton, 1976), p. 248.

3. Danielle M. Turns, "The Epidemiology of Schizophrenia," in *Schizophrenia: Theory, Diagnosis, and Treatment,* ed. Herman C.B. Denber (New York: Marcel Dekker, 1978), p. 20.

4. N. Sartorius and T.A. Lambo, "International Collaboration in Schizophrenia Research," in *Schizophrenia Today,* ed. D. Kemali, B. Bartholini, and D. Richtie (Oxford: Pergamon, 1976), p. 13.

5. Bruce R. Sloan, "Foreword," in *Schizophrenia: The Experience and Its Treatment,* ed. Werner M. Mendel (San Francisco: Jossey-Bass, 1976), p. x.

6. Bellak, "Nature and Interaction," p. 251.

7. Ibid.

8. M.J. Goldstein, E.H. Rodnick, J.S. Evans, and P.R.A. May, "Long-Acting Phenothiazene and Social Therapy in Community Treatment of Acute Schizophrenics," *Psychopharmacology Bulletin* 11(1975):37–38.

9. Manfred Bleuler, "Long Term Course of Schizophrenic Psychoses," in *The Nature of Schizophrenia: New Approaches to Research and Treatment,* ed. Lyman C. Wynne, Rue L. Cromwell, and Steven Matthysse (New York: Wiley, 1978), pp. 633–634.

10. Ann E. Davis, Simon Dinitz, and Ben Pasamanick, *Schizophrenics in the New Custodial Community: Five Years after the Experiment* (Columbus: The Ohio State University Press, 1974), p. 74.

11. P.B. Phillips and R.B. Fischer, "Community Mental Health Centers or Is There a Better Way?" *Journal of the Florida Medical Association* 63(1976):355–356; Bonnie Berry and Ann E. Davis, "Community Mental Health Ideology: A Problematic Model for Rural Areas," *American Journal of Orthopsychiatry* 48(1978):676–677.

12. Alex D. Pokorny, "The Course and Prognosis of Schizophrenia," in *Phenomenology and Treatment of Schizophrenia,* ed. William E. Fann, Ismet Karacan, Alex D. Pokorny, and Robert Williams (New York: Spectrum, 1978), p. 29.

13. Mike Gorman, "Community Absorption of the Mentally Ill: The New Challenge," *Community Mental Health Journal* 12(1976):125.

14. Pasamanick, Scarpitti, and Dinitz, *Schizophrenics in the Community;* Davis, Dinitz, and Pasamanick, *Schizophrenics in the New Custodial Community.*

15. Clair Creer, "Social Work With Patients and Their Families," in *Schizophrenia: Toward a New Synthesis,* ed. J.K. Wing (London: Academic, 1978), pp. 233–251.

16. Alex Pokorny, "Suicide Rates in Various Psychiatric Disorders," *Journal of Nervous and Mental Disorders* 139(1964):499.

17. Eugene B. Brody, "Social Determinants of Schizophrenic Behavior,"

in *Schizophrenia Today,* ed. D. Kamali, G. Bartholini, and D. Richter (Oxford: Pergamon, 1976), pp. 23–48.

18. B. Fish and T. Shapiro, "A Typology of Children's Psychiatric Disorders," *Journal of the American Academy of Child Psychiatry* 4(1965):32–52.

19. Ping-Nie Pao, *Schizophrenic Disorders: Theory and Treatment from a Psychodynamic Point of View* (New York: International Universities Press, 1979), p. 100.

20. Ibid.

21. Lucian A. Buck and Aaron Kramer, "Creative Potentials in Schizophrenia," *Psychiatry* 40(1977):161.

22. Turns, "The Epidemiology of Schizophrenia," p. 21.

23. Brian Cooper, "Epidemiology," in *Schizophrenia: Toward New Synthesis,* ed. J.K. Wing (London: Academic, 1978), p. 42.

24. Silvano Arieti, "The Psychotherapeutic Approach to Schizophrenia," in *The Nature of Schizophrenia: New Approaches to Research and Treatment,* ed. Lyman C. Wynne, Rue L. Cromwell, and Steven Matthysse (New York: Wiley, 1978), pp. 249–250.

25. Julian Leff, "Social and Psychological Causes of the Acute Attack," in *Schizophrenia: Toward a New Synthesis,* ed. J.K. Wing (London: Academic, 1978), p. 163.

26. C. Creer and J.K. Wing, *Schizophrenia at Home* (London: National Schizophrenia Fellowship, 1974).

27. Werner M. Mendel, *Schizophrenia: The Experience and Its Treatment* (San Francisco: Jossey-Bass, 1976), p. 96.

28. Ibid.

17 Psychiatric Aspects of Terrorism in Italy

Franco Ferracuti and
Francesco Bruno

"A [modern] ghost roams around Europe" would be a valid paraphrase of the famous words of Karl Marx in *The Communist Manifesto*. This ghost is represented today by terrorism, a phenomenon that has made Western democracies, although they are strong and modern, fear for their basic foundations. They have been compelled to rally and cooperate against it, overcoming old rivalries and old boundaries. The current wave of terrorism followed the 1968 political and social upheaval that exploded in most advanced societies. Since then, year after year, it has been spreading throughout Europe, and in some nations it has had a dramatic effect on levels of violence. However, terrorism, although it is internationally diffused, underwent a process of differentiation in its manifestations and in various national forms. Thus, terrorism has taken on an ethnosocial format in England, Spain, France, and the Netherlands, while in West Germany, Portugal, and Italy it is characterized by political-ideological trends.

Italian terrorism, the subject of this chapter, is a broad and complex phenomenon, variable in its manifestations and deeply rooted in the inner ganglia of society. Italian society is a variegated and multiform system, presently undergoing an internal political and social crisis while also confronting the worldwide energy crisis and the changes in worldwide political-strategic balance between the East and the West and between the North and the South.

Figure 17–1 shows the number of terrorist events recorded in Italy between 1969 and 1980. The figure includes the best available data on this phenomenon and provides a graphic illustration of both the frequency and the timing of these events. Table 17–1 shows the number of indicted terrorists in Italy. Of 2,107 persons indicted by the judiciary as members of terrorist organizations, 55 percent (1,165) reflect leftist ideology, while 45 percent (942) belong to right-wing organizations. Most of the arrests reflected in table 17–1 have been made recently, with 381 between April and October 1980. Approximately 3.5 percent of the Italian prison population has been charged with political crimes. Most of them reside in maximum-security prisons. Until 1974, the total number of terrorist events averaged about 250 per year; since then, that number rose steadily until 1979, when it reached the maximum figure of 2,500. Note, however, that, for 1980, a sharp decrease is evident. This reflects, at least in

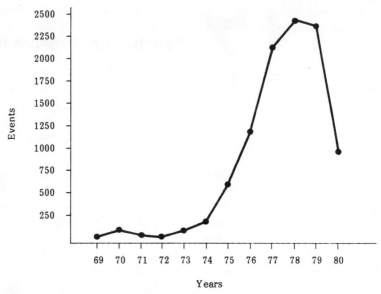

Source: Ministry of Interior, 1980. Data for 1980 are from 1 January to 15 October.

Figure 17–1. Total Number of Terrorist Events in Italy, 1969–1980

part, the tactical success of the antiterrorist forces (police, magistrature, internal-security agencies). However, the number of victims is disproportionately high for 1980, because of the Bologna bombing.

Some observations may be made on the basis of these data. The first concerns the constancy of the phenomenon. From 1974 until now, Italy has been affected by a terrorist phenomenon of such dimensions that it cannot be considered a disease of the system, to be treated through technical operations, sophisticated as they may be, or through ''surgical'' acts, which, by themselves, would mutilate the system.

In fact, Italian terrorism is associated with a large number of political,

Table 17–1
Total Number of Indicted Terrorists in Italy, by
Political Ideology

	Ideology	
Legal Status	*Left*	*Right*
Arrested	851 (73%)	254 (27%)
Free, pending trial	191 (16%)	496 (53%)
Wanted	123 (11%)	192 (20%)
Total	1,165 (100%)	942 (100%)

Source: Ministry of Interior. Data for the year 1980 are through October 15.

economic, social, and cultural crises. Terrorist events are so tightly interwoven into general events and determinants of Italian society, and so many are their dynamic interconnections, that today the terrorism variable cannot be considered independent of the system itself. In other words, the general evolution of Italian society causes or reflects terrorism, which is an integral component of society.

A second consideration, based on the trends of the phenomenon, is in order. The 1968 youth protest and the 1969 workers' struggles had the characteristics of mass movements. They were followed, on one side, by the diffusion of new cultural models among large strata of the population and, on the other, by a police control action that involved thousands of people. In the following years, up to 1974, concomitant with a general political shift to the right, a right-wing terrorism emerged and was accompanied at times by mass protest and eversion, such as the events in Reggio Calabria, Battipaglia, and l'Aquila.[1]

From 1974 to 1979, coinciding with a shift to the left by the electorate and the parliament, a left-wing terrorism emerged, culminating in 1977 and 1978 in youth mass-revolt movements (The 1977 Movement)[2] and in major military actions, such as the kidnapping and murder of Aldo Moro. The current phase, in 1980, is characterized by a new, large-scale social-control activity, by a new shift to the right by the electorate, and, again, by the violent reemergence of right-wing terrorism (for example, the Bologna railroad-station carnage).[3]

Based on an analysis of the diffusion of new cultural models following the 1977 and 1978 movements, as well as the trends just described, it is possible to forecast that, unless the system modifies itself, nationally and internationally, there will be a dramatic transformation of society in 1984 and 1985 (the maturation date of the new generation). This transformation will come about either through the impact of violent protest against the structural foundations of the system or through institutional modifications imposed from above.

If we use a two-dimensional representation of Italian society and include in this model the forms, levels, objectives, and dynamics of terrorism, we have a graphic (although probably oversimplified) representation of reality (see figure 17–2). It should be noted that terrorism is aimed in a cultural-symbolic direction, causing a shift of the system toward decreasing social cohesion. However, a new direction of terrorism is already discernible—that is, against the new structural components of society. These actions, should they become more general and more effective, could lead to the displacement of the existing system and to its restructuring in a form that is impossible to foresee.

The Definition of Terrorism

The Italian Penal Code, in considering crimes against the personality of the state, distinguishes between (1) crimes against the international personality and (2) crimes against the national personality. Article 270 punishes subversive

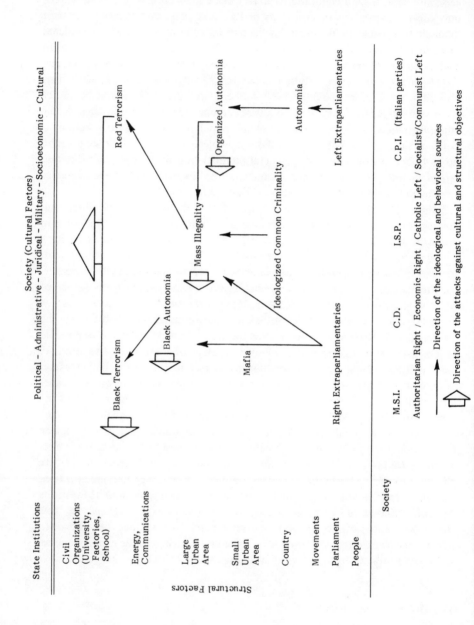

association (directed toward the establishment by violence of a dictatorship of one social class over the others). Article 284 punishes armed insurrection against the powers of the state; Article 285 punishes devastation, looting, and massacre; and Article 286 lists penalties for actions directed toward the incitement of civil war in the territory of the state. Finally, Articles 306 and following define the crimes of establishing or participating in an armed gang. Until 15 December 1979, the Penal Code did not include the crime of terrorism, but since then, by force of Decree No. 265 ("Measures Directed to Safeguard Democratic Order and Public Security"), two articles were added: Article 280, establishing penalties for anybody who "for goals of terrorism or eversion of the democratic order attempts against the life and the safety of a person," and Article 270/bis, which punishes anybody who "promotes, establishes, organises or leads associations directed towards terrorism or the eversion of the democratic order."

The Strasbourg European Convention of 27 January 1977, on the supression of terrorism, lists, in Article 1, a number of crimes that, although belonging to the category of political crimes, are considered to be common crimes and are consequently subject to extradition. The crime of terrorism is now internationally recognized and, from a judicial standpoint, encompasses all those illegal behaviors that are acted out to intimidate or frighten people and institutions for ideological, nationalistic, ethnic, religious, or political goals.

Considering its diffusion and generality, the term *terrorism* has assumed a highly indicative meaning but much less definitional precision. Therefore, if we move from an information-expressive communication to a structural analysis, in order to increase the level of understanding of the phenomenon, a sharper definition is necessary. However, when the definition of terrorism is contemplated, it soon becomes evident that no definition can identify the reality of terrorist behavior unless it is related to a preexisting system of values and established power. The relativity of the term is obvious. Thus, for the French revolutionary, *terror* was equivalent to *justice,* and the same label was used by both the "red" revolutionaries of 1917 and the "white" counterrevolutionaries of Russia. For Hitler, and for Nazism in general, terror was simply the government, the expression of state power.

Finally, it is obvious that terrorists are terrorists only if and when they are defeated; if they win, if they become the leaders of the new order, they become heroes and heads of state. Examples of this can be found in many dictatorships. Canetti defines the "ruler" as the "survivor,"[4] and Enzensberger maintains that the government belongs to anybody who can kill those over whom he rules.[5] In the final analysis, terror is a component of sovereignty and, as such, includes the concept of domination. However, the etymology of the word *terror* includes the active meaning of "fear that is being inflicted" and is very different from the passive meaning of the word *metus,* or "fear that is being felt." But if this is terror, then terrorists are not simply criminals or guerrilla fighters.

Their purpose is to spread terror, since only terror can legitimize a power that they do not really have. Through terror, they portray themselves as "antistate" and reap their only possible harvest—on the emotional-moral level.

If we follow this approach in analyzing one of the most serious terrorist acts, the kidnapping and murder of Aldo Moro,[6] some useful comments can be made. The Moro incident can be divided into three phases: (1) the preparation and the kidnapping, (2) the imprisonment and "trial" of Moro and the negotiations with the state, and (3) the assassination and its political consequences. In the first phase, the Red Brigades acted as guerrilla fighters, ambushing and killing military men whose task it was to protect Moro against attacks. In the second phase, the men of the Red Brigades, through a dreadful blackmail of the state, began using terror to achieve political legitimacy and identification with "red power," which was their main purpose. The third phase, culminating in the dramatic killing of the statesman, was the display of terror. Both the state and the terrorists found themselves in a blind alley: the former for not having been able to save a man who had been the symbol of the institutions, and the latter for having believed that they had attained the moral legitimacy they were seeking, but which they ultimately could not sustain and manage. Subsequent events have shown a widening gap between the people and the institutions (as represented, for example, by a decrease in the percentage of voting) and the continuing deterioration of a terrorist organization that, without enough strength to establish itself as an antistate, found itself carrying too heavy a burden.

In contrast, in the similar Schleyer kidnapping, which saw a confrontation between terrorists and the German state, the terrorists were dramatically defeated, not only on the military level but also on the level of moral legitimacy. Finally, the collective suicide at Stammheim represented, materially and dramatically, the failure of the terrorist action as well as the reinstatement of the dominion of the state over the life and death of its citizens.

These examples illustrate an essential point in the analysis of terrorist events—that not all guerrilla fighters are terrorists and not all terrorists are guerrilla fighters.

It must be understood that the strategies to be used against these two types of behavior are different, just as the behaviors are different, even when they coexist in the same individuals. Whereas guerrilla fighters must be beaten on the military level, terrorists must be beaten specifically at the moral and emotional level. For guerrilla fighters, political solutions are needed, taking into account the causes of their origin and offering possibilities of cooperation within the system; for the terrorists, political, psychological, and cultural solutions are necessary, taking into account the consequences of their actions and preventing them.

In reality, terrorism is a definitional category of a behavior identifiable as terrorist only in relation to the dominating power and value system. As a category, it is not discrete enough to include all events that may be identified as terrorist in all sociopolitical systems. Its relativity, both chronologically (intrasystemic) and politically (intersystemic and intrasystemic), is too wide and too prevalent. It is therefore necessary to assess the basic meaning of *terror* and to discuss its implications on narrower political and strategic levels. At this point, it is possible to assess some of the more strictly psychiatric aspects of Italian terrorism, keeping in mind the limitations and the low explanatory power of a strictly psychopathological approach.

Terrorism as a Psychiatric Category

Since Lombroso, the problem of the relationship between psychiatry and criminal behavior has been formulated but not resolved. Modern psychiatry is the product of the era of enlightenment and positivist rationality. Psychiatry was born as a science when it became obvious that certain human behaviors, disruptive to the community, were not the portentous manifestations of occult forces, nor were they caused by possession by evil spirits; they were, on the contrary, symptoms of a "disease of the mind." Thus, psychiatric hospitals replaced the stakes, and the "witches" were no longer managed by judges of the Inquisition, but by physicians.

By analogy with what was taking place in other branches of medical science, the psychiatric search was on for the "microbe" of mental derangement. This was finally discovered in the brains of subjects affected by general paralysis of the insane (tertiary syphilis, a limited and now disappearing neuropsychiatric illness). This was the first proof that a physical, pathological anomaly of the brain could produce behavioral abnormalities. At that point, general behavioral deviance was no longer considered a definitive concept, and it entered the domain of biological constructs. But the search for biological components of madness did not often meet with success. On the contrary, it was soon evident that most abnormal and deviant behaviors could not be explained by the pathological degeneration of the cerebral organic structure.

At this point, first in the anthropological school (of which Lombroso was one of the foremost members) and then in the psychoanalytic school, the attempt was made to identify the pathogenetic value of morphological and psychodynamic traits in the physical person (in his biological structure) and in the psychological person (including his unconscious components and his personality). Both these approaches, and their subsequent derivations, having based their conceptualizations on untestable theories, inevitably retreated to a definitional approach. Only very recently, through the utilization of new neurophysiological techniques and through the contributions of psychopharmacology, has psychiatry reentered the domain of pathological biology.

This lengthy historical and epistemological discussion was necessary in order to address the question of whether terrorist behavior should be considered

206 The Mad, the Bad, and the Different

the product of a pathological mind or if, instead, it should be viewed (at least in some historical periods and in some sociopolitical contexts) as a normal event—primarily a definitional, relativistic, and political construct. Psychodynamic explanations, for example, could be helpful in understanding the phenomenon at the level of the individual motivations of a single terrorist, within the domain of political psychology, whereas a psychiatric strategy, limited to individual treatment, containment, and isolation, would be unrealistic. The normality of terrorism would reinforce the need for an interdisciplinary approach to its explanatory understanding and to its operational management.

One other consideration is in order. When the analyst must operate without the benefit of a large data base, he is forced to postulate a theory that is only a provisional tool. The analyst must destroy this theory and replace it with increasingly better theory, more suitable for the intended operations, until the necessary knowledge is available. Theories, therefore, and the definitions they provide, are temporary tools, useful only as a transitional stage toward deeper and better levels of knowledge. This is true for any science, from physics to political science, and the analysis of terrorism is no exception.

Lombroso and his contemporaries maintained that the anarchists (the terrorists of the time) were anthropologically very similar to although not the same as, one type of "delinquent man" and that, therefore, terrorist behavior was simply an abnormal variant of criminal behavior.[7] Obviously, this belief has no foundation in reality.

For the psychoanalytic school, the problem shifts from the analysis of violent behavior to the analysis of basic behavioral dynamics. On this level, concepts such as the death instinct or the defense mechanism of projection and the paranoid identification of the persecutor with the state and its institutions are introduced. The etiology of these dynamics is often attributed to a disturbed and conflictual relationship with the father figure. However, these analyses are purely theoretical. Their therapeutic implications are limited to some individual cases, and they carry practically no political or strategic implications. The limitations of psychoanalytic psychobiographies, for example, are well known.

Modern integrated psychiatry seems directed toward the identification of a neurochemical basis for some forms of schizophrenia and for those behaviors defined as borderline because they are between the boundaries of psychopathy and psychosis. Some terrorists may be classified in this rather imprecise category. But again, the practical consequences of this vague classification are minimal. It is obvious that a general psychiatric explanation of terrorism is impossible. To define all terrorists as mentally ill would be an easy way to solve the problem, simply by invoking evil spirits in order to exclude from normality those from whom we want to be as different as possible. This would be an excellent solution to our own problems of identity as compared with terrorists but would not correspond to either clinical or social reality. However, some psychiatric aspects of terrorism are worthwhile for the purposes of this discussion.

Psychiatric Aspects of "Red" and "Black" Terrorism

In Italy, terrorism is divided into two main ideological cores, with different psychiatric aspects. "Red" terrorism, which is the more diffuse and more deeply entrenched, has an ideological matrix that can be defined as Marxist or neo-Marxist and can be further differentiated into two levels. The first level, which is highly organized, has a rather pure Leninist derivation and a rigid conceptual and operational dogmatism. The second level, largely represented by the so-called Autonomia, has more tenuous organizational boundaries and a neo-Marxist derivation, characterized by soft boundaries that are open to contributions from many different sources. Among the main theorists of the Autonomia movement is Toni Negri, currently imprisoned and charged with participation in the political and managerial directorate of Italian "red" eversion.

The philosophy of Autonomia rests on two main ideological tenets: the rejection of work and the proclamation of so-called basic rights. The most recent ideological evolution of the movement appears to be characterized by an increasing emphasis on mass struggle as the engine of the revolutionary transformation of society. In his last ideological tract, *Communism and War,* Toni Negri advocates going beyond terrorism, which he calls "simulation of war," through the political organization of the class struggle (the new class of social laborers, or those who are united by shared marginality, by rejection of work, and by the will to conquer wealth), in order to reach the utopian reality of real communism.[8] In this vision, communism is portrayed as a kind of new era in which all that is utopian today will become possible tomorrow. It is as if the approaching end of this millenium, just as a thousand years ago, holds, for some, the expectation of a supreme event.

In reality, however, the theme of the rejection of work is rather crude and contrasts with the desire for progress shared by humanity as a whole. The theme of basic rights, however, must be fully understood, because it expresses a reality of our times, and it coincides with another basic motive—the drive toward pleasure. A convergence of mass needs and pressures on this theme is therefore possible, particularly for frustrated, unfulfilled, and marginal youths, resulting in the birth of a political organization that is capable of attacking and overthrowing the structure of the system.

This brief description of the ideological foundations of Autonomia illustrates adequately the richness and variety of the political conceptualizations that are possible. Substantial agreement exists between Autonomia and a modern school of thought devoted to the reelaboration of classic Marxism, and this political philosophy lends itself to a cultural model and a value system that is popular in several national contexts, particularly among youth.

Obviously, even extreme adherence to Autonomia cannot, in itself, be considered a symptom of psychopathology. Autonomia's ideology is variable and multifaceted; it proposes utopia but continually accepts criticism and self-criticism. Thus, it helps to overcome or to compensate, not so much for the deep anxieties of individual subjects as for the more superficial, existential anxieties of loosely aggregated groups searching for a value system to supplant the anomie of the youth culture.

Clinical analyses based on the few available case histories of individual left-wing terrorists show that left-wing terrorists rarely suffer from serious personality defects. Normally, they demonstrate a good capacity to withstand stress, to organize themselves into groups, to sustain one another, and to disseminate their ideologies. Their adherence to their ideological beliefs is always firm and very often unshakable. It is interesting that even those who choose to collaborate with the state tend not only to justify but also to rationalize their choice into an ideologically acceptable context. For many young men who wish to protest against the value system of the ruling society, the choice of terrorism as an ideological credo and as a life-style has been an alternative to another popular and self-destructive choice—drug abuse.

Often, entering the drug culture has abruptly ended deviant careers, which began with the rejection of the family and of work and which would have ended, in the normal course of events, in the "armed party." In a few cases, drug abuse has remained as another deviance on the path to terrorism. Ordinarily, however, drug abuse and membership in a left-wing terrorist group do not coexist, particularly in the better organized groups, where drug abuse would reduce one's chances of being selected by the leaders. Drug abuse is much more frequent among right-wing terrorists.

The ideological derivation of right-wing terrorism is unequivocally based on loosely connected Nazi-fascist tenets, not only in their historical roots but also in the works of philosophers and writers belonging to the so-called new right. Among the main figures of this school are Julius Evola and, in Italy, Franco Freda. The ideological core of this school is simple and linear. It is almost solely based on the search for identity and the victory of the superman or hero. The world is sharply dichotomized into all bad (represented by the enemy) and all good (personalized by the hero). The enemy is nonhuman, not good enough. He is the enemy because he is not a hero and is not friendly to the hero. The utopian goal reflects a mythical and reassuring past or a future conceived as a new order in a static society, rigidly structured into classes and corporations, beyond capitalism and communism, and capable of offering the masses the certainty of authority.

This ideology is essentially capable of sustaining delusions of rebirth. So deeply ingrained is it in the "black" terrorist's mentality that he can be motivated to search for the maximum possible destructive power of his attacks against the state in order to bring about the myth of reconstruction of a new society. The dangerousness of this ideology, when transformed into a mass movement, is historically evident upon examination of Hitler and other dictators. Recently, the whole population of Cambodia has been decimated by atrocious massacres designed to destroy the old order to make room for the construction of an unreal, rigidly egalitarian new order.

The ideology of right-wing terrorism can be an easy, safe psychological shelter for restless and even psychologically damaged youth. Clinical experience has clearly confirmed this hypothesis. Among right-wing terrorists (who have been examined more frequently than left-wing terrorists, both during a trial, since they are frequently subjected to expert psychiatric opinion, and clinically, since their parents have requested psychiatric help), disturbed, borderline, or even psychotic personalities have a much higher incidence. They are often individualistic; unable to stand stress, such as imprisonment (they sometimes become suicidal in prison); and unable to organize themselves into a structure, except for loose, pseudomilitary hierarchies. Even when they do not suffer from a psychopathological condition, their basic psychological traits reflect an authoritarian-extremist personality, with the following distinctive features:

1. Ambivalence toward authority (submission-aggression, imbalance);
2. Poor and defective insight;
3. Adherence to conventional behavioral patterns, with poor ability to criticize and a tendency toward emulation and repetition of attitudes and behaviors;
4. Emotional detachment from the consequences of their actions;
5. Disturbances in sexual identity, with role uncertainties;
6. Superstition, "magic," and stereotyped thinking;
7. Etero- and autodestructiveness;
8. Low-level educational reference patterns; and
9. Perception of weapons as fetishes and adherence to violent subcultural values.

The practical implications of this characterological pattern are self-evident: right-wing terrorism can be very dangerous, not only and not mainly because of its eversive ideology, but because of its general unpredictability and destructiveness. In right-wing terrorism, the individual terrorists are frequently psychopathological and the ideology is empty; in left-wing terrorists, ideology is outside reality, and the terrorists are both more normal and more fanatical.

Psychopathological and Sociopolitical Aspects of Terrorism

In 1873, M.A. Bakunin, in his book on the state and anarchy, stated that it is indispensable for the people to share a common ideal that is historically developed from the depths of popular instincts and raised, amplified, and enlightened by a series of significant events, through bitter and hard experiences.[9] It is also necessary for the people to possess a general concept of valid rights and a deep, committed, quasi-religious faith in these rights. When this faith and these ideals meet with poverty and lead to desperation, then social revolution is inevitable, imminent, and irresistible. For the Russian anarchists, therefore, revolutionary behavior was the outcome of other conditions, ideology, experiences, fanaticism, and desperation.

This statement may still be valid and applicable to terrorist behavior. The relationship between the psychopathological and the sociopolitical aspects of terrorism is one of the most interesting issues in the scientific analysis of this phenomenon. To some extent, this issue is linked to the solution of an even more important issue concerning individual and social deviance. What follows is only a preliminary attempt at hypothesis formulation, strictly of heuristic value and without any expectation of explanatory validity.

According to Smith, political behaviors stem from the simultaneous interaction of many factors; early social antecedents interact in the social environment, which is conceived as a basis for personality development and for the introjection of attitudes.[10] Political behavior results from the interplay of these factors with personality processes and basic traits, under the impact of a situation immediately preceding the action. By reason of its very nature, then, political behavior modifies not only the immediate situation but also the social environment and the early social antecedents. Obviously, of the four factors listed by Bakunin, two (ideology and experience) are primarily environmental, and two (fanaticism and desperation) are primarily individual. It is conceivable that psychopathology could interact at either of the two levels of the system—in the environment and in the individual—or at both levels simultaneously. Although it is clearly a biological and personal factor, psychopathology can transfer into the environment as a distorted cultural, subcultural, or ethical value.

All societies are structured around a code or system of values, which can change but cannot be absent. The value system can be more or less permissive and tolerant toward deviant behaviors. When the code is rigid, deviant (including psychopathological) behaviors are repressed and isolated; when the value system is permissive, such behaviors are first tolerated, then accepted, and then can become values of the system and may even become dominant values.

Italian society is currently very tolerant; it has become open and receptive to many deviant behaviors, particularly psychopathologies. Recent laws of the state have closed psychiatric institutions, others have decriminalized drug abuse, and so on. This movement, if conducted too quickly and without adequate evaluation, cost-benefit analysis, and social planning, can lead to environmental psychopathology, which interacts dynamically with introjected deviant behaviors and reacts more or less like a personality threatened by neurotic impulses. From this perspective, it is evident that both forms of psychopathology can interact differently with terrorism, as causal or cocausal factors. When psychopathology acts mostly at the individual level, what results is unpredictable, highly destructive terrorism—limited to the activities of individuals or small, loose groups. However, when psychopathology interacts mostly at an environmental level, diffuse terrorism results—less destructive, more predictable, and more easily kept under control (although politically highly destabilizing). This is typical of the amorphous area usually referred to as mass illegality. A model of this hypothesis is presented in figure 17–3, which portrays the various possible etiologies of pathological terrorism.

A dynamic model of the individual and social etiological factors associated with psychopathological terrorism and of its consequences on the system is shown in figure 17–4. This model integrates that reflected in figure17–3 by expressing its dynamics and by utilizing the concept of anomie. If anomie is conceived as a situation characterized by increasingly sharp dissent between the masses and state institutions, within a context of loose integration marked by

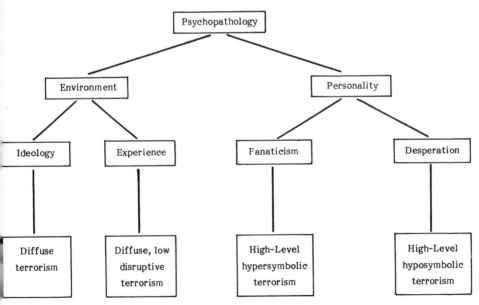

Figure 17–3. Individual and Environmental Etiologies of Pathological Terrorism

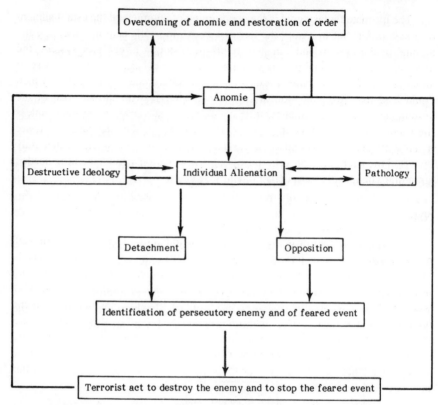

Figure 17–4. Dynamic Model of Psychopathological Terrorism

the disappearance of basic values, then its importance in the etiology of alienation is obvious. Alienation is the resulting individual or collective existential condition of loss of relations, lack of participation, and a decrease in the ability to control pathology and destructive ideologies. The interlocking relationship among pathology, alienation, and destructive ideologies is evident.

Through the mechanisms of emotional and social detachment from residual societal values and through opposition to the system (which is perceived as weak, empty and unsafe), a second process is put into motion in the individual or in the small group. This process consists of identifying the persecutory enemy, or the feared event, with an object or a member of the system. Then, in a destructive and oppositional-reaction pattern against this object or member, the terrorist attack is conceived, becomes psychologically justified, is planned, and is carried out. In this dynamic interplay, the carrying out of the terrorist act not only fails to generate anxiety in the perpetrator but actually functions as a compensatory mechanism for the existential anxiety that precedes the terrorist act itself.

The ultimate fantasy goal is the overcoming of anomie and the establishment of a new order, but in reality the terrorist event, in itself, can only increase the anomie of the system and can only reinforce, through a feedback system, the anomie-generating social process, thus perpetuating and aggravating the existing situation. At this point, a self-reinforcing, dynamic process is triggered, which could lead to a level of anomie that is incompatible with the survival of the system and, therefore, to destruction of or drastic change in the system, unless the needed steps to change it in an orderly way, before disorder takes over, are taken with decisiveness and courage. The hope of the free world is that Italy may find the strength to prevent this disastrous scenario by implementing needed structural changes that are democratically selected.

Notes

1. Reggio Calabria is a city in southern Italy. In 1970, a long period of revolt against the state began there when the city was excluded as the head-quarters of the regional government for the Calabria region. The movement was immediately identified as right-wing, and it channeled the protest of people who were affected by economic underdevelopment. At l'Aquila, a similar movement took place in the same year, culminating in an attack on the city hall and on the federation of the C.P.I. The riots in Battipaglia (also a southern city), however, caused by the firing of the workers, had a left-wing connotation. These riots, which took place in 1969, saw, for the first time in the republic's history, the people pitted against the police forces.

2. In 1977, many violent manifestations and riots took place in Italy, culminating in a large gathering in Bologna. These manifestations were pro-moted by students and youth movements within the ideological framework of *Autonomia* ("Autonomy"), violently opposing the institutional left.

3. This terrorist bombing resulted in 85 deaths and 226 wounded.

4. Elias Canetti, *Masse und Macht* (Hamburg: Veber Verlag, 1960), pp. 259–282.

5. Hans Maguus Enzensberger, *Politik und Verbrechen* (Frankfurt am Main: Surhkamp Verlag, 1964).

6. There are many Italian publications on the Moro case; in addition, a parliamentary commission is investigating the case.

7. Cesare Lombroso, *Gli Anarchici* ("The Anarchists") (Rome: Napo-leone, 1894).

8. Antonio Negri, *Il Comunismo e la Guerra* ("Communism and War"), (Milan: Feltrinelli, 1980).

9. Michail A. Bakunin, *Gosudorstvenost'i Anarchija, Cost I.* (Zurich and Geneva: Izdonie Sociol'no, Revoljucionnoj Party, I., 1973).

10. M. Brewster Smith, *Political Attitudes,* in *Handbook of Political Psy-chology,* ed. J.N. Knutson (San Francisco: Jossey-Bass, 1973), pp. 57–82.

Part V:
Special Issues in
Criminology

Part V consists of several chapters whose scope extends beyond the categories reflected in the first four sections of this book. The issues raised in this section are generic, including the sociology of law, the political nature of criminal-justice programming, and the teaching of criminology and criminal justice.

In chapter 18, Richard L. Schuster analyzes the development of the sociology of law and makes the point that its evolution has been slow and sporadic. A major catalyst to the development of the sociology of law, he argues, has been the recent controversy surrounding what he calls the "conflict-critical approach," which has created a resurgence of interest in the study of law and the legal system, rather than in the etiology of crime. Schuster concludes by assessing the future of the sociology of law, which he views optimistically despite some important obstacles to its continued development.

In 1976, Ohio's Parole Officer Aide Program was selected as one of seventeen "exemplary projects" throughout the United States. However, at the time the announcement was being made that the project had been called exemplary, the Ohio Adult Parole Authority was already moving to abolish it. This paradoxical situation serves as the focus for Joseph E. Scott's chapter. Scott, who published an evaluation of the project in 1975, offers an assessment of why the project was considered exemplary and why, being so honored, it was systematically dismantled by the Adult Parole Authority. What he finds is illuminating with respect to state-federal relations, seed-money grants for action projects, and the politics of state bureaucracies. In pursuit of the reason why an exemplary project should be so readily abandoned by a state agency, Scott's analysis provides a stimulating case study, which certainly has generic implications for evaluation research, criminal-justice reform, and the politics of program implementation.

Sy Dinitz has been honored many times for his excellent teaching, and those of us who have had the privilege of being in his classes and working with him in independent research projects can attest to the fact that he is the consummate teacher. For the final chapter in part V, we therefore thought it appropriate to ask one of Professor Dinitz's former students, who is especially known for his excellent teaching, to contribute an essay on teaching criminology. Tom Foster complied with our request by providing a convincing argument for the benefits of experiential learning in undergraduate criminology and criminal-justice courses and programs. Foster asserts that such learning has pedagogical, economic, and moral-political benefits. Drawing extensively on his own experience as an instructor, as well as on published research on learning and teaching,

Foster skillfully assesses both the advantages and the obstacles associated with the implementation of experiential learning and offers some suggestions for instructors who may wish to enrich their teaching in this way.

The chapters in part V bring us full circle, back to our original focus on generic issues in criminology and deviance. Whether our concern is theoretical explanations, methodological approaches, or teaching, the theme of this book closely reflects Professor Dinitz's emphasis on intellectual diversity and the paramount importance of absolute academic freedom of inquiry. If the chapters in this section and the previous four sections manage to convey that spirit of inquiry, this book will have achieved its purpose.

18 On the Sociology of Law

Richard L. Schuster

The concept of social control has been a central issue for sociological inquiry since the discipline's formation. From this concern, the subdiscipline of the sociology of law, or legal sociology, was developed to examine the nature and functions of the formal aspects of social control. Despite the central notion of social control and the all-encompassing role that law plays in modern social life, the area of legal sociology did not develop to the extent that one would expect until recently; its growth was sporadic, with periods during which it was virtually ignored.[1]

The Sporadic Development of Legal Sociology

The sociology of law has cycled through several calls for revival and periods of moribundity.[2] In 1907, Pound called for the "need of sociological jurisprudence."[3] Thirty years later, in 1937, Timasheff in answering the question, "What is the sociology of law?" argues that "there is room for the new science of the sociology of law."[4] However, a decade later, in 1947, Gurvitch would state that "the sociology of law is still in full course of formulation . . . the sociology of law still has no clearly defined boundaries."[5] Nearly two decades later, in a special issue of *Social Problems,* a journal devoted to the sociology of law, Schwartz proclaimed "the birth of a *new* subdiscipline within the American Sociology"[6] (emphasis added). In the same journal issue, Skolnick modified this statement by claiming that empirical studies done by American legal sociologists were recent but that philosophical work, mainly by law professors, had a much older tradition.[7] The latest resurgence, marked by that special issue of *Social Problems,* has continued for a decade and a half. Whether legal sociology will develop into a mature field or cycle back into oblivion remains to be seen.

In this chapter, I will discuss some possible reasons that have been given for the slow development of the sociology of law in the past and briefly delve into the future for the area. I will also cite the forces in legal sociology that have influenced its latest rebirth. Because of a need for brevity, many of my arguments will be truncated, but I hope they will provide some basis for thought concerning the development of this important area of research.

Reasons for the Slow Development of Legal Sociology

The sociology of law may have had as one of its problems the fact that it is composed of "sociology" and "law." Evan contends that the discipline of sociology has remained so ill defined and has had so little consensus on theory or methodology that is has provided little direction for the sociology of law.[8] The parent discipline of sociology has been so beset with major theoretical and methodological rifts that the sociology of law has had no single paradigm to guide its theory or research. (Although Chambliss argued that the sociology of law was guided by a consensus paradigm,[9] I believe this perspective reflects more a set of assumptions about law and its functions than a paradigm in the true theoretical sense.[10]) Thus, this argument posits that the sociology of law reflects much of the confusion and conflict of its parent discipline.

The argument that sociology's unrest somehow inhibited the development of the sociology of law has two problems. First, other subdisciplines, such as the sociology of the family and criminology, progressed steadily, although they experienced the same conflicts within sociology. Second, one must consider that, although legal sociology was primarily under the purview of sociologists, it was not solely a sociological venture.[11] Law, political science, and economics are three of the other areas that have contributed to the sociology of law. Many of the earliest writers in legal sociology (including Max Weber) were lawyers by training and sociologists by avocation.[12] A perusal of the list of contributors to any major reader or journal devoted to legal sociology will show an assortment of disciplines represented. Thus, it may be presumptuous to claim that sociology's problems account for all legal sociology's problems.

The choice of law as the subject for study may have constituted another major difficulty for legal sociologists. Law has not been an easily defined phenomenon. Gurvitch wrote that the definitions of law were innumerable.[13] Bohannan pointed out that "more scholarship has probably gone into defining and explaining the concept of 'law' than into any other concept still in central use in the social sciences."[14]

Another major source of differences exists between American and European legal sociologists. Americans have tended to rely on a definition that stressed the "law on the books" or the law as a product of political action. European writers used the more literal translation of the European terms *reicht, droit, diritto,* and *ius* to refer to a more moral connotation, or a "what is right" implication.[15] The European definition of law is much broader than the American version, and since much of the early work in legal sociology is of European origin, this distinction has further confused the issue.[16]

It should be noted that scholars in many areas within the social sciences must contend with vaguely defined subject matter, so this difficulty was not unique to legal sociology. Further, many writers have dealt with the problem by accepting one definition and operating under its assumptions or, as Akers and

Hawkins have done, have simply argued that there *is* general agreement on the definition of law.[17]

Another possible reason for legal sociology's slow growth may have been that legal sociologists have been divided on the goal of their field. Should they maintain an essentially value-free, positivist approach, which would divorce them from questions of what law ought to be or could be? Or should they strive to evaluate the law and the legal system with an eye to value positions that might lead to reform or social action? The classic exchange between Black and Nonet summarizes these two positions succinctly.[18] Their debate reflects the major and somewhat competing origins of the sociology of law. On the one hand, the area was a child of sociology, a sociology that, in its early stages attempted to impress other, more established disciplines with its methodological rigor. Since sociologists could contribute their research methods to the study of law, this became a central issue for legal sociologists. The ideal researcher was to apply skills neutrally in order to examine a phenomenon but not to advocate a course of action or even to design the research to have a practical payoff.

On the other hand, a major force in the formation of legal sociology was the legal-realist and sociological-jurisprudence movements within law. The influences of Karl Llewellyn, Jerome Frank, and Justice Oliver Wendell Holmes (legal realism) and Roscoe Pound (sociological jurisprudence) have been marked.[19] These writers emphasized the study of the living law and the law as it ought to be. The questions of values, morals, and, ultimately, evaluation were an integral part of this line of thinking, which was passed on to the fledgling discipline. This position against value neutrality was reinforced later by the debate within sociology concerning value-free research.[20] The debate over this issue was not unique to the sociology of law but, because of the sources of its heritage, was more apparent at an earlier stage.

Schur and others have argued that a possible reason for sociology's failure to study law adequately has been the perceived incompatibility of the disciplines of law and sociology.[21] According to this argument, sociologists shied away from the study of law because they saw it as an area in which they were not properly trained and in which they could not "speak the language." As David Riesman stated, sociologists may have believed that there was a "factual impenetrability resulting from the sheer overwhelming and opaque bulk of data that must be mastered."[22]

Donald Young cites three fundamental reasons for the difficulty social scientists have in working with lawyers: (1) lawyers are advocates and thus committed to one side of a cause, whereas social scientists attempt to be value-free and to consider all evidence; (2) lawyers accept precedent and rely on it, but social scientists are inclined to test all assumptions; and (3) lawyers regard the expertise of social scientists as useful only for expert testimony on specialized matters, not for knowledge *in* the law.[23]

Although Young's reasons may overstate the problem of interaction between social scientists and lawyers, the distance between the two disciplines has traditionally existed, even if it was one of perception rather than reality. Several methods for bridging that gap have emerged recently. One method is for law schools to institute law-and-society programs, such as the one that was begun at the University of Wisconsin in the 1960s, in which students are trained in both law and the social sciences. Other attempts have included collaborative efforts in writing and research between lawyers and social scientists, such as the Davis reader[24] and the increase in the number of individuals with double degrees (for example, J.D. and Ph.D.). Also to be applauded are the law-school deans (such as at The Ohio State University) who opened up their law schools to nonlaw students by allowing graduate students to minor in law.

The Rebirth of Legal Sociology and the Conflict-Critical Approach

The decade and a half from the mid 1960s through the 1970s saw a major resurgence of the sociology of law. This rebirth can be seen in the proliferation of texts and readers in the area.[25] In addition, at least five English-language journals devoted primarily to legal sociology were founded: *Law and Society Review, British Journal of Law and Society, Crime and Social Justice, International Journal of the Sociology of Law,* and *Law and Human Behavior.* This marked increase in material led Currie to proclaim that the sociology of law was "by now an important and well-established enterprise."[26]

Obviously, no single element caused the increase in writing and research in legal sociology, but I believe that one important factor was the rise of the conflict-critical approach. (This approach has been variously labeled "conflict," "radical," "critical," or "Marxist" and covers a wide range of ideologies, so any attempt to characterize it will necessitate some oversimplification.) Until the 1960s, the predominant perspective in the sociology of law was what Chambliss called a consensus approach and others have called a structural-functionalist approach.[27] Simply put, this view saw the formation and functioning of law as the product of group consensus. Freeley notes that two main features have characterized research on the sociology of law: (1) social scientists have studied the discrepancies between the idealized version of law and its actual application, and (2) law is understood as a command supported by sanction.[28] These features illustrate the consensus approach's acceptance of the facticity of law. In other words, the law was considered a given—an accomplished fact—and one did not challenge the assumption that law reflected the collective will.

Although the consensus approach was not a monolithic ideology, the number of opponents of this view remained small until the 1960s. Because there was little ideological controversy within the sociology of law (or the larger field of criminology), the prevailing research went largely unchallenged.[29] As Hunt noted concerning academic law, controversy is the mother of intellectual advance.[30] A field in which the major assumptions remain unchallenged will tend to stagnate.

Since law was accepted as the will of the people, the need was not to study the law, but rather to study the deviants who broke the law. The major research effort was in criminal etiology, not in the analysis of the law (and the enforcement of the law), which defined criminal behavior. Criminologists were not drawn to the study of the law or the legal system—partially because it was not problematic; crime or criminal behavior, however, was. With the exception of a few isolated scholars, the field of criminology was devoted to theorizing about criminal behavior.

With the rise of the labeling perspective in the 1960s, the focus of study began to change. Self-report studies had shown that massive amounts of hidden delinquency and crime existed and that, in many cases, delinquents differed little from nondelinquents. Labeling theory picked up this theme and argued that the process of labeling was more important than the characteristics of the deviant. Although the labeling perspective failed to explain the causes of deviancy, it raised the issue of the process involved in labeling and the source of the labels. The consensus approach had taken that process as a given, but now the process itself came under scrutiny. Research began to focus on the labelers rather than on the labeled. Labeling theory was not a major break with the consensus tradition, but it served as a beachhead for the more radical conflict-critical approach.[31]

In the decade of the 1970s, the conflict-critical approach, as exemplified by the work of Chambliss, Quinney, Turk, and others, shifted the emphasis of analysis from the criminals to the law and the legal system, especially the criminal-justice system, which created and applied the criminal definitions.[32] This is not to argue that the conflict-critical approach emerged complete in the 1970s, but that its adherents reached a "critical mass," which could not be easily ignored.[33] The conflict-critical approach mounted a challenge to the prevailing consensus approach to refocus its attention toward the law. Whether or not one agreed with proponents of the conflict-critical approach, a response to the issues they raised and the accusations they leveled against the legal system was necessary. Consensus followers were compelled to defend their theories and to generate data on topics related to law. These efforts renewed an interest in the law, if for no other reason than for the defense of previously unchallenged ideas.

The conflict-critical approach was important for the revival of the sociology of law because it (1) provided the controversy needed to simulate research and theorizing and (2) redirected the attention of a substantial number of criminologists toward the study of law and the legal system and away from the etiology of crime. By stressing the interest-group nature of law and the role of the state rather than the criminal in creating criminality, the conflict-critical approach focused attention once again on the need to study law. Thus, the conflict-critical school played a crucial role in the resurgence of interest in law and the legal system.

The Future of the Sociology of Law

At present, legal sociology looks promising, but one development presents a possible obstacle for the future of the field. The area called criminal justice or the sociology of criminal justice experienced a phenomenal growth in the 1970s.[34] This growth could be a double-edged sword for the sociology of law. An increased interest in the criminal-justice system has spawned much research into the functions of criminal-justice agencies as enforcers of criminal law. Thus it has aided the latest rebirth in research on law-related topics. However, criminal justice has grown so large that there have been calls for its separation into a discipline distinct from criminology or the sociology of law. An example of this is the formation of separate professional associations (for example, the Academy of Criminal Justice Sciences) and the emergence of separate criminal-justice departments and even separate colleges in some universities, with graduate degrees offered in criminal justice. Further, much research in criminal justice is focused on pure policy formulation, with little regard for theory building or testing. This does little to expand the sociology of law.

Despite the possible effects of criminal justice, the future of the sociology of law looks bright from the standpoint of quantity and quality of research. Sociology of law courses are offered at many universities. As noted earlier, several journals devoted to legal sociology have been founded, and there has been a tremendous increase in the number of textbooks, readers, articles, and papers being written. Although I do not believe that the sociology of law has necessarily come of age, it has developed enough interest and momentum to grow and develop without risk of again quickly lapsing into its seemingly periodic quiescence.

Notes

1. Robert M. Rich, *The Sociology of Law: An Introduction to its Theorists and Theories* (Washington, D.C.: University Press of America, 1978), pp. x–xi.

2. Clive Grace and Philip Wilkinson, *Sociological Inquiry and Legal Phenomena* (New York: St. Martin's Press, 1978), p. 4.

3. Roscoe Pound, "The Need of Sociological Jurisprudence," in *The Sociology of Law,* ed. Rita James Simon (San Francisco: Chandler, 1968), p. 9.

4. N.S. Timasheff, "What Is Sociology of Law?" in *The Sociology of Law*, ed. Rita James Simon (San Francisco: Chandler, 1968), p. 56.

5. Georges Gurvitch, *Sociology of Law* (New York: Philosophical Library, 1942), p. 1.

6. R. Schwartz, "Introduction," in "Law and Society" supplement to *Social Problems* 13(1965).

7. Jerome H. Skolnick, "The Sociology of Law in America: Overview and Trends," in "Law and Society" supplement to *Social Problems* 13(1965).

8. William M. Evan, "Introduction," in *The Sociology of Law*, ed. William M. Evan (New York: Free Press, 1980), p. 1.

9. William J. Chambliss, "Functional and Conflict Theories of Crime," *MSS Modular Publications* 17 (1974):1.

10. Charles E. Reasons and Robert M. Rich, "Part Three: The Sociology of Law: Competing Paradigms," in *The Sociology of Law: A Conflict Perspective*, ed. Charles E. Reasons and Robert M. Rich (Toronto: Butterworths, 1978), p. 139.

11. R.B.M. Cotterrell, "Jurisprudence and Sociology of Law," in *The Sociology of Law*, ed. William M. Evan (New York: Free Press, 1980), p. 21.

12. F. James Davis, "The Sociological Study of Law: in *Society and the Law: New Meanings for an Old Profession*, ed. F. James Davis, Henry H. Foster, Jr., C. Ray Jeffery, and E. Eugene Davis (Westport, Conn.: Greenwood Press, 1962), pp. 18–19.

13. Gurvitch, *Sociology of Law*, p. 50.

14. Paul Bohannan, "Law and Legal Institutions" in *The Sociology of Law*, ed. William M. Evan (New York: Free Press, 1980), p. 3.

15. Roscoe Pound, "Preface," in Gurvitch, *Sociology of Law*, p. ix.

16. Davis, "The Sociological Study of Law," pp. 23–24.

17. Ronald L. Akers and Richard Hawkins, "The Concept of Law," in *Law and Control in Society*, ed. Ronald L. Akers and Richard Hawkins (Englewood Cliffs, N.J.: Prentice-Hall, 1975), p. 5.

18. Donald J. Black, "The Boundaries of Legal Sociology," in *The Sociology of Law: A Conflict Perspective* ed. Charles E. Reasons and Robert M. Rich (Toronto: Butterworths, 1978), pp. 97–113; Philippe Nonet, "For Jurisprudential Sociology," in *The Sociology of Law: A Conflict Perspective*, ed. Charles E. Reasons and Robert M. Rich (Toronto: Butterworths, 1978), pp. 115–133.

19. Edwin M. Schur, *Law and Society: A Sociological View* (New York: Random House, 1968), pp. 37–51.

20. Alvin W. Gouldner, "Anti-minotaur: The Myth of a Value-Free Sociology," *Social Problems*, 9(1962):199–213.

21. Schur, *Law and Society*, pp. 5–6; Davis, "The Sociological Study of Law," p. 34; David Riesman, "Anthropological Science of Law and the Legal Profession," *American Journal of Sociology* 57(1954):121–135; David Ries-

man, "Law and Sociology: Recruitment, Training and Colleagueship," in *Law and Sociology: Exploratory Essays,* ed. William M. Evan (Westport, Conn.: Greenwood Press, 1962); E.W. Robinson, *Law and the Lawyers* (New York: Macmillan, 1935), pp. 1–6; see also Donald Young, cited in Davis, "The Sociological Study of Law," p. 35.

22. Riesman, "Law and Sociology," p. 14.

23. Donald Young, as cited in Davis, "The Sociological Study of Law," p. 35.

24. Davis, "The Sociological Study of Law," p. 34.

25. For an extensive listing of the material generated in the 1960s and 1970s, see Rich, *The Sociology of Law.*

26. Elliot Currie, "The Sociology of Law: The Unasked Questions," *Yale Law Journal,* 18(1971):137.

27. See Chambliss, "Functional and Conflict Theories of Crime," for a delineation of the consensus-conflict perspectives.

28. Malcolm M. Freeley, "The Concept of Laws in Social Science: A Critique of Notes on an Expanded View," in *The Sociology of Law: A Conflict Perspective,* ed. Charles E. Reasons and Robert M. Rich (Toronto: Butterworths, 1978), p. 14.

29. Currie, "The Sociology of Law," p. 134.

30. Alan Hunt, "The Radical Critique of Law: An Assessment," *International Journal of the Sociology of Law* 8(1980):34.

31. Alan Hunt, *The Sociological Movement in Law* (Philadelphia: Temple University Press, 1978), p. 125. For an excellent detailing of the role of the labeling perspective and the emergence of the conflict approach, and their effects on the sociology of law, see John Galliher, "The Life and Death of Liberal Criminology," *Contemporary Crises* 2(1978):245–269.

32. W. Chambliss and R. Seidman, *Law, Order and Power* (New York: Wiley, 1971); W. Chambliss, "Toward a Political Economy of Crime," in *The Sociology of Law: A Conflict Perspective,* ed. Charles E. Reasons and Robert M. Rich (Toronto: Butterworths, 1978), pp. 191–211; Richard Quinney, *Critique of Legal Order* (Boston: Little, Brown, 1973); Richard Quinney, *Class, State, and Crime: On the Theory and Practice of Criminal Justice* (New York: David McKay, 1977); Austin T. Turk, *Criminality and Legal Order* (Chicago: Rand McNally, 1969); Austin T. Turk, "Law as a Weapon in Social Conflict," *Social Problems* 23(1976):276–291. See Charles E. Reasons and Robert M. Rich, eds., *The Sociology of Law: A Conflict Perspective* (Toronto: Butterworths, 1978), for a collection of writings on the conflict approach to the sociology of law.

33. Don C. Gibbons, *The Criminological Enterprise: Theories and Perspectives* (Englewood Cliffs, N.J.: Prentice-Hall, 1979), p. 156.

34. Sheldon R. Olson, *Issues in the Sociology of Criminal Justice* (Indianapolis: Bobbs-Merrill, 1975).

19

The Dismantling of an LEAA Exemplary Project: The Parole Officer Aide Program of Ohio

Joseph E. Scott

In April 1976, the director of the National Institute of Law Enforcement and Criminal Justice (NILECJ), Gerald M. Caplan, announced that the Parole Officer Aide Program of Ohio had been selected as one of seventeen exemplary projects throughout the United States. The NILECJ officially announced the selection in a brochure entitled "Only Ex-Offenders Need Apply: The Ohio Parole Officer Aide Program."[1]

In announcing the selection, Caplan pointed out that the National Advisory Commission (NAC) on Criminal Justice Standards and Goals had urged correctional agencies to take "immediate and affirmative action to employ capable and qualified ex-offenders in correctional roles."[2] He went on to emphasize that the Parole Officer Aide Program of Ohio carried out the spirit of this recommendation and demonstrated its practical value. Caplan cited the mutual benefits such a program offers ex-offenders, departments of correction, and the community at large. Specifically, he cited the fact that this program allowed ex-offenders to attain paid professional positions—jobs that they, their families, and the communities can respect. In addition, the empathy and special perspective of the aides would add a positive new dimension to parole services.[3]

Ironically, by the time the NILECJ was citing Ohio's Parole Officer Aide Program as an exemplary project, the Ohio Adult Parole Authority (APA) had already made the decision to abandon the program.[4] Although the state was still receiving federal monies to support the program, only one more aide would be hired, and five years later, in 1981, the Ohio Adult Parole Authority would have only one parole-officer aide. Moreover, the decision apparently was made in 1975, or no later than 1976, to convert that remaining position into a regular parole-officer position as soon as the aide was promoted, quit, or was terminated.[5] Had the NILECJ been more aware of Ohio's Department of Rehabilitation and Correction's position on the Parole Officer Aide Program, they might more accurately have entitled their brochure "Ex-Offenders Need Not Apply."

The purpose of this analysis is to review the origin of Ohio's Parole Officer Aide Program, its elevation to an LEAA exemplary project, and the Ohio APA's decision to terminate the program, which had been made by the time the program received national recognition. To accomplish these tasks, the growth of the paraprofessional movement in the United States will be examined first.

The Use of Paraprofessionals

Paraprofessionals, under various titles and roles, were participating in New Deal programs as early as 1935, but not until the 1960s did they gain widespread popularity. The modern paraprofessional movement made its major debut in the school system and quickly spread to health agencies and other social-service organizations. These early programs recruited primarily middle-class people to supplement the work of trained professionals. The first major programs were funded via the President's Committee on Juvenile Delinquency and Youth Crime. Mobilization for Youth (MFY), located in New York City's Lower East Side, used local people in school and community work. This program, in fact, led Riessman to publish his first call for "the new nonprofessional."[6]

In 1964, with the enactment of the Economic Opportunity Act and the launching of the Office of Economic Opportunity (OEO), an increasing demand arose for the indigenous paraprofessional. The rash of new programs called for more and better services for the poor and simultaneously provided an opportunity for the employment of these same people. After one year, OEO employed more than 25,000 paraprofessionals in community-action programs and almost twice that number in the Head Start Program.[7]

By the late 1960s, with new and modified legislation, use of indigenous paraprofessionals had become a fact of life in the labor force. Not only did their numbers increase, but the opposition from professionals was diminishing. With the black, civil-rights, antiwar, and student movements of the 1960s, a new awareness of human rights was emerging. Many administrators argued that there were simply too few workers with the requisite training to meet the new demands. Given this situation, the acceptance of a new type of manpower evolved—people with definite community ties but less-formal training.[8] Reiff and Riessman characterized this new worker as a "peer of the client who shares a common background, language, ethnic origin, style and common interests."[9] The indigenous paraprofessional had become a reality almost overnight.

Justifications for the indigenous paraprofessional included the necessity to increase service efficiency and effectiveness. This was to be accomplished by relieving the professional of time-consuming tasks that required little special training and by providing new services not offered by the professionals.[10] It was within this second realm that the paraprofessional was to make his unique contribution to clients and to service agencies. The paraprofessional, it was argued, was capable of providing special services because of his close identity with and understanding of clients' problems and needs. Moreover, it was expected that the paraprofessional would be a resource person for the professionals in understanding and relating to clients.[11]

Originally, the paraprofessionals were viewed as handmaidens of the professionals with whom they worked. Researchers evaluating their effectiveness argued that they were considerably more than that; in fact, they could be as effective as trained professionals in dealing with most problems and clients.[12] It is not surprising that criminal-justice agencies began to explore the feasibility of using paraprofessionals, given the attention they were receiving by the press and the federal government's position on using them. In criminal-justice agencies, the initial use of offenders and ex-offenders as paraprofessionals relied primarily on volunteers rather than paid employees.

Paraprofessionals in Criminal-Justice Agencies

Two early programs were begun in 1964 within correctional facilities. The Draper Project, conducted at the Draper Correctional Center in Elmore, Alabama, initiated a training program run solely by inmates, with many prisoners producing self-instruction educational materials.[13] The Massachusetts Correctional Institution (MCI) at Walpole developed a similar program, in which the prisoners were encouraged to prepare instructional materials for their own use and for use by handicapped children and youth.[14]

In 1964, J.E. Baker, associate warden of the federal prison at Terre Haute, Indiana, reported on the use of inmate self-government programs throughout the United States. Baker noted that the major problem with such programs was their use of inmates as disciplinarians. He proposed the use of inmate advisory councils as a viable alternative, to permit inmates the opportunity to take a more active and constructive role in the improvement of the prison environment while avoiding the difficult role of disciplinarian.[15] The most characteristic element of these early programs was the active involvement of the inmate in self-help or self-improvement activities. Later, programs moved a step further by using the offender and ex-offender in helping not only themselves but others, especially members of their peer groups.

Numerous other inmate-counseling projects began in various prisons in the 1960s, including the Colorado State Penitentiary (BARS Project), San Quentin (Squires Program), and MCI-Walpole (Project Youth). These programs were aimed at helping the youthful segment of the community, especially those singled out as potential offenders.[16]

In a somewhat different vein, the North Carolina Prison Department began a joint venture with the Institute of Government at the University of North Carolina. The Chapel Hill Youth Development and Research Unit was a camp for young felons who were transferred from the state penitentiary; it was staffed entirely by parolees.[17] At about the same time, the Synanon Foundation began assisting a small prison camp on Peavine Mountain, north of Reno, Nevada. Three times a week, the Synanon groups visited the prisoners to conduct discussion sessions or to participate in recreational activities. Some members of the Synanon group were former inmates.[18]

In 1969, the Norfolk Fellowship (a program bringing community members into the Massachusetts Correctional Institute at Norfolk to attend fellowship meetings with inmates) began Project Re-entry. The program allowed ex-offenders who had "made it" on the outside to return to the prison and offer their experience and insights to men who were ready for release.[19] Certainly one of the best known self-help programs staffed by ex-offenders is the Seventh Step Program, begun at the Kansas State Prison as a program for inmates who were within four months of their release date. Today the program extends from New York to California, assisting offenders and ex-offenders with financial matters, employment, housing, and friendship.[20]

A number of groups have been formed by ex-offenders to provide service and support to offenders. Unlike the Seventh Step Foundation, most of these groups are limited to local areas. The Future Association of Alberta, Canada, is one such group, which offers a friendly atmosphere in which previously incarcerated people can meet other people and make new friends who share common fears and problems. The Self Development Group, located in the Deer Island House of Correction in Boston and the Massachusetts Correctional Institute at Concord, provides discussion groups and support to ex-offenders and avoids the use of professionals. Efforts from Ex-Convicts (EFEC), in Washington, D.C., is another such group, although it was organized primarily as a job referral service *by* ex-cons *for* ex-cons.[21] The House of Judah in Atlanta and Youth Development, Inc., are two additional early community programs run by ex-convicts that attempted to provide service to youth in the area.[22]

Paraprofessionals have also been used by law-enforcement agencies on a limited basis. Of particular note is a program initiated by the Los Angeles Police in 1965, shortly after the Watts riot. The indigenous workers employed by the department were all school drop-outs, and 75 percent were ex-offenders. They participated in community activities and aided police in crime and narcotic prevention.[23] Another example of the use of ex-offenders by law enforcement is in Baltimore County, Maryland, where an ex-convict counselor was hired to work with juveniles. Cases were assigned to him in lieu of prosecution, and he worked closely with the police public-relations bureau in giving talks to school and community groups.[24]

The majority of early programs using paraprofessionals in criminal-justice agencies relied primarily on voluntary help or low-paying jobs for the offenders and ex-offenders. The major attribute lacking in such programs was a career path. Not until the development of the New Careers Program in 1967 was the full potential of paraprofessionals in corrections realized. Rather than providing only supplementary helpers or volunteers, the New Careers Program offered permanent jobs and a career-ladder concept. This new direction came about by an important 1966 amendment to the Economic Opportunity Act. The New Careers Program probably did more than any other effort or event to insure the use of offenders as paraprofessionals in the field of corrections. It also changed the direction from using offenders as correctional resources to providing them with meaningful careers. Empey pointed out some of the implications for corrections:

> Our overriding concern is with new careers for offenders, not just with using offenders as a correctional resource. They are already being used as a resource. Our task now is to integrate that use into a larger scheme in which, by being of service to corrections, they might realize lasting career benefits.[25]

The field of corrections was ripe for the New Careers Program. As Clements indicated in his handbook for parole-officer aides, public attention has tended to focus on rising crime rates and punishment of the offender, rather than on opportunities. Moreover, the social distance between parole officers and ex-offenders has often been suggested as one of the major problems resulting in recidivism and even higher crime rates.[26]

The Use of Ex-Offender Paraprofessionals in Corrections

In 1968, the Joint Commission on Correctional Manpower and Training published a report on the employment of offenders and ex-offenders in correctional work in the United States.[27] The report was based on responses from state adult- and juvenile-corrections central offices, institutions, and probation and parole agencies. Seventy-one adult and juvenile offices responded. Sixty-six of these offices indicated that they could hire offenders and ex-offenders, but only 22 reported having such employees. The Joint Commission reported that, of 461 adult and juvenile institutions throughout the United States, only 45 had one or more ex-offenders employed in any type of program. Finally, of the 49 state parole agencies, 7 state probation agencies, and 42 combined state parole and probation agencies responding to the survey, only 15 reported having any ex-offenders as employees (as of 1 March 1967). One obvious conclusion from this survey was the minimal number of ex-offenders working as employees of state correctional agencies. Moreover, this situation was not generally attributable to legal or policy restrictions, but apparently reflected the lack of commitment to such programs on the part of state correctional employees.

California was the only state that had made extensive use of indigenous paraprofessionals in corrections by 1970. California began the Parole Service Assistant Program in 1965 to provide job opportunities to the hard-core unemployed and to improve the quality of parole services. Since that time, well over 300 ex-offenders have worked in that department. As early as 1968, parole aides served as liaison between the parolee and the parole officer. They were expected and able to use their firsthand knowledge and experience in the community.[28]

In 1971, Project MOST (Maximizing Oregon's Services and Training for Adult Probation and Parole) used three ex-offenders as paid staff members, functioning in the capacity of aides performing assignments at a paraprofessional level.[29]

Beginning in October 1968, and extending through September 1972, a two-phase program using ex-offender paraprofessional probation-officer assistants (POAs) was initiated and supervised by the University of Chicago's Center for Studies in Criminal Justice and the U.S. Probation Office for the Northern District of Illinois (Chicago). This project utilized fifty-two part-time indigenous workers, of whom twenty-two were ex-offenders. The POAs, under the supervision of professionally trained probation officers, provided direct services to probationers and parolees.[30] Members of the project advisory committee were so impressed with the results of the program that they recommended to the Judicial Conference Committee on Probation the creation of permanent, full-time paraprofessional positions in the federal probation offices. The Judicial Conference endorsed the idea and recommended funds for fifty such positions for fiscal year 1973. Congress appropriated money for twenty such positions. Gordon's evaluation of this project found that these paraprofessionals "could provide valuable services to most, if not all, of the clients in the probation system."[31]

In 1973, the NAC urged correctional agencies to hire ex-offenders to assist in working with convicted offenders.[32] One possible reason for their strong endorsement of this policy was the claim that the self-help movement in the area of corrections was more rhetorical than apparent.[33] A 1974 study of state parole agencies found limited use of such paraprofessionals. Although sixteen of the fifty states reported the use of ex-offenders as parole officers or aides, many had only one or two such employees. In fact, in 1974, there were only 139 ex-offender parole officers or aides in the United States. Seventy-eight of these were employed in Ohio and Pennsylvania, leaving only 61 such employees in the remaining states. Moreover, it was obvious from this survey that federal funds were primarily responsible for the programs that did exist. Of the sixteen states reporting the use of such paraprofessionals, fourteen indicated that their programs were initiated with federal funds, and all thirteen of the programs started between 1970 and 1972 reported receiving LEAA funds to start their programs.[34]

The concept of using ex-offenders as paraprofessionals in the criminal-justice system received considerable lip service throughout the 1960s and early 1970s. Apparently, it was more an ideal than a reality. As indicated by the two national studies on the states' use of ex-offenders in corrections, very few states had such programs. Certainly one of the most ambitious such programs was begun in Ohio in 1972.[35]

Ohio's Parole Officer Aide Program

The Ohio Parole Officer Aide Program was begun in September 1972 with an LEAA grant of $842,576 and $561,867 in state matching funds. The federal funds were to cover the expenses for the first three years, with step-down funding in the fourth and fifth years of two-thirds and one-third, respectively. During the first three years of the program, the Ohio Adult Parole Authority (APA) contracted with Ohio State University's Program for the Study of Crime and Delinquency to evaluate the effectiveness of the program. Little if any research or evaluation concerning the program has taken place since those initial three years.

The stated goals of the project were to utilize ex-offenders as aides to professional parole officers in order to bridge the gap between the Adult Parole Authority and parolees; to facilitate communication between corrections and the community; to engender trust and confidence in the correctional system; to decrease recidivism; and to reduce parole violations. Another goal often mentioned by APA officials, but never put in writing, was to show the business community that ex-offenders could be dependable and valuable employees.

An original cohort of thirteen aides was hired in August and September 1972. Twenty-three aides were working by the end of the first year,[36] and the same number were on the job after the second year. By the end of the third year (1975), there were still twenty-two aides, but by the end of the fourth year (the year federal funding supported only two-thirds of the cost of the program), only fourteen remained. Following the fifth year of the program (1977), only four parole-officer aides were still employed by the APA, and by 1981, only one parole-officer aide remained; he was one of the original thirteen aides hired in 1972. The last parole-officer aide to be hired by the APA was employed in1976.

The Ohio Parole Officer Aide Program differed from other parole-officer aide programs primarily in the responsibilities given the aides. Each aide was assigned a caseload of thirty parolees during the first year of the program, and by the second year the number had increased to fifty parolees. They were expected to provide supervision parallel to that provided by the parole officers.[37]

The aides were subjected to a number of restrictions that were not imposed on parole officers. They were not allowed to (1) arrest a parolee, (2) own or carry a firearm, or (3) transport an arrested offender. Also, aides were not to assume sole supervisory responsibility over parolees; rather, a senior parole officer and a unit supervisor had the ultimate responsibility for the aides' parolees.

Rather stringent criteria were used in selecting the original aides, although their backgrounds and experience were diversified.[38] Their previous occupations included such positions as sheriff's deputy, undercover agent, employment counselor, salesman, custodian, cab driver, grave digger, and gasoline-station attendant. Their formal education was considerably less than that of the average parole officer. Only one aide of the original thirteen has a college degree, and over a third of them had not completed high school.

The aides' past criminal involvement also varied considerably. The number of arrests for aides varied from one to twenty-one, with an average of 6.2. Convictions for aides ranged from one to twenty-one also, with an average of 4.2 convictions per aide. Time incarcerated ranged from eleven months to ten years, with an average incarceration time of 51.3 months. The offenses for which the aides had been incarcerated also varied considerably, from murder, manslaughter, and armed robbery to such property offenses as burglary, auto theft, and forgery.

The Ohio Parole Officer Aide Program's evaluation used a variety of approaches to assess the program's effectiveness. The major conclusion of the evaluation was that aides' performance, when compared with a control group of Ohio parole officers, was equally effective. There were no claims that the aides did a better job. In fact, the evaluation pointed out that the parolees supervised by aides actually had more additional contacts with the law while on parole than did those supervised by the control group of parole officers. Certainly, a portion of that difference can be accounted for by the fact that the parolees assigned to the aides were worse risks. The aides were assigned multiple-problem cases, parolees with more extensive criminal records, parolees who had been arrested earlier in their lives, and parolees on whom other parole officers had given up and who were about to violate their parole or have it revoked.[39] The parolees assigned to the aides in many ways typified the chronic offender, as identified by Wolfgang, Figlio, and Sellin.[40]

The Ohio Parole Officer Aide Program demonstrated that ex-offender paraprofessionals could perform parole-officer duties as well as typical parole officers could. In fact, one task that aides performed even better than parole officers did was assisting their parolees in securing employment.

The two major questions remaining unanswered, given the modest overall success of the aide program, are (1) how it ever gained LEAA exemplary status and (2) why Ohio abandoned the program completely.

The Creation of an Exemplary Project

The National Institute of Justice received 635 project nominations for exemplary status from 1973 to 1980. Exemplary status was conferred on 34 of these projects, including the Ohio Parole Officer Aide Project.[41] For projects to receive exemplary status, they must be nominated by the regional LEAA officers and the state planning agency. They are then examined by an independent evaluator to verify:

1. Their overall effectiveness in reducing crime or improving criminal justice;
2. Their adaptability to other jurisdictions;
3. Their objective evidence of achievement; and
4. Their demonstrated cost-effectiveness.

Validation results are then submitted to the Exemplary Project Advisory Board, made up of LEAA and state planning-agency officials, which makes the final decision.[42] The Parole Officer Aide Project was only one of the projects the Ohio APA prepared documentation on and submitted to the LEAA regional office and the state planning agency for consideration as an exemplary project. One employee of the Ohio APA thought that it was his job responsibility to submit such documentation on various projects. In fact, this employee believed that any federal recognition for Ohio's APA could only be helpful. Even at the time the documentation for the Ohio Parole Officer Aide Program was submitted, the overwhelming majority of administrators at the APA did not regard the project as a success.[43] The overwhelming conviction was that the project should be terminated as soon as the federal funds were expended and that several other projects were unique and were more deserving of recognition in Ohio than was the Parole Officer Aide Project.[44]

Why was the Parole Office Aide Project recognized as an exemplary project, given the APA administrators' attitudes toward it? The answer to this question may be related, in part, to the lack of rigorous, quantitative evaluation of the more than 100,000 projects and programs supported by LEAA funds.[45] Furthermore, it seems that LEAA officials may have been most receptive to those projects that held any hope of uniqueness, given the status of corrections.[46] Also, LEAA apparently was inclined to recognize as exemplary those projects that were in compliance with the National Standards and Goals.[47] Given that the 1973 NAC Standards and Goals had strongly urged correctional agencies to employ capable and qualified ex-offenders in correctional roles, perhaps any such project with a modicum of success and a quantitative analysis of its operation stood an excellent chance of gaining LEAA exemplary status.

The Dismantling of the Program

It may not be far from accurate to trace the demise of the aide program to its very inception. How could a state agency refuse more than $800,000 in federal funds for a program that would not substantially alter their normal operation and would provide them with certain amenities that were otherwise not available? Based on interviews and discussions with senior administrators at the Ohio Adult Parole Authority, it is my contention that the program never was intended to be a viable part of the Ohio APA. Although a few individuals believed strongly in the program, they were a small minority, and they have been subjected to considerable ridicule for expressing such beliefs and opinions.[48]

A number of empirical indicators support the contention that the project was doomed from its inception. First, when the original project director of the aide program resigned after three years, the person whom he recommended to take over his position was not seriously considered. Instead, his replacement was an individual who had voiced strong opposition to the project. Second, as the federal money supporting the project was reduced in 1976 and 1977, the number of aide positions declined concomitantly. In the first three years of the project, there were twenty-three, twenty-three, and twenty-two aides at the end of each respective year. It was during these first three years that federal monies supported the program. By the end of the fourth year (1976), when step-down funding was in effect and the federal funds would cover only two-thirds of the previous costs, there were only fourteen aides. By the end of the fifth year of the project, when federal funds would cover only one-third of original costs, it is not surprising to find that the APA had only four aides. From 1978 through 1980, when Ohio was no longer receiving federal funds for the aide project, there was only one parole officer aide, and Ohio had decided to abolish that position as soon as possible.

Today, leading Ohio APA personnel attribute the program's failure and its termination to the poor selection of aides. If that were the reason, one would think they would initiate better selection criteria and continue with the program. Nevertheless, numerous stories and newspaper clippings can be cited to illustrate the problems aides encountered and the resulting unfavorable attention to the APA. Headlines such as "Parole Officer Arrested for Trafficking in Narcotics" or "Parole Officer Arrested for Murder" are not uncommon, despite the statement in the LEAA brochure describing the project as exemplary: ". . . according to the Ohio Adult Parole Authority, POAs have proven to be no more of an employment risk than regularly recruited parole officers."[49]

Have the aides been in more trouble with the law since their employment with the APA than "typical" employees have been? This was one question that received considerable attention when the Parole Officer Aide Project was reexamined five years after it received LEAA exemplary status. Without question, the aides as a group have had considerable trouble with the law. Since the program began in 1972, there have been thirty-seven aides. Fourteen of the thirty-seven were promoted to parole-officer status, and six of them are still with the APA. However, six of the thirty-seven aides resigned or were terminated while under administrative investigation for such acts as falsifying travel vouchers, carrying a weapon, or failure to show up for work. (The aide terminated for failure to show up for work also destroyed all his parolees' records, the office log book, and other material before leaving without notice.)

Thirteen of the thirty-seven aides resigned or were terminated with criminal charges pending. Charges ranged from murder, rape, burglary, assault, bribery, and trafficking in drugs to such minor offenses as public intoxication. Compared to parole officers, the aides have had considerable trouble. Since 1975, only one parole officer in Ohio has been arrested for a felony, while nine aides have incurred such problems.

Finally, as a follow-up to the aide program, the driving records of all aides were examined for the past five years. Certainly, this is a different matter from being arrested for a felony, or even a misdemeanor, but it may indicate differences in conformity and risk-taking for terminated aides in comparison with those still employed by the APA. Each of the aides' driving records was checked for the past five years. It is interesting that those who are no longer with the APA have had twice as many moving violations and three times as many automobile accidents per individual than those still employed by the APA. Moreover, five of the twenty-nine no longer employed at APA have had their driver's licenses suspended, compared to none of the ex-offenders still employed by the APA. This may indicate some additional risk-taking or lack of responsibility on the part of those who are no longer with the APA.

Without question, the aides as a group have been in considerably more trouble than have "normal" parole officers with the APA. There are at least two viable explanations for these failures. First, it appears that whatever support may have existed for the program in its first few years vanished with the departure of the original project director. Without a support group, and with many people in the agency complaining about the program, the aides may simply have given up and regressed to their former acting-out patterns, rather than struggling to show the efficacy of the program.

An alternative explanation for the problems aides encountered may be a variation of the burn-out phenomenon.[50] As Freudenberger, Maslach, and others have documented, those working in the helping professions have an extremely high rate of burn-out.[51] This phenomenon is most often experienced by those who work with difficult clients and do not have strong peer and organizational support.[52] If this is the case, the aides would have been subjected to this phenomenon considerably more than would typical parole officers, given the lack of organizational or peer support. It is conceivable that the aides were so disillusioned and burned-out that they reverted to their earlier modes of adaptation.

Notes

1. Office of Technology Transfer, National Institute of Law Enforcement and Criminal Justice, Law Enforcement Assistance Administration, U.S. De-

partment of Justice, "Only Ex-Offenders Need Apply: The Ohio Parole Officer Aide Program," Washington, D.C., 1976.

2. Ibid., p. 2.

3. Ibid., p. 2.

4. Anonymous interviews conducted in December 1980 by Joseph E. Scott with several Adult Parole Authority administrators.

5. Ibid.

6. Frank Reissman, *The Revolution in Social Work: The New Non-Professional* (New York: Mobilization for Youth, 1963).

7. Arthur Pearl and Frank Reissman, *New Careers for the Poor: The Nonprofessional in Human Service* (New York: Free Press, 1965).

8. Alan Gartner, *Paraprofessionals and Their Performance* (New York: Praeger, 1971). See also Robert B. Carkhuff and C.B. Truax, "Lay Mental Health Counseling: The Effects of Lay Group Counseling," *Journal of Consulting Psychology* 29(1965):426–432.

9. Robert Reiff and Frank Reissman, *The Indigenous Non-Professional: A Strategy of Change in Community Action and Community Mental Health Programs* (New York: Behavioral Publications, 1970).

10. Frank Reissman, "The Revolution in Social Work: The New Non-professional," *Transaction* 2 (November-December 1965):12–17.

11. Bruce Bullington, John G. Munns, and Gilbert Geis, "Purchase of Conformity: Ex-Narcotic Addicts Among the Bourgeoisie," *Social Problems* 16 (Spring 1969):456–463.

12. Carkhuff and Truax, "Lay Mental Health Counseling."

13. J. McKee, "Reinforcement Theory and the Convict Culture," *American Correctional Association Proceedings* (1965).

14. Inmates of Massachusetts Correctional Institution, "Prison Days and Nights at MCI Walpole," *The Mentor,* Walpole, Massachusetts, July 1969.

15. J.E. Baker, "Inmate Self Government," *Journal of Criminal Law, Criminology and Police Science* 55 (March 1964):39–47.

16. Albert Morris, "The Involvement of Offenders in the Prevention and Correction of Criminal Behavior," Massachusetts Correctional Association, Bulletin No. 20, October 1970, pp. 6, 7.

17. Paul Keve, *Imaginative Programming in Probation and Parole* (Minneapolis: University of Minnesota Press, 1967), p. 212.

18. Ibid., p. 216.

19. Albert Morris, "The Involvement of Offenders," pp. 6, 7.

20. Bill Sands, *The Seventh Step* (New York: New American Library, 1967).

21. Ronald L. Goldfarb and Linda R. Singer, *After Conviction* (New York: Simon and Schuster, 1973), pp. 598–604. See also EFEC (Efforts From Ex-Convicts), "Statement of Purpose," Washington, D.C., 1966.

22. Edward Sagarin, *Odd Man In: Societies of Deviants in America* (Chicago: Quadrangle Books, 1969).

23. Los Angles Police Department, "An Interim Evaluation of the Community Relations Aides' Performance in the Community Relations Program," Los Angeles, 1969.

24. Joseph R. Gallen and Patricia A. Hanges, "The Effective Use of Formerly Convicted Felons in Police Functions," *Police Chief* 44(1977): 34, 35.

25. LaMar Empey, "Offender Participation in the Correctional Process: General Theoretical Issues," in Joint Commission on Correctional Manpower and Training, *Offenders as a Correctional Manpower Resource* (Washington, D.C.: Superintendent of Documents, U.S. Government Printing Office, 1968).

26. Raymond D. Clements, *Paraprofessionals in Probation and Parole: A Manual for Their Selection, Training, Induction and Supervision in Day to Day Tasks* (Chicago: University of Chicago Press, 1972).

27. Joint Commission on Correctional Manpower and Training, *Offenders as a Correctional Manpower Resource* (Washington, D.C.: Superintendent of Documents, U.S. Government Printing Office, 1968), pp. 88–90.

28. New Careers Development Project, *Final Report* (Los Angeles: Institute for the Study of Crime and Delinquency, 1968).

29. A. Chandler and A. Lee, *Final Report for Project MOST* (Portland, Ore.: Oregon State Corrections Division, 1972).

30. W.S. Pilcher, G. Witkowski, E.R. Rest, and G.J. Busiel, *Probation Officer Case Aid Project, Final Report, Phase II* (Chicago: University of Chicago Law School, 1972).

31. M.T. Gordon, *Involving Paraprofessionals in the Helping Process: The Case of Federal Probation* (Cambridge, Mass.: Ballinger, 1976).

32. The commission cited the urgency of this recommendation to create careers for ex-offenders and to utilize their expertise in improving correctional services.

33. The emphasis here was that, in order to request business to hire ex-offenders, corrections had to demonstrate its willingness to do the same.

34. Joseph E. Scott, *Ex-Offenders as Parole Officers* (Lexington, Mass.: Lexington Books, D.C. Heath and Company, 1975), pp. 77–91.

35. For a detailed discussion of the program, see Ibid., pp. 11–16.

36. Although the first aides were hired in August 1972, they didn't actually begin working as aides until September 1972. When reference is made to the number of aides at the end of each year, the reference is to December of that year.

37. Scott, *Ex-Offenders as Parole Officers*, pp. 11–16.

38. Joseph E. Scott and Pamela A. Bennett, "Background and Development of the Use of Ex-Offenders in Ohio," in *Deviance: Studies in Definition,*

Management, and Treatment, ed. Simon Dinitz, Russell R. Dynes and Alfred C. Clarke, 2nd ed. (New York: Oxford University Press, 1975), pp. 582–588.

39. Scott, *Ex-Offenders as Parole Officers,* pp. 12–13.

40. Marvin Wolfgang, Robert M. Figlio, and Thorsten Sellin, *Delinquency in a Birth Cohort* (Chicago: University of Chicago Press, 1972).

41. Personal communication with Ms. Mary Ann Beck of the National Institute of Justice, January 1981.

42. Office of Technology Transfer, "Only Ex-Offenders Need Apply."

43. Anonymous interviews conducted in December 1980 by Joseph E. Scott with several Adult Parole Authority administrators.

44. Ibid. This was mentioned and emphasized by several of the administrators.

45. Richard S. Allinson, "LEAA's Impact on Criminal Justice: A Review of the Literature," *Criminal Justice Abstracts* 11(December 1979):608–648.

46. Douglas Lipton, Robert Martinson, and Judith Wilks, *The Effectiveness of Correctional Treatment: A Survey of Treatment Evaluation Studies* (New York: Praeger, 1976).

47. Compliance with the National Standards and Goals was repeatedly emphasized by the representative of the independent agency evaluating nominated projects.

48. Anonymous interview conducted in January 1981 by Joseph E. Scott with a key Adult Parole Authority administrator.

49. Office of Technology Transfer, "Only Ex-Offenders Need Apply," p. 10.

50. Ayala Pines and Ditsa Kafry, "Occupational Tedium In the Social Services," *Social Work* 23 (November 1978):500–506. See also Michael R. Daley, "Burnout: Smoldering Problem in Protective Services," *Social Work* 24 (September 1979):375–379.

51. Herbert J. Freudenberger, "Staff Burn-Out," *Journal of Social Issues* 30(1974):159–165; Christina Maslach, "Burned-Out," *Human Behavior* 5 (September 1976):16–22; Christina Maslach, "Job Burnout—How People Cope," *Public Welfare* 36 (Spring 1978):56–58.

52. Maslach, "Job Burnout," pp. 56–58.

20 On Teaching Criminology and Criminal Justice: A Case for Undergraduate Experiential Education

Thomas W. Foster

This chapter advances three broad rationales in support of the utility of experiential learning in undergraduate criminology and criminal-justice courses and programs. The three areas under which arguments for experiential education are subsumed are (1) the pedagogical, (2) the economic, and (3) the moral-political.

This is not a report of research but is, rather, a statement of personal opinion that is largely based on my teaching experiences with undergraduates. It is also an invitation to others—to teaching colleagues and to educational administrators—to make greater use of experiential education, for, aside from its traditional employment in professional and technical training, it remains a promising but unexploited resource in American higher education.[1] I believe that this still-neglected educational resource can prove to be particularly useful in helping students develop sociological and criminological forms of understanding, as well as benefiting them in numerous other, nonacademic ways. It can also be valuably employed, I am convinced, at all levels of undergraduate instruction in criminology and criminal justice and in most courses that are typically included as part of academic majors in these areas.

The potential rewards of experiential learning extend far beyond its educational merits to a variety of social and economic benefits that it can ultimately deliver to various segments of American society, including colleges and universities, job-seeking students, criminal-justice agencies, social-service organizations, offenders, former offenders, and the general public.

What is currently needed, in my view, is the development of an increased awareness of the potentialities of community-based educational experiences, especially on the part of those who can best ensure their successful implementation. This chapter attempts to contribute toward this end by addressing itself principally to educators in criminology and criminal justice, who, it is believed, are in unique and leading positions to undertake the kinds of extra efforts, innovations, and risks that will be required if the promise of experiential education is to be fulfilled in the future.

239

What Is Experiential Education in Criminology and Criminal Justice?

For our purposes, experiential education may be defined as the practice of providing students with off-campus, structured, and supervised personal encounters with offenders, ex-offenders, social-control agents, social agencies, and institutions, and with some of the many community-based organizations and environments that are relevant to the understanding of criminal behavior and to the operation of the criminal-justice system.

Experiential education includes both learning experiences that are designed by individual instructors and integrated into the presentation of specific courses and learning experiences that are designed by academic departments or committees to reflect the focus of entire programs of instruction, or special areas of knowledge, including student internships and work-study programs.

Experiential learning on an academic department level cannot be fully successful, in my opinion, unless it is (1) broadly planned, (2) centrally coordinated, (3) directly supervised, and (4) systematically evaluated. Although I do not intend to provide here a detailed prescription for organizing, supervising, and evaluating field experiences, a few words of caution and some suggestions along these lines seem necessary, both to illustrate my general orientation and to identify some possible areas of difficulty.

First, I must emphasize the importance of cultivating and maintaining amicable relationships with cooperating agencies, organizations, and groups within the community. Without active community involvement and assistance, there simply can be no experiential education as it is defined here.

One of the easiest ways for an academic unit to offend those segments of the community upon whose support it must depend for field-based education is for it to fail to provide an organizational mechanism through which the aforementioned functions of planning, coordination, and the like, may be carried out. For example, this can occur, especially in larger departments, when individual instructors make frequent use of the same community groups or facilities for field trips, without being aware that others are also doing so. The result can be a collective overuse of a community organization, with predictably unpleasant consequences for future working relationships.

Fortunately, these types of problems and many others can generally be averted or resolved through the establishment of departmental or college-wide committees on experiential education. These committees should have broad membership bases, and I would suggest that they be structured to include administrators, instructors, students, and representatives from the community whose groups or facilities are to be visited or otherwise employed.

Although honest disagreements between academic and community participants will inevitably occur (some of which may prove to be irreconcilable), experiential-education committees can at least prevent avoidable errors and keep minor problems from escalating into major issues. If a relationship with a community sponsor must be terminated, it should be terminated only for good cause and only after careful consideration and consultation.

Some of the many functions that experiential-education committees can perform are establishment of general policies and procedures, overall planning and coordination, and community liaison and communication. Community representatives to committees should, of course, be accorded full participatory rights and should be included in all stages of planning and decisionmaking.

A second note of caution involves the need to thoroughly prepare students for field experiences or field placements. Students should always be briefed in advance on why they are observing a phenomenon, how best to observe it, what recording devices may be used (or not used), and what behaviors are appropriate (or inappropriate) for a given situation. Written instruction sheets and guides to observation are helpful preparations for field trips, while extended field placements usually require the preparation of detailed placement manuals. These placement manuals should function to introduce students to the formal or informal norms of the groups or organizations with which they will be working and should explain, among other things, the expectations and field-grading practices of instructors and of community supervisors. In briefing students, it is also extremely important to explain to them the moral and legal rights of human subjects. It is sometimes advisable to have students sign prepared statements acknowledging their understanding of these rights.

Space limitations preclude a further discussion of the practical matters of providing adequate field supervision and follow-up. These are areas, however, in which much can be learned informally from experienced colleagues, including those in social work and education, fields that have long been involved in community-placement activities.

Pedagogical Considerations

Perhaps the most compelling argument for undergraduate experiential education is that most students are motivated to take part in it and, when given the opportunity to do so, a large majority will participate enthusiastically and conscientiously. Thus, questions typically asked of me by undergraduates who are considering enrolling in my introductory courses in criminology or criminal justice are ''Will the class get to visit a prison?'' and ''Will the class get to observe the police?''

These and similar questions are illustrative of what many, if not most, students wish to gain by taking my courses. They want to know what crime, criminals, and the criminal-justice system are ''really like,'' and they are hopeful that their classes will provide them with some opportunities for directly experiencing some of these phenomena.

It is my impression that many of my colleagues are reluctant to employ experiential education, at least in teaching their lower-level courses. Most professors, while paying lip service to the desirability of primary experiences for beginning students, seldom use them or completely omit them from introductory and intermediate courses in favor of secondary forms of information, which are gleaned from professional sources and are usually presented in traditional lecture formats. Although secondary sources are of undeniable educational value and possess the advantage of familiarizing students with the appropriate uses of scientific models and methods, their exclusive employment can have a dampening effect on the typical student's motivation and morale, if only because this practice disappoints the student's desire to experience firsthand something of the phenomenological world of crime, criminals, and the justice system.

Why are many professors nominally supportive of experiential learning but at the same time hesitant to integrate it, on a meaningful scale, into the structure of their most basic undergraduate courses? Several factors seem to obstruct the wider use of experiential education; some of these are apparent, and one of them is rather more subtle.

First, there are the obvious practical obstacles. These include the fact that planning, organizing, and supervising student field experiences is a time-consuming and sometimes difficult task. It is also true that introductory classes tend to be large, that there is usually much essential material to be covered, and that correctional authorities in particular are sometimes less than fully cooperative. Above all, there seldom exists within academic departments any institutionalized procedure for equitably rewarding those faculty members who make the extra effort required to enrich their courses through experiential activities.

Nevertheless, I doubt that any of these practical obstacles are insurmountable and I suspect that, if academicians were to become more convinced of the value of experiential education, they would then find effective ways of circumventing or removing these barriers to its use. I believe a key part of any such effort would necessarily entail the establishment of a fair system of faculty rewards.

A second kind of obstacle to the use of experiential education relates to the obvious forces of tradition and habit in college and university teaching. These forces, together with a customary touch of disdain that academicians sometimes direct toward the practical or the applied, still militate against the adoption of innovative, application-based methods in higher education. Fortunately, the influence of the latter factors appears to be waning, as indicated, in part, by the emergence of a variety of alternative teaching approaches during the past decade. The current economic situation has also played a major role in making both students and educators more aware of the necessity of developing knowledge bases and skills that will permit new graduates to compete more effectively in today's overcrowded job markets.

A third, perhaps more subtle, type of impediment to experiential learning is the epistemological orientation of most professors. I am referring here to our tendency to place a very high value on rational, conceptual, and positivist forms of understanding, which, in some respects, seem far removed from the typical undergraduate's desire to know the world by experiencing it—personally, immediately, and holistically.[2] Professors may thus be hesitant to expose untrained student observers to a phenomenon mainly because they know that naive observers are unlikely to profit as much, in terms of any rational or scientific understanding, as more advanced students. But what we professors sometimes seem to forget is that objective, rational comprehension alone is neither equivalent to nor sufficient for sociological understanding and that even naive observers may derive valuable insights from structured, experiential activities. Although this is not the place to detail Weber's ideas concerning the contribution of subjective elements to social understanding, these are certainly germane to the present discussion, as are Mead's writings on social empathy and on the subjective components of all symbolic representations.

However, what is implied, or stated, in the work of Weber, Mead, Schutz, and many other leading social scientists is that subjective, intuitive forms of understanding are of critical importance, both for grasping certain sociological concepts and for interpreting the meaning of everyday social actions. If this is a valid assumption (and it seems to me to be irrefutable), then the practical problem, for teaching, becomes how best to communicate not only cognitive but also affective meanings to students.

For example, although it is not difficult to communicate rational definitions and explanations of such terms as *maximum-security institution* or *status-degradation ceremony* within the context of a classroom lecture, it is certainly more difficult (for most lecturers, at any rate) to convey adequately the subjective feel and tempo of life in a typical penitentiary or to describe convincingly the common emotional reactions of people who are undergoing a process of status degradation. Yet these same subjective dimensions of sociological meaning can be realistically and effectively imparted to students through some rather easily arranged and commonplace types of field experiences.

I realize, of course, that field experiences are not the sole means by which subjective meanings can be transmitted and that, for example, art forms, such as film, literature, and drama, are also capable of fulfilling this function. But experiential learning, at its best, possesses additional educational as well as practical advantages that can seldom be equaled by these alternative methods of instruction.

In addition to its ability to enlist the enthusiastic cooperation of students and to help them develop *verstehen* comprehension, experiential education can perform at least two other pedagogically valuable functions. First, it can serve as an excellent means of introducing students to the actual use of scientific observational and interviewing techniques within naturalistic settings. Through the exercise of these techniques, students will also have the opportunity to experience for themselves the intellectual excitement that can accompany social-scientific research and the personal discovery of knowledge.

The other educational purpose performed by field-based experience is closely related to its usefulness in scientific training. It can provide a very potent means of demythologizing and dispelling popular prejudices and stereotypes, including those associated with crime, criminals, and the criminal-justice system. The importance of this function is underscored by the fact that most college students come from middle-class or stable working-class backgrounds and are therefore unlikely to have had many previous contacts with offenders or with the workings of the justice system. Consequently, beginning students typically harbor some rather distorted mental images of criminals, crime, and so forth, which reflect both individual misconceptions and cultural stereotypes.

Although the experiences selected for inclusion in field-based learning can never be perfectly typical representations of social reality, if care is taken in their selection, they are likely to provide a more valid foundation for conceptualization than are the a priori ideas of inexperienced students.

The probable reason that other teaching methods (such as lectures, movies, and literature) seem to be generally less effective in changing student attitudes and ideas is that they possess a lower degree of credibility; that is, "seeing is believing." I learned long ago that students sometimes simply refuse to accept well-established sociological facts that are presented in lectures if these facts strongly contradict their existing beliefs or values. They may memorize their lecture notes for the purpose of passing examinations, but, in private, some will freely admit that they considered many of the instructor's "facts" to be little more than an elaboration of his or her personal opinions. Yet, when students must actually confront the existence of these identical facts in the field, through their own senses, they will find it much more difficult to rationalize them away and they will be forced, to some extent, to adjust their thinking and feeling to the demands of empirical realities. In brief, experiential education can be used to teach students to seek truth for themselves by actively testing their ideas against empirical observations. This process lies at the very heart of critical, scientific thinking and stands in direct opposition to the uncritical, passive memorization of facts, which so often occurs in introductory-level courses in the social sciences.

Economic Considerations

Rippetoe has criticized sociology departments for generally failing to provide those undergraduate students who do not plan to attend graduate schools with specific job skills and with meaningful links to employing agencies within the community.[3] Rippetoe is of the opinion that departments of sociology should first seek to identify work-related skills and should then develop supervised field-work experiences that place undergraduates in progressive, change-oriented community organizations.

Although baccalaureate programs in criminology and criminal justice tend to be more occupationally directed than those in sociology, I believe that most of Rippetoe's observations and criticisms are applicable to both areas. Furthermore, in some institutions, criminology and criminal-justice courses are taught within sociology departments, making them subject to those departments' policies.

Rippetoe argues, for example, that, if a department gears its courses and programs to the needs of students who are intending to pursue advanced degrees, it may be neglecting the needs of the vast majority of undergraduates, who will be seeking employment at the B.A. level. In addition, he asks whether it is realistic to expect existing occupational structures and employment opportunities to continue indefinitely into the future, and he suggests that more attention be directed toward placing students in newly emerging types of social agencies, which may be able to provide a greater number of future jobs.[4]

Although I do not think that criminology and criminal-justice programs can or should restrict themselves to placing students in "progressive" community agencies and institutions, I do believe that some of the emerging, nontraditional social agencies, which are involved in less familiar types of work, can provide a promising focus for student field placements as well as for possible future employment. Examples of these organizations that, in my view, could be utilized for the placement of criminology or criminal-justice majors include drug counseling programs; legal-aid services; shelters for runaways or for the victims of domestic violence; victim-compensation programs, and rape-crisis centers.

Community participation can be maximized in securing these and other more traditional types of field-placement sites[5] by utilizing joint-membership experiential-education committees, by carefully matching the needs and interests of individual students with those of sponsoring agencies, and by explaining to agency representatives the potential economic advantages of cooperation. Some of these economic advantages, from the community's perspective, include the availability of low cost or free student help and the development of a convenient pool of future job applicants whose qualifications and performances will be well known to employing organizations.

Some educational institutions also offer economic and other incentives to individual agency personnel who assist with program development or with the supervision of students. These incentives range from cash stipends and tuition rebates to free professional seminars and complimentary tickets to cultural or sporting events.

A Moral-Political Consideration

Finally, there are several moral arguments to be made for experiential education, but I will mention only what I consider to be one of the most important of these. Because the majority of students who take our introductory courses are not criminology or criminal-justice majors, they will probably have few subsequent contacts with offenders, prisons, or the criminal law. If we miss the opportunity to expose these students, who are also citizens and voters, to societal conditions that are related to crime and are in need of public attention and reform, we also miss an opportunity to involve them in the improvement of society.

I say this because I know of no more honest or effective way of generating moral concern and political involvement among students than showing them some of the daily injustices that occur in criminal-justice settings and institutions. I have learned that a single trip to a decaying, century-old county jail, which houses runaway juveniles within sight and sound of adult felons, elicits greater moral indignation from my students than does any lecture I can deliver on the topic of indiscriminate incarceration.

After nearly every field trip that I have arranged, whether to correctional institutions or to community agencies, students have come forward to offer their services as volunteers, often without any solicitation on my part. Conversely, I have had much less success in obtaining student volunteers when I or visiting guest lecturers have attempted to solicit for volunteers within the classroom. In addition, several of my former students have told me that their decision to become involved in such projects as juvenile-justice reform or prisoners' rights was strongly influenced by their field experiences. Still others have decided to pursue careers as criminal-justice professionals as a consequence of their field work. Although most students will not become personally involved in subsequent efforts to improve the system, I am hopeful that their community experiences will at least help them to become better-informed voting citizens.

Notes

1. M.T. Keeton, "Practical Experience in American Higher Education," *Liberal Education*, May 1977, pp. 259–270.

2. Personality testing of college students and professors with the MBTI (Myers Briggs Type Indicator) has consistently shown that broad personality differences exist between these groups and are associated with differential interests and learning styles. In one study of 354 community-college teachers and 335 community-college freshmen, the findings indicated that 63 percent of the teachers were intuitive types, while only 26.5 percent of the students were intuitive. Seventy-three percent of the students were of the nonintuitive, sensing type, which means that they would prefer to learn by employing their five senses

rather than through methods that emphasize speaking and writing (the latter being preferred by intuitionists). For a fuller discussion of the relationship of learning styles to teaching, see C.S. Claxton and Y. Ralston, "Learning Styles: Their Impact on Teaching and Administration," *AAHE-ERIC/Higher Education Research Report* 10(1978):26–27.

3. J.K. Rippetoe, "Undergraduate Education in Sociology: A Case for Experiential Learning," *Teaching Sociology* 4(April 1977):239–250.

4. Rippetoe, "Undergraduate Education in Sociology," pp. 240–242.

5. A comprehensive description of an ongoing, two-semester student internship in criminal justice is to be found in Wornie L. Reed, "A Criminal Justice Internship in Liberal Arts Education" (Paper presented at the Midwestern Association for Criminal Justice Education meeting, October 1980). Reed's paper describes an undergraduate internship in probation and parole in which Washington University students become engaged in a wide variety of professional activities. For example, interns in the Washington University program assist correctional professionals with intake work, individual casework, tutoring, vocational workshops, coordination with halfway houses, group counseling, and presentence investigations.

In Celebration of
Sy Dinitz

Gilbert Geis

I

It is wondrous how a specific assignment and an imminent deadline can focus the mind. I am to add a concluding personal note to this tribute to Sy Dinitz. I have known Sy for more than thirty years, but do I know him well enough to write reasonably about him? We have been neither teaching colleagues at the same university nor research collaborators. Our meetings, since we were together in graduate school, have been in the nature of fleeting passings at this or that conference. That is hardly enough for a Strachey-like pen portrait. I think I know Sy well, and I admire him greatly. But such generalities are not substantial stuff; indeed, they are little more than the shell out of which awkward and unconvincing letters of reference are put together.

There may be something of note, however, in my most vivid recollection of talks I've had with Sy. He and I were perched on the bathtub in Ray Sletto's suite (Ray was then chair of the Sociology Department at Ohio State University) during one of the early 1950s meetings of what was then known, perhaps more felicitously, as the ASS (American Sociological Society). The bathroom provided the only quiet space at this OSU cocktail party given by Sletto. I used the occasion to moan miserably to Sy about the $3,100 I was getting as what I was wont to call "an expendable young instructor" in the Sociology Department at the University of Oklahoma. Besides, I told Sy, during our last faculty meeting, the chairman had asked the head of the recruitment committee about the height of one of the job candidates. "It's been my experience," he said with a tone of supreme assurance, "that big men make the best teachers." I swore that he pointedly looked down at me—far down, from his 6 foot, 3 inch height—when he uttered that pronouncement.

Sy was, as always, enormously sympathetic, even wide-eyed as he probed for further details of my life in academic exile. But before I quite sensed how it had happened, he was counterattacking with a poignant synopsis of his own situation. It wasn't very long before I began feeling much better about Oklahoma. At least, unlike Sy's, my existence was not so forlorn that at virtually any moment I was going to abandon the whole miserable business and take a job in my uncle's clothing factory.

The brief episode was, of course, merely a taste of Sy's magic, his wonderful ability to make a person feel better. He sometimes resorts to self-denigration, and he is truly humble. Sometimes he employs flattery—so blatant that it somehow becomes believable: How could any appraisal so stunning be totally without merit? Maybe it is because Sy wants you to believe these things about yourself and your work, because, if you now feel good, it makes him feel better.

II

At the moment, almost three decades later, as I write the first draft of these pages, Sy and I are part of a conference group in a hotel near Dulles Airport, outside of Washington. At lunch, Sy reported that he would have to leave the meeting a day early. He has been invited as an official delegate to the United Nations crime conference in Caracas. A few days after those sessions he will be off to Australia to deliver the John Barry Memorial Lecture in Melbourne, as well as a number of colloquia throughout the country. It all seems a long way from Ray Sletto's bathroom—and the garment industry.

The group at the conference is listening to a speaker who is droning on mercilessly about his views on research priorities in the field of white-collar crime. Sy is sitting diagonally across the room from me, white-haired, chin-on-elbow-on-table, tie knot pulled far down from his neck. Unlike most of us, he manages to convey the image that he finds the presentation to be of absorbing interest. His contribution over these last two days has largely been confined to livening things up with sprigs of good-natured humor. Because I am trying hard to observe carefully, I notice that Sy has intruded himself ever-so-adroitly into discussions several times in order to rescue a beleaguered speaker. He is able to deflect a discomforting attack on others by broadening the issue, then placing the besieged person's remarks into a perspective where they more properly belong. Anything is reasonable, I muse, if located in its appropriate context. Sy sets out such a context, and he does so as an act of gentlemanly goodwill.

Earlier, at lunch, I had tried to ferret out some information, feeling sheepish about my hidden agenda and also playing a little at being a latter-day Boswell. I know and highly respect Sy's scholarly achievements, and I know his charm and decency as a person. It is his teaching I wanted to learn more about.

He starts by saying offhandedly that he has been working too hard of late; he says this with bemusement as if he is perplexed about the intensity of this drive to work he finds in himself. "If I had my way, I'd like to spend all of my time teaching," he says, obviously meaning it. It is not a popular viewpoint, and a number of the burned-out professors at the lunch table wince notably. They have my sympathy. "The worst of teaching," D.H. Lawrence thought after he tried it for a while in a London suburb, "is that it takes so much out of you and gives you nothing in return. You never know what you've done, or if you've really done anything."[1] Centuries before Lawrence, Samuel Johnson had maintained that "a scholastic and academical life is very uniform and has, indeed, more safety than pleasure,"[2] while the learned jurist Oliver Wendell

Holmes insisted that "academic life is but a half life."[3] Sy would scoff at such views: "I teach ten hours a week now, but I wish I could do at least fifteen and forget the research."

Truly uncomprehending, I ask Sy why he feels this way. But he only kids with me, and I do not want to press the question lest my interest seem more than just a passing curiosity. "My wife won't listen to me. My children won't listen to me either. I've got those students in class where they have to listen." He almost throws away the final and most meaningful line, muttering it because he is a little embarrassed about turning serious after the facetious opening. "They learn what you tell them," Sy says, self-consciously.

Sy's own presentation later during the conference is notable, among other reasons, because it is rather personal, different from the common, antiseptic, third-person academic approach. He talks with obvious pride of research done on white-collar crime by his students and then discusses the contributions of Marshall Clinard, Sy's mentor. He clearly takes satisfaction in the sense of continuity, of intellectual order, and of scholarly heritage that this span of work from Clinard through himself to his students represents.

These are a few clues; with other things that I know as true, they testify to Sy's deep sympathy with and for people, his desire to press a point of view that he thinks is important if we are to have a decent world, his willingness to subordinate himself so that others can shine—all of these supported by a fundamental goodness.

III

A few weeks later, I interrogated a former doctoral student of Sy Dinitz, and I tried to pin him down about his response to Sy. He is one of the most articulate young men I know, but he had great difficulty telling me with any precision why he has such unbounded respect and admiration for Sy. The term "warm" recurs, and he comes back several times to Sy's "openness," particularly his willingness to listen wholeheartedly and sympathetically to young people. The former student grants that Sy is too "middle-of-the-road," his values too "middle-class" for this young man's political taste, but he says this only serves to enhance his admiration for Sy, because the ideological differences between them never even slightly altered Sy's willingness to honor work or be receptive to ideas that are different from his own, provided they were either soundly and logically based or were identified as personal predilections.

His "loyalty" is another quality that this former student well remembers in Sy. "Don't worry, I'm blocking for you," Sy had told him once, during delicate negotiations among members of his dissertation committee. And he knew for certain that he would not be abandoned, even if the fight were costly for Sy. Then he talked of Sy's "wonderful family," his "little jokes" in lectures and seminars, and the office door that was always open to those who sought Sy out.

But I wanted stories, illustrations, and anecdotes that I could use to construct a fuller portrait of the man. I pressed hard but got nowhere. Finally, the former graduate student smiled broadly, sat back, and indicated by his gestures that we had reached an impasse.

"He's great, just great," he said with settled conviction. "He's everything I admire in a person. He's the kind of human being I'd like my kids to be. What else can I say?"

IV

The quality of teaching, a keystone of Sy's life, is a matter difficult to convey, much more so than the information about research achievement that can be put together from scrutiny of published works. To obtain a closer look at Sy's teaching, I commandeered the dust-covered class notes of another former student of Sy's, a woman who, showing that she surely had been taught to think clearly, had moved from Ohio to California. She had taken half a dozen of Sy's courses, and she still glowed with nostalgic pleasure when she thought back on them. " 'Scholars' was what he'd call us," she said. "And he'd end the class with: 'More truth next time.' "

There is a blue-covered notebook that contains the material for Sociology 610 (Sociology of Deviance). Its contents leave no question concerning the instructor's teaching style and skills. He details the diverse views on an issue, then he lets the class know what it all means and what lesson they should take to heart. Sometimes this is done through highlighting the core wisdom by designating it "Dinitz's Law" or "Dinitz's Rule."

On the issue of deviance, for example, Dinitz tells the class that "the more we expect deviance, the more deviance we get." The class notes then read:

1. Becker—no deviance—except as defined by others (state).
2. No human behavior is deviant! But society says some behavior is.
3. Dinitz—*not* just social matter, *some* behaviors are intolerable. But some persons are made outsiders for no reason.

No sensible instructor hedges his lectures with all those scholarly qualifiers that would render incomprehensible virtually any important statement of a complex issue—so embedded would it be in caveats. In addition, no sensible instructor expects nuances to find their way in pristine form into either the notes or the minds of a class of undergraduates. The little homily on deviance (selected from the first page of the first notebook examined, but representative of the group), it could be said, conveys in fine style some extremely important and powerful information—as well as the instructor's identified exception to the orthodoxy.

Deviance, this class was later told, is apt to be defined by some element of a "holy trinity"—psychiatrists, social workers (or psychologists), and authorities in an institution. Then comes the first Dinitz Law: "To find out about a patient, ask the attendants on the ward, not the holy trinity." The students also were told that drug addicts are like diabetics; they should be maintained and let alone. This is shortly followed by the first piece of Dinitz Advice: "Deviate in private"—a hortatory instruction based on the position that visibility is essential for a person to be defined as a deviant. Sy also lets students know that, with Sagarin, he prefers protection of privacy (they are commenting on *Tearoom Trade*) to control of such forms of deviancy as homosexuality.

There are many names in the notes—Becker, Lemert, Szasz, Platt, Lindesmith, Kittrie, Mills—and perhaps a review of all of these together would tell of Sy's philosophical preferences. But I'm impressed with how well he dovetails diverse views and, particularly, how unremittingly he deals with ideas: the functions of deviance, the relationship between the concepts of deviance and normality, and boundary setting in regard to deviance. You see a quick, engaged, active mind at work, having an exciting time intensely scrutinizing a concept, tossing it about to determine what it has to offer, questioning the conventional wisdom, and adding dimensions that are not yet incorporated into the literature on the subject. That the notes themselves offer a coherent and comprehensive overview of the subject is a testament to very good teaching. There is, for instance, some admirable humanism, a blaming of the oppressors rather than, as is common, a condemnation of the victims. Thus, this class was told that distress about Haight-Asbury hippies (how quaint the term sounds already) was based on the fact that they rejected our values.

There are, I grant, some puzzlers. One line reads: "Obscene phone calls— Dinitz solution," with no further enlightenment. And apparently Sy is no better than the rest of us about pausing in his flow of ideas to spell out the name of this or that person with whom the students might not be familiar. Thus, we find that the German sociologist who had some thoughts on Calvinism and capitalism was a fellow named "Max Vaber."

It would have been better, undoubtedly, to have sat through some of those classes personally, to have taken notes for a purpose different from that of getting thorough an exam. Sy Dinitz, by all testimony, is a superb teacher, and I thought by looking at a student's notes I might try to capture an inkling of that classroom charisma.

V

Sy is an Israeliphile—a fervid, intense lover of that tiny, quarrelsome, idealistic, pessimistic, Mideast country that stands as a challenge and a tribute to a postwar act of conscience. It is paradoxically fitting—Sy would see the propriety and the ecumenicism of it—to use an Arabic phrase to encapsulate what I know and what I have found out about a close friend. The Arabs employ the term *baraka* to designate a quality that sometimes appears in a rare person, such as Sy Dinitz. *Baraka* refers to the power of such a person to enhance life, to make it appear better than it was—better than it would be without him.

Notes

1. Jessie Chambers, *D.H. Lawrence* (London: Jonathan Cape, 1935).

2. Mary Frances Wagley and Philip F. Wagley, "Comments on Samuel Johnson's Biography of Sir Thomas Browne," *Bulletin of the History of Medicine* 31:318–326.

3. Mark DeWolfe Howe, *Justice Oliver Wendell Holmes: The Proving Years, 1870–1882* (Cambridge, Mass.: Harvard University Press, 1963).

Simon Dinitz:
Milestones to 1981

The following represents selected honors, awards, and publications authored or coauthored from 1947 to 1981.

1947

B.A., Magna cum Laude, Vanderbilt University

1949

M.A., University of Wisconsin

1950

K.K. Knapp Fellow, University of Wisconsin (1950–1951)

1951

Ph.D., University of Wisconsin
Instructor, Ohio State University (1951–1955)
Lecturer, Ohio State University (1951–1955)

1953

Research grant, Nationwide Insurance Company (1953–1954)

1954

Insurance and Socioeconomic Status. Columbus: The Ohio State University Research Foundation.
"Preferences for Male or Female Children: Traditional or Affectional?" *Marriage and Family Living* 16(May):128–130.

1955

Research Grant, Ohio State University Development Fund (1955–1959)
Insurance and Consumption Patterns. Nationwide Insurance Company.

1956

Assistant Professor, Ohio State University (1956–1959)
"Levels of Aspiration: Some Family Experiences as a Variable." *American Sociological Review* 21(April):212–215.
"Health Insurance Protection and Medical Care Expenditures: Findings from Three Family Surveys." *Social Security Bulletin* (November).
"Self Concept as an Insulator Against Delinquency." *American Sociological Review* 21(December):744–746.

1957

Research Associate in Psychiatry, Ohio State University (1957–1974)
"Teacher Nominations and Evaluations of 'Good' Boys in High Delinquency Areas." *Elementary School Journal,* 57(January):221–223.
"Delinquency Proneness and School Achievement." *Educational Research Bulletin* 32(April):131–136.
"The 'Good' Boy in a High Delinquency Area," *Journal of Criminal Law, Criminology and Police Science* 48(August):18–26.
"The Self Component on Potential Delinquency and Potential Non-Delinquency." *American Sociological Review* 22(October):566–570.

1958

Research grant, National Institute of Mental Health (1958–1959)
"Group Gradients in Delinquency Potential and Achievement Scores of Sixth Graders." *Journal of Orthopsychiatry* 28(July):598–606.
"A Self-Gradient among Potential Delinquents," *Journal of Criminal Law, Criminology and Police Science* 49(September-October):230–233.
"The Ward Behavior of Psychiatrically Ill Patients," *Social Problems* 6(Fall):107–115.
"Correlates and Consequences of Patient Interaction and Isolation in a Mental Hospital." *Journal of Nervous and Mental Disorders* 127(November):437–442.

1959

Associate Professor, Ohio State University (1959–1963)
Research grant, National Institute of Mental Health (1959–1961)
"Integration and Conflict in Self-Other Images as Factors in Mental Illness," *Sociometry* 22(March):44–55.
"Geographic and Seasonal Variation in Births." *Public Health Reports* 74(April):285–289.
"Levels of Aspiration and Family Affection: Religious Preference as a Variable," *Ohio Journal of Science,* April, pp. 103–107.
"Psychiatric Orientation and Its Relation to Diagnosis and Treatment," *American Journal of Psychiatry* 116(August):127–132.
"Hunting for an Insulator Against Delinquency." *Graduate School Record* (Ohio State University) 13(Autumn):20–23.
"Status Perceptions in a Mental Hospital." *Social Forces* 38(December):124–128.
"Decision-Making in a Mental Hospital: Real, Perceived, and Ideal." *American Sociological Review* 24(December):822–829.
"Ward Policies and Practices and Correlates of Patient Behavior," *Regional Research Reports* (American Psychiatric Association) 10:56–61.

1960

"Delinquency Potential of Pre-Adolescents in High Delinquency Areas." *British Journal of Delinquency* 10(January):211–215.
"Social and Medical Characteristics of Hysterectomized and Nonhysterectomized Psychiatric Patients." *Obstetrics and Gynecology* 12(February):209–216.
"Mental Hospital Organization and Staff Evaluation of Patients." *AMA Archives of General Psychiatry* 2(April):462–467.
"Socioeconomic and Seasonal Variations in Birth Rates." *Milbank Memorial Fund Quarterly* 38(July):248–254.
"The 'Good' Boy in a High Delinquency Area: Four Years Later." *American Sociological Review* 25(August):555–558.
"Mate Selection and Social Class: Changes During the Past Quarter Century." *Marriage and Family Living* 22(November):348–351.

1961

"Status Perceptions of Psychiatric Social Workers and Their Implications for Work Satisfaction," *American Journal of Orthopsychiatry* 31(January):102–110.

"The Post-Hospital Psychological Functioning of Former Mental Hospital Patients." *Mental Hygiene* 45(October):579–588.

"Social and Psychiatric Attributes as Predictors of Case Outcome in Mental Hospitalization." *Social Problems* 8(Spring):322–328.

"Rehospitalization of Female Mental Patients: A Study of Social and Psychological Factors" *AMA Archives of General Psychiatry* 4:363–370.

1962

Listed in *American Men of Science,* 10th ed. (also listed in 11th ed., 1968).

"Self Concept as a Predictor of Juvenile Delinquency," *American Journal of Orthopsychiatry,* 32(January):159–168.

"Instrumental Role Expectations and Post-Hospital Performance of Female Mental Patients." *Social Forces* 40(March):248–254.

"Social Class, Expectations and Performance of Mental Patients." *American Journal of Sociology* 68(July):79–87.

"Delinquency Vulnerability: A Cross-Group and Longitudinal Analysis." *American Sociological Review* 27(August):515–517.

"Tolerance of Deviant Behaviors, Post-Hospital Performance Levels, and Rehospitalization." *Proceedings of the Third World Congress of Psychiatry,* pp. 237–241.

"The Outcome of Mental Hospitalization: A Study in Prognosis." *Psychiatric Research Reports* No. 15, American Psychiatric Association.

1963

Professor, Ohio State University (1963-present)

Member, Comprehensive Community Mental Health Center Task Force (1963–1965)

Research grant, National Institute of Mental Health (1963–1966)

"Implementing Two Theories of Delinquency, Value Orientation and Awareness of Limited Opportunity." *Sociology and Social Research* 47(July): 409–416.

1964

Social Problems: Dissensus and Deviation. New York: Oxford University Press.

"Home Versus Hospital Care for Schizophrenics," *Journal of the American Medical Association* 187(January 18):177–181.

"Problems in a Home Care Study for Schizophrenics." *Archives of General Psychiatry* 10(February):143–154.
"Differential Perceptions of Life Chances: A Research Note." *Sociological Inquiry* 34(Winter):60–66.
"L'orientamento dei valori e la consapevolezza della prospettive della vita in giovani americani delinquenti e non delinquenti di classe sociale inferiore e Media." *Quaderni di Criminologia Clinica* 2(April-June).

1965

"Prevention of Hospitalization of Schizophrenics." *American Journal of Orthopsychiatry* 35(January):1–9.
"Psychotherapy with Disturbed and Defective Children: An Evaluation of Changes in Behavior and Attitudes." *American Journal of Mental Deficiency* 69(January):560–567.
"A Sociologist Looks at Suicide." *Ohio's Health* 16(February):1–7.
"Public Health Nurses in a Community Care Program for the Mentally Ill." *American Journal of Nursing* 65(June):89–95.
"Self Concept and Delinquency Proneness." In *Interdisciplinary Problems of Criminology,* ed. Walter C. Reckless and Charles L. Newman, pp. 49–51. Columbus, Ohio: American Society of Criminology.

1966

Editor, *Criminologica,* official journal of the American Society of Criminology (1966–1968)
Member, National Editorial Board, *Excerpta Criminologica* (1966–1968)
Research grant, National Institue of Mental Health (1966–1970)
"Two Years of a Home Care Study for Schizophrenics." In *Psychopathology of Schizophrenia,* ed. Paul Hock and Joseph Zubin, pp. 515–526. New York: Grune and Stratton.
"Former Mental Patients and Their Neighbors: A Comparison of Performance Levels." *Journal of Health and Human Behavior* 7(Summer):106–113.

1967

Hofheimer Prize for Research, American Psychiatric Association
Vice-President, American Society of Criminology (1967–1969)
Schizophrenics in the Community: An Experiment in the Prevention of Hospitalization. New York: Appleton-Century-Crofts.

"Policy Implications of an Experimental Study in the Home Care of Schizophrenics." *Sociological Focus* 1(Winter):1–19.
"The Unmarried Woman after Psychiatric Treatment." *Mental Hygiene*
51(April):175–181.
"Personality Attributes of the Criminal: An Analysis of Research Studies,
1950–1965." *Journal of Research in Crime and Delinquency* 4(July):
185–202.
"Home Care for Schizophrenic Patients: A Controlled Study." *British Journal
of Social Psychiatry* 1(Autumn):270–280.
"Pioneering with Self Concept as a Vulnerability Factor in Delinquency,"
Journal of Criminal Law, Criminology and Police Science 58(December):515–523.

1968

Selected as one of the Big Ten's "Ten Most Exciting Teachers," *Chicago
Tribune*
Outstanding Teacher Award, Ohio State University, Arts College
Visiting Professor, University of Southern California (summer)
Honorary Member, Phi Beta Kappa, Ohio State University
Listed in *World Who's Who in Science*
Associate Editor, *American Sociological Review* (1968–1969; 1970–1971)
Vice-President, Ohio Valley Sociological Association (1968–1969)
Council Member, Section on Criminology, American Sociological Association
(1968–1971)
Critical Issues in the Study of Crime: A Book of Readings. Boston: Little,
Brown.
*Women after Treatment: A Comparison of Treated Mental Patients and Their
Normal Neighbors.* New York: Appleton-Century-Crofts.
"Discussion of Dr. Brody's Paper." In *Social Psychiatry,* ed. Joseph Zubin,
pp. 39–41. New York: Grune and Stratton.

1969

President-Elect, American Society of Criminology (1969–1970)
Visiting Professor, University of Wisconsin (summer)
Consultant, United Nations Social Defense Research Institue (1969–1974;
1978–1979)
Member, Mayor's Urban Community Task Force (Columbus, Ohio)
Research grant, Ohio State University Develoment Fund (1969–1970)
Research grant, New York State Department of Mental Hygiene (1969–1970)

Research grant, State of Ohio, Correctional Information System Grant
     (1969–1970)
Deviance: Studies in the Process of Stigmatization and Societal Reaction. New
     York: Oxford University Press.
"The Social and Bio-Medical Correlates of Sociopathy." *Criminologica*
     5(February):68–75.
"Emerging Issues in Delinquency." In *The Threat of Crime in America*
     (1967–1968 E. Paul de Pont Lectures on Crime, Delinquency and Correc-
     tions). University of Delaware.

1970

President, American Society of Criminology (1970–1971)
Alumni Award for Distinguished Teaching, Ohio State University
Visiting Professor, Institute of Criminology, University of Tel Aviv (fall)
Listed in *Dictionary of International Biography,* 7th ed. (1970–1971)
Listed in *Who's Who in America* (1970–present)
Listed in *Who's Who in the Midwest*
Member, Technical Advisory Committee on Aging (1970–1974)
Research grant, State of Ohio (1970–1972, Sociopathy)
"Antisocial Personality Type with Cardiac Lability." *Archives of General Psy-
     chiatry* 23(September):260–267.

1971

Visiting Professor, Institute of Criminology, University of Tel Aviv (fall)
Chairman, Subcommittee on Institutional Processes, Governor's Task Force on
     Corrections, State of Ohio
"Female Mental Patients and Normal Female Controls: A Restudy Ten Years
     Later." *Psychiatric Spectator.*
"The Simple Sociopath: Physiologic and Sociologic Characteristics." *Biological
     Psychiatry* 3:77–83.
"Hostile and Simple Sociopaths: An Empirical Typology." *Criminology*
     9(May):27–47.
"Community Mental Health as a Boundaryless and Boundary-Busting System."
     Journal of Health and Social Behavior 12(June):99–108.
"The Status of Criminology." *Israeli Quarterly of Criminology, Criminal Law
     and Police Science* 1(Winter):83–88.

1972

Member, Ohio Corrections Advisory Task Force (1972–1973)
The Prevention of Delinquency: An Experiment. Columbus, Ohio: Ohio State
     University Press.

"The Juice Model: A New Look at Sociopathy," *et al.* 2:20–27.

"The Prevention of Hospitalization in Schizophrenia: Five Years After an Experimental Program." *American Journal of Orthopsychiatry* 42(April): 375–388.

"Perceptions of Stigma Following Public Intervention for Delinquent Behavior." *Social Problems* 20(Fall):202–208.

"Female Mental Patients and Their Normal Controls." *Archives of General Psychiatry* 27(November):606–610.

"Crime and Criminal Justice in Small Town USA." In *Politics, Crime and the International Scene,* ed. Freda Adler and Gerhard O.W. Mueller, pp. 269–276. New York: Fred B. Rothman.

1973

Visiting Professor, Institute of Criminology, University of Tel Aviv (winter)

Graduate Teaching Award, Department of Sociology, Ohio State University

Listed in *Contemporary Authors,* Vols. 37–40

Research grant, Law Enforcement Assistance Administration (1973–1974)

"Traditional and Community Psychiatry: The Management of Marginality." In *Research in Comprehensive Psychiatry* (Festschrift for Ralph M. Patterson), ed. Harold Goldman, pp. 45–59. Columbus: College of Medicine, Ohio State University.

"Progress, Crime, and the Folk Ethic: Portrait of a Small Town." *Criminology* 11(May):3–21.

"Interactional and Small-Group Components in Deviant and Criminal Behavior." In *American Criminology: New Directions,* ed. Walter C. Reckless, pp. 37–42. New York: Appleton-Century-Crofts.

"An Empirical Study of the Psychiatric Probation-Commitment Procedure." *American Journal of Orthopsychiatry* 43(July):660–669.

"Motines y Reformas en las Prisones." *Revista Mexicana de Prevencion y Readaptacion Social* 10(Summer):65–82.

"Rivolte Carcerarie Negli U.S.A.—1951–1971." *Quaderni di Criminologia Clinica* 15(September):305–328.

"Measuring Institutional Impact: A Follow-Up." *Criminology* 11(November):417–426.

"Psychopathy and Autonomic Responsivity: A Note on the Importance of Diagnosis." *Journal of Abnormal Psychology* 82:533–534.

"Problemi Penitenziari E. Riforme Negli U.S.A." *Revista Italina Di Diritto E Procedura Penale* 16:651–670.

1974

Edwin H. Sutherland Award for Distinguished Contributions to Criminology, American Society of Criminology

Member, Governor's Advisory Panel for Rehabilitation and Correction (1974–1975)

Schizophrenics in the New Custodial Community. Columbus, Ohio: Ohio State University Press.

A Designed Treatment Program of Sociopathy by Means of Drugs (Studies in Crime and Delinquency). Columbus, Ohio: Ohio State University.

"Compulsive Masculinity and Delinquency: An Empirical Investigation." *Criminology* 11(February):498–515.

"Becoming a Scapegoat: Study of a Deviant Career." *Sociological Symposium* 11(Spring):84–98.

"Reactions to My-Lai: A Visual-Verbal Comparison." *Sociology and Social Research* 58(January):122–129.

"Measuring Perceptions of Organizational Change." *Journal of Research in Crime and Delinquency* 11(July):180–194.

"Conflict and Cooperation in a Community Mental Health Program." In *Sociological Perspectives on Community Mental Health,* ed. Paul M. Roman and Harrison M. Trice, pp. 195–207. Philadelphia: F.A. Davis.

"Home Care for Psychiatric Disorders: Assessment of Effectiveness." In *Sociological Perspectives on Community Mental Health,* ed. Paul M. Roman and Harrison M. Trice, pp. 233–247. Philadelphia: F.A. Davis Co.

"Cross-Cultural Aspects of Delinquent and Criminal Behavior." In *Aggression: Research Publication of the Association for Research in Nervous and Mental Disease,* pp. 287–303. Baltimore: Williams and Wilkins.

1975

Senior Fellow, The Academy for Contemporary Problems (1975–1978)

Research grant, Lilly Endowment (1975–1978, Dangerous Offender Project; 1979–1980)

Delinquents and Nondelinquents in the Puerto Rican Slum Culture. Columbus, Ohio: Ohio State University Press.

Deviance: Studies in Definition, Management and Treatment, 2nd ed. New York: Oxford University Press.

"Inmate Exploitation: A Study of the Juvenile Victim." In *Victimology: A New Focus. Volume V, Violence and Its Victims,* ed. Israel Drapkin and Emilio Viano, pp. 135–142. Lexington, Mass.: Lexington Books, D.C. Heath and Company.

"Games Inmates Play: Notes on Staff Victimization." In *Victimology: A New Focus. Volume V, Violence and Its Victims,* ed. Israel Drapkin and Emilio Viano, pp. 143–156. Lexington, Mass.: Lexington Books, D.C. Heath and Company.

"Staff Exploitation of Inmates: The Paradox of Institutional Control." In *Vic-*

timology: A New Focus. Volume V, Violence and Its Victims, ed. Israel Drapkin and Emilio Viano, pp. 158–168. Lexington, Mass.: Lexington Books, D.C. Heath and Company.
"The Informal Code in a Juvenile Institution." *Journal of Southern Criminal Justice* 1:33–52.

1976

Member, Governor's Youth Services Advisory Committee, State of Ohio (1976–present)
Juvenile Victimization: The Institutional Paradox. New York: Halsted Press, Wiley, a Sage publication.
"The Booty Bandit." *Journal of Homosexuality* 1:203–212.
"Organizational Processing and Inmate Victimization in a Juvenile Training School." In *Victims and Society,* ed. Emilio Viano, pp. 569–578. Visage Press.
"The Centennial of Positivism in Criminology" (Commentary). *The Criminologist* 1(September):6–7.
"The Exploitation Matrix in a Juvenile Institution." *International Journal of Criminology and Penology* 4:257–270.
"Organized and Economic Crime: A Comparison." *CIRCIB* (International Center of Biological and Medico-Forensic Criminology), Official Bulletin 1, No. 12, pp. 10–13. (Based on Proceedings of Second International Symposium on Criminology: The Sociological Model, Sao Paulo, Brazil.)
"Sociopathy: An Experiment in Internal Environmental Control." *American Behavioral Scientist,* November-December, pp. 215–226.
"Analisi Multifattoriale Della Delinquenza Minorile." In *Estratto degli Atti Del V Congress Nazionale Della Soceita' Italiana di Criminologia,* pp. 133–217.
"Prsioners' Unions: A Cross-National Investigation of Public Acceptance." *International Journal of Criminology and Penology,* 4:331–347.

1977

Research grant, National Institute of Corrections (1977–1978)
In Fear of Each Other. Lexington, Mass.: Lexington Books, D.C. Heath and Company.
Criminal Justice Planning. New York: Praeger.
"Economic Crime." In *Criminology in Perspective: Essays in Honor of Israel Drapkin,* ed. S. Landau and L. Sebba, pp. 41–67. Lexington, Mass.: Lexington Books, D.C. Heath.

"The Bottom is in the Hole; A Look at the Dangerous Offender and Society's Effort to Control Him." *American Journal of Correction* 39(January-February):30–31.

"Boys Who Profit: The Limits of Institutional Success." In *Reform in Corrections,* ed. Harry E. Allen and Nancy J. Beran, pp. 8–16. New York: Praeger.

"La Criminalita' Economica." *Quaderni di Criminologia Clinica* 18(October-December):433–458.

"The Incapacitation of the Dangerous Offender: A Statistical Experiment." *Journal of Research in Crime and Delinquency* 14:22–34.

1978

Presidential Fellowship, Ohio State University (1978–1980)

The Violent Few. Lexington, Mass.: Lexington Books, D.C. Heath and Company.

"Thinking about Dangerous Offenders." *Criminal Justice Abstracts* 10(March):99–130.

"Response to Our Critics." *Journal of Research in Crime and Delinquency* 15:135–139.

"White Collar Crime: Conceptual Analysis and Current Status." *Social Science Quarterly* (Israel) 12–19:273–288 (in Hebrew).

"The Prison within a Prison: Discipline at the Impasse." Report to the National Institute of Corrections. Columbus, Ohio: Academy for Contemporary Problems.

"Nothing Fails Like a Little Success." *Criminology* 16(August):225–238.

"Pioneering Innovations in Corrections: Shock Probation and Shock Parole." *Offender Rehabilitation* 3(Winter):113–122.

"I Sindacati dei Detenuti: Una Ricerca Cross-Nazionale Sulla Loro Accettazione da Parte Del Publico." *Quaderni di Criminologia Clinica* 20(1):21–47.

1979

Distinguished Research Award, Ohio State University

Associate Fellow, The Academy for Contemporary Problems (1979–present)

Restraining the Wicked: The Incapacitation of the Dangerous Criminal. Lexington, Mass.: Lexington Books, D.C. Heath and Company.

"Home Care Treatment as a Substitute for Hospitalization: The Louisville Experiment." *New Directions in Mental Health Services* 1(January):1–13.

"Incapacitation of the Chronic Thug." *Journal of Criminal Law and Criminology* 70(Spring):125–136.

1980

Nemzer Award, Ohio State University Chapter of the American Association of
  University Professors
Visiting Professor, University of South Florida (winter)
"The Anti-Social Personality." In *Modern Legal Medicine, Psychiatry and
  Forensic Science,* ed. W. Curry, C. Petty, and L. McGarry, chapter 33.
  Philadelphia: F.A. Davis.
"The Dangerous Two Percent." In *Critical Issues in Juvenile Delinquency,* ed.
  David Schichor and Delos Kelly, pp. 139–155. Lexington, Mass.: Lexing-
  ton Books, D.C. Heath.
"The State's Strongest Medicine." In *An Anatomy of Criminal Justice,* ed.
  Cleon Faust and D. Robert Webster, pp. 237–257. Lexington, Mass.: Lex-
  ington Books, D.C. Heath.

1981

President, North Central Sociological Association (1981–1982)
Named one of the five best professors in the United States, Council for Ad-
  vancement and Support of Education.

Index

Aichhorn, August, 68, 70, 72
Aigner, Stephen M., 89
Akers, Ronald L., 42, 218–219
Albini, Joseph L., 125–134
Alienation. *See* Anomie
Allen, Harry E., 181–187
American Mafia: Genesis of a Legend, The, 125
American Sociological Society, 135
Anomie, 89, 211–213
Arrest rates, 42, 77, 79–84
Asch, Peter, 142
Atavism, 17, 86
Aubert, Vilhelm, 136
Autonomia, 207–8

Bakunin, M.A., 210
Baltimore County, Maryland, 228
Banfield, Edward, 105–106, 107–108
BARS Project (Colorado), 227
Bartollas, Clemens, 159–167
Barzun, Jacques, 8, 9
Beccaria, Cesare, 3–4, 5, 6–7, 8, 9, 10–11, 12
Becker, Howard, 31–32, 42
Bencivengo, Mark, 117
Bentham, Jeremy, 3, 4, 5, 6, 8, 11–12
Beran, Nancy J., 181–187
Biderman, Albert, 138
Biological school, 68, 70; criticism of, 70–71; for women, 86, 87
Bittner, Egon, 29
Black, Donald J., 219
Black, Theodore, 175–176
Blacks: homicide and, 113, 117–118; pawning, 154; in underclass, 107, 108; violence and, 119
Bleuler, Manfred, 190–191
Block, Richard, 116, 117
Bohannon, Paul, 218
Bole, Jacqueline, 86
Bonger, W.G., 68, 73
Boston, murder rate, 112
Boudouris, James, 111
Bowers, William J., 173
Brier, Stephen S., 175
British Journal of Law and Society, 220
Brocker, Paul, 84
Bruno, Francesco, 199–214
Brutalization, 176
Buck v. *Bell*, 16
Buikhuisen, Wouter, 20
Burn-out phenomenon, 235
Bye, Raymond, 169

Cain, James A., 126

California, paraprofessionals in corrections, 229–230
Canetti, Elias, 203
Cantor, David, 171
Capital punishment, 8–11; deterrence and, 169–78; and homicide rate, 169
Caplan, Gerald M., 225
Center for Studies in Criminal Justice, University of Chicago, 230
Cernkovich, Steven A., 89
Chambliss, W.J., 128, 218, 220, 221
Chapel Hill Youth Development and Research Unit, 227
Chicago, homicide in, 114, 115
Child abuse, 34
Chillicothe Correctional Institute, 185
Chronic offender, 232
Cicourel, Aaron V., 28, 30, 34
Clark, John P., 140, 141
Class, State and Crime, 46
Classical school, xii, 5, 6, 7, 15
Clements, Raymond D., 229
Clinard, Marshall, xxii, 135, 142, 143, 251
Cloninger, Dale O., 171–172
Cloward, R.A., 69, 73, 89
Code of Hammurabi, 150
Cohen, Albert K., 69, 88
Cohen, Lawrence, 171
Colorado State Penitentiary, BARS Project, 227
Communism and War, 207
Community mental health, 189–193
Competency to stand trial, 181–182
Comte, August, 15
Conflict-critical approach, 39, 40–43, 220–222
Conflict theory, 40–43
Conrad, John P., 101–110
Conrad, Peter, xxiii, 34
Containment theory, 67–75
Cosa Nostra. *See* Mafia
Count Firmian, 4
Cowie, John, 86
Cowie, Valerie, 86
Creer, Claire, 192
Cressey, Donald, 126, 128, 135
Crime and Conflict, 48
Crime rate, regional variations, 112–113
Crime and Social Justice, 220
Crimes of the Powerful, 48
Criminal identities, 29
Criminal inquiry, methods of, 30–31
Criminality, teaching, 239–247
Criminality and the Legal Order, 42
Criminality of Women, The, 88
Critique of Law: A Marxist Analysis, 48

Critique of Law Group, 48
Culture, Conflict and Crime, 40–41
Curtis, Lynn A., 119
Custodialism, 189–190, 192

Dangerousness, 29, 34
Dangerous Offender project, xxiii, 102, 106–107
Daniels, Arlene Kaplan, 28, 34
Datesman, Susan K., 87, 88–89
Davis, Ann E., 189–198
Death penalty. *See* Capital punishment
DeCavalcante tapes, 129, 132–133
Deinstitutionalization, 1970s, 162
Delinquency. *See* Juvenile delinquency
Delinquency subculture, 69–70
Delinquents and Nondelinquents in the Puerto Rican Slum Culture, xvii
Deterrence punishment, 5–6; and death penalty, 169–178
Detroit, homicide in, 114–115
Deviant identities, 29
Dialectical thought, 44–45, 47
Differential association, 69, 70, 73–74, 89, 135–136
Dinitz, Sy: biographical data, xv; Dangerous Offender project, 101–103; eclecticism, criticism of his, xvii; Hofheimer Prize, xvii, xxiii; milestones, 225–266; multidisciplinary approach, xi; at Ohio State, xi, xv, xxii; personal tribute, Geis, 249–254; prevention of delinquency, 63–64, 72; professional associations, xviii, xxiv; research interests, xi–xii, xvi, 185–186; scope of interests, xv–xvi; Sutherland Award, xvii, xxiii; teaching awards, xviii, xxiv, xxv; University of Wisconsin, xxii
Dixon, M., 58
Documentary interpretation, 29–30, 32
Domestic strife, homicide and, 113, 115
Douglas, Jack D., 29, 34
Draper Correctional Center, 227
Draper Project, 227
Dreitzel, Hans Peter, 33
Drug abuse: and homicide, 116–117; and terrorism, 208
Dugdale, R.L., 17
Durkheim, Emile, 27

Economic crime, 137–138
Economic Opportunity Act, 226, 229
Edelhertz, Herbert, 137–138, 141
Edelman, B., 48
Efforts from Ex-Convicts, 228
Ehrlich, Isaac: critics, 172–176; research, 169–70; supporters, 170–172
Emerson, Robert, 29
Empey, LaMar, 61, 229

England, executions in, 170–171
Enzensberger, Hans M., 203
Epinephrine, effect of on sociopaths, 185
Ermann, M. David, 139–140
Ethnomethodology, xxi, 25–37; definition of, 25–26; and labeling-factors tradition, 31–33
Evan, William M., 218
Evola, Julius, 208
Executions. *See* Capital punishment
Exemplary Project Advisory Board, 233
Ex-offenders: in Ohio Parole Officer Aide Program, 231–235; as paraprofessionals, 227–235
Experiential education, 239–246

Female crime, changes in, 77–93; adult, statistics, 78–81; feminism and, 90–93; juvenile, 81–84
Ferdinand, Theodore N., 112
Ferracuti, Franco, xviii, xxiii, 117, 199–214
Ferri, Enrico, 3, 68
Fienberg, Stephen E., 175
Figlio, Robert M., 232
Filatov, Victor, 174
Fishman, Gideon, 15–23
Forst, Brian, 174
Foster, Thomas, 239–247
Fox, James A., 176
Fragment in Government, A, 4
Frank, Jerome, 8, 219
Frankfurt school, 47, 48
Freda, Franco, 208
Frey, Irwin, 68
Friedlander, Kate, 68
Future Association, 228

Galliher, John F., 126
Gardiner, John A., 127, 128
Garfinkel, Harold, 28, 29, 30
Garofalo, 3, 16
Geis, Gilbert, 5, 249–254
Gelles, Richard J., 116, 119
Gibbons, Don C., 18–19, 39, 87
Gibbs, Jack P., 32
Gilmore, Gary, 9
Girodano, Peggy, 89
Glick, Ruth, 91
Gloser, Daniel, 69, 70, 73
Glueck, Sheldon and Eleanor, 17, 68, 70–71, 87
Goddard, Henry H., 17
Godfather, The, 126, 30–32
Gold, Martin, 84, 85
Gordon, M.T., 230
Goring, Charles, 17
Graham, J.M., 42
Guerilla fighters, 203, 204
Gun ownership, death penalty and, 174

Guns: handguns, 104; and homicide, 116
Gurvitch, Georges, 217, 218

Hagon, J., 42
Halfway houses, 28
Harris, Anthony, 89–90
Hartnett, Catherine M., 149–155
Hawkins, Gordon, 126
Hawkins, Richard, 219
Head Start Program, 226
Helvetius, 4
Hirst, P., 48
Hitler, Adolf, 203
Hofheimer Prize, xvii, xxiii, 189
Hollinger, Richard, 140, 141
Holmes, Oliver Wendell, 219, 250–51
Homicide: and alcohol, 116; blacks and 113,
    117–18; definition of, 25, 111; domestic
    strife and, 113, 115; drugs and, 116–117;
    executions and, 169; guns and, 116;
    ideology of, 113–16; men and, 113,
    114–115; motives, 115; participants'
    attributes, 113; regional variations,
    112–113; sociological explanation of,
    117–120; statistics, 112; technology of,
    116–117; Violence Commission report,
    115, 116; women and, 113, 114
Hooton, Earnest A., 16, 17
House of Judah, 228
Humanism, 5
Hunt, Alan, 220–221
Hutchins, Robert Maynard, xviii
Hyperkinesis, 25–26, 34

Ianni, Francis A.J., 128
Imipramine pamoate, effects of on sociopaths,
    185–186
Indexicality, 27–28, 29, 32, 34
Infanticide, 113
Inmate self-government programs, 227–228
In re Gault, 161–162
Insanity plea, 182–184
Institute of Government, University of North
    Carolina, 227
International Journal of the Sociology of Law,
    220
Israeli Studies in Criminology, xxiii
Italian Penal Code, 201–203
Italy, terrorism in, 199–214

James, Jennifer, 90–91
Johnson, Samuel, 250
Judicial Conference Committee on Probation,
    230
Justice, juvenile, 159–167; history, U.S.,
    159–162; neighborhood, 159. See also
    Juvenile court; Juvenile crime; Juvenile
    delinquency; Juvenile rights
Juvenile court, 160–161

Juvenile crime, 159–167
Juvenile delinquency: current status, 162–164;
    historical attitudes toward, 159–162;
    subculture, 69–70
Juvenile Delinquency prevention, 57–66;
    effectiveness of, 62–65; programs, 57–62
Juvenile Delinquency Prevention and Control
    Act of 1968, 57
Juvenile Delinquency and Youth Offenses Act
    of 1961, 57
Juvenile delinquents, characteristics of, 58–59
Juvenile Justice Act of 1974, 57
Juvenile Delinquency Prevention Act, 1972,
    57
Juvenile Justice and Delinquency Prevention
    Act of 1974, 163

Kansas State Prison, 228
King, David R., 171
Kirkpatrick, Clifford, 169
Kitsuse, John, 30–31, 32, 33, 34
Kleck, Gary, 174
Klein, Laurence R., 174
Knorr, Stephen J., 174–175
Kobrin, S., 61
Konopka, Gisela, 87
Kretschmer, E., 68, 70
Ku Klux Klan, 113

Labeling, 6, 32–33, 34, 35, 39–40, 59, 60,
    64, 89
Lane, Roger, 111, 112, 114, 135, 137
Langbein, John, 7
Lange, Johannes, 21, 68
Law, sociology of, 217–224
Law Enforcement Assistance Administration
    (LEAA), 57, 225–238
Law and Human Behavior, 220
Lawrence, D.H., 250
Law and the Rise of Capitalism, 48
Law-and-society programs, 220
Law and Society Review, 220
Lejins, P., 59
Lester, David, 170
Lester, Marilyn R., 34, 48
Leventhal, Gloria, 91
Llewellyn, Karl, 219
Lombroso, Cesare, 3, 17, 86, 90, 205–6; neo-
    Lombrosianism, 20
Luckenbill, David F., 117
Lumpen-proletariat. See Underclass
Lundman, Richard J., 59, 62, 63, 64,
    139–140

McClelland hearings, 127
McCleary, Richard, 28
McFarlane, P., 59, 62, 63, 64
McKay, Henry D., 97
M'Naghten test, 182

Maestro, Marcello, 9
Mafia, 125–34
Mansfield, Lord, 4
Marcuse, Herbert, 47
Marx, Karl, 107
Marxist perspective, 40, 44–48
Massachusetts, training schools, 162
Massachusetts Correctional Institution (MCI), 227, 228
Matza, D., 40
Mead, George Herbert, 27
Mehan, Hugh, 30
Meier, Robert F., 138
Men: homicide and, 113, 114–115; pawning, 153
Mentally ill offenders, 181–187; competency to stand trial, 181–82; and insanity plea, 182–184. *See also* Sociopath
Mexican-Americans, distribution of heroin, 128
Michalowski, Raymond J., 39–52
Michel, Jerry B., 127–128
Midcity Project, 59
Middle range theory, 67, 71–74
Miller, Jerome, 162
Miller, Martin G., 89
Miller, Stuart J., 159–167
Miller, W., 59
Minnesota Multiphasic Personality Inventory (MMPI), 91
Mobilization for Youth (MFY), 226
Model Penal Code test, 182–183
Molotch, Harvey, 34
Montes Pietatis, 151
Moro, Aldo, murder of, 201, 204

National Institute of Justice, 232
National Institute of Law Enforcement and Criminal Justice (NILECJ), 225
National Juvenile Justice Assessment Center, 162–163
Negri, Toni, 207
Neto, Virginia V., 91
New Careers Program, 228–229
Nonet, Philippe, 219
Norfolk Fellowship, 228
North Carolina, training schools, 165
North Carolina Prison Department, 227
Nuclear secrets, theft of, 141
Nye, F. Ivan, 72

Office of Economic Opportunity, 226
Office of Juvenile Justice and Delinquency Prevention, 57
Ohio, Parole Officer Aide Program, 225–38
Ohio Adult Parole Authority (APA), 225–226, 231
Ohio Penitentiary, 185
Ohio State Award for Distinguished Teaching, xviii

Ohlin, Lloyd, 69, 89
Omnibus Safe Streets and Crime Control Act of 1967, 104
"On Death Punishment," 8
On Law and Ideology, 48
"Only Ex-Offenders Need Apply," 225
Organizational crime, 137–141; research on, 141–143
Organized crime, 125–134; Great Britain, 129
Orsagh, Thomas, 175–176
Ownership of the Image, 48

Paraprofessionals, 226–227; in criminal-justice agencies, 227–229; ex-offenders, 227–235
Parens patriae, 160–161, 164
Parole Officer Aide Program of Ohio, 225, 231–233; dismantling, 233–235
Parole Service Assistant Program, California, 229–230
Pasamanick, Benjamin, xvii, xviii, xxiii
Passell, Peter, 172–173, 174
Patterson, J.A.C., 150
Pawnbroking, 149–155
Pearce F., 48
Penal slavery, 8
Pepinsky, Harold E., 48, 138
Perez, Jacob, 142, 143
Pfohl, Stephen J., 25–37
Philadelphia: homicide in, 112, 114; Zahn and Bencivengo study, 117
Phillips, David P., 162
Pierce, Glenn L., 173
Plea-bargaining, 7
Polk, K., 61
Pollak, Otto, 88, 93
Pollner, Marvin, 28
Positivism, xii, 3, 15–23, 184; biological school, 17–18, 19; classical school, 15–17; contrast with radical theory, 39, 44–46; definition of, 16; neobiological school, 20–21; sociological school, 18–20
Pound, Roscoe, 217, 219
President's Commission on Law Enforcement and Administration of Justice, 57
President's Committee on Juvenile Delinquency and Youth Crime, 226
President's Task Force Commission on Organized Crime, 126–127, 128, 130
Prisons, self-government programs, 227–228
Program for the Study of Crime and Delinquency, Ohio State University, 231
Project MOST (Maximizing Oregon's Services and Training for Adult Probation and Parole), 230
Project Re-entry, 228
Project Youth, 227
Psychological school, 68, 86–87; criticism of, 70
"Psychology of Punitive Justice, The," 27
Psychopath. *See* Sociopath

Punishment to protect society, 16–17
Puzo, Mario, 126, 130–132

Quinney, Earl R., 135, 136, 137, 138, 140
Quinney, R., 43, 46
Quoy, Herbert C., 18

Radical theory, 39, 44–49
Rape, 120
Reckless, Walter C., xvii, xviii, xxii, 63–64, 67–75; with Dinitz, 72
Red Brigades, 204
Redl, Fritz, 68, 70, 72
Redlinger, Lawrence John, 127–128
Reflexivity, 28–29, 32
Refuge, houses of, 160
Rehabilitation model, failure of, 164–165
Reiff, Robert, 226
Reign of Terror, 11
Reimer, David J., 85
Riesman, David, 219
Reiss, Albert J., Jr., 72, 137, 139
Riessman, Frank, 226
Rippetoe, J.K., 244–245
Roby, P., 42
Role convergence theory, 90–92
Rothman, David, 159
Russell, James M., 114

Sacks, Harvey, 36
Salancik, Gerald, 142, 143
San Antonio, distribution of heroin in, 127–128
San Quentin Penitentiary, Squires Program, 227
Savitz, Leonard, 171
Scarpitti, Frank R., xviii, 57–66, 87, 88–89; with Lundman and McFarlane, 59, 62, 63, 64
Schizophrenia, community treatment of, xviii, 189–198; alcohol and drug abuse, 192; genetic factor, 193–195; improvement, 195–196; requisites for care, 193–195; sexual deviance, 192; suicide, 192
Schizophrenics in the Community: An Experimental Study in the Prevention of Hospitalization, 189
Schizophrenics in the New Custodial Community, xviii
Schneider, Kurt, 68
Schroyer, T., 45
Schuessler, Karl, xxii
Schulman, Harry Manuel, 87
Schur, Edwin, 30, 64–65
Schuster, Richard L., 217–224
Schutz, Alfred, 26
Schwartz, R., 217
Scimecca, J.A., 48
Scott, Joseph E., 225–238
Self Development Group, 228

Self-report studies, 84–85, 89, 221
Sellin, Thorsten, 5, 9–10, 40–41, 42, 84, 232
Seneca, J.J., 142
Sentencing disparity, 42
Seventh Step Program, 228
Shaw, Clifford R., 88
Shaw, George Bernard, 49
Shelburne, Lord, 4
Sheldon, William H., 17, 68, 70
Sheleff, Leon Shoskolsky, 3–13
Sherman, Lawrence W., 139, 140–141
Shoham, Shlomo, xxiii
Short, James F., Jr., 88, 138, 139
Shover, Neal, 138–139
Shrager, Laura Shill, 138, 139
Sieverdes, Christopher M., 165
Silverman, Ira J., 77–99
Simons, Ronald L., 89
Skolnick, Jerome H., 217
Slater, Eliot, 86
Sletto, Ray, xxii
Smith, M. Brewster, 210
Social Problems, 217
Societal-reaction perspective, 25, 31–32, 33, 35, 39–40, 60
Sociological school, 68–70; criticism of, 19–21, 69–70; positivism, 18–19; theories of homicide, 117–120; women, 87–90
Sociopath, 18, 184–186; competency to stand trial, 181–182; drugs, effects of on, 185–186; insanity plea, 182–184
Squires Program, 227
Staw, Barry M., 142
Stefensmeier, Darrell, 80–84
Stephenson, Richard M., 88–89
Stern, Irving, 127, 128
Strasbourg European Convention, 1977, 203
Straus, Murray, 119
Street-Corner Society, 69
Strodtbeck, Fred L., 88
Sudnow, David, 27–28
Suicide, right to commit, 9, 29
Sutherland, Edwin H., 69, 70, 73, 89, 135–136, 137, 169
Sutherland Award, xvii, xxiii
Synanon Foundation, 227–228
Szwajkowski, Eugene, 142

Tarde, Gabriel, 69, 70, 73
Tatro, Charlotte, 86
Taylor, John B., 172–173
Terre Haute, Ind., prison, 227
Terrorism: Italy, 199–214; left-wing, 199, 201, 202, 207–208; psychiatric aspects, 207–209, 210–213; right-wing, 199, 201, 202, 207, 208
Thomas, W.R., 150
Thornton, William, 90–91
Tigar, M.E., 48
Timasheff, N.S., 217

Toby, Jackson, 69
Torture, 6, 7. *See also* Plea-bargaining
Trade litigation, 142
Training schools, 165–166; Massachusetts, 162; North Carolina, 165
Treatment, right to (and right to refuse), 183, 186
Tripodi, T., 64
Turk, Austin, 40, 41–42, 43, 221

Underclass, 104–109
Uniform Crime Report (UCR) statistics, 78–89; homicide date, 112. *See also* Arrest rates
University of Wisconsin, xvii, 220
Uomo Delinquente, L', 17
Utilitarianism, 5–6

Valachi, Joseph, 126, 127, 128, 130
Value-neutrality, 43
Van den Berghe, Pierre, 19, 118
Vaughan, Diane, 135–147
Verri, Pietro, 4
Violence Commission report, 115, 116
Visigoth Code, 150
Vital Statistics, homicide data, 112
Vold, G.B., 40, 41, 42, 43
Voltaire, 4

Waldo, Gordon P., 169–178
Wales, time-series study of executions in, 171
Walpole (Mass.) prison, 227
Walsh, Marilyn, 141
Weber, Max, 218, 243
Weider, D. Lawrence, 28
White-collar crime, 135–147; research, 141–143; victims of, 141. *See also* Organizational crime
Williams, F.P., 42
Wiseman, Jacqueline, 29
Witkin, Herman A., 18
Wolfgang, Marvin, 111, 116, 117, 232
Women: homicide and, 113, 114; pawning, 153; psychological school, 86–87
Wood, Houston, 30

Young, Donald, 219–20
Youth crime. *See* Juvenile crime
Youth Development, Inc., 228
Youth Services Bureaus, 162
Yunker, James A., 171, 172, 176

Zahn, Margaret A., 111–123; and Bencivengo, 117
Zeisel, Hans, 176
Zimmerman, Joel, 84

About the Contributors

Joseph L. Albini is a professor in the Department of Sociology at Wayne State University. He received the B.A. from The Pennsylvania State University in 1954, the M.A. from Louisiana State University in 1956, and the Ph.D. from The Ohio State University in 1963. He served on the sociology faculty of the University of Kentucky, Bowling Green State University, World Campus Afloat, the University of Windsor, Ontario, and as senior visiting researcher in criminology at the University of Glasgow. He is the author of *The American Mafia: Genesis of a Legend* and has published several articles in professional journals. His areas of specialization include criminology, collective behavior, sexual behavior, and medical sociology.

Harry E. Allen is professor and chairperson, Administration of Justice Department, San Jose State University. He received the B.A. from Stetson University, the M.A. from Vanderbilt University, and the Ph.D. from The Ohio State University. He was formerly professor of public administration and director of the Program for the Study of Crime and Delinquency, The Ohio State University. His areas of interest and publications are in corrections, particularly community corrections, halfway houses, and probation and parole.

Clemens Bartollas is associate professor, Department of Sociology, University of Northern Iowa. He received the Ph.D. from The Ohio State University in 1973. A student of Simon Dinitz, Professor Bartollas coauthored a number of articles and a book, *Juvenile Victimization: The Institutional Paradox,* with Professor Dinitz. He also coauthored textbooks on juvenile corrections, correctional administration, actors in the justice system, and adult corrections.

Nancy J. Beran is associate professor of sociology and the first Lavelle Professor of Criminal Justice at Ohio Dominican College. Her primary field of scholarly interest within criminology is the coincidence of mental disorder and criminality and the special problems and issues generated by this dual status. She has conducted extensive research in this area and is the senior author of *Mentally Ill Offenders and the Criminal Justice System: Issues in Forensic Services.*

Francesco Bruno, M.D., is researcher in criminological medicine and forensic psychiatry, University of Rome Medical School. He has conducted research on addiction, youth culture, and deviance.

Alfred C. Clarke is professor of sociology at The Ohio State University and codirector of the Visual Research Laboratory. He has served in a wide variety of administrative, research, and editorial capacities, often extending beyond the boundaries of a single discipline. His research interests have focused chiefly on the sociology of the family and the emerging area of visual sociology. He holds a joint appointment in the Department of Photography and Cinema at The Ohio State University, where his research is on interrelationships between imagery and society. He is coauthor (with Timothy Curry) of *Introducing Visual Sociology.* His other publications include *Social Problems: Dissensus and Deviation in an Industrial Society* and *Deviance: Studies in Definition, Management, and Treatment,* coauthored with Simon Dinitz and Russell Dynes.

Marshall B. Clinard was educated at Stanford University and the University of Chicago (Ph.D. in sociology, 1941). Dr. Clinard served as chief, Criminal Statistics, U.S. Bureau of the Census, and, during World War II, as chief of analysis and reports, Enforcement Department, Office of Price Administration, Washington, D.C. He served on the faculties of the University of Iowa and Vanderbilt University and, from 1946 until 1979, the University of Wisconsin— Madison. Since 1979 he has been Emeritus Professor of Sociology, University of Wisconsin, and Distinguished Research Professor, University of New Mexico. Dr. Clinard was consultant to the Ford Foundation in India and taught and did research in East Africa under the Rockefeller Foundation. He also conducted comparative research in Switzerland, Sweden, and other countries. He is a former president of the Society for the Study of Social Problems and the Midwest Sociological Society. He has authored numerous books and articles including *Sociology of Deviant Behavior, Cities with Little Crime: The Case of Switzerland,* and *Slums and Community Development.* He was editor of *Anomie and Deviant Behavior;* coauthor of *Criminal Behavior Systems, Crime in Developing Countries,* and *Corporate Crime;* and recipient of the Edwin H. Sutherland Award for Distinguished Contributions to Criminology.

John P. Conrad is currently associated with the American Justice Institute. He received the B.A. from the University of California (1934) and the M.A. (1940) from the University of Chicago. He is widely known as a researcher, author, and expert on corrections. He has served as chief of research for the California Department of Corrections and for the U.S. Bureau of Prisons. He also was chief of the Center for Crime Prevention and Rehabilitation, Law Enforcement Assistance Administration. More recently, he was codirector of the Dangerous Offender Project for the Academy for Contemporary Problems in Columbus, Ohio.

Ann E. Davis is professor of sociology at Miami University, Oxford, Ohio. Her areas of specialization are medical and psychiatric sociology. She received the

B.A. from The Ohio State University; the M.A. in social work from the University of Louisville; and the Ph.D. from The Ohio State University. She is the senior author, with Simon Dinitz and Benjamin Pasamanick of *Schizophrenics In The New Custodial Community*. She has also published numerous articles and book chapters in the areas of alienation, sex roles, the family, and social theory. She is the former secretary of the North Central Sociological Association and a founder of the Association for Humanist Sociology. She is currently writing a book on narcissism in America, its etiology and implications for the future survival of the system.

Russell R. Dynes is executive officer of the American Sociological Association. He received the B.A. and M.A. from the University of Tennessee and the Ph.D. from The Ohio State University. He is author or coauthor of five books and many articles. His current research interests are in the relation of social science to policy and the sociology of crises and disaster.

Franco Ferracuti, M.D., is professor of criminological medicine and forensic psychiatry, University of Rome Medical School. He was a former U.N. staff member in the Social Defence Section and a consultant to the U.N. Social Defence Research Institute. He has published 160 papers and monographs in criminology and forensic psychiatry and was the recipient of the Sellin-Glueck Award of the American Society of Criminology. He has been visiting professor at several American universities, including The Ohio State University.

Gideon Fishman is senior lecturer in sociology, University of Haifa, Israel. He received the B.A. in sociology and political science from the Hebrew University, Israel, in 1968; the M.A. in sociology from Carleton University, Ottawa, in 1971; and the Ph.D. in sociology from The Ohio State University in 1974. He is currently a visiting professor in criminal justice at the University of South Florida, Tampa (1980–1981). His main areas of research interest are social policy, community treatment, judicial decisionmaking, crime trends, and forms of violent behavior. He has published papers in such journals as *Social Policy, Social Indicators Review, International Journal of Criminology and Penology, British Journal of Criminology, Social Psychiatry,* and *Review of Modern Sociology.* He has also contributed chapters to several books on criminology.

Thomas W. Foster is assistant professor of sociology at The Ohio State University and a faculty research associate of the University's Program for the Study of Crime and Delinquency. He received the B.S. in psychology from the University of Illinois; the M.A. in sociology from Bowling Green State University; and the Ph.D. in sociology from The Ohio State University. His special fields of study and areas of publication include sociopathic offenders, prison subcultures, and the control of deviant behaviors within traditional societies. He is also interested in improving the quality of undergraduate instruction in criminology and criminal justice through the increased use of community-based experiential education.

Gilbert Geis is professor, Program in Social Ecology, University of California, Irvine. He received the Ph.D. from the University of Wisconsin in 1953. His primary field of concentration is white-collar crime, and he has written extensively about a wide variety of criminological and legal issues. He is a former president of the American Society of Criminology and has held visiting appointments at the Institute of Criminology, Cambridge University; Faculty of Law, Sydney University; Harvard Law School; and the School of Criminal Justice, State University of New York.

Catherine M. Hartnett is chairperson of the Department of Criminal Justice, Albany State College, Georgia. She also directs the Criminal Justice Institute, which the Board of Regents of the University System of Georgia established at Albany in 1979. She received the M.A. in sociology from Illinois Institute of Technology and the Ph.D. from The Ohio State University. In addition to white-collar criminality, she is interested in comparative criminology and juvenile delinquency. Her published works include studies of juvenile delinquency in India.

Raymond J. Michalowski is associate professor of sociology at the University of North Carolina at Charlotte. He received the B.A. and M.A. in sociology from Fordham University and the Ph.D. in sociology from The Ohio State University in 1973. His published works include articles on vehicular homicide, shock probation, political repression, alternative world futures, criminological theory, and critical criminology.

Stuart J. Miller is associate professor of sociology at Washington and Jefferson College in Washington, Pennsylvania. He received the Ph.D. in sociology from The Ohio State University in 1971. He has published a number of articles in the area of criminal justice and is coauthor of *Juvenile Victimization: The Institutional Paradox; The Juvenile Offender: Control, Correction and Treatment; Correctional Administration: Theory and Practice; Careers of the Violent;* and *Practitioners in the American Criminal Justice System: A Behavioral Approach.* He also has served as a consultant to the Dangerous Offender Project of the Academy for Contemporary Problems in Columbus, Ohio, and currently is studying violence in America.

Stephen J. Pfohl is assistant professor of sociology at Boston College. He received the B.A. from the Catholic University of America and the M.A. and Ph.D. (1976) from The Ohio State University. He is author of *Predicting Dangerousness: The Social Construction of Psychiatric Reality* (Lexington Books, 1978) and is currently completing a second book on theoretical, methodological, and policy dimensions in the study of deviance and social control. Other of his recent publications have focused on child abuse, criminal violence, ethnomethodology, predictions of dangerousness, the implications of right-to-treatment litigation, and critical criminology. He has also been involved in research on health services for migrant farm workers, served as an evaluation-research consultant for the Ohio Division of Mental Health, and participated in the 1976 court-ordered classification of inmates in the Alabama prison system. In 1979 he was appointed by the governor of Massachusetts to chair the state's Juvenile Justice Advisory Committee. At present he is coordinating a study of the control of violent juvenile offenders in Massachusetts.

Walter C. Reckless is Professor Emeritus of Sociology at The Ohio State University. He received undergraduate and graduate education from the University of Chicago (Ph.D. in sociology, 1925). He initiated the program of academic instruction and research in criminology at The Ohio State University after joining the faculty in 1940. Professor Reckless has published numerous books, including the classic *Vice in Chicago* (1931); *Juvenile Delinquency* (1931); *Social Psychology* (1931); and five editions of *The Crime Problem* (1950–1973). His social-psychology and juvenile-delinquency books were among the first few published on those subjects in the United States. Professor Reckless is past-president of the American Society of Criminology; has served as chairman of the criminology section of the American Sociological Association; and was a consultant to the President's Crime Commission. His distinguished career has been honored by many awards, including the Sutherland Award. Walter Reckless holds a special place of honor at The Ohio State University and nationally as one of the pioneers of American criminology, and he is widely known and admired in international criminology as well.

Frank R. Scarpitti is professor of sociology at the University of Delaware. He received the B.A. from Cleveland State University and the M.A. and Ph.D. (1962) from The Ohio State University. He is the author or coauthor of a number of books, including *Social Problems* (1980); *Women, Crime and Justice* (1980); and *Drugs and the Youth Culture* (1980). He has published numerous articles and was cowinner of the American Psychiatric Association's Hofheimer Prize for Research in 1967. He currently serves as president of the American Society of Criminology (1980–1981). His research interests include the deinstitutionalization of juvenile status offenders.

Richard L. Schuster is assistant professor of sociology at Virginia Polytechnic

University. He received the B.A. from the University of Wisconsin—White-water, the M.A. from Arizona State University, and the Ph.D. from The Ohio State University. While at Arizona State University, he was awarded a National Science Foundation Fellowship. He is coauthor of *The Violent Few* (Lexington Books, 1978) and several articles on criminal-justice concerns. His research interests include the sociology of law and criminal justice.

Joseph E. Scott is associate professor of sociology at The Ohio State University. He received the B.A. from the University of Utah (1967) and the M.A. (1968) and Ph.D. (1972) from Indiana University. He is executive secretary of the American Society of Criminology and has served as counselor of the Criminology Section of the American Sociological Association. He has received both the OSU Alumni Distinguished Teaching Award and the OSU Arts and Sciences Teaching Award. He has published two books and articles in several journals, including *Journal of Criminal Law and Criminology, Journal of Sex Research, Public Opinion Quarterly, British Journal of Criminology, International Sociological Review,* and *Sociology and Social Research.* He is currently involved in cross-cultural research on criminology and deviance.

Leon Shaskolsky Sheleff has a joint appointment as senior lecturer in the Department of Sociology and The Institute of Criminology and Criminal Law at Tel Aviv University. He received a law degree from the University of Cape Town and the Ph.D. in sociology from The Ohio State University. He has published articles in journals of sociology, law, and criminology and is the author of *The Bystander: Behavior, Law, Ethics* (Lexington Books, 1978) and *Generations Apart: Adult Hostility to Youth.* His current research is on the use of capital punishment, particularly for political purposes, and on the sociological study of criminal law.

Ira J. Silverman is currently associate professor of criminal justice at the University of South Florida. He received the Ph.D. from The Ohio State University in 1970. He also taught in the Sociology Department at the State University of New York College at Cortland. He is the coauthor of *The Nature of Crime.* Two other texts, *Modern Criminology* and *Modern Corrections* are to be completed in the next year. He has also done research and published in the areas of the female offender, delinquency, sexual behavior, and women in law enforcement. In addition, since 1977, he has served as editor and publisher of the *LAE Journal of the American Criminal Justice Association.* He has been a member of many governmental and civic boards and committees in both Florida and New York.

Diane Vaughan is a National Institute of Mental Health postdoctoral fellow at Yale University. She received the B.A., M.A., and Ph.D. (1979) from The

Ohio State University. Her areas of specialization include criminology, complex organizations, and methodology. She is currently engaged in research on the social control of organizations in the Department of Sociology, Yale University. Her research and publications have been on such varied topics as corrections, crime between organizations, methods for studying organizations, and divorce. She is the author of *On the Social Control of Organizations: A Case Study* (forthcoming).

Gordon P. Waldo is professor of criminology at Florida State University. He received the B.A. in 1960 from the University of North Carolina, Chapel Hill, and the M.A. and the Ph.D. in sociology (1965 and 1967) from The Ohio State University. He has published extensively in such journals as *American Sociological Review, Social Forces, Social Problems, Criminology, Journal of Criminal Law and Criminology, Journal of Research in Crime and Delinquency,* and *Evaluation Quarterly.* His research interests are in the empirical testing of criminological theories, deterrence, capital punishment, and evaluation research.

Margaret A. Zahn is associate professor of sociology at Temple University and director of a nationwide study on the nature and patterns of American homicide. She received the B.A. in 1963, the M.A. in 1964, and the Ph.D. in 1969, all from The Ohio State University. She has published numerous articles in professional journals, dealing primarily with violence and factors associated with it; the most recent article is "Homicide in the Twentieth Century United States." She is currently working on a book on homicide in the United States. She has also studied the Italian women's movement and women in politics, an interest that arose when she coordinated a sociology program at Temple Abroad in Rome. She has served on the executive boards of the American Society of Criminology and the American Sociological Association.

About the Editors

Israel L. Barak-Glantz is assistant professor of sociology at Wayne State University. He received the B.A. in sociology and criminology from the Bar-Ilan University, Israel, and the M.A. and Ph.D. in sociology from The Ohio State University in 1973 and 1978, respectively. His publications include chapters in the first volume of *Israel Studies in Criminology* and the *International Handbook of Contemporary Developments in Criminology,* as well as papers and reports in professional journals and at meetings. He is a coauthor of a forthcoming volume, *The Dangerous Offender in Custody.* His primary research interests have been the social organization and management styles of correctional institutions, patterns of prisoner behavior, incompetence and criminal liability, comparative criminology, and penology and evaluation research.

C. Ronald Huff is associate professor of public administration and sociology and director of the Program for the Study of Crime and Delinquency at The Ohio State University. He received the B.A. in psychology from Capital University in 1968; the M.S.W. from the University of Michigan in 1970; and the Ph.D. in sociology from The Ohio State University in 1974, where he was a student of Simon Dinitz. Prior to joining the OSU faculty, he held faculty positions at the University of California, Irvine, and Purdue University. He is coauthor of *Attorneys as Activists* (1979) and *Planning Correctional Reform* (1975) and is editor of *Contemporary Corrections* (1977). He has also published approximately twenty articles and book chapters in sociological, criminological, psychiatric, and governmental journals and books, and has served as associate editor of *Criminology* (1978–1981) and as a member of the executive board of the American Society of Criminology.